THE ISLAMIC LAW OF NATIONS

Shaybānī's Siyar

By the Same Author

WAR AND PEACE IN THE LAW OF ISLAM
The Johns Hopkins Press

INDEPENDENT IRAQ
Oxford University Press

LAW IN THE MIDDLE EAST
(Edited, in collaboration with H. J. Liebesny, for The Middle East Institute)

ISLAMIC JURISPRUDENCE: Shāfiʿī's *Risāla*
The Johns Hopkins Press

MODERN LIBYA: *A Study in Political Development*
The Johns Hopkins Press

THE GOVERNMENT OF IRAQ
(Arabic and English)

AMERICAN WRITINGS ON THE MIDDLE EAST
(Edited in Arabic for the Franklin Publications)

THE ALEXANDRETTA QUESTION
(Arabic Publication)

THE ISLAMIC LAW OF NATIONS

Shaybānī's Siyar

TRANSLATED WITH AN INTRODUCTION, NOTES, AND APPENDICES BY

Majid Khadduri

THE JOHNS HOPKINS PRESS, Baltimore, Maryland

Baltimore, Md. 21218

Printed in the United States of America

Library of Congress Catalogue Card No. 66-14377

DEDICATED

IN FRIENDSHIP TO

Abd al-Razzaq Ahmad al-Sanhuri

FOREWORD

by Philip C. Jessup
Judge, the International Court of Justice

There are dangers in trying to write a Foreword to a volume dealing with a body of material which lies quite outside the ken and competence of the writer. The danger is enhanced when fascinating details tempt one to venture generalizations which should rest upon conclusions only the expert is entitled to draw. Surely I would not venture to embark on such a task if I were confronted only by the translation of old Arabic texts—and it must be noted that the core of this book is the annotated translation of the teachings on the law of nations of an eighth-century Islamic jurist. But in this case, Professor Majid Khadduri has prefaced the translation with an "Introduction on Islamic Law and the Law of Nations" which provides a key enabling the reader to unlock the gate to unknown areas—even though these areas are indeed ones whose general contours the author has made known to a wide audience of international lawyers through his previous writings, especially his *War and Peace in the Law of Islam*, the second edition of which appeared eleven years ago. These prefatory remarks I must make because I write this Foreword as a student of international law and not even as a tyro in Arabic studies.

The appearance of this text of Shaybānī's teachings is particularly timely because there is now so much interest in the debate over the question whether the international law of which Hugo Grotius is often called the father is so completely Western-European in inspiration and outlook as to make it unsuitable for universal application in these days of a much wider and more varied international community of states. The attention recently paid—both in scholarly writings and in international arbitral awards—to Asian, Middle Eastern, and Islamic precursors of the law of nations has revealed how widely certain concepts have influenced man's thought as problems concerning the interrelationships of various groups have been faced throughout history. Professor Khadduri points to current emphasis on the comparative law approach, which a book like this is bound to stimulate and encourage. He points out also the relevance of such comparative studies to the interpretation of Article 38 (1) (b) of the Statute of the International Court of Justice, under which the Court applies " the general principles of law recognized by civilized nations."

It is not that we need to find exact parallels or precedents, since law has always responded to contemporary conditions and objectives. Professor Khadduri shows how Islamic concepts of the legal relations between Islam and the rest of the world changed as it became apparent that the expectations of the early period—when Islam was a vigorously proselytizing, expansionist entity, unified and unifying—yielded in the face of practical necessities when the relative power balance changed and when Islam itself became divided. He notes that the decentralization trends of the tenth century of the Christian era brought about " a long transitional period of coexistence which Don Juan Manuel characterized in the thirteenth century as *guerra fria* (cold war) " before Islam and Christendom " tacitly arrived at an agreement to conduct their relations on the basis of equality and mutual interest."

Shaybānī was himself a product of the " universal " phase which characterized the 'Abbāsid dynasty and spread from the time of Shaybānī's birth in 750 A. D. to about 900. He was primarily a teacher although he also served as a judge and as an adviser to the Caliph Hārūn al-Rashīd. As Professor Khadduri points out, he taught by what we in the United States now call the " case method," although in our writings we do not use the dialogue form which Shaybānī employs in his " siyar " (law of nations). He was a recorder and interpreter of prior teachings and traditions, incorporating his own opinions based on analogy and pure juristic reasoning. Many of the problems which he poses and answers are highly complicated. Since he lived at a time when the normal relationship between Islam and other peoples was war (the jihād—holy war, or *bellum justum* as later European jurists would have called it), most of the problems deal with situations arising from war. To quote from the Introduction:

> The scholars of the early ʿAbbāsid period began to study the conduct of the Prophet and his early successors as models so as to learn from their practices. They interested themselves in . . . the campaigns and military expeditions of the Prophet and the early military commanders, and sought to discover the legal norms underlying those military exploits. Some confined their study to narratives of the past, while others sought to reformulate legal rules for the future relationships of Islam with other peoples. Those inquiries introduced into Islamic learning a new concept of the siyar which transformed it from a narrative to a normative character.

The analysis of rights to captured persons and property leads to much detailed exposition of property rights in general, including rights by marriage and by inheritance. One finds also material on what the private international lawyers of today would call "choice of law" and the limits of jurisdictional power. While "the law of Islam is essentially personal and binding on Muslims regardless of territory," Professor Khadduri notes that Abū Ḥanīfa, "who was the first to introduce Shaybānī to the study of law, . . . introduced the notion of territoriality in the relationships between Muslims and non-Muslims." The public international lawyer finds evidence of the deeply rooted principle of *pacta sunt servanda,* of postliminy, the contraband trade (even though neutrality was not recognized), and the treatment of prisoners and of the wounded. Chapter V of Shaybānī's Siyar deals with peace treaties and in many places there is detailed discussion of safe-conducts which apparently could be granted more freely and be more widely respected than in this twentieth century.

Professor Khadduri tells us of the efforts of Western scholars as early as 1825 and as late as 1955 to identify Shaybānī as the " Hugo Grotius of the Muslims," but he himself, while hailing Shaybānī as " the most eminent Muslim jurist who wrote on Islam's legal relationships with other nations," leaves us with a more balanced and more instructive picture: " To identify the names of Shaybānī and Grotius," he writes, ". . . will not add laurels necessarily to a classical author whose place in the history of jurisprudence is assured " even though he is insufficiently known to students of comparative jurisprudence and the history of law.

This book affords the welcome opportunity for many of us to become better acquainted with this great eighth-century scholar, his method and his times.

PREFACE

Nations that uphold the sovereignty of God seem to take for granted the potential capacity of men to be governed by one law, eternal and just, given by a Divine Legislator. The history of mankind provides many examples of nations which felt constrained to put God's authority into practice and to extend the benefits of His revealed law to other nations, even at the point of the sword.

Islam was neither the first nor the last of the nations that sought to establish a world public order based on divine legislation and to enforce it by the "jihād." The jihād is the Islamic *bellum justum* and may be regarded as the very basis of Islam's relationships with other nations. Christendom, a prototype of divine public order and an object of the jihād, counteracted with the Crusades. But neither Islam nor Christendom could achieve exclusive control of the governance of mankind. The East-West conflict that ensued and lasted for centuries taught Muslims and Christians alike that an ever-continuing adaptation of ideology to reality was necessary if the rival systems under which they lived were to survive. A long period of hostility was followed by competition and coexistence which gradually superseded exclusive legal doctrines, and the sovereignty of God no longer remained the monopoly of a single nation.

In the dispersed sovereignty of the modern states the law that replaced transcendental law and regulated the newly formed family of nations is based on reciprocity and mutual interest and is enforced by all, individually and collectively, and not merely by a single nation. This law, whether called the modern law of nations, *droit des gens*, or *Völkerrecht*, is a positive law derived from the experiences of nations over the last four centuries. It had contributed its modest share to the maintenance of peace during that period as well as to the mitigation of the scourges of war by providing rules which regulated the conduct of hostilities among combatants.

Today the modern law of nations, under the impact of two world wars, is no longer able to cope adequately with the problems of a society of nations that is rapidly growing and a world that is correspondingly shrinking. Some jurists have sought to expand the scope of the law of nations by suggesting the merging of private and public international law into "un droit intersocial unifié" (George Scelle); others have called for a thorough re-examination of existing concepts and principles and suggested its transformation into "transnational law" (Jessup) or a "common law of mankind" (Jenks) or simply "world law." The methods of achieving this objective have varied from a revival of natural-law concepts to improvisation by trial and error.

The latter includes the comparative method. Students of private law have for long been deepening their study of the law by drawing on foreign experiences. But text writers on the modern law of nations, although appreciating the value of the comparative method, have drawn almost exclusively on Western experience. This bias was perhaps fully justified at a time when the family of nations was made up principally of Western nations and the battleground of diplomatic conflicts was confined essentially to Europe and to the Western hemisphere. This situation is no longer true, and the community of nations is rapidly growing into a world-wide society of nations. To draw on the experiences of an increasing number of other nations is as logical as it is pragmatic, for diversity of experience serves the common interests of an expanding community of nations. The authors of the Statute of the International Court of Justice had probably implied more than the clause literally meant when they stated that the court makes decisions, in addition to custom and conventions, on the basis of "the general principles of law recognized by civilized nations." To achieve that purpose, the study of "general principles" of the public orders of various nations would be needed. It is the purpose of this work to present an annotated text in translation as well as a study of the jurisprudence of an original writer on the public law of Islam—a nation that played an important role in the past and produced a system of law that was no less significant than the Roman.

It is a pleasure to acknowledge the assistance of many a friend. I should like to thank Shaykh Muhammad Abu Zahra and Shafiq Shihata (Chehata) of Egypt for initial helpful suggestions. I am grateful for the valuable comments received from Muhammad Hamidullah of Hyderabad, now residing in Paris, who read the entire work; Harold Glidden, who read the main part of the translation; and Emil Lang, who read the translator's introduction. I wish to acknowledge the grant extended by the Rockefeller Foundation, which enabled me in the summer of 1963 to visit Istanbul and Cairo and work on the Shaybānī manuscripts in the rich libraries of those cities as well as on other works connected with this study. Needless to say, none of these is responsible for any errors or opinions which the work contains.

MAJID KHADDURI

July 12, 1965

School of Advanced International Studies
The Johns Hopkins University

CONTENTS

THE ISLAMIC LAW OF NATIONS

Shaybānī's Siyar

TRANSLATOR'S INTRODUCTION

Islamic Law and the Law of Nations

Islam and the Community of Nations

The modern law of nations presupposes the existence in the world of sovereign territorial groups gathered together to form a community of nations, each possessing its own internal or municipal law and exercising an authority subject to no restrictions save those provided by the law of nations. This law, designed to regulate the relationships among nation-states, is enforced not by any supreme power, but by the members of the community of nations themselves, individually or collectively. The law of nations, in its present form, is therefore the public law of a community of sovereign territorial groups.

This law is essentially a relative term. It describes the latest stage in a process of evolution that has been in progress for centuries. Its development began as a European and Christian law and for over three centuries it governed the interrelationships of European nations essentially, before it became the law of a wider circle of nations, no longer European or Christian alone. In its present form, it tends to be universal, because it has the potential capacity of extending its advantages to all mankind. But in a rapidly growing world community, this public law has outgrown traditional limitations. A number of writers have suggested a re-examination of its scope and basic concepts if it is to become truly the public law of mankind.[1] Some have noted that contemporary law

[1] See C. W. Jenks, *The Common Law of Mankind* (London, 1958), Chap. 1.

is limited in scope and includes as its subjects only states and not individuals.[2] Others have deplored its inadequacy to serve as an expression of the life of a true society of nations.[3] But all the writers have hopefully stressed the need for further development, so as to meet the growing demands of a world society of nations.[4]

The developing nature of the modern law of nations reflects its potential capability of cumulative growth, as well as the history behind it more remote than its immediate European background. The history of the contemporary law of nations can be traced back through the Renaissance and the age of discoveries, through the Greco-Roman periods, back to the days of ancient Egypt and Babylonia, and perhaps to even earlier times. The earliest records of history provide ample evidence that ancient states and peoples applied a body of rules and practices in their relationships with one another. Some broad principles and maxims of justice, if not specific rules and practices, evolved in early societies and may be regarded as the very basis of the law of nations. A law governing the relationships among nations existed in the Near East in early days as well as in Greece and Rome, the legacy of which had subsequently been bequeathed to the West.[5]

Earlier systems of the law of nations, however, in contrast with the contemporary, were not world-wide in character. Each system concerned itself essentially with regulating the relationship of entities and nations within a limited area of the world and within one civilization or more. It has been

[2] Philip C. Jessup, *A Modern Law of Nations* (New York, 1948); *Transnational Law* (New Haven, 1956); P. E. Corbett, *The Individual and World Society* (Princeton, 1953).

[3] Sir Alfred Zimmern, *The League of Nations and the Rule of Law* (London, 1936), Chap. 9.

[4] Q. Wright, *The Strengthening of International Law* (Leiden, 1959); P. E. Corbett, *Law and Society in the Relations of States* (New York, 1951).

[5] See Arthur Nussbaum, *A Concise History of the Law of Nations* (New York, 1947); T. W. Walker, *A History of the Law of Nations* (Cambridge, Eng., 1899); Robert Ward, *An Enquiry Into the Foundation and History of the Law of Nations in Europe from the Time of the Greeks and Romans* (London, 1795).

observed that in each civilization the population tended to develop within itself a community of political entities—a family of nations—whose interrelationships were regulated by a set of customary rules and practices, rather than being a single nation governed by a single authority and a single system of law. Several families of nations existed or coexisted in areas such as the ancient Near East, Greece and Rome, China, Islam, and Western Christendom, where at least one distinct civilization had developed in each of them. Within each civilization a body of principles and rules developed for regulating the conduct of states with one another in peace and war.

These systems, however, were not truly "international," in the modern sense, for each was exclusive and failed to recognize the principles of legal equality and reciprocity which are essential to any system if it is to become world-wide. The possibility of the various systems integrating into a single coherent system was virtually nil. Though each necessarily borrowed from the others without acknowledgments, each claimed an exclusive superiority of its moral and religious values over the others. Small wonder, therefore, if each classical system vanished with the disappearance of the civilization (or civilizations) under which it had flourished.[6]

The rise of Islam, with its universal appeal to mankind, necessarily raised the problem for the Islamic state as to how to conduct its relations with non-Islamic states as well as with the tolerated religious communities within its own territory. The special branch of the sacred law—the siyar—developed by the Muslim jurists to meet the need may aptly be called the Islamic law of nations. The experiences of Islam, like those of earlier nations, provided a system of law designed to maintain order and justice throughout the world. The Islamic law of nations, the product of centuries of stored experiences, reveals Islam's efforts to cope with the problem of constructing a stable and an ordered world society. Every

[6] For the nature of the law of nations among Asiatic states, see Q. Wright, "Asian Experience and International Law," *International Studies Quarterly*, Vol. I (1959), pp. 71-87.

matured system of law reflects the ways by which nations endeavored to achieve such an end. The experiences of Islam, like those of other nations, are worthy of a close examination, if the process of the development of the modern law of nations is to be meaningful.

Islamic Conception of the Law of Nations

The annals of ancient nations provide ample evidence that they observed some form of law, customary or otherwise, in their relationships with one another, which may fall under the collective name "the law of nations." "The mere fact of neighborly cohabitation," says one writer, "creates moral and legal obligations, which in the course of time crystallize into a system of international law." [7] Even among primitive peoples, rules or precepts seem to have existed as a part of the mores before they were developed into a coherent system governing the relations of civilized nations. Even when conflict and anarchy reigned perennially among them, agreement on certain rules such as the exchange of prisoners and abstention from certain practices for fear of retaliation proved to be in their common interest. The records of the ancient Egyptians and Babylonians contain agreements signed with their neighbors dealing with such problems as the use of water, the settlement of frontier disputes, and the exchange of prisoners.[8] From the Old Testament we learn how the ancient Israelites regulated their relations with their neighbors, in peace as in war.[9] The Greeks, in their relations with Rome and other states, applied a system of law no less impressive, whether in the form of *jus naturale* or *jus gentium*.[10] The

[7] Baron S. A. Korff, "An Introduction to the History of International Law," *American Journal of International Law*, Vol. XVIII (1924), p. 248.

[8] J. H. Wigmore, *A Panorama of the World's Legal Systems* (St. Paul, 1928); G. R. Driver and John C. Miles, *The Babylonian Laws* (Oxford, 1956).

[9] H. Schrey, H. Walz, and W. A. Whitehouse, *The Biblical Doctrine of Justice and Law* (London, 1955); Walker, *A History of the Law of Nations*, Vol. I, pp. 31-36.

[10] Coleman Phillipson, *The International Law and Custom of Ancient Greece and Rome* (London, 1911).

contemporaries of Islam—India,[11] China,[12] and Christendom—created similar systems for the regulation of their external relations with other nations. Montesquieu did not stray far from the truth in stating that all nations, not even excepting the Iroquois, who, he claimed, devoured their prisoners, had a law of nations.[13]

The Islamic faith, born among a single people and spreading to others, used the state as an instrument for achieving a doctrinal or an ultimate religious objective, the proselytization of mankind. The Islamic state became necessarily an imperial and an expansionist state striving to win other peoples by conversion. At the very outset, the law of war, the jihād, became the chief preoccupation of jurists. The Islamic law of nations was essentially a law governing the conduct of war and the division of booty. This law was designed for temporary purposes, on the assumption that the Islamic state was capable of absorbing the whole of mankind; for if the ideal of Islam were ever achieved, the *raison d'être* of the law of war, at least with regard to Islam's relations with non-Islamic states, would pass out of existence. The wave of Islamic expansion did not succeed, however, in encircling the globe and the Islamic state had to accommodate its relations with other nations on grounds other than those envisaged in the jihād or law of war. A law regulating peaceful relations with other nations, although temporary in theory, sprang from the realities of life which imposed themselves on Islam. The concept of the siyar, or the Islamic law of nations, was necessarily broadened to include peaceful as well as hostile relationships with other nations. Rules and practices governing the termination or suspension of hostilities, the making of treaties, and the movement of individuals from

[11] P. Bandyopadhyay, *International Law and Custom in Ancient India* (Calcutta, 1920); S. V. Viswanatha, *International Law in Ancient India* (London, 1925).

[12] Siu Tchoan-pao, *Les droits des gens et la Chine antique* (Paris, 1926); Chan Nay Chow, *La doctrine du droit international chez Confucius* (Paris, 1940).

[13] Baron de Montesquieu, *The Spirit of the Laws*, trans. Th. Hugent (London, 1900), Vol. I, p. 5.

one territory to another for commercial and other peaceful purposes developed from necessity.

The Islamic law of nations, however, is not a system separate from Islamic law. It is merely an extension of the sacred law, the sharīʿa, designed to govern the relations of Muslims with non-Muslims, whether inside or outside the territory of Islam. In a word, an Islamic law of nations does not exist as a separate system in the sense that modern municipal (national) law and international law, based on different sources and maintained by different sanctions, are distinct from one another. The siyar, if taken to mean the Islamic law of nations, is but a chapter in the Islamic *corpus juris*, binding upon all who believed in Islam as well as upon those who sought to protect their interests in accordance with Islamic justice. But just as the *jus gentium*, an extension of the *jus civile*, was designed by the Romans to regulate their relations with non-Romans, so was the siyar, an extension of the sharīʿa, designed to govern the relationships of Muslims with non-Muslims at a time when Islam came into contact with them. The siyar, in other words, was the sharīʿa writ large.

The binding force of the siyar was not based essentially on reciprocity or mutual consent, unless non-Muslims desired to avail themselves of Islamic justice, but was a self-imposed system of law, the sanctions of which were moral or religious and binding on its adherents, even though the rules might run counter to their interests. Unlike Mosaic law, which was equally binding upon Jews and Gentiles when they came into contact with one another,[14] Islamic law was binding essentially upon those who professed the faith of Islam. Some rules, necessarily the product of reciprocity, such as the exchange of prisoners, diplomatic immunity, and custom duties,[15] were mutually acceptable to Muslims and their neighbors.

Finally, the Islamic law of nations was binding on territorial groups as well as individuals. Like all ancient law, the

[14] Cf. my *War and Peace in the Law of Islam* (Baltimore, 1955, 1962), p. 46. See J. M. Powis Smith, *The Origin and History of Hebrew Law* (Chicago, 1931).

[15] See paragraphs 774-81, below.

law of Islam was inherently personal rather than territorial, for if Islam were intended for all mankind, the territorial basis of law would be irrelevant. However, since many non-Islamic lands remained outside the pale of Islamic law, the siyar was bound to grant consideration to the territorial basis and to regulate the relationships among Muslims and non-Muslims, both on the personal and territorial levels. It is true that only a single school of law, the Ḥanafī, stressed the territorial character of the law, while others, like the Shāfi'ī school, stressed the personal; but all accepted territorial limitations in varying degree.[16]

Nature and Sources of the Islamic Law of Nations

The viewpoint that law is the product of the immediate needs and aspirations of society is founded on the assumption that men are capable of creating binding acts which would translate these needs and aspirations into a normative system. This kind of law, which mirrors the ideas and ideals of society, is called positive law. Man-made law, common or civil, is admittedly imperfect and society endeavors to perfect it by a continuing process of legislation. The ideal law remains a mirage, and the real one develops by improvisation from generation to generation.

In a society which assumes that man is incapable of rising above his evil propensities or of determining what his ultimate good may be, the idea that fallible man can legislate for others is scarcely acceptable. In such a society, a superhuman or a divine power is invoked to provide guidance and security for its members. The ancient Hebrew, Christian, and Islamic societies were committed to this viewpoint—God disclosed Himself through a revealed law and communicated His will and justice to men through prophets. This law, regarded as applicable to all men and embodying divine wisdom, forms another category of law. In contrast with positive law, it may

[16] See Abū Ja'far Muḥammad b. Jarīr al-Ṭabarī, *Kitāb Ikhtilāf al-Fuqahā'* (*Kitāb al-Jihād*), ed. J. Schacht (Leiden, 1933), pp. 60-64. See also paragraphs 442-45, below.

be said to fall into the category of natural law. It is not the product of pure reason necessarily, as natural law is often taken to mean, but of intuition or divine inspiration uttered or transmitted by a prophet. Rational justification for such a law is not needed and men seek to justify it with mere self-conviction.

In Islamic legal theory, the law proceeded from a divine source. It was regarded as perfect and eternal, designed for all time and for universal application to all men. The ideal way of life was led in strict conformity with this law. Islamic law so called may be regarded as a form of natural law, derived partly from the Qur'ān, the very word of God, and from the Prophet Muḥammad's utterances, inspired by divine wisdom. In practice, however, the raw material of Islamic law was derived in the main from the sunna, the prevailing customary (or tribal) law of Arabia, and from the local custom and practices of the occupied provinces outside Arabia. This legal raw material was transformed with meticulous care by the legal speculation of leading jurists into what was virtually a positive system of law based on the broad ethical principles of the Qur'ān and the model behavior of the Prophet.

The Islamic law of nations, or the siyar, as an integral part of Islamic law, was based in theory on the same sources and maintained by the same sanctions of that law. In practice, however, if the term siyar is taken to mean the sum total of the principles, rules, and practices governing Islam's relationships with other nations, one should look for evidence beyond the conventional roots (uṣūl), or sources, of Islamic law. Some principles and rules may be found in treaties and peace agreements made by Muslim rulers with non-Muslims; [17] others in public utterances and official instructions of the caliphs to commanders in the field which the jurists subsequently incorporated in the law; [18] still others in the rules and practices necessarily evolving from reciprocity and mutual relations with other nations or derived from Islam's direct experiences with neighboring countries. Above all, the juristic writings

[17] See Chap. V, below.

[18] See Chap. I, below.

of eminent Muslim jurists and judges provided a legal rationale of Islam's relationships with other nations within the general framework of Islamic ethical principles and helped to formulate rules and principles based on analogical reasoning (qiyās) and juristic preference (istiḥsān). Some of these writings were highly abstract and theoretical, reflecting the medieval character of scholastic speculation, but others dealt with concrete answers to specific questions that had arisen, or were considered likely to arise, in Islam's intercourse with other nations. Not infrequently, Muslim rulers sought the legal advice of leading jurists on questions of the day. Those juridical opinions, or fatwas, were given either in the form of an interpretation of an already established principle, or of rulings establishing a new precedent which subsequent generations followed.

In terms of the modern law of nations, the sources of the Islamic law of nations conform generally to the same categories defined by modern jurists and specified in the Statute of the International Court of Justice.[19] These may be grouped under the general headings of custom, authority, agreement, and reason. The sunna and local practices are equivalent to custom; the Qur'ān, the Prophet's utterances, and the caliph's decisions and instructions represent authority; principles and rules enshrined in treaties with non-Muslims fall in the category of agreement; and juristic writings, based on analogical deduction and other forms of juristic reasoning in accordance with Islamic legal methodology, may be said collectively to represent reason. As the present work of Shaybānī indicates, not all of the Islamic authoritative sources were drawn upon as heavily for the development of an Islamic *jus gentium*; the siyar, evolving almost as a separate branch of the law, was derived from custom and reason, in great degree, more than from the other conventional sources. We shall, however, have more to say on this point in our discussion of Shaybānī's works.[20]

[19] See Article 38 of the Statute of the International Court of Justice.
[20] See pp. 41 ff., below.

Theory of the Islamic Law of Nations

The Islamic Conception of World Order

In order to reconstruct an Islamic theory of the law of nations we should recall that Islam is not merely a set of religious ideas and practices but also a political community (the umma) endowed with a central authority. That authority was originally derived from a high divine source and charged with the duty of regulating the conduct of the political community with the outside world in accordance with its sacred law. The umma, composed of all who profess the Islamic faith, is the immediate point of reference for every believer, but the ultimate point of reference is the belief in one God and in the universal message of the Prophet Muḥammad. The umma was therefore potentially capable of embodying the whole of mankind, and the Islamic state, whether it engulfed the whole of the umma or only a part, was the instrument which would achieve the ultimate religious objective.

It follows that only the members of the umma are the subject of the Islamic legal and ethical system. All other communities are the object of that system, although they are by no means denied certain advantages of the system when they come into contact with Islam. The ultimate objective of Islam was to establish peace and order in accordance with Islamic justice within the territory brought under the pale of its public order, and to expand the area of the validity of that order to include the whole world.

But the Islamic universal state, not unlike other universal states, did not include the whole world. Outside it, communities remained with which Islam had to deal permanently. Even in its early period, Islam entered into peaceful arrangements with communities beyond its frontiers in accordance with a set of rules and practices, before some of those communities were brought under its sovereignty.

Conformity with the legal and ethical standards of Islam was required of believers who resided in the territories that had come under Islamic rule, as well as of believers dwelling in territories which had not yet come under that rule. Islam as a religion was spread by trade and cultural connections beyond the frontiers of the state and believers owed legal but not necessarily political allegiance to it. Islamic law, though in practice enforced upon believers residing within Islamic territory, was also observed by believers outside its territories. In theory, the law was personal in character, since territorial limitation is irrelevant to the concept of a state claiming to be ecumenical in nature, but in practice territorial limitations necessarily affected the enforcement of the law. Non-Muslims domiciled in Islamic territory were not bound by all the ethical and legal rules of Islam unless they wished to avail themselves of its justice. Islamic authority, however, had to deal with legal problems arising from the interrelationships of non-Muslims with Muslims.

In Islamic theory, the world was split into two divisions: the territory of Islam (the dār al-Islām), which may be called *Pax Islamica*, comprising Islamic and non-Islamic communities that had accepted Islamic sovereignty, and the rest of the world, called the dār al-ḥarb, or the territory of war. The first included the community of believers as well as those who entered into an alliance with Islam. The inhabitants of those territories were Muslims who formed the community of believers (the umma), and non-Muslims of the tolerated religious communities collectively called the " People of the Book " or Dhimmīs (Christians, Jews, and others known to have possessed scriptures), who preferred to hold fast to their own law and religion at the price of paying a poll tax (jizya) to Islamic authority. The Muslims enjoyed full rights of citizenship while the followers of the tolerated religions enjoyed only partial civil rights, but all enjoyed full status as subjects of the Imām, or caliph, the head of state, in their claim to internal security and to protection from foreign attack. The Imām, in the discharge of his responsibilities in the foreign conduct of the state, spoke in the name of all subjects, Muslim and non-Muslim alike. Relations between the Islamic and non-Islamic communities within the Islamic legal superstructure were regulated in accordance with special agreements issued by the caliphs (which were in the nature of constitutional charters), recognizing the canon law of each tolerated religious community bearing on matters of personal status. But any member of these communities, in contrast to contemporary practice elsewhere, could join the Islamic community at any moment by merely pronouncing the Islamic formula for the profession of the faith. Moreover, they were not denied access to Islamic courts if they wished to avail themselves of Islamic justice.[21]

The world surrounding the Islamic state, composed of all other nations and territories that had not been brought under its rule, was collectively known as the "territory of war." The territory of war was the object, not the subject, of the Islamic legal system, and it was the duty of Muslim rulers to bring it under Islamic sovereignty whenever the strength was theirs to do so. The communities of the dār al-ḥarb were regarded as being in a "state of nature," for they lacked legal competence to enter into intercourse with Islam on the basis of equality and reciprocity because they failed to conform to its ethical and legal standards. It followed that arrangements made between the dār al-Islām and the dār al-ḥarb must be short-lived by necessity because they carry with them no implied recognition of status under Islamic law.[22] However, not all Muslim jurists held to the theory that the world was split into two divisions. Some, especially Shāfiʿī jurists, devised a third temporary division called the dār al-ṣulḥ (territory of peaceful arrangement) or dār al-ʿahd (territory of covenant), giving qualified recognition to non-Muslim communities if they entered into treaty relations with Islam on conditions agreed upon between the two parties (such as the payment of annual tribute to Islamic authorities). Most jurists, however, especially the Ḥanafī school, did not recognize the third division, arguing that if the inhabitants of a territory concluded a peace treaty and paid tribute, it became part of the

[21] For a discussion of the legal status of these communities, see my *War and Peace in the Law of Islam*, Chap. 17.

[22] See A. Abel, "Dār al-Ḥarb" and "Dār al-Islām," *Encyclopaedia of Islam* (2nd ed.; London and Leiden, 1960), Vol. II, pp. 155-57, 170-71.

dār al-Islām and its people were entitled to the protection of Islam.[23]

The dār al-Islām, in theory, was in a state of war with the dār al-ḥarb, because the ultimate objective of Islam was the whole world. If the dār al-ḥarb were reduced by Islam, the public order of *Pax Islamica* would supersede all others, and non-Muslim communities would either become part of the Islamic community or submit to its sovereignty as tolerated religious communities or as autonomous entities possessing treaty relations with it.[24]

But the dār al-ḥarb, though regarded as in the state of nature, was not treated as a no-man's land. Its hostile relations with the dār al-Islām were regulated with the Islamic law of war just as Romans observed the rules of the *jus fetiale* in their hostile relations with other nations. Thus Muslims were under legal obligation to respect the rights of non-Muslims, both combatants and civilians, whenever fighting was in progress. During the short intervals of peace, when hostilities were suspended, Islam took cognizance of the authority or authorities that existed in countries which it could not claim to have brought under its control. But this cognizance of the need of authority in the dār al-ḥarb did not constitute recognition, in the modern sense of the term, for recognition implied Islam's acceptance of non-Islamic sovereignties as equal entities under the Islamic legal system. Islam's cognizance of non-Islamic sovereignties merely meant that some form of authority was by nature necessary for the survival of mankind, even when men lived in territories in the state of nature, outside the pale of the Islamic public order. Thus, if a Muslim entered the dār al-ḥarb as a merchant, or as a visitor under a safe-conduct (amān), he was under obligation to respect the authority of that territory and observe its laws as long as he remained in that territory

[23] D. B. Macdonald and A. Abel, "Dār al-Ṣulh," *Encyclopaedia of Islam* (2nd ed.), Vol. II, p. 131.

[24] See Shams al-Dīn Muḥammad b. Aḥmad b. Sahl al-Sarakhsī's exposition of the object of Islam's relationships with other communities in *Kitāb al-Mabsūṭ* (Cairo, 1324/1906), Vol. X, pp. 2-3.

enjoying the benefits of security granted him by a safe-conduct or a treaty with Muslim authorities. The Muslim was in the meantime under obligation to observe his own law, except perhaps certain rules not strictly obligatory in enemy territory; [25] but if conflicts arose between his own law and that of the territory, no doubt existed where his choice would lie.

The state of war existing between the dār al-Islām and the dār al-ḥarb, however, does not necessarily mean that actual hostilities must occur. Whenever fighting came to an end, the state of war was reduced to a situation equivalent under the modern law of nations as a state of nonrecognition. Strictly speaking, it meant that the dār al-ḥarb was denied legal status under Islamic law as long as it failed to conform to Islam's legal and ethical standards or to attain the status of the tolerated religious communities. But this state of nonrecognition did not imply, as it would in the modern sense of the term, that direct negotiations could not be conducted or that treaties could not be concluded. Such activities did not imply equality between the two parties nor did they possess a permanent character. Perhaps the nearest equivalent under the modern law of nations is the recognition of insurgency. Such recognition does not preclude a later *de facto* or *de jure* recognition nor does it represent approval of the regime's conduct under insurgency. It merely means that authority to enforce law and order in a particular territory was necessary in certain circumstances. Nor did the Islamic state, in entering into diplomatic relations with a non-Islamic state, intend to extend the full advantages of its legal system to the inhabitants of non-Islamic lands, for such actions would imply neither equality of status nor recognition of the conduct of the administering authority of the enemy territory so long as the inhabitants of that territory remained outside the Islamic legal system.

[25] See Ṭabarī, *Kitāb Ikhtilāf*, pp. 60-61.

The Doctrine of the Jihād

The instrument which would transform the dār al-ḥarb into the dār al-Islām was the jihād. The jihād was not merely a duty to be fulfilled by each individual; it was also above all a political obligation imposed collectively upon the subjects of the state so as to achieve Islam's ultimate aim—the universalization of the faith and the establishment of God's sovereignty over the world.[26] Thus the jihād was an individual duty, especially in the defense of Islam, as well as a collective duty upon the community as a whole, and failure to fulfill it would constitute a gross error.[27]

The jihād, in the broad sense of the term, did not necessarily call for violence or fighting, even though a state of war existed between Islamic and non-Islamic territories, since Islam might achieve its ultimate goal by peaceful as well as by violent means. The jihād was equivalent to the Christian concept of the crusade, or a war of words as well as of the sword. In technical language, it was an " exertion " of one's own power to fulfill a prescribed duty, and the believers' recompense, in addition to worldly material rewards, would be the achievement of salvation, for the fulfillment of such a duty means the reward of Paradise.[28] This participation might be fulfilled by the heart, the tongue, or the hands, as well as by the sword. The jihād was accordingly a form of religious propaganda carried out by spiritual as well as by material means.[29]

[26] See Abū 'Abd-Allāh Muḥammad b. Ismā'īl al-Bukhārī, *Ṣaḥīḥ*, ed. M. L. Krehl (Paris, 1864), Vol. II, p. 280.

[27] Abū 'Abd-Allāh Muḥammad b. Idrīs al-Shāfi'ī, *Kitāb al-Umm*, Vol. I, p. 51; *Kitāb al-Risāla*, ed. Aḥmad Muḥammad Shākir (trans. Khadduri, *Islamic Jurisprudence: Shāfi'ī's Risāla* [Baltimore, 1961], pp. 82-86). For the significance of the jihād as a collective duty, see my *War and Peace in the Law of Islam*, pp. 60-62.

[28] Q. LXC, 10-13. A promise of Paradise is given to every believer who fulfills the basic duties, but none would enable him to gain Paradise as surely as participation in the jihād. See Sarakhsī, *Sharḥ Kitāb al-Siyar al-Kabīr li-Muḥammad b. al-Ḥasan al-Shaybānī*, ed. Salah al-Dīn al-Munajjid (Cairo, 1957), Vol. I, pp. 24-25.

[29] The believers may fulfill the jihād duty by heart in their efforts

Islam prohibited war in every form save in the fulfillment of a religious purpose, the jihād. The idea that certain wars are just, as Aristotle pointed out, and should therefore be distinguished from others is an old one.[30] It is implied in the *jus fetiale,* and regarded not only as *justum,* but also as *pium,* prescribed in the commands of gods and sanctioned by religion. Like the concept of the crusade in Christendom, the jihād was the Islamic *bellum justum.* It was enjoined by God upon all believers "to slay the polytheists whereever you may find them," [31] and the Prophet's utterance "to fight polytheists until they say: 'There is no god but God.'" [32] In Islamic legal theory, the jihād was a permanent obligation upon the believers to be carried out by a continuous process of warfare, psychological and political, even if not strictly military. No other form of fighting was lawful, whether within Islamic territory or outside it.[33] The Imām was empowered to decide when the jihād was to commence or stop. No essential difference among leading jurists is to be found on this fundamental duty, whether in orthodox or heterodox doc-

---

to combat the devil and to escape his persuasion to evil; by their tongue and hands in their attempt to support the right and correct the wrong; and by the sword in taking part in actual fighting and by sacrificing their "wealth and lives" (Q. LXI, 11) in the prosecution of war. See 'Alī b. Aḥmad b. Ḥazm, *Kitāb al-Faṣl fī al-Milal wa al-Niḥal* (Cairo, 1347/1928), Vol. IV, p. 135. See also my *War and Peace in the Law of Islam,* pp. 56-57.

[30] Aristotle, *Politics,* trans. Ernest Barker (New York, 1946), Bk. I, Chap. 8.

[31] Q. IX, 5.

[32] Bukhārī, *Ṣaḥīḥ,* Vol. I, p. 111; Abū Muḥammad 'Abd-Allah b. 'Abd al-Raḥman b. Faḍl b. Bahram al-Dārimī, *Sunan* (Damascus, 1349/1930), Vol. II, p. 218.

[33] Ibn Khaldūn, in describing the forms of war that existed in Islamic history, noted four different types: (1) tribal warfare, such as that which existed in the Arabian desert; (2) feuds and raids which are characteristic of primitive people; (3) wars prescribed by the sacred law; (4) war against rebels and dissenters. Considering the first two types to have been caused by purely selfish and material motives, he condemned them as unjustified and regarded only the last two, in pursuance of maintaining an ethical or religious standard, as just wars. ('Abd al-Raḥmān Ibn Khaldūn, *al-Muqqadima,* ed. W. M. de Slane [Paris, 1858], Vol. II, pp. 65-79; Eng. trans. F. Rosenthal [London, 1958], Vol. II, pp. 73-88.)

trine.[34] The concept, however, has undergone many alterations and adjustments in modern times, a subject to which we shall return.[35]

Conditions of Peace

In accordance with Islamic legal theory a state of war exists between the dār al-Islām and the dār al-ḥarb until the time when the former overcomes the latter. The state of war should, accordingly, come to an end when the dār al-ḥarb has disappeared. At such a stage the dār al-Islām, as the abode of peace, would reign supreme in the world. It may be argued, therefore, that the ultimate objective of Islam is the achievement of permanent peace rather than the perpetuation of war. Thus the jihād, in Islamic theory, was a temporary legal device designed to achieve Islam's ideal public order by transforming the dār al-ḥarb into the dār al-Islām. In practice, however, the two dārs—the dār al-Islām and the dār al-ḥarb—proved to be more permanent than the jurists had envisaged, and the Muslims became more accustomed to a state of dormant jihād rather than to a state of open hostility. In the meantime, contacts between Muslims and non-Muslims, personal and official, were conducted by peaceful means, although a state of war continued to exist between Islam and other countries.

In accordance with the law of Islam, brief spans of peace may be offered the inhabitants of the dār al-ḥarb, whether by a peace treaty concluded between Muslims and non-Muslims or by an amān (safe-conduct). A treaty, not exceeding ten years in duration, rendered enemy territory immune from Muslim attack and conferred upon its inhabitants the right of entering Islamic lands unmolested. In the absence of a

[34] For the Shī'ī doctrine of the jihād, see Qāḍī al-Nu'mān b. Muḥammad, *Da'ā'im al-Islām*, ed. Āṣif A. A. Fayḍī (A. A. A. Fyzee) (Cairo, 1951), Vol. I, pp. 399-466; A. Querry, *Recueill de lois concernant les Musulmans Schyites* (Paris, 1881), Vol. I, pp. 331-53. For a summary of the Shī'ī and Khārijī doctrines, see my *War and Peace in the Law of Islam*, pp. 60-69.

[35] See pp. 57 ff., below.

treaty, the ḥarbī—a person from the territory of war—may enter the territory of Islam under an amān, obtained beforehand from any Muslim. Such an amān, if granted, transforms the status of the ḥarbī from a state of war to one of temporary peace and security, with respect to his own private relations with the inhabitants of the territory of Islam. For the ḥarbī, subject to molestation owing to the state of war between his territory and Islam, becomes under Islamic law a musta'min, a person who is clothed with security as long as he remains in Islamic lands.[36] It is to this device that we must attribute the ease with which Muslims and non-Muslims crossed frontiers from one land to another for trade and for cultural and other purposes.

Non-Muslims who permanently resided in the dār al-Islām were given a special status defined in peace treaties of indefinite duration, called 'ahds or covenants, by which their lives and property were secured and religious tolerance enjoyed. Such treaties took the form of constitutional charters, since non-Muslims obtained a special status of citizenship, called Dhimmīs, provided they paid the poll tax (jizya) and accepted certain legal disabilities.[37]

Communities seeking to maintain neutrality had no place in the Islamic legal order, if neutrality were taken to mean the attitude of a state which voluntarily desired to refrain from hostile relations with belligerent parties. Since all communities were in a state of war with Islam, according to the Islamic legal theory, none would be immune from the jihād or allowed to enjoy the privileges of a neutral position if they failed to gain recognition as part of the dār al-Islām. Only Ethiopia attained a special status in its relationship with Islam and was declared immune from the jihād by virtue of doctrinal and historical considerations.[38]

Other countries that were spared an offensive jihād or enjoyed peaceful relations with Islam could do so only by virtue of peace treaties. But all such treaties, regardless of

[36] See Chap. VI, below.
[37] See Chap. V, below.
[38] See my *War and Peace in the Law of Islam*, pp. 253-58.

the number of renewals, were regarded as temporary arrangements, while the state of war was regarded as the normal relationship between the dār al-Islām and the dār al-ḥarb.[39]

The Relevance of Legal Theory to Historical Circumstances

The classical theory of the Islamic law of nations is found neither in the Qur'ān nor in the Prophet's utterances, although its basic assumptions were derived from these authoritative sources; it was rather the product of Islamic juridical speculation at the height of Islamic power. Islam, which had incorporated a complex of ethnic and cultural groups, was conceived by Muslim jurists as an ecumenical society, and they formulated a theory of state rationalizing existing conditions and aspirations. The expansion of Islam, by virtue of trade and cultural propaganda especially, was still in progress at the time, and the state, as the instrument of a universal religion, was considered capable of expanding *ad infinitum*.

In its early development, the state made no claim to be ecumenical, although it conceived of religion to be universal in nature. The Islamic state passed through various stages of evolution until it acquired universal attributes. It began as a city-state in Madīna (A. D. 622) and expanded later to incorporate Arabia and the neighboring countries as well as a vast area in southern Asia and northern Africa. It culminated in a golden age of ascendancy with the establishment of the 'Abbāsid dynasty (A. D. 750), often referred to as the Islamic classical period, and then began to be subdivided into political entities which accommodated themselves to surrounding conditions, until these entities were finally integrated as sovereign states in the modern community of nations. The stages through which the Islamic state evolved took the following forms:

[39] See Muḥammad Hamidullah, *Muslim Conduct of State* (3rd ed.; Lahore, 1953), pp. 292 ff., for the viewpoint that the state of war was not the normal relationship with other nations.

Stage	Years (A. D.)
1. City-state	622-632
2. Imperial	632-750
3. Universal	750-*ca.* 900
4. " Decentralization "	*ca.* 900-*ca.* 1500
5. " Fragmentation "	*ca.* 1500-1918
6. National	1918-

In the first two stages, especially under Umayyad rule, the Islamic state possessed an Arabian ethnic bias and its rulers depended heavily on the support of Arabian tribes. Subject races of non-Arabian origin who adopted Islam in the hope of attaining equality of status were often discriminated against in such matters as taxation and service to the state. In the middle of the eighth century, when the 'Abbāsid dynasty was established, the Islamic state began to change from an exclusive to a universal character. A revolution, led by elements stressing the religious and ecumenical character of Islam, produced the change. Had the Islamic state failed to transform itself from the exclusive into the ecumenical, it would probably have broken into two or more political entities. The transformation helped to preserve the outward unity of the Islamic community.

The Islamic state was compelled in practice to accommodate itself to the realities of surrounding conditions and to accept certain limitations, notwithstanding that in theory it recognized no state besides itself. Unable to incorporate the whole of mankind, the Islamic state tacitly accepted the principle of coexistence with others and conducted its external relations in accordance with principles derived from Islamic doctrine and from its long experience with other states. The overriding principle of coexistence compelled Islam to accept territorial limitations, although many a jurist continued to view them as irrelevant. Hence, the law was bound to become territorial as well as personal in character, and territorial differences created binding legal acts. It was in this period that leading jurists began to devote attention to the law governing the relations of the Islamic state with contemporary political communities and created works dealing with the problems arising from the encounters of Muslims with non-Muslims in war and peace.

Changes in the character and structure of the Islamic state occurred for internal reasons no less than for external considerations. The internal changes arose in the main out of a conflict between centrifugal and centripetal forces. Over a long period controversy raged between two schools of thought as to the nature of central authority. One school advocated a monistic doctrine of authority, stressing the necessity of a unified caliphate, while the other stressed a pluralistic theory allowing the rise of more than one caliphate within the legal superstructure. The advocates of central authority, represented by leading orthodox jurists, argued that since there was one God who was the source of divine power, and one law (the sharīʿa), there must be one caliph and one authority. The pluralistic school, or the advocates of the division of the political community into two (or more) political entities, argued that whenever Islamic territory is divided by the sea (which may be reformulated as natural barriers) it should be divided into two (or more) political communities, each headed by an independent caliph who would enforce the sacred law in his own realm. Leading jurists and theologians rejected the pluralistic view, while the doctrine of central authority was modified to permit the rise of subentities, each governed by a head who acknowledged the ultimate authority of the central caliphate. This interpretation represented a compromise school of thought, perhaps best expressed in the writings of the Shāfiʿī jurist al-Māwardī (974-1058), which sought to adjust the monistic doctrine of the caliphate to the realities of political conditions of the time. In his well-known work on the principles of government Māwardī stressed the ultimate authority of the caliph, but he advised that self-appointed provincial rulers be recognized so as to preserve the outward unity of the state.[40] This school of

[40] Abū al-Ḥasan ʿAlī b. Muḥammad b. Ḥabīb al-Māwardī, *Kitāb al-*

thought represented the emerging " decentralization " trends of the tenth century of the Christian era and culminated in the permanent division of Islam into separate political entities by the opening of the sixteenth century. During the " decentralization " stage the dār al-Islām and the dār al-ḥarb passed through a long transitional period of coexistence, which Don Juan Manuel characterized in the thirteenth century as *guerra fria* (cold war), before they tacitly arrived at an agreement to conduct their relations on the basis of equality and mutual interest.[41] The dār al-Islām accepted the state of peace rather than the state of war as the permanent basis for its relations with the dār al-ḥarb. This radical departure from the classical doctrine occurred in the sixteenth century when Muslim rulers agreed to deal with Christian princes on the basis of reciprocity and mutual interest. Before discussing this significant change, which made possible the incorporation of Islamic states within the emerging community of nations, we must first examine Shaybānī's works and his exposition of the classical theory.

Shaybānī's Life and Writings

Shaybānī's Forerunners

Shaybānī may be regarded as the most important jurist to write on the siyar, although he was not the first. Nor was the siyar before him a *corpus juris* studied systematically as a separate body from other parts of the sacred law. Formerly,

---

Aḥkām al-Sulṭānīya, ed. M. Enger (Bonn, 1853). For a discussion of Māwardī's theory, see H. A. R. Gibb, " al-Māwardī's Theory of the Khilāfah," *Islamic Culture,* Vol. XII (1937), pp. 291-302.

[41] Don Juan Manuel, Crown Prince and nephew of Ferdinand II and cousin of Alphonse X of Spain, distinguished between " hot war," which he said always ended by a peace treaty, and " cold war," which " does not bring peace." The latter concept, Don Juan thought, characterized the situation of his time (thirteenth and fourteenth centuries) which was the era of permanent hostility between the Christians and Muslims. See Louis Garcia Arias, *El Concepto de Guerra y la Denominade " Guerra Fria "* (Zaragoza, 1956), p. 67.

it was treated under the general heading of the jihād and attracted but a few of those who studied the sharī'a in the formative period. Some, like Ibrāhīm al-Nakha'ī (d. 95/714) and Ḥammād b. Sulaymān (d. 120/738), whose opinions influenced the early development of law, paid little attention to questions relating to the law of war; but others, like al-Sha'bī (d. 104/723) and Sufyān al-Thawrī (d. 161/778),[42] seem to have given greater attention to the subject and their ideas influenced Abū Ḥanīfa (d. 150/768) and his disciples, especially Abū Yūsuf and Shaybānī, who dealt more fully with it.[43] Mālik b. Anas (d. 179/796), the leading jurist of the Ḥijāz, devoted a relatively short chapter to the jihād.[44] His immediate predecessors, such as Zuhrī (d. 124/742) and Rabī'a (d. 136/754), displayed even less interest in the subject.[45] The Ḥijāzī jurists, somewhat remote from the areas in which Muslims and non-Muslims came into direct contact, paid little or no attention to the questions arising from the encounters between Islam and other communities.[46]

One of the early jurists who wrote a work on the siyar, treating it as an independent subject, was 'Abd al-Raḥmān al-Awzā'ī (d. 157/774). Awzā'ī's opinions, formulated in Syria under the Umayyad dynasty (for he spent the greater part of his life under that regime), represented the pattern of legal reasoning in that period. His doctrines were based primarily

[42] No specific works seem to have been written by these jurists but their opinions on specific questions relating to the law of war have been preserved in the fragment of Ṭabarī's *Kitāb Ikhtilāf*.

[43] A more detailed discussion on these Ḥanafī jurists will be found in the following section. In his book *al-Majmū'*, Zayd b. 'Alī (d. 122/744) devotes a chapter to the siyar, but this book, though ascribed to Zayd, was probably composed a century after his death. If it were authentic, the book would be the earliest on the subject. See J. Schacht, *Origins of Muhammadan Jurisprudence* (Oxford, 1950), p. 262.

[44] Mālik b. Anas, *al-Muwaṭṭa'*, ed. M. Fuād 'Abd al-Bāqī (Cairo, 1370/1951), Vol. II, pp. 443-71.

[45] See Ṭabarī, *Kitāb Ikhtilāf, passim.*

[46] In his work on Mālikī law in *al-Mudawwana* (Cairo, 1323/1905) Saḥnūn (d. 240/855) dealt more extensively with questions relating to the law of war, because Islam in North Africa and Spain came into direct contact with non-Muslim communities, but his treatment reflects no less the influence of Ḥanafī than Mālikī jurists on the subject.

on the sunna of the Prophet, which to him meant a narrative handed down from the Prophet, as well as the sunna or the practice of Muslims of his time, including official orders.[47] Awzā'ī wrote a treatise on the siyar which has failed to reach us, but its text is preserved in at least two works on the subject, the one from the pen of Abū Yūsuf and the other from Shāfi'ī's. Abū Yūsuf first cites Abū Ḥanīfa's differences with Awzā'ī and then presents his argument in support of Abū Ḥanīfa's opinions as well as his own, which differed but slightly from the latter's.[48] Shāfi'ī quotes the entire text of Awzā'ī, with commentaries and glossaries by Abū Ḥanīfa and Abū Yūsuf, and gives his own differences with the two Ḥanafī jurists. Shāfi'ī's opinions, based on the principle that only authoritative Traditions from the Prophet are binding, agree with Awzā'ī's opinions,[49] but the latter draws no distinction between the so-called authentic Traditions from the Prophet and narratives from his Companions, which Shāfi'ī had stressed.[50] Additional legal materials from Awzā'ī, confined almost exclusively to the siyar, are preserved in Ṭabarī's works.[51]

However, Awzā'ī's treatise on the siyar deals with practical questions relating to the law of war, especially the treatment of enemy persons and the distribution of spoils, and it could scarcely be regarded as a comprehensive study of the law governing Islam's external relations. Awzā'ī addressed himself to specific problems arising from the wars of conquest in early Islam, not with general principles, although one might well discern the general principles underlying the treatment of specific problems. Nor was his treatise speculative in nature, in the sense that it provided legal arguments in support of his opinions or a systematic method of reasoning such

[47] Cf. Schacht, *Origins of Muhammadan Jurisprudence*, pp. 34-35.

[48] Abū Yūsuf Ya'qūb b. Ibrāhim al-Anṣārī, *Kitāb al-Radd 'ala Siyar al-Awzā'ī*, ed. Abū al-Wafa al-Afghānī (Cairo, 1357/1939).

[49] Shāfi'ī, "Kitāb Siyar al-Awzā'ī," *Kitāb al-Umm* (Cairo, 1325/1907), Vol. VII, pp. 303-36.

[50] Khadduri, *Islamic Jurisprudence*, Chap. IX.

[51] See Ṭabarī, *Kitāb Ikhtilāf*, *passim*.

as that which was developing at the time among contemporary jurists in 'Irāq.[52]

Abū Ḥanīfa, representing a higher level of juristic speculation, was perhaps the first to develop a set of principles governing Islam's external relations with other communities as well as a coherent system of relationships between the Islamic and non-Islamic communities. His system may be regarded as essentially the product of personal opinion (ra'y) and analogical deduction rather than narratives related from the Prophet and his Companions, as reflected, for instance, in Awzā'ī's exposition of the subject. The text of the translated section of this book demonstrates that the principal sources of Abū Ḥanīfa's jurisprudence were personal opinion and analogical deduction, and only infrequently Traditions, which perhaps Shaybānī had provided. The text in translation, which will be more fully discussed in the following pages, is essentially an exposition of Abū Ḥanīfa's system of the siyar, although some of his opinions may be found in other works.[53] Abū Ḥanīfa's disciples and contemporaries, stimulated by a growing interest in a subject touching on Islam's relationship with other nations at the height of its power, carried further their master's work and provided us with elaborate studies.

Abū Ḥanīfa's principal disciples who paid special attention to the siyar were Abū Yūsuf and Shaybānī. In addition to committing to writing Abū Ḥanīfa's doctrines on the siyar in the *Kitāb al-Aṣl*—the text in translation in this book—Abū Yūsuf wrote a reply to Awzā'ī's book on the siyar, as we noted earlier. In the *Kitāb al-Āthār* he reported some of Abū Ḥanīfa's opinions on questions relating to the law of war,

[52] We know very little about Awzā'ī's opinions on other legal questions, for none of his works has reached us, nor do we know much about his life. Some light has been thrown on it recently by the publication of an anonymous manuscript edited by Shakīb Arslān, entitled *Maḥāsin al-Masā'ī fī Manāqib al-Imām Abī 'Amr al-Awzā'ī* (Cairo, n.d.), but it is not a critical study of his life, much less of his legal thought. See Schacht, "al-Awzā'ī," *Encyclopaedia of Islam* (2nd ed.), Vol. I, pp. 772-73 [bibliography].

[53] A summary of Abū Ḥanīfa's opinions on the siyar, compared with other contemporary jurists, is preserved in Ṭabarī, *Kitāb Ikhtilāf, passim.*

based on narratives and his predecessors' opinions.[54] Most important, perhaps, is his book *Kitāb al-Kharāj* which, though entitled *A Book on Taxation*, dealt with a variety of legal subjects, including the law governing Islam's relations with other communities. The significance of the work lies in that the author did not ascribe all of his opinions to Abū Ḥanīfa, as other disciples were in the habit of doing, but that he presents independently the opinions of other jurists as well as his own. Where his opinions are in agreement with Abū Ḥanīfa's, he does not enter into the reasons for it. But in cases of disagreement, whether with Abū Ḥanīfa or with others, he presents the arguments of Abū Ḥanīfa and his reasons for disagreement.[55] This book, written at the request of the Caliph Hārūn al-Rashīd, reflects the mature thought of a leading jurist as well as his long experience with the Islamic administration of justice. Abū Yūsuf's differences with Abū Ḥanīfa and Shaybānī will be noted in the translated portion of this book.

Another disciple of Abū Ḥanīfa who wrote a work on the siyar was Abū Isḥāq Ibrāhīm b. Muḥammad al-Fazārī.[56] Like Abū Yūsuf, he based his work on that of several other jurists, but we know very little about him.[57] He died after Abū Yūsuf in 186/802.

Shaybānī contributed more elaborate studies on the siyar than other disciples, and his works and ideas will be the subject of our discussion in the following pages, preceded by a brief account of his life.

Shaybānī's Life

Little is known of Shaybānī's childhood and early years in

[54] Abū Yūsuf, *Kitāb al-Āthār* (Cairo, 1355/1936), pp. 192-95.

[55] See Abū Yūsuf, *Kitāb al-Kharāj* (Cairo, 1352/1933), pp. 64, 84-85, 93.

[56] A copy of this work, dated 270/883, is to be found in the Qarawiyyīn Library, the second volume of which I have seen. Four other volumes are in fragments. For the life and works of Fazārī, see Abū Nu'aym al-Isfāhānī, *Ḥilyat al-Awliyā'* (Cairo, 1938), Vol. VIII, pp. 253-66.

[57] Fazārī states that he had based his work on the books of maghāzī by Ibn 'Utba, Ibn Isḥāq, 'Abd al-Razzāq Abī al-Namr, Ibn Shihāb, and on the siyar of Awzā'ī.

Kūfa, although a number of biographical accounts have given us fairly detailed accounts mixed with legends. The earliest accounts of Ibn Sa'd (d. 320/845)[58] and Ibn Qutayba (d. 276/890)[59] are devoid of legends, and very brief; but by the time al-Khaṭīb al-Baghdādī (d. 403/1013),[60] Ibn 'Abd al-Barr (d. 463/1070),[61] and al-Shirāzī (d. 476/1084)[62] wrote their biographies, legend and fact in the story of Shaybānī's life were already mixed. Later accounts, such as those of Ibn Khallikān (d. 681/1283),[63] al-Dhahabī (d. 748/1348),[64] al-Kirdarī (d. 827/1424),[65] and Ibn Quṭlubughā (d. 879/1474),[66] use the earliest sources, but the historical account is flavored with legend. Modern studies, such as that of Muḥammad Zāhid al-Kawtharī, are uncritical.[67] An attempt to study Shaybānī's life with a certain degree of detachment has already been made,[68] but a full critical study of his life and juris-

[58] Muḥammad Ibn Sa'd, *Kitāb al-Ṭabaqāt al-Kabīr* (Beirut, 1957), Vol. VI, pp. 336-37.

[59] Abū Muḥammad 'Abd-Allāh b. Muslim Ibn Qutayba, *Kitāb al-Ma'ārif*, ed. Tharwat 'Ukkāsha (Cairo, 1960), p. 500.

[60] Abū Bakr Aḥmad b. 'Alī al-Khaṭīb al-Baghdādī, *Ta'īkh Baghdād* (Cairo, 1349/1931), Vol. II, pp. 172-82.

[61] Abū 'Umar Yūsuf b. 'Abd-Allāh b. Muḥammad Ibn 'Abd al-Barr, *Kitāb al-Intiqā' fī Faḍā'il al-Thalātha al-A'imma al-Fuqahā'* (Cairo, 1350/1931), pp. 174-75.

[62] Abū Isḥāq al-Shīrāzī, *Ṭabaqāt al-Fuqahā'* (Baghdad, 1356/1938), pp. 114-15.

[63] Abū al-'Abbās Shams al-Dīn Aḥmad b. Muḥammad b. Abī Bakr Ibn Khallikān, *Wafayāt al-A'yān*, ed. M. Muḥī al-Dīn 'Abd al-Ḥamīd (Cairo, 1948), Vol. III, pp. 324-25.

[64] Abū 'Abd-Allāh Muḥammad b. Aḥmad b. Uthmān Dhahabī, *Manāqib al-Imām Abī Ḥanīfa wa Ṣaḥibayhi Abī Yūsuf wa Muḥammad b. al-Ḥasan*, ed. M. Zāhid al-Kawtharī and Abū al-Wafā al-Afghānī (Cairo, 1366/1947), pp. 50-60.

[65] Ibn al-Bazzāz al-Kiradarī, *Manāqib al-Imām al-A'zam* (published together with Abū al-Mu'ayyad al-Muwaffaq b. Aḥmad Makkī's *Manāqib al-Imām al-A'zam Abī Ḥanīfa* [Hyderabad, 1321/1904]), Vol. II, pp. 146-67.

[66] Zayn al-Dīn Ibn Quṭlubughā, *Tāj al-Tarājum* (Baghdad, 1962), p. 159.

[67] Muḥammad Zāhid b. al-Ḥasan al-Kawtharī, *Bulūgh al-Amānī fī Sīrat al-Imām Muḥammad b. al-Ḥasan al-Shaybānī* (Cairo, 1355/1937).

[68] See Abū Zahra's introduction to Sarakhsī's *al-Siyar al-Kabīr lil-Imām Muḥammad b. al-Ḥasan al-Shaybānī*, ed. Muḥammad Abū Zahra and Muṣṭafa Zayd (Cairo, 1958), Vol. I, pp. 7-36; *Abū-Ḥanīfa* (Cairo, 1947), pp. 206-17; W. Heffening, "al-Shaibānī," *Encyclopaedia of Islam* (1st ed.; Leiden and London, 1934), Vol. IV, pp. 271-72.

prudence remains to be written.[69]

The earliest authorities disagree as to whence his ancestors came—whether from al-Jazīra, in northern 'Irāq, or from Ḥarasta, near Damascus, Syria. Ibn Sa'd gives the Jazīra as the place of origin and states that Shaybānī's father served in the Syrian army before moving to 'Irāq, where Shaybānī was born in the town of Wāsiṭ in 132/750.[70] Al-Khaṭīb al-Baghdādī states that Shaybānī's father came from Ḥarsta, a suburb of Damascus, and that he was in the service of the Syrian army during Umayyad rule, although his ancestors had come originally from the Jazīra, where the tribes of Banū Shaybān had gone and with whom Shaybānī's grandfather had been associated and whose client he became.[71] But neither Ibn Sa'd nor Baghdādī states whether Shaybānī's ancestors were Arabian or non-Arabian in origin. The silence of authorities on this matter, contrary to the conclusion drawn by a modern writer,[72] should mean rather that his ancestors were likely to have been non-Arabian in origin, since his grandfather sought to become the client of an Arabian tribe. From Syria, Shaybānī's father, who seems to have become well-to-do in the meantime, moved to Kūfa, a center of political and religious activities under the newly established 'Abbāsid dynasty. Shaybānī was born in Wāsiṭ, so-called as a midway town between Kūfa and Baṣra,[73] to which Shaybānī's father may have gone on business or on a visit. But Shaybānī was soon taken to Kūfa, where he grew up and spent the greater part of his life as a diligent student of the sacred law.[74]

[69] For works on Shaybānī's life and jurisprudence, see Select Bibliography, p. 302.

[70] Ibn Sa'd, *Ṭabaqāt*, Vol. VII, p. 336.

[71] Baghdadi, *Ta'rīkh Baghdād*, Vol. II, p. 172.

[72] Abū Zahra's introduction to Sarakhsī's *al-Siyar*, p. 8.

[73] Founded by al-Ḥajjāj, the Umayyad governor of 'Irāq, as a military center in 83/702.

[74] The early authorities are agreed that Shaybānī was born in 132/750, but Ibn 'Abd al-Barr states that he was born in 135/753 (see Ibn 'Abd al-Barr's *al-Intiqā'*, p. 174). This date has apparently been quoted uncritically by Ibn Khallikān (see Ibn Khallikān's *Wafayāt al-'Āyān*, Vol. III, p. 324).

Kūfa was one of the two principal centers of learning in 'Irāq and played a significant role in the development of the sharī'a. A number of jurists, such as Ibrāhīm al-Nakha'ī (d. 95/714), Sha'bī (d. 104/723), Ḥammād b. Sulaymān (d. 120/738), and Abū Ḥanīfa (d. 150/768) won reputations there by stressing personal reasoning and analogical deduction while their contemporaries in the Ḥijāz claimed to follow Traditions in judicial decisions. Abū Ḥanīfa, the founder of a school of law bearing his name, perhaps tended to use analogy as the basis of legal reasoning more than others, but Mālik b. Anas (d. 179/795), the founder of another school of law in the Ḥijāz, used personal reasoning no less than his contemporaries did in 'Irāq. The legal reasoning of the jurists of these early centers of learning, contrary to what their disciples maintained, did not differ radically in one center from another, regardless of whether they used analogy or Traditions.

It was in this milieu that Shaybānī grew up and came to play so significant a role in the development of the sharī'a. Growing up in Kūfa, the seat of Abū Ḥanīfa's circle, he became a follower first of Abū Ḥanīfa and then of his disciple Abū Yūsuf. As a young student of law he learned of Mālik's reputation as the leading jurist of the Ḥijāz. He went to Madīna to study under him and was exposed to the legal reasoning of the Ḥijāzī jurists. However, the greater part of Shaybānī's career was devoted to writing and lecturing rather than to service as a judge. In the final decade of his life, he reluctantly agreed to serve as a qāḍī (judge) but was interrupted by lecturing for two years. Shaybānī's career falls, therefore, into three well-marked periods. The first, the period of study and preparation, began with his attachment to the circles of Abū Ḥanīfa and Abū Yūsuf, where he was given a thorough training in legal reasoning, and extends to Abū Yūsuf's appointment as Chief Qāḍī. The second, when Shaybānī became the brilliant lecturer in Kūfa, extended to his appointment as Qāḍī of Raqqa. The third, in which he combined judicial experience with intellectual maturity and became, after Abū Yūsuf's death, the master, ended with his death.

The early authorities scarcely tell us anything of significance about Shaybānī's life before he joined Abū Ḥanīfa's circle, except that he was brought up in a relatively prosperous family and that he was devoted to learning from his youth. At fourteen he joined Abū Ḥanīfa's circle in 146/764, for, according to Shaybānī's biographers, he had studied only four years when Abū Ḥanīfa died in 150/768. Shaybānī seems to have attended the circles of other scholars, whether in Kūfa or elsewhere, for Ibn Sa'd cites the names of Mis'ar b. Kidām (d. 153/770), Sufyān al-Thawrī (d. 161/778), Awzā'ī (d. 157/774), Ibn Jurayj (d. 150/767), and others;[75] al-Khaṭīb al-Baghdādī, who confirms these names, adds Mālik b. Anas,[76] with whom Shaybānī read the *Muwaṭṭa'*, a *corpus juris* reputed to have been based on the Traditions known to the Ḥijāzī jurists. The authorities do not state when Shaybānī made the journey to Mālik, but while in the Ḥijāz he studied under Ibn Jurayj of Makka, who died in 150/767, and hence the journey must have taken place before that year. On his way to the Ḥijāz, Shaybānī probably stopped in Syria to study under Awzā'ī, author of a work on the siyar, from whom the inspiration to write a separate work on the subject may have derived.[77] That Shaybānī made a journey to the Ḥijāz to study under Mālik is attested by the fact that a version of the *Muwaṭṭa'*, transmitted by Shaybānī, has been preserved.[78]

Abū Ḥanīfa, who was the first to introduce Shaybānī to the study of law, died in 150/768 when Shaybānī was eighteen

[75] Ibn Sa'd, *Ṭabaqāt*, Vol. VII, p. 336.

[76] Baghdādī, *Ta'rīkh Baghdād*, Vol. II, p. 172.

[77] Sarakhsī relates an anecdote, perhaps circulated by Shaybānī's disciples, telling that when Awzā'ī came across a book on the siyar by Shaybānī he made a derogatory remark to the effect that the 'Irāqī jurists were not acquainted with this subject. This remark, according to this anecdote, prompted Shaybānī to write an enlarged work on the siyar. But such stories were often told by disciples to enhance the prestige of their masters and deprecate the importance of rival jurists. See Sarakhsī, *Sharḥ Kitāb al-Siyar al-Kabīr*, ed. Munajjid, Vol. I, p. 3.

[78] Muḥammad b. al-Ḥasan al-Shaybānī, *al-Muwaṭṭa'* (Lucknow, 1297 and 1306; Cairo, 1962).

years old. At that tender age he could scarcely have comprehended in full Abū Ḥanīfa's sophisticated legal reasoning; it devolved therefore upon Zufar and Abū Yūsuf, who succeeded Abū Ḥanīfa as lecturers, to train the promising young disciple. Zufar went to Baṣra soon after Abū Ḥanīfa's death and he died in 158/775. It was to Abū Yūsuf, therefore, that Shaybānī was mainly indebted for his training in the law, and through his lectures Abū Ḥanīfa's doctrines passed to Shaybānī. In Abū Yūsuf's circle, Shaybānī distinguished himself as a diligent disciple and a brilliant debater. Even before Abū Yūsuf relinquished the chair as lecturer (*ca.* 170/786), when he went to Baghdad to serve as qāḍī, Shaybānī proved an attractive lecturer and seems to have competed with his master in popularity among those who attended his lectures. This may have prompted Abū Yūsuf to get him the office of qāḍī which he then reluctantly accepted. Shaybānī remained in Kūfa as a lecturer until 180/797, when he became the Qāḍī of Raqqa at the age of forty-eight. Even as qāḍī he continued to write and to lecture; he seems to have been a born teacher and was completely devoted to research and writing.

In 180/797 Shaybānī was suddenly and unexpectedly ordered by the authorities to proceed to Baghdad. The order seems to have upset him, for he went straight to Abū Yūsuf upon his arrival in Baghdad to voice his complaint. Abū Yūsuf stated, according to a traditional story, that he had been consulted about a candidate for the office of qāḍī in Raqqa—a town on the Euphrates and a summer resort for the Caliph Hārūn al-Rashīd—and that he had suggested the name of Shaybānī. His reason was, Abū Yūsuf emphasized, that legal knowledge of the Ḥanafī doctrine had spread in the eastern provinces, and that he thought it right that it should spread beyond the Euphrates into Syria and other provinces. Shaybānī replied that a call without a prior knowledge of the reason was repugnant to him, but Abū Yūsuf replied that the sudden call was issued by the authorities. Shaybānī told his master that an official position did not interest him and Abū Yūsuf took him to Yaḥyā b. Khālid b. Barmak, the

Caliph's First Minister, to discuss the matter. Ibn Barmak seems to have threatened Shaybānī and compelled him to accept the office against his desire. This, according to traditional accounts, was the reason for the estrangement between master and disciple.

But if master and disciple grew estranged on account of the appointment, a second reason must have played a part. It was well-known that Shaybānī, following the precedent of his former master Abū Ḥanīfa, was more interested in scholarly pursuits than in service as a judge. Scholars did not look with favor upon the office of judge because it would entail the subordination of their consciences to official pressures. This consideration seems to have affected Shaybānī and he preferred to follow the precedent of Abū Ḥanīfa rather than Abū Yūsuf. Like Abū Ḥanīfa, he had inherited wealth from his father; unfettered by family demands, he could afford to put aside the material temptations that an official position offered.

Against this background Shaybānī's injured feelings when Abū Yūsuf, without prior consultation, suggested his name to the authorities as a judge in Raqqa, become understandable. But Shaybānī's biographers seem to have exaggerated the rift, and have interpreted the recommendation of his name by Abū Yūsuf as an act of jealousy of the disciple's growing reputation as a scholar. But in his service as a judge, contrary to traditional accounts, Shaybānī gave up neither teaching nor writing. The story of the estrangement between master and disciple must therefore be discounted, for the personal injury felt by Shaybānī at the outset had probably been superseded by the advantages gained from an official position. Moreover, the spread of Ḥanafī doctrines west of the Euphrates, as Abū Yūsuf had hoped, must have come as a satisfaction to Shaybānī and his followers. Shaybānī held the position of Qāḍī in Raqqa for seven years, from 180/797 to 187/803. Scarcely two years had passed in that office when Abū Yūsuf, Chief Qāḍī of Baghdad, passed away. Shaybānī was in Raqqa at the time. He did not attend the funeral in Baghdad and failed therefore to recite the funeral prayer for his master on that occasion. His absence led critics to remark that the two had remained estranged, but this was not likely, as noted earlier. Shaybānī seems to have been too pleased with his work in Raqqa to feel any grudge against his master. Furthermore he must have realized that his experiences as a judge were invaluable in his research and writings and the deference attached to an official position was probably an added attraction. After his dismissal in 187/803, he seems to have been anxious to return to the bench two years later.[79]

In 187/803 Shaybānī was dismissed as Qāḍī of Raqqa. The reason given was a legal opinion issued by him on the validity of an amān (pledge of security) granted by the Caliph Hārūn al-Rashīd to the Zaydī Imām Yaḥya b. 'Abd-Allāh in 176/793, which thereafter, it seems, had not been fully observed. The Caliph held a conference in Raqqa, his summer capital, in which the Zaydī Imām affair was the subject of discussion. Abū al-Bakhtarī Wahb b. Wahb, then Chief Qāḍī, attended the conference. Shaybānī, Qāḍī of Raqqa, and al-Ḥasan b. Ziyād al-Lu'lu'ī (d. 204/819), a well-known jurist, were also invited. Shaybānī stated in no uncertain terms that the amān was valid but al-Ḥasan b. Ziyād hesitated to give a clear answer, althongh he seems to have shared Shaybānī's opinion. Abū al-Bakhtarī, in supporting the Caliph's position, stated that Imām Yaḥya's conduct justified the withdrawal of the amān. Imām Yaḥya, whom the Caliph apparently wanted to put to death, was thrown into prison and died thereafter. The Caliph dismissed Shaybānī as he suspected him of possible sympathy with the Zaydī Imām.[80] He went to Baghdad where he spent the next two years in lecturing and writing. Some authorities maintain that Shaybānī was deprived of the right, after his dismissal, to issue legal opinions. It was during this period that Muḥammad b. Idrīs al-Shāfi'ī, who

[79] See Abū Zahra's introductory essay on the life of Shaybānī in Sarakhsī's *al-Siyar*, p. 12.

[80] Kirdarī, *Manāqib al-Imām al-A'zam*, Vol. II, pp. 163-65; Muḥammad b. Khalaf b. Ḥayyān Wakī', *Akhbār al-Quḍāt* (Cairo, 1947), Vol. I, p. 249.

seems to have also sympathized with the Zaydī Imām, had arrived in Baghdad and made the acquaintance of Shaybānī and studied his works.[81]

Shaybānī's loyalty to the Caliph must have been demonstrated after settling in Baghdad. The Caliph seems to have appreciated his attitude and moral integrity and, very soon after, restored him to grace. Some say that Shaybānī was appointed Chief Qāḍī of Baghdad at this time, but the authorities are unclear. If al-Bakhtarī, the Chief Qāḍī, lived in Baghdad until his appointment as Governor of Madīna in 192/807, Shaybānī, who died in 189/804, could scarcely have succeeded him as Chief Qāḍī.[82] However, authorities agree that in the last year of Shaybānī's life the Caliph Hārūn al-Rashīd appointed him as Qāḍī of Rayy (Khurāsān). Shaybānī accompanied the Caliph on an expedition to suppress a rebellion in Samarqand, led by Rāfi' b. al-Layth, and died in Rayy when the Caliph was there.

It is possible that Shaybānī had given legal opinions to the Caliph on public matters before his reappointment as qāḍī. In a conflict with the Byzantines, the Caliph seems to have suspected that the sympathy of the Christians of the tribe of Banū Taghlib lay with the Byzantines and sought to punish them by revoking the covenant granted them by the Caliph 'Umar. In an effort to justify his action, the Caliph Hārūn maintained that the Banū Taghlib had baptized their children in violation of their covenant with Islam that they would become Muslims. Shaybānī supported the position of the Banū Taghlib, based on the practice of 'Umar and his successors, which, he argued, had been followed since 'Umar's time. If this act violated the covenant of 'Umar and his successors, Shaybānī said, the covenant could have been revoked by them long ago. But Shaybānī was cautious in expressing

[81] See my introduction in *Islamic Jurisprudence*, p. 12. Cf. Schacht, "On Shāfi'ī's Life and Personality," *Studia Orientalia Ioanni Pedersen* (Copenhagen, 1963), p. 320, who questions the involvement of the two jurists—Mālik and Shāfi'ī—in the affair of the Zaydī Imām Yaḥya b. 'Abd-Allāh.

[82] Wakī', *Akhbār al-Quḍāt*, Vol. I, pp. 243-44.

his opinion to the Caliph, who held the highest authority, by remarking that the latter's pronouncement would be supreme.[83] The flexible nature of the reply, in contrast to his earlier opinion on the Zaydī Imām, must have pleased the Caliph. It is possible that before Shaybānī was appointed a qāḍī of Rayy, he held an official position in Baghdad, for he seems to have been frequently called to the Court for consultation. The span between Shaybānī's dismissal from Raqqa in 187 to his death in 189 might be regarded as covering the peak of his prestige and reputation as a great Ḥanafī jurist and perhaps as the leading jurist of his day, for Abū Yūsuf and Mālik had both passed away and Shāfi'ī had not yet emerged as a rival to the Ḥanafī jurists.

Shaybānī is described as having been very handsome from his youth and as an adult he was quite conscious of his appearance. He was relatively short and fat but possessed an attractive personality. A traditional story has it that Shāfi'ī said of him that he had never seen a fat person as light-hearted and attractive as Shaybānī.[84] He seems to have been an able speaker and a persuasive debater, for his discourses and lectures attracted many students. In disputations with rival jurists he is depicted as patient and understanding, although traditional accounts imply that other jurists were impatient with rival debaters. He is also described as speaking eloquently and reciting the Qur'ān in a pleasing voice.

From early childhood Shaybānī displayed a sharp intelligence, a good memory, and a passionate desire for knowledge. It is true that he was attracted to the legal method of Abū Ḥanīfa, which stressed analogical reasoning, but he showed a desire to collect Traditions, perhaps under the influence of Abū Yūsuf. There was a growing interest in the study of Traditions and Shaybānī combined analogy and Traditions as sources for his legal reasoning. But this legal methodology will be discussed later. Although the study of law was his

[83] Baghdādī, *Ta'rīkh Baghdād,* Vol. II, p. 174; Kirdarī, *Manāqib al-Imām al-A'zam,* Vol. II, p. 150.
[84] Baghdādī, *Ta'rīkh Baghdād,* Vol. II, pp. 175; Kirdarī, *Manāqib al-Imām al-A'zam,* Vol. II, p. 156.

main concern, he paid attention to other branches of learning and to the Arabic language and Arabic sciences in particular. He was said to be a great friend of al-Kisā'ī, the well-known grammarian, and they seem to have discussed questions of grammar.[85]

Traditional accounts give the impression that Shaybānī was throughout his life averse to judicial offices. The fact is particularly stressed in connection with the traditional story of the estrangement with Abū Yūsuf. While Shaybānī's attitude toward the office of qāḍī may have been true in Kūfa, where teaching and writing seem to have absorbed him completely, it shifted after he occupied the office. It is true that he never lost interest in teaching and writing even after going to Raqqa. Indeed, his reputation and prestige were enhanced and his maturity and practical experiences enriched his writings. From Raqqa Shaybānī went to Baghdad rather than to Kūfa, where he could exert an influence in official as well as nonofficial circles. While in Baghdad he seems to have been anxious to return to official work, for he remained attached to the authorities and agreed to resume his judicial functions two years later and perhaps earlier. If the traditional account that Shaybānī was appointed Chief Qāḍī of Baghdad is true, he must have filled in the last year or two of his life the highest judicial position that a jurist of his caliber could aspire to. At that time Ḥanafī jurists reached perhaps the highest point of their prestige in official circles, centuries before the school of the law they represented became official under the Ottoman sultans.

Shaybānī's Writings

Shaybānī was a prolific writer who set down the Ḥanafī doctrines, as well as those of other jurists, as his version of Mālik's *Muwaṭṭa'* attests. It is true that he was not the first to write juridical works, since Awzā'ī, Mālik, and Abū Yūsuf had preceded him. Indeed, Abū Yūsuf is credited with numer-

[85] Kirdarī, *Manāqib al-Imām al-A'zam*, Vol. II, p. 152.

ous works, although but few have reached us. Shaybānī began to write when he was still a disciple and proved the most productive in the formative period of the sharī'a.

Some of his books, especially those written when he was studying under Abū Yūsuf, were in the main compilations of the views of Abū Ḥanīfa as he heard them from Abū Yūsuf or as they were dictated to him by Abū Yūsuf. All the books described as al-ṣaghīr, such as *al-Jāmi' al-Ṣaghīr* and *al-Siyar al-Ṣaghīr*, were said to have been dictated by Abū Yūsuf, while those described as al-kabīr, such as *al-Jāmi' al-Kabīr*, and *al-Siyar al-Kabīr*, were written by Shaybānī on his own responsibility without supervision.[86] However, this distinction between Shaybānī's own works and those written under Abū Yūsuf's supervision seems too simple. Some of Shaybānī's early works, such as *Kitāb al-Aṣl* and *Kitāb al-Āthār*, were written under Abū Yūsuf's direction,[87] but neither was called al-ṣaghīr.

Shaybānī's principal works are often called "the books of zāhir al-riwāya," whether written by him or under the supervision of Abū Yūsuf, on the ground that they are authentic and were transmitted by his disciples. But Shaybānī's other works, though they carry his name and contain some of his opinions, are not regarded as authentic because they were not contributed by him.[88]

Some of Shaybānī's works, like *Kitāb al-Āthār* and *Kitāb al-Radd 'ala Ahl al-Madīna*, are authentic writings, although not considered to be in the category of zāhir al-riwāya. The *Kitāb al-Āthār*, consisting of Traditions related by Shaybānī, may have been recorded by a disciple, but *Kitāb al-Radd 'ala Ahl al-Madīna*, which failed to reach us, seems to have been written by Shaybānī. Shāfi'ī wrote a critical commentary on the book and reported with the full text his commentary on it, which now may be found in his collected works, known

[86] Muḥammad Amīn Ibn 'Ābidīn, *Majmū'at Rasā'il: al-Risāla al-Thāniya: Sharḥ al-Manzūma al-Musammāt Bi'uqūd Rasm al-Muftī* (Istānbūl, 1325/1907), Vol. I, pp. 16, 19.

[87] Baghdādī cites a statement from Shaybānī to the effect that only *Kitāb al-Jāmi' al-Ṣaghīr* was dictated to him by Abū Yūsuf. See Baghdādī, *Ta'rīkh Baghdād*, Vol. II, p. 180.

[88] *Ibid.*, p. 17.

as *Kitāb al-Umm.*[89] Shaybānī's works which have direct bearing on the present study are the *Kitāb al-Aṣl* (the portion pertaining to the siyar is given in this work in translation) and the *Kitāb al-Jāmiʿ al-Ṣaghīr.* The *Kitāb al-Siyar al-Kabīr,* whose original text seems to have been lost, is known to us only through the elaborate commentary, known as *Sharḥ Kitāb al-Siyar al-Kabīr,* by Sarakhsī.

Shaybānī and the Islamic Law of Nations

THE CONCEPT OF SIYAR

In the second century of the Islamic era, especially after the establishment of the ʿAbbāsid dynasty (132/750), scholars began to develop an interest in the study of Islam's achievements and to take note of the enormous changes that had set in after Muḥammad's death. The scholars took a critical attitude toward the Umayyad caliphs and weighed their conduct in the scales of the ethical and religious standards of their predecessors—the Prophet and the early Orthodox caliphs. The only jurist who grew up under the Umayyads and took a relatively unbiased attitude toward them was Awzāʿī, who wrote a treatise on the law of war, as we noted earlier, based on the sunna of the Prophet and his successors, including the Umayyad caliphs.

The scholars of the early ʿAbbāsid period began to study the conduct of the Prophet and his early successors as models so as to learn from their practices. They interested themselves in fields such as the siyar and maghāzī, consisting of the campaigns and military expeditions of the Prophet and the early military commanders, and sought to discover the legal norms underlying those military exploits. Some confined their study to narratives of the past, while others sought to reformulate legal rules for the future relationships of Islam with other peoples. These inquiries introduced into Islamic learning a

[89] Shāfiʿī, *Umm,* Vol. VII, pp. 277-303.

new concept of the siyar which transformed it from a narrative to a normative character.

The term siyar, plural of sīra, gained two meanings in the second century of the Islamic era, one used by chroniclers in their narrative accounts to mean life or biography, and the other, used by jurists, to mean the conduct of the state in its relationships with other communities.[90] The term literally meant motion, before scholars came to formulate the new meanings. In the Qur'ān, where the word can be found in six verses, it is used in the sense of "travel" or "to move,"[91] or in the sense of "form."[92] In the Prophet's time, it had not yet acquired a technical meaning.

The early jurists treated the subject matter of the siyar either under the general heading of the jihād, or under such particular subjects as maghāzī (campaigns), ghanīma (spoil), ridda (apostasy), and amān (safe-conduct); but almost all confined their treatment to the law of war.[93] Who was the first to use the term siyar in the normative sense is not known, but the Ḥanafī jurists were known to be the first to popularize the term. It is likely that the legal meaning began to evolve in the formative period of the sharī'a, and Abū Ḥanīfa used it in his lectures in Kūfa. It is said that these lectures were committed to writing by disciples of Abū Ḥanīfa, such as al-Ḥasan b. Ziyād al-Lu'lu'ī, Abū Isḥāq al-Fazārī, and Muḥammad b. al-Ḥasan al-Shaybānī. Perhaps it was the work of the latter, according to a traditional story, that Awzā'ī had seen and on which he wrote a critical commentary which came to be known as *The Siyar of al-Awzā'ī*. Awzā'ī's treatise, as we noted earlier, was commented upon by Abū Yūsuf in defense of Abū Ḥanīfa's doctrines, but the original text has failed to reach us. Some parts of Awzā'ī's exposition, it is true, read like a reply to Abū Ḥanīfa, but the original text

[90] Nāsir b. 'Abd-Allāh al-Muṭarrazī, *al-Mughrib* (Hyderabad, 1328/1910), Vol. II, p. 272.

[91] Q. III, 131; VI, ii; XII, 30; XVI, 38; XXXIV, 17.

[92] Q. XX, 22.

[93] Mālik, *al-Muwaṭṭa'*, Vol. II, pp. 443-71, 736; Ṭabarī, *Kitāb Ikhtilāf*, *passim*; Shāfi'ī, *Umm*, Vol. IV, pp. 82-147.

may have been written without reference to the latter. An inquiry into the external relations of Islam seems to have attracted a number of early jurists who speculated searchingly on the subject before the time of Abū Ḥanīfa, among them Nakha'ī, Sha'bī, and Ḥammād, as the fragments of Ṭabarī's *Ikhtilāf al-Fuqahā'* demonstrate, but it seems they wrote no treatises on the subject.[94] Thus, Abū Ḥanīfa might well be regarded as the first who treated the subject systematically, and the material of his lectures was incorporated in the writings of his disciples.

The scholar who took a keen interest in the siyar and wrote a number of works on it was Shaybānī. He committed to writing the doctrines of Abū Ḥanīfa and Abū Yūsuf on the subject and incorporated his own opinions as well.

Shaybānī never defined the term siyar nor gave a precise meaning to it. It was his successors, in their comments or glosses on his writings, who tried to give the term a specific definition. Sarakhsī (d. 483/1101), in a copious commentary on Shaybānī's siyar, defined the term as follows:

> The siyar is the plural of sīra and this book is called after this term. It describes the conduct of the believers in their relations with the unbelievers of enemy territory as well as with the people with whom the believers had made treaties, who may have been temporarily (musta'mins) or permanently (Dhimmīs) in Islamic lands; with apostates, who were the worst of the unbelievers, since they abjured after they accepted [Islam]; and with rebels (baghīs), who were not counted as unbelievers, though they were ignorant and their understanding [of Islam] was false.[95]

Another Ḥanafī jurist, Kāsānī (d. 587/1191), defined the term as: "The ways of conduct of the warriors and what is incumbent upon them and for them [i. e., the rules binding upon them and others]." [96]

[94] Ṭabarī, *Kitāb Ikhtilāf, passim.*
[95] Sarakhsī, *Mabsūṭ*, Vol. X, p. 2.
[96] 'Alā al-Dīn Abū Bakr b. Mas'ūd al-Kāsānī, *Kitāb Badā'i' al-Ṣanā'i'* (Cairo, 1328/1910), Vol. VII, p. 97.

These definitions, though stressing the law of war, approached nearest what is called nowadays the law of nations. The siyar was obviously law regulating relationships among political entities as well as among individuals. It was a law which Muslims declared to be binding upon themselves, regardless of whether non-Muslims accepted it. However, when Muslims entered into peace treaties with other communities both parties observed the principle *pacta sunt servanda* as well as other rules derived from reciprocity. Essentially, the siyar formed an Islamic law of nations, not a law binding on all nations in the modern sense of the term.

Shaybānī's Works on the Siyar

Shaybānī's works deal with nearly every aspect of the law and more extensively than earlier writers had done. In most of his works a portion is devoted to the siyar as a whole or to some of its aspects, at least. Most important, of course, are the two treatises which he devoted to the siyar exclusively. No other jurist in the formative period seems to have contributed more to this field than Shaybānī, and on that account his writings are of particular interest to students of the law of nations.

Shaybānī's first book, the *Kitāb al-Siyar al-Ṣaghīr,* was dictated to him by Abū Yūsuf, it is said.[97] The work is often called the *Siyar of Abū Ḥanīfa,* since it embodied the latter's doctrines, notwithstanding that the authors were Abū Yūsuf and Shaybānī. It is said that the work had prompted Awzā'ī to compose his book, *The Siyar of al-Awzā'ī,* in the form of a reply to Abū Ḥanīfa's doctrines, and that Abū Yūsuf had rejoined by writing the *Kitāb al-Radd 'alā Siyar al-Awzā'ī,* in which he refuted the critical remarks. Unfortunately, neither Shaybānī's *Siyar al-Ṣaghīr* nor Awzā'ī's *Siyar* has reached us. *Al-Siyar al-Ṣaghīr* may have been a label attached to Shaybānī's work after he had written his *magnum opus* on

[97] Having committed the book to writing, Shaybānī is said to have read it to Abū Yūsuf, who approved of the text.

the subject, the *Kitāb al-Siyar al-Kabīr*. The *Siyar of Abū Ḥanīfa* may also have been an early name, although the work of that name might likely have been another which Abū Yūsuf committed to writing and to which Awzā'ī replied. Shaybānī may also have written a second variant of Abū Ḥanīfa's lectures called *al-Siyar al-Ṣaghīr*.[98] The confusion between the two books may be traceable to this, for some state that Awzā'ī had seen Abū Ḥanīfa's *Siyar* and replied to it while others mention that Shaybārī wrote his *Kitāb al-Siyar al-Kabīr* as a reply to a derogatory remark made by Awzā'ī on his *Siyar al-Ṣaghīr*. As related by Sarakhsī, the story betrays an inner contradiction. Awzā'ī could scarcely have read Shaybānī's *Siyar al-Kabīr* since he had died before it was composed. It is clear, at any rate, that Shaybānī's *Siyar al-Ṣaghīr*, whether it was a version of Abū Ḥanīfa's *Siyar* or a dictation by Abū Yūsuf, was essentially an exposition of Abū Ḥanīfa's doctrines on the siyar.

The most elaborate of Shaybānī's works on the siyar was the *Kitāb al-Siyar al-Kabīr*. Sarakhsī, who wrote a commentary on the work, stated that the composition was prompted by the following:

> As to the reason which led to the composition of this book, it happened that the *Siyar al-Ṣaghīr* fell into the hands of 'Abd al-Raḥmān b. 'Amr al-Awzā'ī, the scholar of Syria, who asked: "Who is the author of this book?" "Its author is Muḥammad, the 'Irāqī," he was told. "How is it that the people of 'Irāq compose books on such a subject, since they have no knowledge of the siyar, and the maghāzī [campaigns] of the Apostle of God and his Companions took place in the Ḥijāz and Syria, not in 'Irāq." These words of Awzā'ī, which came to the knowledge of Muḥammad, annoyed him and he set forth to compose this book for his own satisfaction. It is said that when Awzā'ī glanced through the book, he remarked that had he [Shaybānī] not supported everything by Traditions, I would

[98] It is said that other disciples, such as al-Ḥasan b. Ziyād al-Lu'lu'ī, committed to writing other variants of Abū Ḥanīfa's *Siyar*.

have said that he has laid down knowledge out of himself and that God put forth the right opinions in his mind.[99]

In addition to the inner contradiction in Sarakhsī's statement, as we stated earlier, the reason given by Sarakhsī as to why Shaybānī wrote the *Siyar al-Kabīr* appears too simple. Shaybānī displayed an interest in the study of the law governing Islam's external relations early in life and set forth his ideas on the subject in several works. His *magnum opus* on the siyar, called the *Kitāb al-Siyar al-Kabīr*, seems to have been written toward the end of Shaybānī's life, when he was still qāḍī in Raqqa or perhaps after he had settled in Baghdad in 187/802. It is said that he sent a copy of the work to the Caliph Hārūn al-Rashīd, who was impressed by it and ordered his two sons, al-Amīn and al-Ma'mūn, to read it under Shaybānī's guidance. If the story is true, the work must have been completed in Baghdad. It is also said that the substance of the work was transmitted by Ismā'īl b. Tawba al-Qazwīnī, the tutor of the Caliph's sons, who had heard it when Shaybānī read the text before the latter,[100] and by Abū Sulaymān al-Juzjānī (d. *ca.* 200/815).[101] This book, written in Shaybānī's mature years, represents his final reflections on the subject, although the original text has been lost.

Two commentaries on Shaybānī's major work have been written. One was by al-Jamāl al-Huṣayrī, an obscure jurist who resided in Damascus, it appears, and died in the seventh century of the Islamic era (thirteenth century A.D.). His commentary has failed to reach us. The other was by Muḥammad b. Aḥmad al-Sarakhsī (d. 483/1101), who received his training in the sharī'a in Bukhāra where he came into conflict with the authorities. He spent some fifteen years in the prison of Uzjund, it is said, and from memory, since books

[99] Sarakhsī, *Sharḥ Kitāb al-Siyar al-Kabīr*, ed. Munajjid, Vol. I, p. 3.

[100] Abū al-Wafā al-Qurashī, *al-Jawāhir al-Muḍīya* (Hyderabad, 1332/1913), Vol. I, p. 147.

[101] Aḥmad b. Ḥafs, who transmitted other works of Juzjānī, but not this work, was in Bukhāra when Shaybānī moved to Baghdad and composed the *Siyar al-Kabīr*. *Ibid.*, p. 67; Kawtharī, *Bulūgh al-Amānī*, p. 64.

were unavailable, dictated his commentaries on Shaybānī's works to his disciples who had heard his lectures outside the prison. But Sarakhsī's commentary amounts virtually to a new book; he failed to reproduce Shaybānī's original text, to which access was denied him in the prison, although it may be regarded as an exposition of Shaybānī's doctrines on the siyar as he understood them. Shaybānī's text, despite efforts by modern editors to distinguish it from the commentary, may well be regarded as lost.[102] Sarakhsī's commentary represents Ḥanafī doctrines as they were understood in the fifth century of the Islamic era (eleventh century A. D.), and not in the second century (eighth century A. D.) when Shaybānī was alive.[103]

We must therefore fall back on Shaybānī's other works in dealing with the siyar. Fortunately, an important part of the *Kitāb al-Aṣl,* also called *Kitāb al-Mabsūt,* one of Shaybānī's early and most comprehensive works, is devoted to the subject. This work, said to have been dictated to Shaybānī by Abū Yūsuf, takes the form of a discourse between master and disciple, and presents Abū Ḥanīfa's replies to the legal questions put to him. The work was intended to embody only the legal doctrines of Abū Ḥanīfa, and not of others, for whenever Abū Yūsuf and Shaybānī differed from Abū Ḥanīfa, they recorded separately their points of difference with the master. Not infrequently, Abū Ḥanīfa's differences with other jurists were also given. The portion on the siyar in *Kitāb al-Aṣl* represents the development of the subject from the discussions in Abū Ḥanīfa's circle. Abū Ḥanīfa was in the habit of presenting his legal opinions to his disciples for discussion, and the questions were committed to writing by his disciples after critical study. The book on the siyar in the *Kitāb al-Aṣl* may therefore be regarded as essentially the

[102] The two attempts to distinguish Shaybānī's text and Sarakhsī's commentary may be found in the Hyderabad edition, *Kitāb Sharḥ al-Siyar al-Kabīr* (Hyderabad, 1335/1916), 4 vols., and Munajjid's edition, *Sharḥ Kitāb al-Siyar al-Kabīr* (Cairo, 1957), 3 vols. (incomplete).

[103] A new edition of Sarakhsī's commentary, *al-Siyar al-Kabir,* prepared by Abū Zahra and Muṣṭafa Zayd, makes no distinction between the text and commentary. Only one volume has been published in Cairo, in 1958.

contribution by Abū Ḥanīfa and his circle. The text may be the writing of Shaybānī, but the substance was the product of the collective legal reasoning in which Abū Yūsuf and Shaybānī had also participated. This work, the text of which has been preserved in full, represents the opinions of Abū Ḥanīfa and his principal disciples—Abū Yūsuf and Shaybānī in particular—more closely than does Sarakhsī's reconstruction of Shaybānī's doctrines.[104]

The *Kitāb al-Aṣl* was transmitted by two of Shaybānī's disciples, Aḥmad b. Ḥafs and Abū Sulaymān al-Juzjānī (*ca.* 200/815). The *Kitāb al-Siyar* itself seems to have been the part transmitted by Juzjānī. Numerous copies of this work are in existence, and the oldest, dated 638/1240, will be examined in the following pages.

Other works by Shaybānī dealing with the siyar are *Kitāb al-Jāmiʿ al-Ṣaghīr* and *Kitāb al-Jāmiʿ al-Kabīr.* In the first, Shaybānī presents a brief summary of Abū Ḥanīfa's opinions without discussion; [105] the second, though original and highly speculative in nature, treats but few questions pertaining to the siyar.[106] The *Kitab al-Āthār,* a book consisting essentially of Traditions and narratives, contains a section on the siyar concerning Islam's relationships with unbelievers.[107] In the first chapter of the siyar in the *Kitab al-Aṣl,* Shaybānī presents a larger collection of Traditions than those in the *Kitāb al-Āthār.*[108]

[104] At the end of the commentary on the chapters of the siyar in his book *Mabsūṭ,* Sarakhsī says that he has "ended his commentary on the *Siyar al-Ṣaghīr* [of al-Shaybānī]" (see Sarakhsī's *Mabsūṭ,* Vol. X, p. 144). Since it is well-known that Sarakhsī's *Mabsūṭ* is a commentary based on the *Kitāb al-Mukhtaṣar al-Kāfī* of al-Ḥākim, which is a résumé of Shaybānī's *Kitāb al-Aṣl,* it is likely that Shaybānī's *Siyar al-Ṣaghīr* was either written before his *Kitāb al-Aṣl* and later incorporated in it, or that the *Siyar al-Ṣaghīr* was an expanded version of the chapters on the siyar of the *Kitāb al-Aṣl.*

[105] Shaybānī, *Kitāb al-Jāmiʿ al-Ṣaghīr* (Cairo, 1310/1892), pp. 85-92.

[106] Shaybānī, *al-Jāmiʿ al-Kabīr* (Cairo, 1336/1937), pp. 229, 360-63.

[107] Shaybānī, *Kitāb al-Āthār* (Lucknow, n.d.), pp. 150-51.

[108] See Chap. I, below.

The Vocabulary of Shaybānī's Siyar

The vocabulary of Shaybānī's siyar, like other classical legal studies, raises questions of legal nomenclature, as well as of literary and philosophical terminology. Shaybānī rarely defined his terms, assuming that they would be familiar to his readers from the context of his writings or from the common usage of the time. It may be useful to define some of the principal terms and expressions before we discuss the fundamental ideas of Shaybānī's siyar. Three sets of terms deserve particular examination.

To begin with, a number of general terms in jurisprudence call for clarification. The meaning of terms such as the Qur'ān, ḥadīth (Traditions), qiyās (analogy), ijmā' (consensus), and others was explained when discussing the sources of Islamic law, but some, like ḥadīth and a few others, need additional explanation. Shaybānī, like some of his contemporaries, used the term ḥadīth to mean any narrative or precedent, whether it originated with the Prophet or a Companion or successor, not an authentic Tradition from the Prophet as it was later established by Shāfi'ī. Shaybānī uses also the terms athar (plural āthār) and khabar (plural akhbār) as synonymous with Tradition and rarely uses the term sunna, which means custom or practice, and not necessarily the sunna of the Prophet.[109] Qiyās is a form of analogical reasoning through which Abū Ḥanīfa used opinion as a source of law and his disciples, especially Abū Yūsuf and Shaybānī, followed his example, although they too used Traditions. Istiḥsān, in the form "I approve of," (or conversely, "I disapprove of"), is another kind of analogical reasoning, by which Abū Ḥanīfa and his disciples showed preference for one precedent over another. The term makrūh is used to express objection to a certain act which, though not prohibited by law, is objected to on ethical or religious grounds by Abū Ḥanīfa and his followers. Finally, Abū Ḥanīfa and his contemporaries were accustomed to use expressions such

[109] For the development of the meaning of sunna and Tradition, see my *Islamic Jurisprudence*, pp. 30-31.

as "ara'yta" ("what do you think") and "alā tara" ("do you not think"), which discuss legal questions considered likely to arise, or to speculate on purely hypothetical questions to which they framed replies. Speculative legal reasoning of this kind, which the early Ḥanafī jurists excelled in, was classified as objectionable by jurists who advocated a heavier dependence on Traditions. Some critics labeled Abū Ḥanīfa and his disciples as the jurists of opinion and called them the "ara'ytas," using the term in a derogatory sense.[110]

A second set of terms is made up of those used by Shaybānī in his discussion of the conduct of the Islamic state and its relations with other states. Terms such as siyar, jihād, dār al-Islām, and dār al-ḥarb have already been discussed. Other terms in the same category, such as ḥarbī, amān, musta'min, khārijīs, baghīs, ṣulḥ, and hudna, require explanation.

Ḥarbī, a person belonging to the territory of war, is equivalent to an alien in modern terminology, but may be regarded as an enemy as well since he was also in a state of war with the Muslims. He could attain a state of temporary peace by means of an amān (safe-conduct), which he could obtain from an official or from a private person before entering Islamic lands and becoming a musta'min. The musta'min enjoys a status of temporary peace for a period not to exceed one year, while in the dār al-Islām. Should he decide to remain for a longer span, he would be required to become a Dhimmī and pay a poll tax as non-Muslim subject of the Islamic state. Dhimmīs (Christians, Jews, Sabians, Zoroastrians, and others who claimed to have possessed scriptures) were originally inhabitants of occupied territories who agreed to pay the jizya (poll tax) and to observe certain rules embodied in peace agreements made after they passed under Islamic rule. Persons who chose to become Dhimmīs were bound by those rules.

Believers who followed a heterodox creed or who might rise in rebellion against the established authority were called

[110] Sarakhsī, *Uṣūl*, ed. Abū al-Wafa (Cairo, 1372/1952), Vol. II, p. 121; Muḥammad Abū Zahra, *Abū Ḥanīfa: Ḥayatuh wa 'Aṣruh, Arā'uh wa Fiqhuh* (2nd ed.; Cairo, 1947), p. 230.

khārijīs (dissenters), baghīs (rebels), or murtadds (apostates). As a khārijī, the person was entitled to remain a subject of the state but was liable to punishment if he opposed authority. A person who became a murtadd would be subject to execution, unless he repented or escaped to the territory of war.

The inhabitants of the territory of war were eligible to enter into a peace treaty with Islam, which placed them in a state of temporary peace for a period not exceeding ten years, according to some jurists. They could enter the territory of Islam without an amān, since they were already at peace with the Muslims, but they were required to observe the rules applicable to musta'mins. Temporary peace with non-Muslims is called muhādana or muwāda'a, and the instrument of peace, ṣulḥ or hudna.

In the third set of terms some used by Shaybānī in his discussions of the law of war and the conduct of fighting belong to private rather than to public law, but they are essential to the study of the siyar, since the Islamic law of nations governs the relationships of groups as well as individuals. The most important of those terms are ghanīma, fay', jizya, kharāj, and 'ushr.

The distinction between ghanīma and fay' has given rise to differences of opinion. Jurists are agreed that ghanīma means property taken from the enemy by force ('anwatan), and fay' property taken without force. But is property taken by force without the Imām's permission a ghanīma? The Ḥanafī jurists required the Imām's permission, for property taken without it would be viewed as theft,[111] but other jurists, such as Awzā'ī and Shāfi'ī, did not require such permission.[112] Fay' literally means "that which came back," property which passed into the hands of Muslims from unbelievers without resort to war. Some mention that it is property taken after hostilities have ended, but that it would not be divided among the warriors; it belonged to the community and was

[111] See p. 250, below.
[112] Ṭabarī, *Kitāb Ikhtilāf*, pp. 78-80.

viewed as revenue for the public treasury.[113] According to 'Alī b. 'Īsa, fay' is more general than ghanīma and was applicable to every kind of property taken by Muslims from unbelievers.[114] The division of the ghanīma, which has given rise to the difference in opinions, will be discussed in this volume according to the Ḥanafī doctrine, although these differences are essentially in details.[115]

The terms jizya and kharāj are perhaps more ambiguous. Shaybānī often uses kharāj to mean a tax on land (kharāj al-arḍ) or a poll tax (kharāj 'ala al-ra's) although infrequently he uses jizya for poll tax specifically and kharāj for land tax. Early jurists seem to have used the two terms interchangeably before they gained their technical meanings. Moreover, jizya in original usage was equivalent to tribute, as demonstrated in the case of the people of Najran, before it was applied specifically to poll tax.[116]

Structure and Substance of Shaybānī's Siyar

A brief summary of the content of Shaybānī's siyar scarcely does it justice, for only a complete translation of the text, as it is provided in the following pages, can present a full expression of the ideas and method of reasoning of its author. In this section fundamental doctrines and principles rather than the specific questions dealt with in Shaybānī's siyar will be discussed.

In structure, the book falls into four separate though not unrelated parts. The first, Chapter I, is a compilation of Traditions from the Prophet and narratives from his Companions and successors. Nearly all the citations deal with specific questions pertaining to the law of war. As such they set forth specific decisions and cases and not basic principles

[113] Māwardī, *Kitāb al-Aḥkām*, pp. 217-45; Khadduri, *War and Peace in the Law of Islam*, pp. 118-25.

[114] Muṭarrazī, *al-Mughrib*, Vol. II, p. 80.

[115] See Chap. III, below. See Frede Løkkegaard, "Fay," and "Ghanīma," *Encyclopaedia of Islam* (2nd ed.), Vol. II, pp. 869-70, 1005-06.

[116] For a critical discussion on the meanings of jizya and kharāj, see my *War and Peace in the Law of Islam*, pp. 187-93.

and rules, although the use of them is implied in these cases.

The narratives transmitted by Shaybānī were all on the authority of Abū Yūsuf, except the first, which was related on the authority of Abū Ḥanīfa. Nor did Abū Yūsuf relate the narratives from Abū Ḥanīfa, but rather from other authorities such as Sha'bī, Ibn Isḥāq, and Kalbī, who were well-known to be versed in Traditions. In contrast, Abū Yūsuf and Shaybānī sought to combine Abū Ḥanīfa's methodology with a knowledge of Traditions and narratives, perhaps under the impact of the rising influence of Traditionists. Indeed, Abū Yūsuf began his study of the law under Ibn Abī Layla, who stressed Traditions, it was reputed, in his decisions as Qāḍī of Kūfa. He had sought a knowledge of Traditions from Ibn Isḥāq and other Traditionists while studying under Abū Ḥanīfa. Shaybānī had also attended the lectures of Mālik, and perhaps Awzā'ī, in addition to those of Abū Ḥanīfa and Abū Yūsuf. These two distinguished jurists, though essentially representing the school of analogical reasoning, sought to validate their legal deductions by an authoritative source. Perhaps their interest in Traditions was provoked by the criticism of jurists who claimed that Abū Ḥanīfa paid no attention to Traditions, or by a genuine interest in the study of them which had become a favorite field of inquiry for a number of distinguished scholars. Small wonder then that Shaybānī devoted the first chapter of his *Abwāb al-Siyar* (the text in translation) to a careful selection of narratives bearing on the siyar. His heavy dependence on Traditions in the *Kitāb al-Siyar al-Kabīr* is striking, but perhaps the hand of Sarakhsī is responsible, since the latter's commentary is essentially his own exposition of the subject, rather than a precise reproduction of Shaybānī's original text, as was noted earlier. Shaybānī's own ideas and methodology are perhaps demonstrated more clearly in the translated text of his work rather than in the one reproduced by Sarakhsī.

The second part, (Chapters II–VIII), is the largest and the most interesting portion of the book. By itself, it forms a separate, coherent, and systematic study of the law of nations, based essentially on Abū Ḥanīfa's doctrines, qualified in matters of detail by the points of difference expressed by his disciples. Discussion takes the form of a dialogue covering all the relevant questions. The method employed is the "case method," a discussion of specific situations, highly speculative and scholastic in nature, and bearing on every conceivable question that may have arisen, or was believed likely to arise, in the relationships between Islam and other nations.

Hypothetical speculation, a medieval method of reasoning well-known to schoolmen, was a discipline in which Muslim theologians had excelled. Abū Ḥanīfa was a theologian whose jurisprudence was influenced by thinkers who accepted reason as a source of knowledge in addition to divine revelation. As a jurist, Abū Ḥanīfa applied this method, mainly through analogical reasoning, and his method was followed by his disciples as well as by jurists of other schools of law, in varying degree. His disciple Zufar is said to have shown nearly equal talent in analogical reasoning, but it seems that he never wrote a work on law and died relatively young as a judge in Baṣra.[117] Abū Yūsuf and Shaybānī sought to combine analogical reasoning with precedents (narratives) and their approach exercised greater appeal to a society that revered the growing influence of traditionalism.

Abū Ḥanīfa seems to have discussed basic principles with his disciples, but they committed only problems to writing. In his *Kitāb al-Kharāj,* Abū Yūsuf not infrequently presents some of Abū Ḥanīfa's arguments, specially those pertaining to questions on which he had disagreed with contemporary jurists. In his siyar, however, Shaybānī rarely formulates general principles, although it is not difficult to discern the underlying principles on which his discussion is based.

Abū Ḥanīfa and his disciples seem to have been the earliest jurists to view Islam's external relationships as a coherent system and to discuss its problems in terms of comprehensive doctrines. Muslims and non-Muslims were viewed as juridical personalities, both as individuals and territorial groups. Terri-

[117] See Kawtharī, *Lamḥāt al-Nazar fī Sīrat al-Imām Zufar* (Cairo, 1368/1948).

torial separation created legal effects in the relationships between Islam and other nations. Thus, while the law of Islam is essentially personal and binding on Muslims regardless of territory, Abū Ḥanīfa introduced the notion of territoriality in the relationships between Muslims and non-Muslims. Legal decisions were to be made on the basis of custom or analogy, as well as on territoriality (the dār). This principle seems to be the underlying one and explains the legal differences between Abū Ḥanīfa and Abū Yūsuf on the one hand and Awzā'ī on the other in the *Kitāb al-Radd 'ala Siyar al-Awzā'ī*. For example, Awzā'ī held that the Imām may divide the spoils of war in the dār al-ḥarb while the army was still in occupation, but Abū Ḥanīfa and Abū Yūsuf maintained that the Imām should divide the spoils only after they were carried to the dār al-Islām. Abū Ḥanīfa stressed the principle of territorial segregation and argued that Muslims may acquire the spoils in enemy territory but will gain legal possession only after their transfer to the territory of Islam.[118] Accordingly, the Imām has no legal right to divide the spoils in the dār al-ḥarb but can do so only after they reach a place of security in the territory of Islam.[119]

From this basic principle stems another that the rulings of non-Muslims should be accepted as binding by Muslims whenever the latter reside in non-Muslim territory. Abū Ḥanīfa considered acts by Muslims in non-Muslim territory which violated the latter's laws as acts of banditry or theft.[120] He even accepted as valid certain transactions, e. g., marriage, if the parties became Muslims and entered the dār al-Islām.[121] If a Muslim and a non-Muslim ruler entered into a treaty, all the previous acts of the latter would be regarded as valid by the former.

The principle that a state of war exists between the dār al-Islām and the dār al-ḥarb is not discussed in Shaybānī's siyar, but it is taken for granted in the dialogue between

[118] Abū Yūsuf, *Kitāb al-Radd*, p. 1.
[119] See paragraph 55, below.
[120] See paragraphs 1546-49, below.
[121] See paragraphs 862-65, 1679, below.

master and disciple. The unbeliever from a non-Muslim territory is invariably called ḥarbī, a belligerent, and his territory, the territory of war (dār al-ḥarb). The ḥarbī would be subject to killing if he entered the dār al-Islām, unless he first obtained an amān which would give him protection in traveling through Islamic lands, or if his ruler made a peace agreement, which of necessity would be temporary in duration. Normal relations between Islamic and non-Islamic territories were not peaceful, and a state of hostility existed which jurists nowadays call a state of war.

Abū Ḥanīfa and his disciples accepted the principle of reciprocity, even where temporary peace was not established between Islam and other nations. He advised the Imām that non-Muslims entering the dār al-Islām should be treated reciprocally with Muslims. He should exempt from the payment of customs duty non-Muslim merchants in the dār al-Islām if Muslims in the dār al-ḥarb were exempted. Where exemption was not practiced, the Imām should collect from non-Muslim merchants the corresponding levies imposed on Muslims by non-Muslim authorities.[122] The reciprocal treatment of diplomatic emissaries is stressed, although diplomatic immunity is an old practice recognized by ancient custom.[123] Finally, the principle of reciprocity is observed in the exchange of prisoners, the payment of ransom, and related practices.

The object of war was the achievement of an ultimate religious purpose and not the annihilation of the enemy; an invitation to accept Islam must therefore precede fighting. Muslim commanders were advised to negotiate if the enemy agreed to do so as an alternative to fighting. Even if Islam were not accepted, and the unbelievers agreed to pay tribute (if they were scripturaries), a peace treaty would become the basis of temporary relations. Unnecessary damage in the prosecution of the war was disapproved and practices such as killing noncombatants, mutilation, and treacherous attacks were prohibited.

The offer of peace was necessarily a device to achieve certain

[122] See paragraphs 774-81, below.
[123] See paragraphs 732-33, below.

specific objectives, since the state of permanent war was the normal relationship between Islam and other nations. Shaybānī states that peace should last for a definite period without specifying the length, while Sarakhsī, in his commentary on Shaybānī's *Siyar al-Kabīr*, states that the duration should not exceed ten years.[124] The early Ḥanafī jurists, it seemed, deemed it unnecessary to specify a maximum period, for Abū Yūsuf confirmed Shaybānī's statement that the treaty should be limited in duration without specifying the length, although he cited the precedent of the Ḥudaybiya treaty and stated that it ran for ten years.[125]

Peace does not supersede the state of war, for the jihād is a legal duty prescribed by the law; peace means the grant of security or protection to non-Muslims for certain specified purposes, and the achievement of them brings the grant of peace to an end. Protection may be granted to an individual in the form of an amān (safe-conduct), or to a group in the form of a treaty (muhādana or muwāda'a). The person (the ḥarbī) who obtains an amān enjoys protection as long as he remains in the dār al-Islām, but the status is ended when he returns to the dār al-ḥarb. He needs a new amān to return to the dār al-Islām. A group of ḥarbīs may gain a similar status by a peace agreement with the Muslims. Such an agreement would extend protection to persons as well as to the territory they lived in and would validate acts performed in that territory. The people and the territory would lose the grant of protection when the agreement expired, and the state of war, suspended during the term of the treaty, would be resumed. Only in the case of scripturaries who made a peace treaty with Muslims called 'ahd (pact or covenant), by which their territories became part of the dār al-Islām, would the treaty be regarded as permanent and become what might be called today a constitutional charter.

Muslim authorities concluded peace treaties with the enemy only when it was to the advantage of Islam, whether because

[124] Sarakhsī, *Kitāb Sharḥ al-Siyar al-Kabīr* (Hyderabad) Vol. IV, p. 61.
[125] Abū Yūsuf, *Kitāb al-Kharāj*, pp. 207-12.

it found itself in a state of temporary weakness following a military defeat or because of engagement in war in another area. An amān could be granted to a ḥarbī by any Muslim, but a peace treaty must be concluded by a responsible Muslim authority, such as the Imām or his commanders on the battlefield. Once concluded, the treaty must be observed by the Muslims to the end of the specified period unless the other party violates it. The Imām may terminate the treaty, but a notice to the enemy demanding denunciation of it must first be sent, together with the reason for it. The principle of *rebus sic stantibus* seems to be applied here; otherwise, the Imām must abide by the treaty on the strength of the principle *pacta sunt servanda.*[126]

The third part of Shaybānī's siyar is an addendum (Chapter IX), in which he summarizes Ḥanafī doctrines on the subject. This chapter seems to add practically nothing new other than to provide a brief exposition of the Islamic law of nations and its inclusion is redundant.

The fourth part (Chapters X–XI) deals with taxation, and, strictly speaking, is not an integral part of the siyar. The two chapters on the subject overlap necessarily because each was written by a different author. The first seems to be a summary of Abū Ḥanīfa's doctrines as transmitted by Abū Yūsuf to Shaybānī, while the second is a brief exposition of the subject by Ibn Rushayd, a disciple of Shaybānī. These chapters are included in a work on the siyar, mainly because they deal with the status of the Dhimmīs (scripturaries) and the taxes imposed upon them by the state. The first of these two chapters is important for providing us with Abū Ḥanīfa's doctrines on the subject. Abū Yūsuf, it is true, often cited Abū Ḥanīfa's ideas in his *Kitāb al-Kharāj,* but essentially the work was an exposition of his own doctrines. The second chapter was from the pen of Dāwūd b. Rushayd, a disciple of Shaybānī. He lived in Baghdad and was associated with

[126] This is based on Q. IX, 4; and Q. XVI, 93. For a brief account of Shaybānī's doctrine of muwāda'a based on Sarakhsī's commentary on *al-Siyar al-Kabīr,* see Hans Kruse, "al-Shaybānī on International Instruments," *Journal of the Pakistan Historical Society,* Vol. I (1953), pp. 90-99.

Shaybānī, it seems, after the latter was dismissed as judge in Raqqa. He died in Baghdād in 239/853.[127] His chapter on taxation is a direct transmission of Shaybānī's doctrines on the subject.

Shaybānī as the Founder of the Science of the Siyar

Shaybānī tried to commit to writing the legal knowledge handed down to him from Abū Ḥanīfa and Abū Yūsuf. As a jurist in his own right, Shaybānī made a contribution to the sharī'a and provided source material for succeeding generations. For students of the Islamic law of nations, Shaybānī's contribution is invaluable for he was the first to consolidate all the legal materials relevant to the subject and to provide perhaps the most detailed and thorough study of it.

A Turkish translation of Sarakhsī's commentary on the *Siyar al-Kabīr* was published in 1825.[128] Joseph Hammer von Purgstall reviewed the work and called the author the Hugo Grotius of the Muslims.[129] However, the theme of Islam's legal relationships with other nations stirred no great interest at a time when its territories had fallen under the political influence of European nations. In 1917, almost a century later, Sarakhsī's commentary on the *Siyar al-Kabīr* became available to scholars when it was published in Hyderabad, Deccan, in four volumes. In the years that followed, scholars began to study the works of Shaybāni and of other writers on the subject. The attempt to designate Shaybānī as the Hugo Grotius of Islam was renewed. "However surprising," writes Hans Kruse, "the bestowal of such a title of honour on a Muslim jurist . . . by so great a scholar as Purgstall may have been, it did not find an echo among European scholars. . . ." Hans Kruse made another attempt to "secure for al-Shaybānī that place in the history of international law which he rightfully deserves according to his importance," [130] and he founded

[127] Qurashī, *al-Jawāhir al-Muḍīya*, Vol. I, p. 237.

[128] Translated and published in two volumes by Muḥmūd Munīb 'Ayntābī (Istānbūl, 1241/1825).

[129] *Jahrbücher der Literatur* (Wien, 1827), Vol. 40, p. 48.

[130] Kruse, "The Foundation of Islamic International Jurisprudence,"

the Shaybānī Society of International Law in 1955. But scholars did not appear disposed to regard Shaybānī as the Hugo Grotius of Islam nor did Kruse follow up his pioneering effort to co-ordinate the work of the Shaybānī Society after he had founded it.

In designating Shaybānī as the Hugo Grotius of Islam, it is questionable whether Joseph Hammer had more in mind than to call the attention of scholars to the master's works. Shaybānī (d. 804) preceded Grotius (d. 1645) by some eight centuries and composed his works on a system of law whose appeal to students of the history of law is greater than to students of the modern law of nations. But a study of the Islamic law of nations would certainly be of interest to all who seek to broaden the scope and subject matter of the modern law of nations. Shaybānī will always be remembered as the most eminent Muslim jurist who wrote on Islam's legal relationships with other nations and may well be called the father of the science of the Islamic law of nations. But to identify the name of Shaybānī with Grotius, even though the latter is the most illustrious writer on the modern law of nations, will not necessarily add laurels to a classical author whose place in the history of jurisprudence is assured, notwithstanding the fact that he is insufficiently known to students of comparative jurisprudence.

Changes in the Concepts of the Siyar After Shaybānī

Shaybānī's Successors

We have seen how Abū Ḥanīfa and his disciples, especially Shaybānī, laid down general rules and principles governing Islam's external relations, based on the assumption that a normal state of war existed between Islamic and non-Islamic territories; but they made no explicit statements that the

---

Journal of the Pakistan Historical Society, Vol. III (1955), p. 238; "Die Begründung der Islamischen Völkerrechtslehre," *Saeculum*, Vol. V, heft 2, pp. 238-39.

jihād was a war to be waged against unbelievers solely on account of their disbelief (kufr). On the contrary, the early Ḥanafī jurists seem to have stressed that tolerance should be shown unbelievers, especially scripturaries, and advised the Imām to prosecute war only when the inhabitants of the dār al-ḥarb came into conflict with Islam.[131]

It was Shāfiʿī who first formulated the doctrine that the jihād had for its intent the waging of war on unbelievers for their disbelief and not merely when they entered into conflict with Islam.[132] The jihād was thereby transformed into a collective duty enjoined on Muslims to fight unbelievers "wherever you may find them" (Q. IX, 5), although not every individual Muslim was necessarily obligated to fight.[133] This legal principle provoked a discussion among Shāfiʿī's contemporaries and led to a division of opinion among the Ḥanafī jurists who followed Shaybānī. Some, like Ṭaḥāwī (d. 321/933), adhered more closely to the early Ḥanafī doctrine that fighting was enjoined only in a conflict with unbelievers;[134] but Sarakhsī, the great commentator on Shaybānī's works, accepted the Shāfiʿī doctrine that fighting the unbeliever was "a duty enjoined permanently until the end of time."[135] Jurists who came afterward, and up to the very decline of Islamic power, merely introduced refinements and elaborations of these basic principles.

Commentaries upon the early writers on the siyar began to undergo a good deal of adjustment to realities when conditions in the dār al-Islām began to change radically. From the tenth

[131] This was also the position of Awzāʿī, Mālik, and other early jurists.

[132] Shāfiʿī, *Umm*, Vol. IV, pp. 84-85.

[133] The distinction between the collective and individual duty of fighting was fully explained by Shāfiʿī, who pointed out that if the duty were fulfilled by some, the others would be relieved, but if none fulfilled the duty, all would be subject to punishment. See Shāfiʿī's *Risala*, ed. Shākir (Cairo, 1958), pp. 364-68; Eng. trans. Khadduri, *Islamic Jurisprudence*, pp. 84-86.

[134] Ṭaḥāwī formulated the doctrine thus: "The jihād is a duty, but the Muslims are relieved of it, unless called upon to fulfill it" (Abū Jaʿfar Aḥmad b. Muḥammad b. Salama al-Ṭaḥāwī, *Kitāb al-Mukhtaṣar*, ed. Abū al-Wafā al-Afghānī [Cairo, 1370/1950], p. 281).

[135] Sarakhsī, *Mabsūṭ*, Vol. X, pp. 2-3.

century onward Islam could no longer expand without impairing its internal unity. We have seen how the decentralization of authority found its expression in the writings of Māwardī, who advised the Caliph that he should recognize self-appointed provincial governors so as to preserve his own ultimate authority.[136] More serious dangers arose when superior forces from the dār al-ḥarb (the Crusades and Mongol invasions in the tenth through the thirteenth centuries) invaded the dār al-Islām and threatened its very existence. In the altered circumstances, juridical writings began to turn on the question whether the jihād against unbelievers was justified on the ground of their infidelity alone or of their hostility (i. e., aggression) against Muslims. The principle that the jihād was a collective duty permanently imposed upon the community to fight the unbeliever wherever he might be found retained little of its substance. Ibn Taymīya (d. 728/1327), with all his fidelity to classical thought, understood the futility of waging a permanent war against disbelief at a time when foreign enemies were menacing at the gates of Islam. He made a concession to reality by reinterpreting the jihād to mean a defensive war against unbelievers whenever they threatened Islam.[137] Unbelievers who made no attempt to encroach upon the dār al-Islām, Ibn Taymīya explained, would not have Islam imposed upon them by force for, he said, "if the unbeliever were to be killed unless he becomes a Muslim, such an action would constitute the greatest compulsion in religion" which would run contrary to the Quranic rule that "no compulsion is prescribed by religion" (Q. II, 257). But unbelievers who encroached upon Islam would be in a different position altogether.[138]

A long period of decentralization set in as early as the tenth century and produced the division of Islam into several

[136] See pp. 21-22, above.

[137] Taqī al-Dīn Abī al-'Abbās Aḥmad b. 'Abd al-Ḥakīm Ibn Taymīya, "Qā'ida fī Qitāl al-Kuffār," *Majmū'at Rasā'al*, ed. M. Ḥamīd al-Fiqqī (Cairo, 1368/1949), pp. 115-46; and *al-Siyāsa al-Shar'īya*, ed. 'Alī al-Nashshār and A. Z. 'Atīya (Cairo, 1951), pp. 126-53.

[138] Ibn Taymīya, "Qitāl al-Kuffār," p. 123.

political entities, although the outward legal unity was maintained in theory. The central authority of the 'Abbāsid caliphs in Baghdad was challenged by *de facto* independent rulers (sultans) and was at times defied by rival caliphs in Spain and Egypt. The *de facto* independent rulers in Islam differed but little in position from the Christian princes in medieval Europe who were independent within their own realms yet in theory derived their authority from Emperor or Pope. The rival authority of Byzantium resembled that of Faṭimid Egypt or Umayyad Spain, but though Byzantium rejected the overlordship of the Western Empire, it did not challenge the theoretical unity of Christendom. For a long span, especially following the disappearance of the 'Abbāsid dynasty in the thirteenth century, the dār al-Islām abounded in political entities, great and small. Many a state waged battles of life and death, and as an outcome two principal states emerged, the Ottoman and the Persian, each rationalizing its existence by one of the two principal Islamic creeds, the Sunnī or Shī'ī. This territorial division was the first of lasting consequence and coincided with the absorption by neighboring powers of peripheral territories of Islam. A third division, whose people upheld the Sunnī creed, has been ruled by several dynasties to the present day, although the greater portion of its territory fell under non-Islamic rule. The fragmentation of Islam, whether regretted as the breakdown of a great ecumenical society or hailed as the progressive evolution of a public legal order adjusting itself to the ever-changing conditions of life, was necessary for the Islamic state to survive.

The Islamic State System

The break-up into independent political entities of the dār al-Islām marked a new development in the Islamic law of nations. For Muslim rulers the problem arose of how to regulate their relationships with other Muslim heads of state as well as with non-Muslim princes. One independent ruler (sultan) after another rose in Islam before the sixteenth century, although the outward unity of the dār al-Islām was maintained. But after the sixteenth century, the division of Islam into three entities, each of which in turn divided or subdivided into others, became permanent and the divisions were consolidated by the trends of political development within Islam as well as by its relationships with the Christian world. The Islamic universal state became transformed into an Islamic state system, following a long process of decentralization and break-up, just as Western Christendom was transformed from a universal into a European state system.[139] This change is one of the most revolutionary that has occurred in the Islamic public order since the formative period itself.

The transformation of Islam into a set of sovereign states brought in its train changes in concept of the Islamic law of nations, produced by the new circumstances of life. First and foremost was the acceptance of the principle that the control of religious doctrines should be separated from that of external relations. This principle, which relegated religion to the domestic level, was the product of disputation in creed within Islam. Doctrinal schism was far from being a new phenomenon. It was recurrent in Islamic society and had resulted in the rise of rival religious-political parties. But permanent territorial divisions did not accompany doctrinal differences.[140] At the opening of the sixteenth century, however, a permanent split began which divided Islam into three political entities. The rise of two rival dynasties—the Ottoman and Persian—each advocating a different creed, compelled them to separate doctrinal differences from the exercise of external relations and to regulate their relationships on a nonsectarian (i. e., secular) basis, following a long period of conflict and rivalry. The separation of religious doctrine from the external relations of the state of Islam was not unlike the schisms in Christianity arising from the religious conflicts at

[139] For the stages of development of the Islamic state, see p. 20, above.

[140] If the followers of a heterodox creed opposed authority with arms they were treated as dissenters and suppressed as rebels, but jurists were not prepared to recognize them as separate political entities. See pp. 230 ff., below.

the time of the Reformation, and the subsequent agreement among the Christian princes to relegate religious doctrine to the domestic level and to regulate their external relations on a secular basis. This step completed the transformation of the European public order from a medieval to a modern one. The principle *cuius regio, eius religio,* first adopted at the Peace of Augsburg in 1555, became the basis of the European system after the Peace of Westphalia (1648) and helped to co-ordinate first the Christian states of Europe, and later states of different faiths throughout the world, into a community of nations.

The emergence of an Islamic state system gave rise to complex legal problems pertaining to the recognition of Muslim states by one another, the equality and reciprocity of their interrelationships, and the treatment of the subjects of each Muslim state in the other. When the split in Islam began at the opening of the sixteenth century, neither Turkey nor Persia was prepared to recognize the other, nor to regulate their relationships on the basis of equality and reciprocity. The Ottoman Porte, resenting Persia's declaration of Shī'īsm as its official religion, expelled or executed persons who adhered to the Shī'ī creed in its territory and *mutatis mutandis* the Sunnīs in Persia were mistreated no less by Persian authorities. Only when these Muslim states, from their contacts with European nations, began to learn the principle of individual allegiance based on territorial rather than religious affiliation, did they treat aliens on a par with their subjects, regardless of religious differences.

Perhaps an even more significant change in the relationships of Islam with other nations was the adoption by Islam of the principle of peaceful relations among nations of different religions, replacing the classical principle of the permanent state of war between Islamic and non-Islamic territories. The jihād, as we noted earlier, became inadequate as a basis for Islam's relations with other nations. Peace treaties extending beyond the ten-year period provided under the classical law of nations necessarily replaced the jihād as a normal relationship between Islam and other states.

The most notable instrument that recognized peace as the normal relationship between Islamic and non-Islamic states was the Treaty of 1535, concluded by Sultan Sulaymān the Magnificent with Francis I, the King of France.[141] This treaty provided quite a few innovations in relationship between Islam and other nations. The preamble treated the King of France and his envoys on an equal footing with Sultan Sulaymān and his representatives. Article 1 provided for the establishment of "valid and certain peace" (*bonne et sûre paix*) between the Sultan and the King "during their lives" and granted the subjects of each sovereign reciprocal rights in the territory of the other. The French were to enjoy exemption from the payment of poll tax, the right to practice their religion, and the right of trial in their own consulates by their own law. The King of France was given the right to:

> send to Constantinople or Pera or other places of this Empire a bailiff—just as at present he has a consul at Alexandria. The said bailiff and consul shall be received and maintained in proper authority so that each one of them may in his locality, and without being hindered by any judge, qaḍi, soubashi, or other, according to his faith and law, hear, judge, and determine all causes, suits and differences, both civil and criminal, which might arise between merchants and other subjects of the King [of France]. . . . The qaḍi or other officers of the Grand Signior may not try any difference between the merchants and subjects of the King, even if the said merchants should request it, and if perchance the said qaḍis should hear a case their judgment shall be null and void (Article 2).

The siyar had permitted ten years of peace but Ottoman practice extended the period to the lifetime of the sultan who had concluded the treaty. The Treaty of 1535 viewed the signatories as equal partners and recognized the mutuality of

[141] For the text of the treaty, see Baron I. de Testa, *Recueil des traités de la porte Ottomane* (Paris, 1864), Vol. I, pp. 15-21; and G. Noradoungian, *Recueil d'actes internationaux de l'empire Ottoman* (Paris, 1897), Vol. I, pp. 83-87.

their interests. This might be regarded as a special privilege granted to the King of France, as some writers have contended, to the exclusion of other Christian princes. Article 15 stated, however, that such privileges would be extended to other sovereigns if they adhered to the treaty, thereby indicating that the Sultan sought to establish a principle applicable to other Christian princes. Article 15 reads:

> The King of France has proposed that His Holiness the Pope, the King of England, his brother and perpetual ally, and the King of Scotland should be entitled to adhere to this treaty of peace if they please, on condition that when desirous of doing so they shall within eight months from date send their ratifications to the Grand Signior and obtain this.[142]

Nor was this all. The treaty modified yet another classical principle by exempting from the poll tax French subjects who resided in the Ottoman Empire, even for a period exceeding one year. With respect to the right of trial granted to Frenchmen (later extended to other Europeans) of being tried by their own consulates, the treaty first expressed the classical principle of the personality of the law; but in subsequent treaties (especially after 1740) the assertion of the *clausula capitula,* by which lawsuits involving foreigners and Muslims were to be tried by foreign consulates, marked a radical change in the fundamental principle that Islamic law must be applied in cases involving Muslim interests.[143] The Treaty of 1535, concluded at a time when the modern law of nations had just emerged from its formative stage, might have provided an excellent opportunity for reconciling the

[142] The King of England preferred to sign a separate treaty with the Sultan in 1580 while the Pope and the King of Scotland failed to adhere to the treaty of 1535.

[143] For a discussion of foreign privileges in Islamic lands, see Nasim Sousa, *The Capitulatory Regime in Turkey* (Baltimore, 1933); and H. J. Liebesny, "The Development of Western Judicial Privileges," *Law in the Middle East,* ed. Khadduri and Liebesny (Washington, 1955), Vol. I, pp. 309-33.

Islamic and Christian laws of nations. However, neither Islam nor Christendom was ready to meet the other on common ground and to harmonize their laws of nations so as to make them applicable to both.

The third important change in the concept of the siyar was the adoption by Islam of the principle of territorial sovereignty and territorial law necessitated by territorial segregation. Like the medieval Christian concepts of state and law, the classical Islamic state was universal and its law essentially personal rather than territorial.[144] To a state with a world outlook territorial limitations are irrelevant. But when the Islamic state disintegrated, the constituent entities emerged fully sovereign and each tended to divert the mode of loyalty of its subjects from universal to territorial values. Moreover, the secular character of Western law which influenced the legal and judicial systems in Islamic lands contributed to the assertion of territorial sovereignty. As a result the Western concept of territorial segregation replaced the ecumenical character of Islamic sovereignty and introduced territory as a basic element in the composition of the state. This gave rise to a set of complex problems proceeding from the concept of territorial sovereignty, such as frontier and boundary questions and the movement of nationals. In the absence of guidance from the classical doctrines of Islam, Muslims felt compelled to draw on the experiences of Western nations.

The Ottoman Empire and the Modern Law of Nations

Despite radical changes in the pattern of Islam's external relationship with Christendom, the Ottoman Empire was not regarded as part of the European system nor subject to its law of nations. The European powers often concluded treaties or special conventions with Muslim rulers to regulate their relationships on matters governed then by customary rules among European nations, on the ground that European customs were

[144] Abū Ḥanīfa and Shaybānī, it will be recalled, recognized some aspect of the principle of territorial limitations, but classical jurists as a whole asserted the principle of the personality of the law.

not binding on non-European nations.[145] The laws and customs of Islam differed so much from European traditions that the modern law of nations was not deemed applicable to the Ottoman Empire. In the *Madonna del Burso* case, Sir William Scott argued that the law of nations should not be applied in its full rigor to nations outside Europe, for, as he explained:

> The inhabitants of those countries [Ottoman Empire] are not professors of exactly the same law with ourselves: in consideration of the peculiarities of their situation and character, the Court has repeatedly expressed a disposition not to hold them bound to the utmost rigour of that system of public law, on which European states have so long acted, in their intercourse with one another.[146]

During the latter part of the nineteenth century the European powers deemed it necessary to treat the Ottoman Empire as a member of the European community, and it was admitted "to participate in the public law and concert of Europe" on the invitation of the powers signatory to the Treaty of Paris (March 30, 1856). The meaning of this clause apparently was a source of confusion to European jurists. Most of them contended that Turkey at last had become subject to the law of nations, although a few argued that the clause meant merely that Turkey had been admitted to the European community of nations but that the admission had no bearing on the subject of her participation in the operation of the law of nations.[147] Over a long span before 1856 the

[145] Ward, *An Enquiry into the Foundation and History of the Law of Nations in Europe*, Vol. II, pp. 321-22.

[146] *The Madonna del Burso*, High Court of the Admiralty, 1802, 4C. Rob. 169. In *The Fortuna*, 1803, Sir William Scott said: "Considering this case as merely between the British and Algerian claimants, I do not, at the same time, mean to apply to such claimants the exact rigour of the law of nations as understood and practised among the civilized states of Europe; it would be to try them by a law not familiar to any law or practices of theirs . . ." (2C. Rob. 92). See also the *Hurtige Hane* (1801) and *The Helena* (1801).

[147] Hugh M. Wood, "The Treaty of Paris and Turkey's Status in International Law," *American Journal of International Law*, Vol. XXXVII (1943), pp. 262-74.

Ottoman Empire had begun to participate in the operation of the law of nations by establishing diplomatic intercourse with European nations and by entering into treaty relationships with them. But prior to the middle of the nineteenth century this participation was considered to extend to the Ottoman Empire only partial advantages of the law of nations. Her admission to the Concert of Europe in 1856 must have fully entitled her (subject to foreign capitulatory rights) to the full advantages of that law. It is tempting to conclude that Turkey and other Islamic states had been recognized only by slow stages as subjects of the modern law of nations, and the European powers, without perhaps becoming aware of this process at the outset, had slowly arrived at this conclusion.

Islam and the Modern Community of Nations

Twentieth-century Islam has reconciled itself completely to the Western secular system, a system which had also undergone radical changes from its medieval origins. Even Muslim thinkers who have objected to the secularization of the law governing Islam's domestic affairs have accepted marked departures from the law and traditional practices which governed external relations. Some called for a complete separation between religion and the state, others advocated the establishment of an Islamic subsystem within the community of nations,[148] but none advocated the restoration of the traditional Islamic system of external relations. This attitude is consistent with the trend toward a world-wide community of nations developing over a long period, and the active participation of Muslim states in international councils and organizations has committed Islam to the cause of peace and international security.

After World War II a few Muslim thinkers began to reflect on the enormous changes that had taken place in Islam under

[148] The exponent of the principle of separation between state and religion is 'Alī 'Abd al-Rāziq in his work *al-Islām wa Uṣūl al-Ḥukm* (Cairo, 1925), and the exponent of Islam as a subsystem is 'Abd al-Razzāq al-Sanhūrī in his work *Le Califat: son évolution vers une société des nations orientales* (Paris, 1926).

the impact of the West. To look back on one's own achievements so as to resolve certain doubts or to gain momentum for further strides is not a sign of ill health. Some have regretted that Islam became divided and weak; others have taken a critical view of the complete integration of Islam's public order within the larger world order. But all seem to agree that Muslim states should assert a certain degree of solidarity in international councils which would enhance their prestige and serve their common interests.

The rise to statehood of Muslim territories, such as Pakistan and Indonesia, to mention but two, has added impetus to the trend. A few Muslim leaders have called for the holding of Islamic conferences and the formation of regional pacts and alliances among Muslim states. This new trend, called neo-Pan Islamism, is not aimed at the restoration of Islamic unity, as was the Pan-Islamic movement in the nineteenth century, nor does it indicate a desire to reinstate the exercise of the Islamic traditional system in external relations. It is rather an aspiration, perhaps not yet shared by all, to cooperate as an Islamic bloc within the community of nations.

Furthermore, a few Muslim thinkers, who advocate an active participation in international councils, envisage the possibility of a contribution by Islam to the development of a peaceful and more stable world order. The reconciliation between the Christian and Islamic systems could set a precedent for reconciliations between other rival systems. What could Islam's centuries of experiences contribute to an expanding world order, it might be asked?

First, the conflict and competition between Islam and Christendom, which endured over a long period, demonstrated that diverse systems could coexist and ultimately become integrated into a world-wide system, whenever both parties were prepared to accommodate themselves to changing circumstances. In the emerging world community, diverse systems of public order, the Islamic included, should be closely studied so as to draw upon the historical experiences of the nations that had lived under those systems, for every matured system records the stored experiences of its people in coping with the problem of the maintenance of a stable public order.

Secondly, in the Islamic experience of international relations the individual was viewed as a subject of the law governing external relations, and central authorities dealt with him directly, apart from the state. In the past, Islam recognized the individual as a subject because its system was personal, but in a shrinking world it would seem that the individual's claim to protection under the modern law of nations has become a pressing necessity. It can be taken for granted that Muslims would welcome the adoption of such a principle in the modern law of nations, as reflected in their acceptance of the Declaration of Human Rights, since traditionally Islamic law recognized the individual as a subject on the international plane.

Thirdly, Islam as a way of life stresses moral principles, apart from religious doctrine, in the relations among nations. The historical experiences of Islam demonstrate a paradox: that religious doctrine as a basis for the conduct of the state promoted conflict and continuous hostilities with other nations, but religion as a sanction for moral principles prompted Muslims to adopt a tolerant attitude toward non-Muslims and to observe humane principles embodied in the laws of war during hostilities with other nations. The historical experiences of Islam, indeed the historical experiences of all mankind, demonstrate that any system of public order, on the national as well as the international plane, would lose its meaning were it divorced completely from moral principles.

The stress on moral principles in intercourse among nations does not imply the reintroduction of religious doctrine in the conduct of states. The historical experiences of Christendom and Islam demonstrate that the fusion of religion or of any form of an ideology with the foreign conduct of states can become dangerous indeed. Divergent ideologies can hamper the development of relations among nations on the basis of rules and practices derived from their historical experiences and their common interest. It is unfortunate that when Islam and Christendom, following a long period of competition and rivalry, finally learned to divorce ideology from the principles and practices governing their foreign relations, both find themselves confronted by the rise of a new ideology which its followers appear to insist on reintroducing in the intercourse among nations. Islam's past competition and present coexistence with Christendom should be food for thought indeed to countries seeking to infuse ideology into the relations between nations during the crisis through which the community of nations is currently passing.[149]

The Text of The Siyar

Manuscripts

The treatise on al-siyar by Shaybānī, as we have pointed out earlier, is a portion of a larger work on Islamic law by the same author called the *Kitāb al-Aṣl* and often also called the *Kitāb al-Mabsūṭ*. This treatise, entitled "Abwāb al-Siyar fī Arḍ al-Ḥarb" ("Chapters on the Siyar in the Territory of War"), follows the chapter on usurpation or the "Kitāb al-Ikrāh."

Several manuscripts of the *Kitāb al-Aṣl* are in existence; some are in Istanbul, others in Cairo, and perhaps still others elsewhere.[150] But the manuscripts are not all complete and those examined by me in Cairo and Istanbul do not all contain the treatise on al-siyar. It is likely that others are to be found in private libraries, for the *Kitāb al-Aṣl*, a basic book on Islamic law, had been in wide use as a text book for centuries and many copies were preserved in many parts of the Islamic world where the Ḥanafī school of law prevailed.

[149] The writer has drawn freely from his book *War and Peace in the Law of Islam*, and from his articles "Islam and the Modern Law of Nations," *American Journal of International Law*, Vol. 50 (1956), pp. 358-72, and "The Islamic System: Its Competition and Co-Existence with Western System," *Proceedings of the American Society of International Law*, 1959, pp. 49-52.

[150] For the manuscripts of *Kitāb al-Aṣl*, see Schacht's list in *Abhandlungen der preussischen Akademie der Wissenschaften* (Berlin, 1928), No. 8, pp. 12-15; 1931, No. 1, pp. 10-11.

بسم الله الرحمن الرحيم الحمد لله الواحد الابد

ابواب السير في ارض الحرب

ابو سليمن عن محمد بن الحسن عن ابي حنيفة عن علقمة بن مرثد عن عبد الله بن بريدة عن ابيه
قال كان رسول الله صلى الله عليه اذا بعث جيشا او سرية اوصى صاحبهم بتقوى الله تعالى في
خاصة نفسه واوصى بمن معه من المسلمين خيرا ثم قال اغزوا بسم الله وفي سبيل الله قاتلوا من
كفر بالله لا تغلوا ولا تغدروا ولا تمثلوا ولا تقتلوا وليدا واذا لقيتم عدوا من المشركين
فادعوهم الى الاسلام فان اسلموا فاقبلوا منهم وكفوا عنهم ثم ادعوهم الى التحول من دارهم
الى دار المهاجرين فان فعلوا فاقبلوا منهم وكفوا عنهم والا فاخبروهم انهم كاعراب المسلمين
يجرى عليهم حكم الله تعالى الذي يجرى على المسلمين وليس لهم من الفيء ولا في الغنيمة نصيب
فان ابوا ذلك فادعوهم الى اعطاء الجزية فان فعلوا ذلك فاقبلوا منهم وكفوا عنهم واذا
حاصرتم اهل حصن او مدينة فارادوكم على ان تنزلوهم على حكم الله تعالى فلا تنزلوهم فانكم
لا تدرون ما حكم الله تعالى ولكن انزلوهم على حكمكم ثم احكموا فيهم بما رايتم واذا حاصرتم
اهل حصن او مدينة فارادوكم ان تعطوهم ذمة الله تعالى وذمة رسوله صلى الله عليه فلا تعطوهم
ذمة الله تعالى ولا ذمة رسوله ولكن اعطوهم ذممكم وذمم ابائكم فانكم ان تخفروا ذممكم
وذمم ابائكم اهون محمد عن ابي يوسف عن الكلبي عن ابي صالح عن ابن عباس ان الخمس كان يقسم
على عهد رسول الله صلى الله عليه على خمسة اسهم لله وللرسول سهم ولذي القربى سهم وللمساكين
سهم ولليتامى سهم ولابن السبيل سهم قال ثم قسمه ابو بكر وعمر وعثمان وعلي رضي الله عنهم
اجمعين على ثلثة اسهم لليتامى والمساكين وابن السبيل محمد عن ابي يوسف عن محمد بن اسحق
عن ابي جعفر قال قلت ما كان راي علي بن ابي طالب في الخمس قال كان رايه راي اهل بيته ولكنه
كره ان يخالف ابا بكر وعمر محمد عن ابي يوسف عن ابي اسحق عن اسمعيل بن ابي امية عن عطا بن

The first page of the Murād Mulla MS, Istanbul.

بسم الله الرحمن الرحيم   ابواب السير في ارض الحرب

ابو سليمان عن محمد بن الحسن عن ابي حنيفة عن علقمة بن مرثد عن عبد الله بن بريدة عن ابيه قال
كان رسول الله صلى الله عليه وسلم اذا بعث جيشا او سرية اوصى صاحبهم بتقوى الله تعالى في خاصة نفسه
واوصى بمن معه من المسلمين خيرا ثم قال اغزوا بسم الله وفي سبيل الله قاتلوا من كفر بالله لا تغلوا
ولا تغدروا ولا تمثلوا ولا تقتلوا وليدا واذا لقيتم عدوكم من المشركين فادعوهم الى الاسلام فان
اسلموا فاقبلوا منهم وكفوا عنهم ثم ادعوهم الى التحول من دارهم الى دار المهاجرين فان فعلوا فاقبلوا
منهم وكفوا عنهم والا فاخبروهم انهم كاعراب المسلمين يجري عليهم حكم الله تعالى الذي يجري على المسلمين
وليس لهم من الفيء ولا من الغنيمة نصيب فان ابوا ذلك فادعوهم الى اعطاء الجزية فان فعلوا ذلك فاقبلوا
منهم وكفوا عنهم فاذا حاصرتم اهل حصن او مدينة فارادوكم على ان تنزلوهم على حكم الله تعالى
فلا تنزلوهم فانكم لا تدرون ما حكم الله تعالى ولكن انزلوهم على حكمكم ثم احكموا فيهم بما رايتم واذا
حاصرتم اهل حصن او مدينة فارادوكم ان تعطوهم ذمة الله تعالى وذمة رسول الله صلى الله عليه وسلم
فلا تعطوهم ذمة الله ولا ذمة رسوله ولكن اعطوهم ذممكم وذمم ابائكم فانكم ان تخفروا ذممكم وذمم ابائكم
اهون   محمد عن ابي يوسف عن الكلبي عن ابي صالح عن ابن عباس ان الخمس كان يقسم على عهد
رسول الله صلعم على خمسة اسهم لله وللرسول سهم ولذي القربى سهم وللمساكين سهم ولليتامى
سهم ولابن السبيل سهم قال ثم قسمه ابو بكر وعمر وعثمان وعلي رضي الله عنهم اجمعين على ثلثة اسهم
لليتامى والمساكين وابن السبيل   محمد عن ابي يوسف عن محمد بن اسحق عن ابي جعفر قال
قلت ما كان راي علي رضي الله عنه في الخمس قال كان رايه راي اهل بيته ولكنه كره ان يخالف
ابا بكر وعمر   محمد عن ابي يوسف عن ابي اسحق عن اسمعيل عن ابي امية عن عطاء بن ابي رباح
عن ابن عباس رضي الله عنهما قال عرض علينا عمر رضي الله عنه ان نزوج من الخمس ايمنا وان نقضي منه
عن مغرمنا فابينا الا ان يسلمه لنا فابى عمر ذلك علينا   محمد عن ابي يوسف عن محمد بن اسحق عن
الزهري عن سعيد بن المسيب قال قسم رسول الله صلى الله عليه وسلم الخمس يوم خيبر فقسم سهم ذوي
القربى بين بني هاشم وبين بني المطلب فكلمه عثمان بن عفان وجبير بن مطعم رسول الله صلى الله عليه وسلم
فقالا نحن وبنو المطلب اليك في النسب سواء واعطيتهم دوننا فقال رسول الله صلعم انا لم نزل نحن وبنو
المطلب في الجاهلية والاسلام معا   محمد عن ابي يوسف عن الاشعث بن سوار عن ابي الزبير عن جابر
انه قال كان يحمل الخمس في سبيل الله تعالى ويعطى منه نائبة القوم فلما كثر المال جعل في غير ذلك   محمد عن
ابي يوسف عن الحسن بن عمارة عن عبد الملك بن ميسرة عن طاوس عن ابن عباس رضي الله عنهما ان رجلا
وجد بعيرا له في المغنم قد كان المشركون اصابوه قبل ذلك فسال عنه رسول الله صلى الله عليه وسلم فقال ان وجدته
قبل القسمة فهو لك وان وجدته بعد القسمة اخذته بالثمن ان شئت   محمد عن ابي يوسف عن عبد الله
بن عمر عن نافع عن عبد الله بن عمر رضي الله عنهما ان عبدا لابن عمر ابق وانفلت له فرس فاخذه العدو
فظهر عليهم خالد بن الوليد فرد العبد والفرس على ابن عمر في عهد رسول الله صلى الله عليه وسلم   محمد عن ابي يوسف
عن عبد الله بن عمر ان عبدا لابن عمر اخذه الروم فافتداه خالد بن الوليد بدرهمين ثم رده الى ابن عمر

The first two pages of the ʿĀṭif MS, Istanbul.

بسم الله الرحمن الرحيم
ابواب السير في ارض الحرب

ابو يوسف عن محمد بن الحسن عن ابي حنيفة عن علقمة بن مرثد عن عبد الله بن بريدة عن ابيه
قال كان رسول الله صلى الله عليه وسلم اذا بعث جيشا او سرية اوصى صاحبهم بتقوى الله تعالى
في خاصة نفسه واوصى بمن معه من المسلمين خيرا ثم قال اغزوا باسم الله وفي سبيل الله
قاتلوا من كفر بالله لا تغلوا ولا تغدروا ولا تمثلوا ولا تقتلوا وليدا واذا لقيتم عدوكم من
المشركين فادعوهم الى الاسلام فان اسلموا فاقبلوا منهم وكفوا عنهم ثم ادعوهم
الى التحول من دارهم الى دار المهاجرين فان فعلوا فاقبلوا منهم وكفوا عنهم والا فاخبروهم انهم
كاعراب المسلمين يجري عليهم حكم الله تعالى الذي يجري على المسلمين وليس لهم من
الفيء ولا من الغنيمة نصيب فان ابوا ذلك فادعوهم الى اعطاء الجزية فان فعلوا ذلك
فاقبلوا منهم وكفوا عنهم فاذا حاصرتم اهل حصن او مدينة فارادوكم على ان تنزلوهم على
حكم الله تعالى فلا تنزلوهم فانكم لا تدرون ما حكم الله تعالى ولكن انزلوهم على حكمكم ثم
احكموا فيهم بما رايتم واذا حاصرتم اهل حصن او مدينة فارادوكم ان تعطوهم ذمة الله
تعالى وذمة رسول الله صلى الله عليه وسلم فلا تعطوهم ذمة الله تعالى ولا ذمة رسوله
ولكن اعطوهم ذممكم وذمم اباءكم فانكم ان تخفروا ذممكم وذمم اباءكم اهون محمد عن ابي
يوسف عن الكلبي عن ابي صالح عن ابن عباس ان الخمس كان يقسم على عهد رسول الله
صلى الله عليه وسلم على خمسة اسهم لله وللرسول سهم ولذي القربى سهم وللمساكين
سهم ولليتامى سهم ولابن السبيل سهم قال ثم قسمه ابو بكر وعمر وعثمان وعلي رضي الله
عنهم اجمعين على ثلثة اسهم لليتامى والمساكين وابن السبيل محمد عن ابي يوسف عن
محمد بن اسحق عن ابي جعفر قال قلت ما كان راي علي بن ابي طالب رضي الله عنه في الخمس
قال كان رايه مثل راي اهل بيته ولكنه كره ان يخالف ابا بكر وعمر محمد عن ابي يوسف
عن ابن اسحق عن اسمعيل عن ابي امية عن عطاء بن ابي رباح عن ابن عباس رضي الله
عنهما قال عرض علينا عمر رضي الله عنه ان نزوج من الخمس ايمنا ونقضي منه عن مغرمنا
فابينا الا ان يسلمه لنا فابى ذلك علينا محمد عن ابي يوسف عن محمد بن اسحق عن
الزهري عن سعيد بن المسيب قال قسم رسول الله صلى الله عليه وسلم الخمس يوم خيبر
فقسم سهم ذوي القربى بين بني هاشم وبني المطلب فكلمه عثمان بن عفان وجبير بن
مطعم رسول الله صلى الله عليه وسلم فقالا ... وبنو المطلب اليكم في النسب سواء فاعطيتهم
دوننا فقال رسول الله صلى الله عليه وسلم انا لم نزل نحن وبنو المطلب في الجاهلية
والاسلام معا محمد عن ابي يوسف عن الاشعث بن سوار عن ابي الزبير عن جابر انه قال

The first page of the Fayḍ-Allāh MS, Istanbul.

The first page of the Cavala MS (Dar al-Kulub), Cairo.

Brockelmann and Schacht have already given us virtually a full description of the manuscripts now available to scholarship and no attempt to describe them will be made.[151]

In reconstructing an Arabic version for the text in translation I have selected five manuscripts, three from Istanbul and two from Cairo. In Istanbul, I used the Murād Mulla manuscript, Volume III (no. 1040/1024), pp. 131-78; the Fayḍ-Allāh manuscript (no. 664), pp. 190-222; and the 'Ātif manuscript, Vol. III (no. 743), pp. 71-98. In Cairo I used two manuscripts, both in the Dār al-Kutub, the National Library. The first is in one volume and may be found in the Cavala collection (no. 200), and the other, though in four volumes, is incomplete. The latter contains, however, the section on the taxation system.

The oldest manuscript in existence is that of Murād Mulla; the date of the portion of the siyar which appears in the manuscript is given as Ramaḍān, 638/1240. The date of the Fayḍ-Allāh manuscript is 753/1352, but the dates of the 'Ātif and Cairo manuscripts are unknown, although the style of writing and the quality of the paper make it clear that they are much more recent.

The Murād Mulla manuscript is the most complete of those I have seen. The handwriting, though not as clear as some of the others, is legible enough and rarely is it obscure or impossible to read. In two or three instances the copyist had repeated a few lines, and these obviously do not appear in the translation. Accordingly I have used the Murād Mulla as the basic manuscript, verified by others wherever necessary (as indicated in the text in translation), and its pages are indicated in the margin beside the text in translation.

Editions

To my best knowledge, a full edition of the *Kitāb al-Aṣl* has not appeared in print to date. A portion of the *Kitāb al-Buyū' wa al-Salam,* edited by Shafīq Shiḥāta, was published

[151] *Ibid.*, and C. Brockelmann, *Geschichte der arabischen Literatur* (2nd ed.; Leiden, 1944-49), Vol. I, p. 178; Supplement I, p. 289.

in Cairo in 1954 as a single volume of text. A second volume, scheduled to include an introduction and appendices, has not yet appeared. This edition is based on the Murād Mulla and Fayḍ-Allāh manuscripts of Istanbul and the Dār al-Kutub (Cavala) manuscript of Cairo.

A full edition of the *Kitāb al-Aṣl* seems to be in preparation at the Dā'irat al-Ma'ārif al-Niẓāmīya of Hyderabad, as I have learned only recently. The publication of this comprehensive *corpus juris* of the Ḥanafī school would be a welcome and long overdue event.

Translation

Translation into English from a foreign tongue, especially from one in which the classical writers were accustomed to express themselves in a synoptic style, confronts the translator with a number of difficulties. Some translators tend to recast the original in a modern style in an effort to clarify the archaic style of an old writer and to make his abstract ideas intelligible. Commendable though this method may be, it deprives the reader of a deeper understanding of the spirit and thought of the original author and perhaps of a touch of his literary talent. As H. A. R. Gibb pointed out in his review of Franz Rosenthal's translation of Ibn Khaldūn's *Muqaddima* (Prolegomena), the recasting of Ibn Khaldūn's elegant original into modern style deprived the reader of the "lively, direct, colorful, brilliantly imaginative, exuberantly eloquent [style of] Ibn Khaldūn."[152] With all its defects, literal translation is perhaps the safest way for a thorough understanding of the spirit and thought of writers of different cultural background and social milieu from those of our age.

At the other extreme, a closely literal translation may distort the original meaning or render the broad or abstract concept in the English language more specifically than the author intended. In translating the *Risāla,* a treatise on jurisprudence, by Shāfi'ī, who was a jurist fond of expressing his

[152] Gibb, "Franz Rosenthal, trans., Ibn Khaldūn: *The Muqaddimah,*" *Speculum,* Vol. 35 (1961), p. 139.

ideas in terse and often in incomplete sentences, I tried to provide the reader with "the equivalent in English in as close and literal a translation as is possible with occasional words and sentences added in parentheses to complete the meaning of a sentence or to clarify an abstract concept. No attempt was made to recast the original in a completely modern style."[153] But this statement elicited the protest of one reviewer who asked: "Might we appeal to him to reconsider that decision next time?"[154]

Fortunately, Shaybānī's text, though often as obscure as Shāfi'ī's, is less involved in style. It is possible therefore to modify in some degree the method followed in the translation of Shāfi'ī's *Risāla* and to maintain a balance between clarity and fidelity to the original text. It is hoped that this introduction will provide the background necessary for the understanding of the theme and content of the text in translation. The definitions of basic terms and concepts and the supplementary material in the notes may also help to explain the meaning of the text. The notes are also intended to indicate the principal classical sources available for the material discussed in the text.

The original text appears to be fairly coherent and the ideas, though occasionally repeated, are set forth systematically. No attempt has been made in this translation to omit repetitions of ideas, although the repetition of an entire passage or paragraph, obviously made by a copyist, has been omitted. Four sections (or subdivisions of chapters) do not appear to fit into the logical order of the text. The first, on "The Killing of Captives and the Destruction of Enemy Fortifications" (paragraphs 94-123), which follows the section on "Trade between the Territory of Islam and the Territory of War" (paragraphs 374-407), has been transposed from Chapter IV to Chapter II. The second, on "The Granting of Amān by Muslims in the Territory of War" (paragraphs

[153] See my *Islamic Jurisprudence*, p. 52.

[154] W. J. D. Holland, "Islamic Jurisprudence: Shāfi'ī's *Risāla*; translated with an Introduction, Notes and Appendices by Majid Khadduri," *Royal Central Asian Society*, Vol. 50 (January, 1963), p. 90.

628-47), which follows the section on "Muslim Merchants in the Territory of War Seeking to Recover Their Women or Property" (paragraphs 434-45), has been transposed from Chapter IV to Chapter VI. The third, the section on "Slave Girl Captured by a Single Warrior Starting from the Muslim Camp and Making an Incursion in the Territory of War" (paragraphs 336-73), following the section on "The Granting of Amān by Muslims in the Territory of War" (paragraphs 628-47), has been transposed from Chapter IV to Chapter III. Finally, the section on "Penalties in Territory of War and the Shortening of Prayer" (paragraphs 124-47), following the section on "Slave Girl Captured by a Single Warrior Starting from the Muslim Camp and Making an Incursion in the Territory of War" (paragraphs 336-73), has been transposed from Chapter IV to Chapter II. In order to preserve the character and the general scheme of the work as laid down by Shaybānī, no other attempts have been made to change or recast the order of the book, although certain additional changes might have improved the structure.

None of the original texts is divided into basic chapters nor into numbered paragraphs, as is provided in the text in translation. Shaybānī was satisfied with sectional divisions, supplying no major divisions under which the sections might be regrouped.

Translation of Shaybānī's Siyar

Chapter I

[TRADITIONS RELATING TO THE CONDUCT OF WAR][1]

Murād Mulla MS Vol. III, folio 131

In the Name of God, the Merciful, the Compassionate. Praise Be to God, the One, the Just.[2]

1. Abū Sulaymān [al-Juzjānī][3] from Muḥammad b. al-Ḥasan [al-Shaybānī][4] from Abū Ḥanīfa[5] from 'Alqama b. Marthad from 'Abd-Allāh b. Burayda from his father [Burayda b. al-Ḥuṣayb al-Aslamī], who said:[6]

Whenever the Apostle of God[7] sent forth an army or a detachment,[8] he charged its commander personally to fear

[1] In this chapter Shaybānī reproduces the relevant Traditions that have bearing on the siyar. See pp. 49 ff., above.

[2] The second line of the blessing appears only in the Murād Mulla MS, not in the others.

[3] One of Shaybānī's disciples who transmitted *Kitāb al-Aṣl.* See pp. 43, 45, above.

[4] In all the MSS, Shaybānī is referred to either as Muḥammad or Muḥammad b. al-Ḥasan.

[5] Abū Ḥanīfa al-Nu'mān b. Thābit (d. 150/768). See pp. 25-26, *passim,* above.

[6] This Tradition, related on the authority of 'Alqama b. Marthad and Ibn Burayda, was transmitted by several other authorities. See Abū al-Ḥusayn Muslim b. al-Ḥajjāj Muslim, *Ṣaḥīḥ* (Cairo, 1929), Vol. XII, pp. 37-40; Ibn Māja Abū 'Abd-Allāh Muḥammad b. Yazīd al-Qazwīnī, *Sunan,* ed. M. Fu'ād 'Abd al-Bāqī (Cairo, 1373/1954), Vol. II, pp. 953-54; Abū Dāwūd Sulaymān b. al-Ash'ath, *Sunan* (Cairo, 1935), Vol. II, p. 137; Abū Yūsuf, *Kitāb al-Kharāj,* pp. 193-94, reproduces similar instructions to commanders of the army issued by the Caliph 'Umar b. al-Khaṭṭāb.

[7] The blessing "Peace be upon him" is omitted throughout this translation.

[8] Muslim publicists distinguish between jaysh, a large armed force, and sarīya, a small detachment. The latter, due to its small numerical strength, was ordinarily employed for surprise attacks at night, and was to retire to hiding during the day. See Sarakhsī, *Mabsūṭ,* Vol. X, p. 4, and *Sharḥ Kitāb al-Siyar al-Kabīr,* ed. Munajjid, Vol. I, p. 33.

God, the Most High, and he enjoined the Muslims who were with him to do good [i. e., to conduct themselves properly].[9]

And [the Apostle] said:

Fight in the name of God and in the "path of God" [i. e., truth].[10] Combat [only] those who disbelieve in God. Do not cheat or commit treachery, nor should you mutilate anyone or kill children.[11] Whenever you meet your polytheist enemies, invite them [first] to adopt Islam.[12] If they do so, accept it, and let them alone. You should then invite them to move from their territory to the territory of the *émigrés* [Madīna]. If they do so, accept it and let them alone.[13] Otherwise, they should be informed that they would be [treated] like the Muslim nomads (Bedouins) [who take no part in the war] in that they are subject to God's orders as [other] Muslims, but that they will receive no share in either the ghanīma (spoil of war)[14] or in the fay'.[15] If they refuse [to accept Islam], then call upon them to pay the jizya (poll tax); if they do, accept it and leave them alone.[16] If you besiege the inhabi-

[9] This order, as pointed out by Sarakhsī, was intended to inspire confidence in the army and respect for its commander. See Sarakhsī, *Mabsūṭ*, Vol. X, p. 5.

[10] This is intended to show the religious purpose of war and that fighting should begin by invoking the name of God. See Sarakhsī, *Mabsūṭ*, Vol. X, p. 5; and Khadduri, *War and Peace in the Law of Islam*, pp. 94-95.

[11] In another version of the Tradition, the Prophet prohibited the killing of women, children and aged men (paragraphs 28-30, below). See Bukhārī, *Ṣaḥiḥ*, Vol. II, p. 251; Sarakhsī, *Mabsūṭ*, Vol. X, p. 5; Khadduri, *War and Peace in the Law of Islam*, pp. 103-4.

[12] This is based, as Muslim publicists assert, on the Quranic injunction: "We never punished anyone until we first sent them an Apostle" (Q. XVII, 16); and on other Traditions from the Prophet. See Sarakhsī, *Mabsūṭ*, Vol. X, p. 6; and Khadduri, *War and Peace in the Law of Islam*, pp. 96-98.

[13] Muslims who migrated from Makka to Madīna, where the Prophet Muḥammad established his seat of government, were called al-Muhājirūn, or *émigrés*; those in Madīna who became Muslims were called al-Anṣār, or supporters. Before Makka fell into Muslim hands, everyone who became a Muslim was ordinarily ordered to emigrate to Madīna; but after Makka was taken by Muḥammad (8/630), the migration order was repealed. See Sarakhsī *Mabsūṭ*, Vol. X, pp. 6-7.

[14] See p. 106, below.

[15] See pp. 48-49, above.

[16] The jizya (poll tax) was imposed only on the "People of the Book,"

tants of a fortress or a town and they try to get you to let them surrender on the basis of God's judgment, do not do so, since you do not know what God's judgment is, but make them surrender to your judgment and then decide their case according to your own views.[17] But if the besieged inhabitants of a fortress or a town asked you to give them a pledge [of security] in God's name or in the name of His Apostle, you should not do so, but give the pledge in your names or in the names of your fathers; for, if you should ever break it,[18] it would be an easier matter if it were in the names of you or your fathers.[19]

2. Muḥammad [b. al-Ḥasan] from Abū Yūsuf[20] from [Muḥammad b. al-Sā'ib] al-Kalbī from Abū Ṣāliḥ [al-Sammān] from ['Abd-Allāh] b. 'Abbās [who said]:

The one-fifth [share of the spoil] was divided in the time of the Apostle of God into five parts: one for God and the Apostle, one for the near of kin, one for the poor, one for the orphans, and one for the wayfarer.[21]

He [Ibn 'Abbās] said that [the Caliphs] Abū Bakr, 'Umar, 'Uthmān, and 'Alī divided [the one-fifth share] into three

---

as we stated before; Sarakhsī points out that its general meaning in this statement was intended to apply specifically to the People of the Book (Sarakhsī, *Mabsūṭ*, Vol. X, p. 7).

[17] Abū Yūsuf held that divine legislation and the Prophet's decrees have dealt with such situations. Shaybānī, however, who disagreed with his master on this point, held that the ruling was still binding. See Sarakhsī, *Mabsūṭ*, Vol. X, p. 7.

[18] This order was obviously not intended to imply encouragement to break pledges, but was meant as a warning not to involve the names of God and his Apostle in making pledges to the enemy (see Sarakhsī, *Sharḥ Kitāb al-Siyar al-Kabīr*, ed. Munajjid, Vol. I, pp. 38-39; and his *Mabsūṭ*, Vol. X, p. 8).

[19] See Muslim, *Ṣaḥīḥ*, Vol. XII, pp. 37-40; Ibn Māja, *Sunan*, Vol. II, pp. 953-54; Abū Ḥanīfa al-Nu'mān b. Thābit, *Kitāb al-Musnad*, ed. Ṣafwat al-Saqqā (Aleppo, 1382/1962), pp. 153-54; Abū Yūsuf, *Kitāb al-Āthār*, pp. 192-93; Sarakhsī, *Sharḥ Kitāb al-Siyar al-Kabīr*, ed. Munajjid, Vol. I, pp. 38-39.

[20] Ya'qūb b. Ibrāhim al-Anṣārī, better known as Abū Yūsuf. See pp. 25, *passim*, above

[21] This was known as the share of the Prophet, orphans, and the poor, based on divine legislation as provided in a Quranic communication (Q. VIII, 42). It was in effect the share of the state to be distributed among the poor. For the division of this share, see Chap. III, below.

parts; one for the orphans, one for the poor, and one for the wayfarer.

3. Muḥammad [b. al-Ḥasan] from Abū Yūsuf and Muḥammad b. Isḥāq, from Abū Ja'far [Muḥammad b. 'Alī b. al-Ḥusayn] [from Yazīd b. Hurmuz], who said: [22]

I asked [Ibn 'Abbās]: "What was [the Caliph] 'Alī b. Abī Ṭālib's opinion concerning the one-fifth [share]?" He [Ibn 'Abbās] replied: "His ['Alī's] opinion was like the opinion of his House [the House of the Prophet Muḥammad], but he disliked to disagree with Abū Bakr and 'Umar [on the subject]." [23]

4. Muḥammad [b. al-Ḥasan] from Abū Yūsuf from Abū Isḥāq from Ismā'īl b. Abī Umayya from 'Aṭā' b. Abī Rabāḥ from ['Abd-Allāh] b. 'Abbās, who said:

[The Caliph] 'Umar offered to defray the expenses of marriage for [the unmarried members of] our House and to pay our debts [from the one-fifth share]. When we insisted that [the share] instead should be handed over to us [*in toto*], he refused.[24]

5. Muḥammad [b. al-Ḥasan] from Abū Yūsuf from Muḥammad b. Isḥāq from [Muḥammad b. Shihāb] al-Zuhrī from Sa'īd b. al-Musayyib, who said:

The Apostle of God, in dividing up the one-fifth [share] of the spoil after the campaign of Khaybar,[25] divided between

[22] The chain of authorities for this Tradition seems to be incomplete, for Abū Ja'far did not relate the Tradition directly from Ibn 'Abbās, but from Yazīd b. Hurmuz. See paragraph 49, below.

[23] Abū Yūsuf, *Kitāb al-Kharāj*, p. 20; Dārimī, *Sunan*, Vol. II, p. 225; Sarakhsī, *Mabsūṭ*, Vol. X, pp. 10-11.

[24] Abū Yūsuf, *Kitāb al-Kharāj*, pp. 19-20. The Caliph Abū Bakr, followed by his successors, made a decision against giving the one-fifth share to the Prophet's house after the Prophet's death on the strength of a Tradition from the Prophet to the effect that his share, not considered to be his private property, could not be inherited. See Muslim, *Ṣaḥīḥ*, Vol. XII, pp. 74-82; and Sarakhsī, *Mabsūṭ*, Vol. XII, p. 11.

[25] Khaybar, a Jewish settlement about eighty miles northeast of Madīna, was brought under Muslim domination in 7/628. See Abū Muḥammad 'Abd al-Malik Ibn Hishām, *Kitāb Sīrat Sayyidina Muḥammad Rasūl Allāh*, ed. Ferdinand Wüstenfeld (Göttingen, 1858-60), Vol. II, pp. 755 ff.; Eng. trans. A. Guillaume, *The Life of Muhammad* (London, 1955), pp. 510 ff.

the Banū Hāshim and the Banū al-Muṭṭalib the part assigned to the near kin.[26] Thereupon, 'Uthmān b. 'Affān and Jubayr b. Muṭ'im asked the Apostle to treat them on equal footing on the ground that they were as closely related to him as Banū al-Muṭṭalib. The Apostle replied: "We and the Banū al-Muṭṭalib have stood together in [the days of] both al-Jāhilīya [27] and of Islam." [28]

6. Muḥammad [b. al-Ḥasan] from Abū Yūsuf from al-Ash'ath b. Sawwār from Abū al-Zubayr [Muḥammad b. Muslim] from Jābir [b. 'Abd-Allāh], who said:

He [the Prophet] used to assign the one-fifth to "the path of God" [i. e., religious purposes] and out of it he gave to some members of the community,[29] but when the revenue increased, he included others.[30]

7. Muḥammad [b. al-Ḥasan] from Abū Yūsuf from al-Ḥasan b. 'Umāra from 'Abd al-Malik b. Maysara from Ṭāwūs [b. Kaysān] from ['Abd-Allāh] b. 'Abbās [who said]:

A man once found in the spoil [taken from the enemy] a camel of his that the unbelievers had captured, and he asked the Apostle [whether he could take it back]. He [the Prophet]

[26] The house of the Banū Hāshim and the house of the Banū al-Muṭṭalib were descendants of 'Abd Manāf. 'Abd Manāf, a son of Quṣayy, belonged to the tribe of Quraysh. Hāshim and Muṭṭalib were brothers. 'Uthmān descended from 'Abd Shams and Jubayr from Nawfal, but all the four (Hāshim, Muṭṭalib, Nawfal, and 'Abd Shams) were brothers. See Muṣ'ab b. 'Abd-Allāh al-Zubayrī, *Kitāb Nasab Quraysh*, ed. E. Lévi-Provençal (Cairo, 1953), pp. 14-17, 17-20, 15-91.

[27] Al-Jāhiliya, or the Days of Ignorance, is a term traditionally used for the pre-Islamic or pagan period.

[28] This Tradition concerning the part of the one-fifth share given to the near of kin was interpreted to mean that the share was given to the near of kin who supported the cause of Islam, not to all the near of kin. See Bukhārī, *Ṣaḥīḥ*, Vol. II, p. 286; Ibn Māja, *Sunan*, Vol. II, p. 961; Sarakhsī, *Mabsūṭ*, pp. 12-13; Abū 'Ubayd al-Qāsim Ibn Sallām, *Kitāb al-Amwāl*, ed. M. Ḥamīd al-Fiqqī (Cairo, 1353/1954), p. 331.

[29] "Nā'ibat al-Qawm" has been interpreted to mean either the near of kin (dhawū al-Qurbā)—which is more likely—or the warriors (al-ghuzāt) who took part in the fighting. See Sarakhsī, *Mabsūṭ*, Vol. X, p. 14. Cf. Bukhārī *Ṣaḥīḥ*, Vol. II, p. 283.

[30] In his *Kitāb al-Kharāj*, p. 20, Abū Yūsuf cites the latter part of the Tradition to read: "But when the share increased in quantity, he included the orphans, the poor, and the wayfarer."

replied: "If you found it before the spoil was divided, it is yours; but if you found it after it was divided, you can take it by paying its price, if you so desire." [31]

8. Muḥammad [b. al-Ḥasan] from Abū Yūsuf from 'Abd-Allāh b. 'Umar from Nāfi' [freed slave of Ibn 'Umar] from 'Abd-Allāh b. 'Umar [who said]:

A runaway slave who belonged to him [Ibn 'Umar] went over to the enemy [the unbelievers] and his horse was captured by them. When Khālid b. al-Walīd [the commander of a Muslim force] defeated them, he returned the slave and the horse to Ibn 'Umar in the time of the Apostle of God.[32]

9. Muḥammad [b. al-Ḥasan] from Abū Yūsuf from 'Abd-Allāh b. 'Umar, who said:

A slave belonging to Ibn 'Umar was captured by the Rūm [Byzantines], but Khālid b. al-Walīd ransomed him by releasing two Byzantine [prisoners] and returned him to Ibn 'Umar.[33]

10. Muḥammad [b. al-Ḥasan] from Abū Yūsuf from al-Mujālid b. Sa'īd from ['Āmir b. Sharāḥīl] al-Sha'bī [who said]:

[The Caliph] 'Umar b. al-Khaṭṭāb decreed that the inhabitants of [the territory of] al-Sawād [34] would be regarded as Dhimmīs.[35]

[31] In either case, the Tradition recognizes the principle that the unbelievers had owned the camel by capture and that its recapture by the believers rendered it part of the spoil that belonged to the community of Islam. Since its capture by the unbeliever constituted a loss to one individual believer, he could take it back free of charge before the division of the spoil on the basis of the right of postliminium; but after the division, the original owner could recover it only by paying its price. See Abū Yūsuf, *Kitāb al-Kharāj*, p. 200, and *Kitāb al-Āthār*, p. 195; Sarakhsī, *Mabsūṭ*, Vol. X, pp. 14-15.

[32] Abū Yūsuf, *Kitāb al-Kharāj*, p. 200; Bukhārī, *Ṣaḥīḥ*, Vol. II, p. 265. Khālid's campaign may have taken place either during the iconoclastic expedition at the time of the conquest of Makka or the expedition against Najrān commanded by Khālid.

[33] In 'Āṭif MS, the latter part of the Tradition reads: "two Byzantine female [prisoners]." Cf. Abū Yūsuf, *Kitāb al-Kharāj*, p. 200.

[34] Southern 'Irāq. It was called al-Sawād (the black) because it was covered with dark green vegetation. See Muṭarrazī, *al-Mughrib*, Vol. I, p. 267.

[35] See Abū Yūsuf, *Kitāb al-Kharāj*, p. 28; Sarakhsī, *Mabsūṭ*, Vol. X,

11. Muḥammad [b. al-Ḥasan] from Abū Yūsuf, from Hishām b. Sa'īd from Muḥammad b. Zayd from al-Muhājir [b. 'Umayra] from 'Umayr, freed slave of Abī al-Laḥm, who said:

When I was a slave, I came to the Apostle and asked him to give me something [from the spoil] while he was dividing the spoil of the battle of Khaybar. He said: "Hold this sword," which I did, and I dragged it over the ground [as an evidence of my strength]. Thereupon, he gave me something of no great value.[36]

12. Muḥammad [b. al-Ḥasan] from Abū Yūsuf from Muḥammad b. Isḥāq from Ismā'īl b. Umayya from 'Aṭā' b. Abī Rabāḥ from 'Abd-Allāh b. 'Abbās [who said]:

[Nadja b. 'Āmir] [37] wrote to him requesting his opinion [about the following questions]:

"Is the slave entitled to a share of the spoil?

"Did women ever participate in war in the time of the Apostle of God?

"When is a minor entitled to a share of the spoil?

"[What is the status of] the share of the near of kin?" 132

Ibn 'Abbās replied:

"The slave is not entitled to a share of the spoil, but he should be given a little something [as compensation].

"Women used to accompany the Apostle [in his campaigns] in order to take care of the wounded and were given something [in compensation].

"The minor is not entitled to a share of the spoil until he attains puberty.

"As to the share belonging to the near of kin,[38] 'Umar

---

pp. 15-16. The Dhimmīs were the People of the Book, or scripturaries (see note 16 and Chap. V).

[36] It is held that 'Umayr, either because he was a minor or a slave, was not entitled to a regular share of the spoil, but the Prophet gave him compensation. See Abū Yūsuf, *Kitāb al-Kharāj*, p. 198; and *Kitāb al-Radd*, p. 120; Ibn Sa'd, *Ṭabaqāt*, Vol. II, p. 114; Dārimī, *Sunan*, Vol. II, p. 226; Sarakhsī, *Mabsūṭ*, Vol. X, p. 26.

[37] Najda b. 'Āmir, a follower of the Khārijī sect, wrote Ibn 'Abbās requesting his opinion about a number of controversial legal questions. See Abū Yūsuf, *Kitāb al-Kharāj*, pp. 20-21; and *Kitāb al-Radd*, pp. 38, 43.

[38] See paragraph 2, above.

[b. al-Khaṭṭāb] offered to pay from it the marriage expenses of the members of our family and to pay our debts. We demanded that the [whole] share should be given to us, but he refused to do so." [39]

13. Muḥammad [b. al-Ḥasan] from Abū Yūsuf from [Muḥammad b. al-Sā'ib] al-Kalbī and Muḥammad b. Isḥāq [both of whom said]:

The Apostle of God [once] gave a woman, who belonged to [the tribe of] Aslam, a necklace from the spoil taken at the campaign of Khaybar.[40]

14. Muḥammad [b. al-Ḥasan] from Abū Yūsuf from al-Ḥajjāj b. Arṭāt from 'Amr b. Shu'ayb from Sa'īd b. al-Musayyib, who said:

'Umar [b. al-Khaṭṭāb] held that the slave had no right [to a share] in the spoil.[41]

15. Muḥammad [b. al-Ḥasan] said: "As to the division of the spoil in enemy territory," Abū Yūsuf related from [Muḥammad b. al-Sā'ib] al-Kalbī and Muḥammad b. Isḥāq, both of whom said:

The Apostle of God himself [established the precedent that the spoil should be divided in the territory of Islam] by dividing the spoil [of the battle of] Badr after his return to Madīna.[42] 'Uthmān [b. 'Affān] requested [the Prophet] to assign for him from that spoil and he gave him a share. Ṭalḥa

[39] Muslim, *Ṣaḥīḥ*, Vol. XII, pp. 190-91; Sarakhsī, *Mabsūṭ*, Vol. X, pp. 16-17.

[40] The woman's name was Ghifār. See Ibn Hishām, *Kitāb Sīrat Rasūl Allāh*, Vol. II, p. 768.

[41] The slave has no right to a full share of the spoil, but he is entitled to compensation if he takes part in war by permission of his master. If he does not obtain permission, he is not entitled to compensation and would be held liable for not obtaining such permission. See Sarakhsī, *Mabsūṭ*, Vol. X, p. 17.

[42] There was a controversy among jurists as to whether the spoil of war should be divided after the return of the army from enemy territory or whether it could be divided while the army was still in enemy territory. The Ḥanafī school held that the spoil should be divided after the return of the army from enemy territory; but others, like Awzā'ī, held that the spoil might be divided while the army was still in enemy territory. See Abū Yūsuf, *Kitāb al-Radd*, pp. 1-15; Shāfi'ī, *Umm*, Vol. VII, pp. 303-4. See also paragraph 17, below, and p. 52, above.

b. 'Abd-Allāh [likewise] requested a share and was given one, although neither 'Uthmān nor Ṭalḥa had taken part [in the battle of] Badr. 'Uthmān was ordered by the Apostle to stay behind [in order to take care of] Ruqayya [wife of 'Uthmān and daughter of the Prophet], who was sick and died before the Apostle returned from Badr. Ṭalḥa was [then] in Syria.[43]

16. Muḥammad [b. al-Ḥasan] from Abū Yūsuf from [Muḥammad b. al-Sā'ib] al-Kalbī and Muḥammad b. Isḥāq from Usāma b. Zayd, who said:

Zayd b. Ḥāritha [father of Usāma b. Zayd] returned [to Madīna] announcing the good news of the victory [in the battle] of Badr when we had just finished putting the [sun-dried] bricks in place over [the grave of] Ruqayya, daughter of the Apostle of God. And [Zayd] said that 'Utba b. Rabī'a, Shayba b. Rabī'a, Abū Jahl b. Hishām, and Umayya b. Khalaf had been killed [in the battle]. He [Usāma] asked his father [Zayd]: "Is that right, father?" [Zayd] replied: "Yes—by God—[it was], my son."[44]

17. Muḥammad [b. al-Ḥasan] from Abū Yūsuf from al-Ḥasan b. 'Umāra from al-Ḥakam [b. 'Utayba] from Miqsam [b. Bujra] from ['Abd-Allāh] b. 'Abbās [who said]:

The Apostle of God divided the spoil [of the campaign of Ḥunayn] at al-Ji'rāna after his return from al-Ṭā'if.[45] As to Khaybar, [the Prophet] conquered it and his rule prevailed over it. So the Apostle of God divided up the spoil there before he left the town. He also divided the spoil of [the tribes of] Banū al-Muṣṭaliq in their land after he had conquered it.[46]

[43] It is held that 'Uthmān was entitled to a share because he stayed behind by an order of the Prophet to take care of his wife (also daughter of the Prophet), and Ṭalḥa was dispatched to Syria to obtain intelligence on the movement of the enemy before the battle of Badr took place. See Abū Yūsuf, *Kitāb al-Kharāj*, p. 196; Sarakhsī, *Mabsūṭ*, Vol. X, pp. 17-18; Bakhārī, *Ṣaḥīḥ*, Vol. II, pp. 282-83; Vol. III, p. 114.

[44] Abū Yūsuf, *Kitāb al-Kharāj*, p. 196; Sarakhsī, *Mabsūṭ*, Vol. X, pp. 17-18.

[45] Al-Ji'rāna, a suburb of Makka, was in the territory under Islamic rule and the Prophet, having passed out of enemy territory, divided the spoil there. See Bukhārī, *Ṣaḥīḥ*, Vol. III, pp. 150-55; Sarakhsī, *Mabsūṭ*, Vol. X, p. 18.

[46] Bukhārī, *Ṣaḥīḥ*, Vol. III, pp. 128-30.

18. Muḥammad [b. al-Ḥasan] from Abū Yūsuf from al-Ḥasan b. 'Umāra from al-Ḥakam [b. 'Utayba] from Miqsam [b. Bujra] from ['Abd-Allāh] b. 'Abbās [who said]:

The Apostle of God assigned two shares [of the spoil] to the horse-rider and one to the foot-warrior in [the battle of] Badr.[47]

19. Muḥammad [b. al-Ḥasan] said that Abū Yūsuf said that the same Tradition was related by Muḥammad b. Isḥāq and by [Muḥammad b. al-Sā'ib] al-Kalbī.[48]

20. Muḥammad [b. al-Ḥasan] from Abū Yūsuf from al-Juwaybir [Jābir b. 'Abd-Allāh] from al-Ḍaḥḥāk b. Muzāḥim [who said]:

[The Caliph] Abū Bakr sought the advice of the Muslims as to what should be done with the share of the near of kin [which reverted to the treasury after the Prophet's death], and they held [49] that it should be expended in [providing] horses and weapons.[50]

21. Muḥammad [b. al-Ḥasan] from Abū Yūsuf from Abū Isḥāq from al-Ḥasan b. 'Umāra from al-Ḥakam [b. 'Utayba] from Ibrāhīm [b. Yazīd al-Nakha'ī] [who said]:

While he [Ibrāhīm] was residing in a fortified post [on the frontier], he [and his company] were called upon to take part in an expedition; [Ibrāhīm] hired someone and paid scutage [instead].[51]

22. [Muḥammad b. al-Ḥasan from] [52] Abū Yūsuf from [Abū] Ṣāliḥ [al-Sammān] from a Shaykh from Abū Isḥāq al-

[47] Abū Yūsuf, *Kitāb al-Kharāj*, p. 18; *Kitāb al-Radd*, p. 17; Muslim, *Ṣaḥīḥ*, Vol. XII, p. 83; Sarakhsī, *Mabsūṭ*, Vol. X, p. 19.

[48] Abū Yūsuf, *Kitāb al-Kharāj*, pp. 18-19; cf. Bukhārī, *Ṣaḥīḥ*, Vol. III, p. 114.

[49] In another version "they agreed" (Abū Yūsuf, *Kitāb al-Kharāj*, p. 21).

[50] *Ibid.*, p. 21.

[51] "Al-Ju'l" is a scutage or contribution to the war effort in lieu of fighting, especially if the contribution were in the form of weapons which enable unarmed men to participate in war. See Sarakhsī, *Sharḥ Kitāb al-Siyar al-Kabīr*, ed. Munajjid, Vol. I, pp. 138-44, and *Mabsūṭ*, Vol. X, pp. 19-20; Muṭarrazī, *al-Mughrib*, Vol. I, pp. 86, 259; N. P. Aghnides, *Mohammedan Theories of Finance* (New York, 1916), Part II, Chap. 4.

[52] Not in the Arabic MSS.

Sabī'ī from someone who told it from ['Abd-Allāh] b. 'Abbās [who said]:

A man once asked me: "We are obligated to provide a fighting force; out of every ten [men], five, six, or seven are under obligation to go and those who stay behind [should] give contribution to those who go. But," he asked, "what should the one who stays behind contribute to those who go, for some contribute [something that would be expended in providing] horses and weapons while others contribute house provisions or servants [which would be used in the war]."

Ibn 'Abbās replied:

Contributions which would be expended for horses and weapons are satisfactory, but house provisions are unsatisfactory.[53]

23. Muḥammad [b. al-Ḥasan] from Abū Yūsuf from someone[54] who related from Ḥammād [b. Abī Sulaymān] from Ibrāhīm [b. Yazīd al-Nakha'ī], who said:

Scutage [as a substitute for fighting] is all right.[55]

24. Muḥammad [b. al-Ḥasan] from Abū Yūsuf from 'Āṣim [b. Sulaymān] al-Aḥwal from Abū 'Uthmān al-Nahdī [who said]:

'Umar b. al-Khaṭṭāb made unmarried men go to war instead of the married ones and he used to give the warrior the horse of him who stayed behind.[56]

25. Muḥammad [b. al-Ḥasan] from Abū Yūsuf from a shaykh from Maymūn b. Mihrān, who said:

Contribution [as a substitute for fighting] is all right, but it is objectionable to me to take a contribution and hire

[53] Bukhārī, *Ṣaḥīḥ*, Vol. II, p. 241; Sarakhsī, *Mabsūṭ*, Vol. X, p. 20, and *Sharḥ Kitāb al-Siyar al-Kabīr*, ed. Munajjid, Vol. I, p. 138.

[54] Perhaps Abū Ḥanīfa.

[55] Sarakhsī, *Mabsūṭ*, Vol. X, p. 20.

[56] Sarakhsī, *Sharḥ Kitāb al-Siyar al-Kabīr*, ed. Munajjid, Vol. I, p. 138. In commenting on 'Umar's decision, Sarakhsī states that some authorities held that 'Umar asked those who stayed behind to contribute horses as a voluntary act, for, if those who stayed behind failed to contribute, the warriors were supplied by the state. See Sarakhsī, *Mabsūṭ*, Vol. X, p. 20.

another person [to fight] for an amount less than that contribution.[57]

26. Muḥammad [b. al-Ḥasan] from Abū Yūsuf from 'Abd al-Raḥmān b. 'Abd-Allāh from someone who related to him from Jarīr b. 'Abd-Allāh al-Bajalī [who said]:

[The Caliph] Mu'āwiya b. Abī Sufyān ordered the inhabitants of Kūfa to raise an army but he exempted Jarīr [b. 'Abd-Allāh] and his son.[58] Jarīr said: "We would not accept [the exemption] but would give to the warrior a contribution from our property."[59]

27. Muḥammad [b. al-Ḥasan] from Abū Yūsuf from Muḥammad b. Isḥāq from Yazīd b. Abī Ḥabīb from Abū Marzūq from one of the Prophet's Companions,[60] who said that upon his capture of a town in al-Maghrib,[61] he stood up and made a speech to his company assuring them that he would not transmit to them save what he had heard the Apostle of God say in the battle of Khaybar. I heard him say:

He who believes in God and in the Last Day should not go into a woman [taken as a spoil] who is pregnant, nor should he sell [a part of] the spoil before it is divided. He should not ride an animal belonging to the Muslims [i. e., before the spoil is divided] until it is emaciated and then bring it back to them, nor should he wear a garment belonging to the Muslims' booty and return it worn out.[62]

28. Muḥammad [b. al-Ḥasan] from Abū Yūsuf from al-Ḥajjāj b. Arṭāt from Abū al-Zubayr [Muḥammad b. Muslim] from someone who took part in battle, said:

[57] Sarakhsī, *Sharḥ Kitāb al-Siyar al-Kabīr*, ed. Munajjid, Vol. I, p. 139.

[58] Jarīr, a companion of the Prophet Muḥammad who settled in Kūfa, was exempted by Mu'āwiya on the ground of respect and veneration for one of the Prophet's Companions.

[59] Sarakhsī, *Mabsūṭ*, Vol. X, pp. 20-21, and *Sharḥ Kitāb al-Siyar al-Kabīr*, ed. Munajjid, Vol. I, p. 139.

[60] His name is Ḥanash al-Ṣan'ānī.

[61] The name of the town is Jirba, an island near Qābis. Al-Maghrib was the name applied to the whole North African sector from Tunisia to Morocco, but more specifically to the latter in modern times.

[62] Ibn Hishām, *Kitāb Sīrat Rasūl Allāh*, Vol. II, pp. 758-59 (Guillaume's translation, p. 512). See also Dārimī, *Sunan*, Vol. II, p. 227; *Sarakhsī, Mabsūṭ*, Vol. X, pp. 21-22.

I heard the Apostle of God in the campaign against Banū Qurayza saying: "He [of the enemy] who has reached puberty[63] should be killed, but he who has not should be spared."

He who related this Tradition to Abū al-Zubayr, said that he had not reached puberty, so he was spared.[64]

29. Muḥammad [b. al-Ḥasan] from Abū Yūsuf from 'Āsim b. Sulaymān [al-Aḥwal] from al-Ḥasan [b. al-Ḥasan al-Baṣrī] said:

The Apostle of God prohibited the killing of women.[65] 133

30. Muḥammad [b. al-Ḥasan] from Abū Yūsuf from al-Ḥajjāj [b. Arṭāt] from Qatāda [b. Du'āma al-Sadūsī] from al-Ḥasan [b. al-Ḥasan al-Baṣrī], who said:

The Apostle of God said: "You may kill the adults of the unbelievers, but spare their minors—the youth."[66]

31. Muḥammad [b. al-Ḥasan] from Abū Yūsuf from Yaḥya b. Abī Unaysa from 'Alqama b. Marthad from ['Abd-Allāh] b. Burayda from his father [Burayda b. al-Ḥuṣayb al-Aslamī], who related from the Apostle of God a Tradition similar to that of Abū Ḥanīfa [on the prohibition of killing women].[67]

32. Muḥammad [b. al-Ḥasan] from Abū Yūsuf from Ash'ath b. Sawwār from [Muḥammad] b. Sīrīn, who said:

The Apostle of God used to assign to himself a choice article from the spoil before it was divided, such as a sword, a horse, an armor, or any other article.[68]

33. Muḥammad [b. al-Ḥasan] from Abū Yūsuf from Muḥammad b. Isḥāq and [Muḥammad b. al-Sā'ib] al-Kalbī, who said:

[63] This was regarded as evidence for minors who have come of age.

[64] Sarakhsī, *Mabsūṭ*, Vol. X, p. 27. For a different chain of transmitters, but essentially the same Tradition, see Abū Ḥanīfa, *Musnad*, pp. 154-55.

[65] For different chains of transmitters, see Abū Yūsuf, *Kitāb al-Kharāj*, p. 195 (related on the authority of Ibn 'Abbās); Bukhārī, *Ṣḥīḥ*, Vol. II, p. 251; Muslim, *Ṣaḥīḥ*, Vol. XII, p. 48.

[66] See Abū Yūsuf, *Kitāb al-Kharāj*, p. 195 (related on the authority of Ibn 'Abbas and Mujāhid).

[67] *Ibid.*, p. 195.

[68] *Ibid.*, pp. 22, 23.

The share of the Apostle of God from the spoil of the battle of Khaybar was included in the lot of 'Āsim b. 'Adī.[69]

34. Muḥammad [b. al-Ḥasan] from Abū Yūsuf from [Muḥammad b. al-Sā'ib] al-Kalbī and Abū Isḥāq, both of whom said that the Apostle of God once said:

"By God it is not lawful for me to take anything from the booty [before it is divided], not even this tuft of hair"—and he picked up a tuft of hair from the hump of a camel—"save [my part of] the one-fifth [share], and that one-fifth [too] will be returned to you. You should [therefore] return [even] the thread and needle [that you may have taken], for treachery would be a shame and a disgrace on the Day of Resurrection to those who had committed it." Thereupon, a man from the Anṣār (helpers)[70] who had taken a bundle of [camel hair] thread, came [to the Prophet] and said: "I took this ball to repair the saddle of a camel of mine." The Apostle replied: "You may have my own share of it!" Thereupon, [the man] said: "If the matter has reached this point, I have no need of it."[71]

35. Muḥammad [b. al-Ḥasan] from Abū Yūsuf from Muḥammad b. 'Abd al-Raḥmān b. Abī Layla from al-Ḥakam [b. 'Utayba] from Miqsam [b. Bujra] from ['Abd-Allāh] b. 'Abbās [who said]:

An unbeliever fell into the trench [of the believers] and died. The Muslims were given money in exchange for the corpse. When the Apostle was consulted on the matter, he prohibited this [deal].[72]

36. Muḥammad [b. al-Ḥasan] from Abū Yūsuf from 'Abd-

[69] The Prophet was entitled to three categories of shares: (1) the choice article before the division of the spoil; (2) his part of the one-fifth share; and (3) his share as a participant in war with other warriors, and this was ordinarily assigned to him and to one of the warriors. See Abū Yūsuf, *Kitāb al-Kharāj*, p. 23; Ibn Sallām, *Kitāb al-Amwāl*, p. 7; Ṭabarī, *Kitāb Ikhtilāf*, p. 140; Sarakhsī, *Mabsūṭ*, Vol. X, p. 27.

[70] The Anṣār were the supporters of the Prophet in the city of Madīna; those who migrated with him from Makka were the Muhājirūn (*émigrés*).

[71] Mālik, *al-Muwaṭṭa'*, Vol. II, pp. 20-21; Abū Yūsuf, *Kitāb al-Radd*, p. 48; Dārimī, *Sunan*, Vol. II, p. 230; Sarakhsī, *Mabsūṭ*, Vol. X, p. 27.

[72] Abū Ḥanīfa, *Musnad*, p. 155; Abū Yūsuf, *Kitāb al-Kharāj*, p. 199; Sarakhsī, *Mabsūṭ*, Vol. X, p. 22.

Allāh b. Abī Ḥumayd from Abū Mulayḥ from Abū Usāma [Zayd b. Ḥāritha] who related that the Apostle said in the last Pilgrimage:[73]

All the usury [of the Days] of Ignorance[74] [still payable] is canceled and the first usury to be canceled is the usury of 'Abbās b. 'Abd al-Muṭṭalib [all the blood shed in the Days of Ignorance is to be left unavenged].[75]

37. Muḥammad [b. al-Ḥasan] from Abū Yūsuf from Muḥammad b. 'Abd-Allāh from al-Ḥakam [b. 'Utayba] from Miqsam [b. Bujra] from ['Abd-Allāh] b. 'Abbās, who related a similar Tradition.

38. Muḥammad [b. al-Ḥasan] from Abū Yūsuf from Mujālid b. Sa'īd from ['Āmir b. Sharāḥil] al-Sha'bī and Ziyād b. 'Ilāqa [who said] that [the Caliph] 'Umar b. al-Khaṭṭāb wrote to Sa'd b. Abī Waqqāṣ [saying]:

I have sent you reinforcements from the people of Syria; whoever of them arrives before the dead [bodies] disintegrate should be included [among the recipients of] the spoil.[76]

39. Muḥammad [b. al-Ḥasan] from Abū Yūsuf from Muḥammad b. Isḥāq from Yazīd b. 'Abd-Allāh b. Qasīṭ [who said]:

[The Caliph] Abū Bakr dispatched 'Ikrima b. Abī Jahl with 500 men to the Yaman to reinforce the men with Ziyād b. Labīd al-Bayāḍī and Muhājir b. Umayya al-Makhzūmī. These arrived when [the town of] al-Nujayra was captured and

[73] "Ḥujjat al-Widā'" is a term applied to the last pilgrimage performed by the Prophet in the year 10/632 and in which, according to traditional reports, he made his last testament. For an account of this pilgrimage, see Ibn Hishām, *Kitāb Sīrat Rasūl Allāh*, Vol. II, pp. 66 ff. (Guillaume's translation, pp. 649 ff.), and Ibn Ḥazm, *Ḥujjat al-Widā'*, ed. M. Zakī (Damascus, 1956).

[74] Al-Jāhilīya. See note 27, above.

[75] Full text in Ibn Hishām, *Kitāb Sīrat Rasūl Allāh*, Vol. II, p. 968 (Guillaume's translation, p. 651). This Tradition indicates that the Prophet decreed that the law of the pre-Islamic period was no longer valid in matters of usury and bloodshed under Islam (see Sarakhsī, *Mabsūṭ*, Vol. X, p. 28).

[76] Abū Yūsuf, *Kitāb al-Radd*, pp. 6-7, 35-36; Sarakhsī, *Sharḥ Kitāb al-Siyar al-Kabīr*, ed. Munajjid, Vol. III, p. 1007, and *Mabsūṭ*, Vol. X, p. 22.

they were included [among the recipients of] the spoil.[77] The prime [of encouragement] offered was one-fourth [of the spoil] at the onward journey [of the expedition] and one-third during the return journey.[78]

40. Muḥammad [b. al-Ḥasan] from Abū Yūsuf from al-Ḥasan b. ʻUmāra from al-Ḥakam [b. ʻUtayba] from Miqsam [b. Bujra] from [ʻAbd-Allāh] b. ʻAbbās [who said]:

The Apostle of God sought the assistance of the Jews of the tribe of the Banū Qaynuqāʻ against the [Jews of] Banū Qurayza, but he gave them nothing from the booty.[79]

41. Muḥammad [b. al-Ḥasan] from Abū Yūsuf from Juwaybir [Jābir b. Zayd] from al-Ḍaḥḥāk [b. Muzāḥim] [who said]:

The Apostle of God [while on his way to the battle of Uḥud in 3/625] encountered a goodly company of men. He asked: "What are these?" He was told that they were such-and-such [a company, i. e., unbelievers]. Thereupon he said: "We do not seek an assistance from the unbelievers." [80]

42. Muḥammad [b. al-Ḥasan] from Abū Yūsuf from [Muḥammad b. al-Sā'ib] al-Kalbī [who said]:

Two unbelievers went forth with the Apostle of God [while once on an expedition]. The Apostle of God told them: "Nobody would be allowed to take part in the fighting along with us who is not follower of our religion." Thereupon they became Muslims.[81]

43. Muḥammad [b. al-Ḥasan] from Abū Yūsuf from al-Ḥajjāj b. Arṭāt from al-Ḥakam [b. ʻUtayba from Miqsam b. Bujra, who said]: [82]

[77] Abū Yūsuf, *Kitāb al-Radd*, p. 36; Sarakhsī, *Sharḥ Kitāb al-Siyar al-Kabīr*, ed. Munajjid, Vol. III, p. 1005, and *Mabsūṭ*, Vol. X, p. 23.

[78] The prime, or additional shares of the spoil, was promised to raise the morale of the army. The practice of giving additional shares was called tanfīl (supererogatory shares). See Sarakhsī, *Mabsūṭ*, Vol. X, p. 28.

[79] Sarakhsī, *Mabsūṭ*, Vol. X, p. 23.

[80] Muslim, *Ṣaḥīḥ*, Vol. XII, p. 198; Dārimī, *Sunan*, Vol. II, p. 233; Sarakhsī, *Mabsūṭ*, Vol. X, p. 24.

[81] See ʻAbd-Allāh b. ʻUmar al-Wāqidī, *Kitāb al-Maghāzī*, ed. A. von Kremer (Calcutta, 1856), pp. 40-41; Sarakhsī, *Mabsūṭ*, Vol. X, p. 23.

[82] The chain of transmitters is not complete in the Arabic MSS.

[A commander] wrote to [the Caliph] Abū Bakr inquiring whether a prisoner of war taken from the Rūm (the Byzantines) [might be ransomed]. He replied that he should not be ransomed, even at the price of two mudds of gold,[83] but that he should be either killed or become a Muslim.[84]

44. Muḥammad [b. al-Ḥasan] from Abū Yūsuf from Ash'ath b. Sawwār from al-Ḥasan [b. al-Ḥasan al-Baṣrī] and 'Aṭā' b. Abī Rabāḥ, both of whom said:

The prisoner of war should not be killed, but he may be ransomed or set free by grace.[85]

However, Abū Yūsuf held that the opinions of al-Ḥasan and 'Aṭā' did not count for anything [on this matter].[86]

45. Muḥammad [b. al-Ḥasan] from Abū Yūsuf from Abū Bakr b. 'Abd-Allāh from [Muḥammad b. Muslim] al-Zuhrī, who said:

The Apostle of God prohibited the hamstringing of horses in enemy territory.[87]

46. Muḥammad [b. al-Ḥasan] from Abū Yūsuf from Ash'ath b. Sawwār from Muḥammad b. Mujālid, who said:

I asked 'Abd-Allāh b. Abī Awfī: "Was the food captured at Khaybar divided into five shares?" He replied: "No, because it was too little, but if any one of us needed anything he took enough to satisfy his need." [88]

47. Muḥammad [b. al-Ḥasan] from Abū Yūsuf from Juwaybir [Jābir b. 'Abd-Allāh] from al-Ḍaḥḥāk [b. Muzāḥim], who said:

Whenever the Apostle of God sent forth a detachment he

[83] Literally: "Even if paid by two mudds of gold," a large measure of gold. See Muṭarrazī, *al-Mughrib*, Vol. II, p. 180.

[84] Sarakhsī, *Mabsūṭ*, Vol. X, p. 24, states that Abū Bakr was consulted about two prisoners of war taken from the Rūm (Byzantines).

[85] This is based on Q. XLVII, 5. See Sarakhsī, *Mabsūṭ*, Vol. X, p. 24.

[86] Abū Yūsuf held that the decision concerning the fate of prisoners of war should be left to the Imām to decide whether they should be killed or ransomed on the basis of the interests of Muslims (see Abū Yūsuf, *Kitāb al-Kharāj*, pp. 195-96).

[87] Abū Yūsuf, *Kitāb al-Radd*, pp. 88-89.

[88] Sarakhsī, *Mabsūṭ*, Vol. X, p. 25.

said to it: "Do not cheat or commit treachery, nor should you mutilate or kill children, women, or old men."[89]

48. Muḥammad [b. al-Ḥasan] from Abū Yūsuf from 'Abd-Allāh b. 'Umar from Nāfi' [freed-slave of Ibn 'Umar] from ['Abd-Allāh] b. 'Umar [who said]:

He [Ibn 'Umar] prohibited the entry of the Book [the Qur'an] into enemy territory.[90]

49. Muḥammad [b. al-Ḥasan] from Abū Yūsuf from Muḥammad b. Isḥāq from Abū Ja'far [Muḥammad b. 'Alī b. al-Ḥusayn] and [Muḥammad b. Muslim] al-Zuhrī and Ismā'īl b. Umayya from Yazīd b. Hurmuz, who said:

I am [the man] who wrote the replies of Ibn 'Abbās to Najda's [questions]. You wrote to Ibn 'Abbās asking about the killing of children in battle and cited the case of the learned [guide] of Moses who had killed a child, whereas the Apostle of God prohibited the killing of children. [Ibn 'Abbās replied] "Had you known concerning children what the learned [guide] of Moses knew, you would be in a position to do so."[91] You also wrote inquiring whether women used to participate in war along with the Apostle of God and whether they were assigned a share or were merely given a portion as compensation. "They did participate in war with the Apostle and received a portion as compensation" [Ibn 'Abbās replied]. Ismā'īl b. Umayya added to the Tradition:
"You wrote inquiring whether the slaves participated in war 134
along with the Apostle of God and whether they were assigned

[89] This is part of the Tradition related on the authority of Burayda. See paragraph 1, above.

[90] Bukhārī, *Ṣaḥīḥ*, Vol. II, p. 245; Muslim, *Ṣaḥīḥ*, Vol. XIII, p. 13. Abū Dāwūd gives the authorities of this Tradition as follows: 'Abd-Allah b. Maslama al-Qa'nabī from Mālik [b. Anas] from Nāfi' from 'Abd-Allah b. 'Umar (Abū Dāwūd, *Sunan*, Vol. III, p. 36). See Sarakhsī, *Mabsūṭ*, Vol. X, p. 29; and Ṭaḥāwī, *Mushkil al-Āthār* (Hyderabad, 1333/1914), Vol. II, pp. 368-70.

[91] For Quranic citations concerning the guide of Moses, see Q. XVIII, 59-81. The Khārijīs kill enemy children, including Muslims, whom they consider as unbelievers and apostates, on the basis of the Quranic verse concerning the guide of Moses. Ibn 'Abbās rejected this argument on the basis of the precedent of the guide of Moses.

a share [of the spoil]." I [secretary to Ibn 'Abbās] wrote in reply an opinion about the slaves similar to that I had written concerning women [namely, that they were not entitled to a share, but merely to a portion of it as compensation]. You also asked: "When does an orphan cease to be regarded as such [i. e., a minor]?" [Ibn 'Abbās] replied that when the orphan attains puberty he ceases to be regarded as such, and he is entitled to a share [of the spoil, if he takes part in war].[92]

50. Muḥammad [b. al-Ḥasan] from Abū Yūsuf from al-Ḥajjāj b. Arṭāt from 'Amr b. Shu'ayb from his father [93] from the Prophet, who said: [94]

Muslims should support one another against the outsider; the blood of all Muslims is of equal value, and the one lowest in status [i. e., a slave] can bind [all] the others if he gives a pledge [of security]. The vanguard can make a treaty binding on them all, and the rearguard makes available its captured booty to them all also.[95]

51. [The same Tradition is reproduced as in paragraph 7.] [96]

52. Muḥammad [b. al-Ḥasan] from Abū Yūsuf from al-Ḥasan b. 'Umāra from al-Ḥakam [b. 'Utayba] from Miqsam [b. Bujra] from ['Abd-Allāh] b. 'Abbās, who said:

The Apostle of God launched a campaign against al-Ṭā'if at the beginning of [the sacred month of] Muḥarram and

[92] Najda seems to have often written Ibn 'Abbās requesting his opinion on a variety of legal questions. Some of these questions were grouped together in one narrative by Hurmuz (Sarakhsī, *Mabsūṭ*, Vol. X, pp. 16-17, 29-30). For a different narrative, see Abū Yūsuf, *Kitāb al-Kharāj*, p. 198, and *Kitāb al-Radd*, p. 38; Sarakhsī, *Mabsūṭ*, Vol. X, pp. 29-30; Ibn Sallām, *Kitāb al-Amwāl*, pp. 332-35; Muslim, *Ṣaḥīḥ*, Vol. XII, pp. 190-94.

[93] The name of 'Amr b. Shu'ayb is incorrectly cited in the Arabic MS as 'Umar b. Shu'ayb, and the latter related Traditions from the Prophet on the authority of his grandfather 'Amr b. al-Āṣ rather than from his father (see Abū al-Wafā's comments in Abū Yūsuf, *Kitāb al-Āthār*, p. 12, n. 4).

[94] The order of words of the Tradition is slightly changed to conform to other transmissions. See Abū Yūsuf, *Kitāb al-Radd*, pp. 59-61; Sarakhsī, *Mabsūṭ*, Vol. X, pp. 25-26.

[95] Abū Yūsuf, *Kitāb al-Radd*, pp. 60-61, and his *Kitāb al-Kharāj*, p. 205.

[96] This may have been a mistake of the copyist, for the Tradition is repeated *verbatim*.

continued it for forty days until he captured the city in [the month of] Ṣafar.[97]

53. Muḥammad [b. al-Ḥasan] from Abū Yūsuf from al-Ḥasan b. 'Umāra from Ibn Abī Najīḥ [Yasār] from Mujāhid [b. Jābir], who said:

The prohibition of fighting during the sacred months[98] [as laid down in the Qur'ān[99]] was abrogated by God, the Most High (in another text of the Qur'ān) which says: "Slay the polytheists wherever you may find them."[100]

Abū Yūsuf added: This is also the opinion of Abū Ḥanīfa. However, [Muḥammad b. al-Sā'ib] al-Kalbī, according to Abū Yūsuf, held that the prohibition [of fighting during the sacred months] was not abrogated. But, according to Muḥammad b. al-Ḥasan, Abū Yūsuf held that al-Kalbī's opinion was not to be followed.

54. Muḥammad [b. al-Ḥasan] from Abū Yūsuf from al-Ḥajjāj b. Arṭat from Makḥūl [Abū 'Abd-Allāh, who said]:

The Apostle of God, in dividing the spoil of Khaybar, gave the horse-rider two shares and the foot-warrior one share. But God knows best.[101]

[97] Sarakhsī, *Mabsūṭ*, Vol. X, p. 26.

[98] Singular in the Qur'ān (Q. II, 214) and in the Arabic MS. The sacred months are Shawwāl, Dhū al-Qi'da, Dhū al-Ḥijja, and Muḥarram.

[99] Q. II, 214: "They will ask you about the sacred month and fighting in it. Say, fighting in it is a heinous thing."

[100] Q. IX, 5. It is held that this divine legislation was provided after the other and therefore it abrogated it. See Sarakhsī, *Mabsūṭ*, Vol. X, p. 26, and *Sharḥ Kitāb Siyar al-Kabīr*, ed. Munajjid, Vol. I, p. 93; Ṭabarī, *Tafsīr* (Cairo, 1374/1955), Vol. IV, pp. 299-316; and Vol. XIV, pp. 133-37. Cf. Abū al-Khayr Nāsir al-Dīn al-Bayḍāwī, *Anwār al-Tanzīl wa Asrār al-Ta'wīl* (Cairo, 1305/1887), pp. 46 (margin), 247 (margin).

[101] Bukhari, *Ṣaḥīḥ*, Vol. III, p. 114; cf. Abū Yūsuf, *Kitāb al-Kharāj*, p. 19.

Chapter II

ON THE CONDUCT OF THE ARMY IN ENEMY TERRITORY[1]

[*General Rules*]

55. If the army [of Islam] attacks the territory of war and it is a territory that has received an invitation to accept Islam, it is commendable if the army renews the invitation, but if it fails to do so it is not wrong.[2] The army may launch the attack [on the enemy] by night or by day and it is permissible to burn [the enemy] fortifications with fire or to inundate them with water.[3] If [the army] captures any spoil of war,

[1] Literally: "A chapter on the army whenever it attacks the territory of war."

[2] It is agreed among jurists that an invitation to accept Islam before battle is obligatory, but a second invitation is commendable only to Mālikī and Ḥanafī jurists. See paragraph 1; Abū Yūsuf, *Kitāb al-Kharāj*, p. 191; Ṭabarī, *Kitāb Ikhtilāf*, pp. 2-3; Sarakhsī, *Sharḥ Kitāb al-Siyar al-Kabīr*, ed. Munajjid, Vol. 1, pp. 75-80, and *Mabsūṭ*, Vol. X, p. 30. This practice, equivalent to a declaration of war, existed from antiquity (See Deut. XX, 10-12; and Phillipson, *International Law and Custom of Ancient Greece and Rome*, Vol. I, pp. 96-97); but its adoption by Muslim jurists is said to have been based on the Qur'ān, which states: "We never punished any people until we first sent them an Apostle" (Q. XVII, 16), and on a Tradition from the Prophet, which states: "I have been ordered to fight the polytheists until they say there is no god at all but Allah; if they say it, they are secured in their blood and property (Bukhārī, *Ṣaḥīḥ*, Vol. II, p. 236). Like the *jus fetiale* of ancient Rome, which required that a set of rules must be followed so that war would be lawful, the jihād was regarded as lawful only if it were preceded by an invitation to adopt Islam. If the enemy refused (or if they were People of the Book and refused to pay the poll tax), fighting would become lawful for the Muslims. See Hamidullah, *Muslim Conduct of State*, pp. 190-92; Khadduri, *War and Peace in the Law of Islam*, pp. 96-98.

[3] Abū Yūsuf, *Kitāb al-Kharāj*, pp. 192, 194; Ṭabarī, *Kitāb Ikhtilāf*, p. 3; Sarakhsī, *Mabsūt*, Vol. X, pp. 30-31.

it should not be divided up in enemy territory until [the Muslims] have brought it to a place of security and removed it to the territory of Islam.[4]

56. Abū Yūsuf said: I asked Abū Ḥanīfa [his opinion] concerning the food and fodder that may be found in the spoil and whether a warrior in need may take from that spoil [before division] any of the food for himself and fodder for his mount.

57. He [Abū Ḥanīfa] replied: There is no harm in all that.[5]

58. I asked: If there were weapons among the spoil, [do you hold that it would be permissible] for a Muslim [warrior] who needed a weapon with which to fight to take one without the permission of the Imām?

59. He replied: There is no harm in it, but he should return the weapon to the spoil after the battle is over.[6]

60. I asked: Why have you held that it is permissible [for the warrior] to take food and fodder [from the spoil]?

61. He replied: Because a narrative from the Apostle of God has come to my knowledge to the effect that in [the campaign of] Khaybar the believers captured some food and ate from it before it was divided. Fodder falls in the same category as food, for both provide the strength necessary for the warrior [while fighting against the enemy].[7]

62. I asked: Why do you hold that it is permissible [for the warrior] to take a weapon with which to fight?

[4] See paragraphs 15 and 17; Abū Yūsuf, *Kitāb al-Kharāj*, p. 196, and *Kitāb al-Radd*, pp. 1-12; Sarakhsī, *Kitāb Sharḥ al-Siyar al-Kabīr* (Hyderabad), Vol. II, p. 254, and *Mabsūṭ*, Vol. X, pp. 32-34. However, al-Awzā'ī and Shāfi'ī held that the Prophet's practice was in favor of dividing it up in the territory of war. See Ṭabarī, *Kitāb Ikhtilāf*, pp. 129-30; Shāfi'ī, *Umm*, Vol. VII, p. 303.

[5] Cf. paragraph 34 and see Abū Yūsuf, *Kitāb al-Kharāj*, p. 197, and *Kitāb al-Radd*, p. 16; Sarakhsī, *Mabsūṭ*, Vol. X, p. 34. For opinions of Awzā'ī, Mālik, and Shāfi'ī, see Ṭabarī, *Kitāb Ikhtilāf*, pp. 86-93.

[6] Abū Yūsuf, *Kitāb al-Radd*, pp. 13-16; Ṭabarī, *Kitāb Ikhtilāf*, p. 102; Sarakhsī, *Mabsāṭ*, Vol. X, pp. 34-35.

[7] See paragraph 46. Abū Ḥanīfa used analogical reasoning on the strength of a Tradition giving general permission, within the context of which Abū Ḥanīfa gave his own opinion. Cf. opinions of Awzā'ī, Mālik, and Shāfi'ī in Ṭabarī, *Kitāb Ikhtilāf*, pp. 99-101.

63. He replied: Do you think that it would be objectionable if the unbelievers shot an arrow at one of the believers and the latter shot it back at the enemy, or if one of the unbelievers attacked a believer with a sword and the latter snatched it from him and struck him with it?

64. I said: No.

65. He said: The latter situation is similar to the former.[8]

66. I asked: Do you think that it is objectionable for a person to take clothings and goods from the spoil for his own use before it is divided?

67. He replied: I disapprove of that for him.[9]

68. I asked: If the believers were in need of clothing, animals, and goods, would it be incumbent on the Imām to divide the spoil among them before they returned to the territory of Islam (dār al-Islām)?

69. He replied: If they were [really] in need, it would be all right to divide it among them, but if they were not in need I should disapprove of dividing it.

70. I asked: Why?

71. He replied: Because [the believers] had not yet taken [the spoil] to a secure place so long as they remained in the territory of war (dār al-ḥarb). Besides, do you not think that if another [Muslim] army entered the territory of war [and took part in the fighting] it would be entitled to participate in that spoil?[10]

72. I asked: Do you think that the Imām should divide up the captives before the believers returned to the territory of Islam, if the believers need them?

73. He replied: No.[11]

74. I asked: What should the Imām do with the captives, if the believers do not need them? Should he sell them?

75. He replied: If I held that it would be permissible for

[8] See Sarakhsī, *Mabsūṭ*, Vol. X, p. 35.
[9] See paragraph 34 and Sarakhsī, *Mabsūṭ*, Vol. X, p. 35.
[10] Ṭabarī, *Kitāb Ikhtilāf*, p. 130.
[11] *Ibid.*, p. 131.

the Imām to sell them [before the believers returned to the territory of Islam], I should hold that it would be permissible for him to divide them up [there].[12]

76. I asked: What should [the Imām] do about transporting them?

77. He replied: If [the Imām] possesses surplus means of transport he should use it to carry [the captives]; if there is none he should see if there is any surplus means among the Muslims. If he finds such means he should get them to carry it with them of their own free will.[13]

78. I asked: If neither the Imām nor the Muslims possess surplus means of transport but some [private] individuals among them [have their own means], should the Imām cause the spoil to be transported on the animals belonging to those particular persons?

79. He replied: Yes, provided those persons are willing to do so. Otherwise, the Imām should hire means of transport rather than force the owners of private means to carry the spoil. As to the captives, the Imām should oblige them to go on foot if they are able to do so.[14]

80. I asked: And if they are unable to walk?

81. He replied: He [the Imām] should kill the men and spare the women and children, for whom he should hire means for carrying them.[15]

Muḥammad [b. al-Ḥasan] held that it would be permissible to the Imām [in these circumstances] to divide the spoil in the territory of war, since the jurists have disagreed on the matter.[16]

82. I asked: If the believers in the territory of war capture spoil in which there are [animals such as] sheep, riding animals, and cows which resist them and they are unable to drive

[12] Cf. Opinions of Awzā'ī and Shāfi'ī, *ibid.*, pp. 129-30.
[13] *Ibid.*, p. 133.
[14] *Ibid.*; Sarakhsī, *Mabsūṭ*, Vol. X, p. 36.
[15] Ṭabarī, *Kitāb Ikhtilāf*, p. 133.
[16] For opinions of other jurists, see *ibid.*, pp. 131-33.

them to the territory of Islam, or weapons which they are unable to carry away, what should they do [with them]?

83. He replied: As to weapons and goods, they should be 135
burned, but riding animals and sheep should be slaughtered and then burned.[17]

84. I asked: Why should not [the animals] be hamstrung?

85. He replied: Because that is mutilation, which they should not do because it was prohibited by the Apostle of God. However, they should not leave anything that the inhabitants of the territory of war could make use of.[18]

86. I asked: Do you think that they should do the same with whatever [other] animals refuse to be driven away or with whatever weapons and goods are too heavy to carry?

87. He replied: Yes.[19]

88. I asked: Do you think that it is objectionable for the believers to destroy whatever towns of the territory of war that they may encounter?

89. He replied: No. Rather do I hold that this would be commendable. For do you not think that it is in accordance with God's saying, in His Book: "Whatever palm trees you have cut down or left standing upon their roots, has been by God's permission, in order that the ungodly ones might be humiliated." [20] So, I am in favor of whatever they did to deceive and anger the enemy.[21]

90. I asked: If the Imām attacked an enemy territory and took possession of it, do you think that he should divide the land [among the warriors] as he divides the spoil of war?

91. He replied: The Imām is free either to divide the land into five shares, distributing the four-fifths among the warriors who participated in conquering it, or not to divide it up

[17] Abū Yūsuf, *Kitāb al-Radd*, pp. 88-89; Ṭabarī, *Kitāb Ikhtilāf*, p. 107; Sarakhsī, *Mabsūṭ*, Vol. X, pp. 36-37.

[18] Abū Yūsuf, *Kitāb al-Radd*, pp. 88-89; Ṭabarī, *Kitāb Ikhtilāf*, p. 110; Sarakhsī, *Mabsūṭ*, Vol. X, p. 37.

[19] Ṭabarī, *Kitāb Ikhtilāf*, p. 110.

[20] Q. LIX, 5.

[21] Ṭabarī, p. 107.

[i. e., hold it as state-owned land] as [the Caliph] 'Umar did in [the case of] the land of al-Sawād [of southern 'Irāq].[22]

92. I asked: Should [the Imām] leave it [immobilized] while its inhabitants paid the kharāj?

93. He replied: Yes. So it was related to us that 'Umar b. al-Khaṭṭāb did. But God knows best! [23]

The Killing of Captives and the Destruction of Enemy Fortifications [24] 139

94. I asked: If male captives of war were taken from the territory of war, do you think that the Imām should kill them all or divide them as slaves among the Muslims?

95. He replied: The Imām is entitled to a choice between taking them to the territory of Islam to be divided [among the warriors] and killing them [while in the territory of war].[25]

96. I asked: Which is preferable?

97. He replied: [The Imām] should examine the situation and decide whatever he deems to be advantageous to the Muslims.[26]

98. I asked: If killing them were advantageous to the Muslims, [do you think that the Imām] should order their killing?

99. He replied: Yes.[27]

[22] Agricultural lands in the occupied territories of Syria and Egypt were divided among the believers, while the lands of southern 'Irāq became state lands subject to annual tribute. See Abū Yūsuf, *Kitāb al-Kharāj*, pp. 28-39, 39-41; Shaybānī, *Kitāb al-Jāmi' al-Ṣaghīr*, p. 88; Sarakhsī, *Mabsūṭ*, Vol. X, p. 37; Ibn Sallām, *Kitāb al-Amwāl*, pp. 143 ff.

[23] On the land policy of 'Umar, see Abū Yūsuf, *Kitāb al-Kharāj*, pp. 35-39.

[24] This section, falling more appropriately under the general subject of the conduct of the army in enemy territory, has been moved from the chapter on the intercourse between the dār al-Islām and the dār al-ḥarb (Chap. IV), as it appears in the Arabic MSS.

[25] Abū Yūsuf, *Kitāb al-Kharāj*, pp. 196, 202; Sarakhsī, *Mabsūt*, Vol. X, p. 37.

[26] Ṭabarī, *Kitāb Ikhtilāf*, p. 144.

[27] *Ibid.*, p. 144.

100. I asked: If all of them became Muslims, would he be entitled to kill them?

101. He replied: He should not kill them if they became Muslims; they should be regarded as booty to be divided among the Muslims.[28]

102. I asked: If they did not become Muslims, but they claimed that they had been given a safe-conduct and a few Muslims declared that they had given such a pledge to them, would such a claim be accepted?

103. He replied: No.[29]

104. I asked: Why?

105. He replied: Because both [merely] stated their own claim.

106. I asked: If a group of Muslims known to be of just character testified that a safe-conduct had been given by a party of warriors to the prisoners of war who were still capable of resistance [in a fortification before their surrender], would that testimony be valid?

107. He replied: Yes.[30]

108. I asked: Would the prisoners of war be set free?

109. He replied: Yes.

110. I asked: Do you think that the blind, the crippled, the helpless insane, if taken as prisoners of war or captured by the warriors in a surprise attack, would be killed?

111. He replied: [No], they should not be killed.[31]

112. I asked: Would it be permissible to inundate a city in the territory of war with water, to burn it with fire, or to attack [its people] with mangonels[32] even though there may be slaves, women, old men, and children in it?

113. He applied: Yes, I would approve of doing all of that to them.[33]

[28] *Ibid.*, pp. 40, 144.

[29] Abū Yūsuf, *Kitāb al-Radd*, p. 63, and *Kitāb al-Kharāj*, pp. 202-3.

[30] Ṭabarī, *Kitāb Ikhtilāf*, pp. 40, 43.

[31] *Ibid.*, p. 144; Ṭaḥāwī, *Mukhtaṣar*, p. 283; Sarakhsī, *Mabsūṭ*, Vol. X, p. 64.

[32] Anglicized from Manjanīq, a hurling machine.

[33] Abū Yūsuf, *Kitāb al-Kharāj*, pp. 194-95; Ṭabarī, *Kitāb Ikhtilāf*, pp. 6-7; Sarakhsī, *Mabsūṭ*, Vol. X, p. 65.

114. I asked: Would the same be true if those people have among them Muslim prisoners of war or Muslim merchants?

115. He replied: Yes, even if they had among them [Muslims], there would be no harm to do all of that to them.[34]

116. I asked: Why?

117. He replied: If the Muslims stopped attacking the inhabitants of the territory of war for any of the reasons that you have stated, they would be unable to go to war at all, for there is no city in the territory of war in which there is no one at all of these you have mentioned.

118. I asked: If the Muslims besieged a city, and its people [in their defense] from behind the walls shielded themselves with Muslim children, would it be permissible for the Muslim [warriors] to attack them with arrows and mangonels?

119. He replied: Yes, but the warriors should aim at the inhabitants of the territory of war and not the Muslim children.[35]

120. I asked: Would it be permissible for the Muslims to attack them with swords and lances if the children were not intentionally aimed at?

121. He replied: Yes.

122. I asked: If the Muslim [warriors] attack [a place] with mangonels and arrows, flood it with water, and burn it with fire, thereby killing or wounding Muslim children or men, or enemy women, old men, blind, crippled, or lunatic persons, would the [Muslim warriors] be liable for the diya (blood money) or the kaffāra (expiation or atonement)?

123. He replied: They would be liable neither for the diya nor for the kaffāra.[36]

[34] Ṭabarī, *Kitāb Ikhtilāf*, p. 6; Sarakhsī, *Mabsūṭ*, Vol. X, p. 65.

[35] Abū Yūsuf, *Kitāb al-Radd*, p. 65; Ṭabarī, *Kitāb Ikhtilāf*, p. 7.

[36] Abū Yūsuf, *Kitāb al-Radd*, p. 7; Ṭaḥāwī, *Mukhtaṣar*, p. 284; Sarakhsī, *Mabsūṭ*, Vol. X, p. 65.

Penalties in the Territory of War and the Shortening of Prayer[37] 142

124. I asked: If a [Muslim] army entered the territory of war led by a commander, do you think he would be [competent] to enforce the religious penalties (ḥudūd)[38] in his army camp?

125. He replied: No.[39]

126. I asked: If the governor of a city or a province, such as al-Shām or 'Irāq, entered the territory of war at the head of an army, would he be [competent] to impose religious penalties or retaliation in his army camp?

127. He replied: Yes.[40]

128. I asked: Would he be [competent] to order the cutting off of the hand for theft and enforce the penalty for false accusation (qadhf)?[41]

129. He replied: Yes.

130. I asked: And [also] to enforce the penalties for zina (adultery or fornication) and [the drinking of] wine?

131. He replied. Yes.[42]

132. I asked: If there was at the head of the army a commander—not the governor of al-Shām or 'Irāq—and [the army] was four or five thousand strong, would he be [competent] to enforce any of the [religious penalties] stated above?

133. He replied: No.[43]

[37] This section has been moved from the chapter on the intercourse between the dār al-Islām and the dār al-ḥarb (Chap. IV), as it appears in the Arabic MSS.

[38] Ḥudūd (plural of ḥadd) are fixed penalties for certain crimes as specified in the Qur'ān. Ḥudūd cases can be heard only by higher authorities. See *Law in the Middle East*, ed. Khadduri and Liebesny (Washington, 1955), Vol. 1, pp. 227-29.

[39] Abū Yūsuf, *Kitāb al-Radd*, p. 7; Shāfi'ī, *Umm*, Vol. VII, p. 332; Sarakhsī, *Mabsūṭ*, Vol. X, p. 75.

[40] Abū Yūsuf, *Kitāb al-Radd*, p. 80; Sarakhsī, *Mabsūṭ*, Vol. X, p. 75.

[41] Qadhf is a false accusation of unchastity and illegitimacy such as zina (adultery).

[42] Sarakhsī, *Mabsūṭ*, Vol. X, p. 75.

[43] *Ibid.*, p. 75.

134. I asked: Would the same be true for the commanders of detachments, that they are [incompetent] to enforce penalties?

135. He replied: Yes [that is right].

136. I asked: If the governor of al-Shām or 'Irāq were at the head of a large army laying siege to a city for over a month, should he celebrate [the conquest] in the Friday prayer or perform them in their complete form?

137. He replied: He is [under obligation] neither to celebrate Friday prayer nor to perform them completely, because he is on travel status.[44]

138. I asked: If a group of Muslims desired to attack the territory of war but did not have the [sufficient] force or the finances to do so, do you not think that it would be lawful for them to help each other and the ones who would not go forth to battle to contribute [supplies] to those who take the field?

139. He replied: It would be lawful to do so in such a situation; but if the Imām had the wherewithal and the Muslim had the forces, I would neither approve of it nor should I permit it. However, if the Imām lacked the means, it would be lawful [for some to contribute to others who take the field].[45]

140. I asked: Which [act] is more commendable to you: guarding [i. e., to act as sentinel] or performing a supererogatory prayer?

141. He replied: If sentineling were sufficiently provided for, performance of the [supererogatory] prayer would be the more commendable to me; but if those who act as sentinels were not sufficient, then the performance of guarding would be the more commendable.[46]

[44] *Ibid.*, p. 76. When on travel, one is authorized to pray only three times daily instead of five times, combining the second and the third, the fourth and the fifth. In this instance, it seems, the combination of prayers includes the Friday congregational prayer. See Sarakhsī, *Kitāb Sharḥ al-Siyar al-Kabīr* (Hyderabad), Vol. III, pp. 251-52.

[45] Sarakhsī, *Mabsūṭ*, Vol. X, p. 76.

[46] Abū Yūsuf, *Kitāb al-Radd*, p. 89; Shāfi'ī, *Umm*, Vol. VII, p. 324; Sarakhsī, *Mabsūṭ*, Vol. X, p. 76.

142. I asked: If a [Muslim] warrior is run through by a lance, would you disapprove if he advances—though the lance be piercing him—in order to kill his adversary with the sword?

143. He replied: No.[47]

144. I asked: Do you not think that he helped against his own life by so doing [i. e., that he committed suicide, which is forbidden]?

145. He replied: No.[48]

146. I asked: If a group were on board a ship that was set on fire, do you think that it would be more commendable if they resigned themselves to being burned to death or if they threw themselves into the sea?

147. He replied: Either one of the two [courses] would be permissible.[49]

[47] Sarakhsī, *Mabsūṭ*, Vol. X, p. 77.
[48] *Ibid.*, p. 77.
[49] Ṭaḥāwī, *Mukhtaṣar*, p. 293; Sarakhsī, *Mabsūṭ*, Vol. X, p. 77.

Chapter III 135 Folio

[ON THE SPOIL OF WAR]

Division of the Spoil [1]

148. I asked: What do you think about the one-fifth [state share]? How should the Imām divide it and among whom should he distribute it?

149. He replied: He should divide it among those named by God in His Book [the Qur'ān].[2] It has been related to us that [the Caliphs] Abū Bakr and 'Umar [b. al-Khaṭṭāb] used to divide the one-fifth [share] into three parts: [one] for the orphans, [another] for the poor, and [the third for] the wayfarer.[3]

150. I asked: In dividing the spoil, how much, do you think, should be given to the horse-rider and how much to the foot-warrior?

151. He replied: The horse-rider should be given two shares [one for the mount and one for himself] and the foot-warrior one.[4]

152. I asked: [Do you think], therefore, that [riders of] mules and foot-warriors are equal?

153. He replied: Yes.[5]

[1] Literally: "Division of the one-fifth [share] and the [warrior's] shares and those who are not entitled to a share."

[2] Q. VIII, 42.

[3] Abū Yūsuf, *Kitāb al-Kharāj*, pp. 20-21; Ibn Sallām, *Kitāb al-Amwāl*, pp. 303-8; Kāsānī, *Badā'i' al-Ṣanā'i'*, Vol. VII, pp. 125-26.

[4] Abū Yūsuf, *Kitāb al-Kharāj*, p. 19; *Kitāb al-Radd*, p. 17; *Kitāb al-Āthār*, p. 171; Sarakhsī, *Mabsūṭ*, Vol. X, p. 41; Ṭaḥāwī, *Mukhtaṣar*, p. 258.

[5] Abū Ḥanīfa, contrary to the opinion of other jurists, held that the horse (or any other animal) should not be assigned more than what a man would receive. See Abū Yūsuf, *Kitāb al-Kharāj*, p. 19, and *Kitāb al-Radd*, p. 40. For opinions of other jurists, who allot as much as three

154. I asked: [Do you think that] the jade-rider[6] and horse-rider are equal?

155. He replied: Yes, the jade-rider should be given two shares and the horse-rider two.[7]

156. I asked: Why do you think that the horse-rider should be given two shares and the foot-warrior one?

157. He replied: Because it has been related to us that this was the practice of [the Caliph] 'Umar b. al-Khaṭṭāb. This is also the opinion of Abū Ḥanīfa.[8]

However, Abū Yūsuf and Muḥammad [b. al-Ḥasan] held that the horse-rider should be given three shares, two for the mount and one for himself. The foot-warrior receives [only] one share.[9]

158. I asked: If a man entered the territory of war as a mounted warrior with the army and if his horse died of exhaustion or was hamstrung, so that when the spoil was taken to a place of security [i. e., to the dār al-Islām] he was a foot-warrior—though it was recorded in the diwān (army list) that he had a horse—or if he had brought a horse before entering the territory of war and it died of exhaustion in the dār [al-Islām], should he be allotted the share of a horse-rider?

159. He replied: Yes.[10]

160. I asked: What would be your opinion if his name was entered in the diwān as a foot-warrior and he entered the territory of war as such, but thereafter he bought a horse and took part in the fighting as a horse-rider and he was as such when the spoil was taken to a place of security?

---

shares to the horse-rider, see Ṭabarī, *Kitāb Ikhtilāf*, pp. 80-81; Shāfi'ī, *Umm*, Vol. IV, p. 74; Sarakhsī, *Mabsūṭ*, Vol. X, pp. 41-42.

[6] Birdhawn: "A horse of mean breed or of coarse make—a jade." See *Arabic-English Lexicon*, ed. E. W. Lane (Edinburgh, 1863), Vol. I, p. 186.

[7] Abū Yūsuf, *Kitāb al-Radd*, p. 19; Ṭabarī, *Kitāb Ihktilāf*, p. 82; Sarakhsī, *Kitāb Sharḥ al-Siyar al-Kabīr* (Hyderabad), Vol. II, pp. 175-83.

[8] Abū Yūsuf, *Kitāb al-Kharāj*, p. 19, and *Kitāb al-Āthār*, p. 171.

[9] Abū Yūsuf, *Kitāb al-Kharāj*, p. 18; Ṭabarī, *Kitāb Ikhtilāf*, p. 81; Ṭaḥāwī, *Mukhtaṣar*, p. 285.

[10] Ṭabarī, *Kitāb Ikhtilāf*, p. 85; Sarakhsī, *Mabsūṭ*, Vol. X, pp. 42-44.

161. He replied: I should not allot him save the share of a foot-warrior.[11]

162. I asked: If a group [of believers], consisting of horse-riders and foot-warriors, undertook an expedition by sea, carrying horses [on board the ship], and took possession of spoil, how many shares do you think that the horse-rider and the foot-warrior should receive?

163. He replied: The horse-rider should be given two shares and the foot-warrior one.

164. I asked: Why, since the foot-warrior and the horse-rider on the [high] seas would be on an equal footing?

165. He replied: If they [the foot-warriors and the horse-riders] were in a camp in the territory of war and the men went forth and took possession of spoils, would you not allot the horse-rider two shares and the foot-warrior one?

166. I said: Yes.

167. He said: This situation and the other are alike.[12]

168. I asked: If a man died or was killed in the territory of war after the spoil was taken [from the enemy], but before [the Muslims] carried it to a place of security in the territory of Islam, do you think that his share could be inherited?

169. He replied: No.

170. I asked: Why?

171. He replied: Because he died before the spoil was [owned and] taken to the territory of Islam.[13]

172. I asked: If he died after [the spoil] was taken to the territory of Islam, do you thing that his share could be inherited?

[11] Abū Yūsuf, *Kitāb al-Radd*, p. 22; Ṭabarī, *Kitāb Ikhtilāf*, p. 85; Sarakhsī, *Mabsūṭ*, Vol. X, p. 44; Ṭaḥāwī, *Mukhtaṣar*, p. 285.

[12] Abū Ḥanīfa, on the basis of qiyās, considering the status of the horse-rider on board ship to be the same as on land, held that he should receive the same amount of compensation from the spoil. See Ṭabarī, *Kitāb Ikhtilāf*, pp. 86 ff.; Sarakhsī, *Mabsūṭ*, Vol. X, p. 44.

[13] Shaybānī, *al-Jāmi' al-Ṣaghīr*, p. 92; Abū Yūsuf, *Kitāb al-Radd*, p. 23; Ṭabarī, *Kitāb Ikhtilāf*, p. 77.

173. He replied: Yes [because the spoil was then carried to a place of security and owned].[14]

174. I asked: If an army attacked a territory of war and took spoil, but before taking the spoil to the territory of Islam it was joined by another army [of believers] but [neither] encountered the enemy on the way back until the spoil was carried to the territory of Islam, do you think that the [second] army is entitled to participate in the spoil?

175. He replied: Yes [because the spoil was not yet carried to a place of security before the second army arrived].[15]

176. I asked: If a slave took part in the war with his master against the enemy, do you think that he would be entitled to a share?

177. He replied: No, but he would be entitled to compensation, and so would a mukātab.[16]

178. I asked: If a Dhimmī took part in the fighting on the side of the Muslims at their request, do you think that he would be entitled to a share of the spoil?

179. He replied: No, but he would be entitled to compensation.[17]

180. I asked: If a woman took care of the sick and wounded and was useful to the men [in the war], do you think that she would be entitled to a share of the spoil?

181. He replied: No, but she would be entitled to compensation.[18]

182. I asked: Do you think that merchants in the [Muslim]

[14] The guiding principle, as Abū Ḥanīfa pointed out, is that placing in security occurs only after the spoil is taken to the territory of Islam. Since the warrior died after the spoil was owned, his shares would be inherited by his heirs. See Shaybānī, *al-Jāmi' al-Ṣaghīr*, p. 92; Sarakhsī, *Mabsūṭ*, Vol. X, p. 44.

[15] Abū Yūsuf, *Kitāb al-Radd*, p. 34; Ṭabarī, *Kitāb Ikhtilāf*, p. 70.

[16] A mukātab is a slave who has made a contract with his master to purchase his freedom by installments. Sarakhsī, *Mabsūṭ*, Vol. X, p. 45; Ṭaḥāwī, *Mukhtaṣar*, pp. 285-86.

[17] Abū Yūsuf, *Kitāb al-Radd*, pp. 39-40; Sarakhsī, *Mabsūṭ*, Vol. X, p. 45.

[18] Abū Yūsuf, *Kitāb al-Radd*, p. 37; Sarakhsī, *Mabsūṭ*, Vol. X, p. 45; Ṭaḥāwī, *Mukhtaṣar*, p. 286.

army camp are entitled to a share of the spoil or to compensation?

183. He replied: I hold that they are entitled to neither a share nor compensation, unless they take part in the fighting. Those of them who do so are entitled to a share.[19]

184. I asked: Would the slave who serves his master [when the latter is taking part in war] be entitled to compensation?

185. He replied: No [because the slave is not participating in the fighting].[20]

186. I asked: If a warrior takes two horses [into the battle], how many shares do you think that he would be entitled to?

187. He replied: I hold that he would be entitled to no more than the share of one horse-rider, for if he would be entitled to the shares of two horses he should likewise be entitled to the shares of three or more, and I disapprove of putting the animal on the same footing as a Muslim. This is the opinion of Abū Ḥanīfa and Muḥammad b. al-Ḥasan.[21]

However, Abū Yūsuf held that a man [with two horses] would be entitled to the shares of two horse-riders, but no more [for any additional horse].[22]

188. I asked: Do you think that a minor is entitled to a share of the spoil?

189. He replied: No.[23]

190. I asked: Do you think that the helpless insane person 136
is entitled to a share?

191. He replied: No.

192. I asked: If a man, having taken part in the fighting, comes out of it wounded and remains sick until the Muslims are victorious and take possession of the spoil and carry it to the territory of Islam, do you think that he would be entitled to a share?

[19] Abū Yūsuf, *Kitāb al-Radd*, p. 44; Sarakhsī, *Mabsūṭ*, Vol. X, p. 45.
[20] Sarakhsī, *Mabsūṭ*, Vol. X, p. 45.
[21] Abū Yūsuf, *Kitāb al-Radd*, p. 40; Ṭabarī, *Kitāb Ikhtilāf*, p. 83.
[22] Abū Yūsuf, *Kitāb al-Kharāj*, p. 18; Ṭabarī, *Kitāb Ikhtilāf*, p. 83; Ṭaḥāwī, *Mukhtaṣar*, p. 285.
[23] Abū Yūsuf, *Kitāb al-Radd*, p. 42; *Sarakhsī, Mabsūṭ*, Vol. 8, p. 45.

193. He replied: Yes.[24]

194. I asked: If a detachment was sent forth by the Imām from a camp to fight, and both those who remained in the camp as well as the detachment took possession of spoil, do you think that each group would be entitled to share in the other's?

195. He replied: Yes, all the spoil would be gathered together, one-fifth would be taken out and the rest divided among those in the camp and the detachment.[25]

196. I asked: If a man is taken prisoner and afterward the Muslims capture some spoil, but then he [escapes and] comes back, and he and the army return to the territory of Islam with the spoil without further fighting, do you think that he would be entitled to participate in the division of the spoil?

197. He replied: Yes, he would be entitled to his share.[26]

198. I asked: Do you hold the same opinion concerning an unbeliever who became a Muslim and joined the Muslims' camp?

199. He replied: I hold that he would not be entitled unless he participated with the Muslims in a subsequent battle.[27]

200. I asked: In what respect is this latter situation different from the former?

201. He replied: In the former situation the man was a Muslim and was fighting [alongside the Muslims] against the enemy until he was taken prisoner. If he were a slave who had committed an unintentional tort or had destroyed property which made him liable to debt and then were taken prisoner by the unbelievers who subsequently were converted to Islam, the slave would be lawfully owned by them and the tort would be waived, but the debt would have to be paid by them. If they were not converted to Islam and the slave was

[24] Sarakhsī, *Mabsūṭ*, Vol. X, p. 46.
[25] *Ibid.*, p. 46.
[26] *Ibid.*
[27] Abū Yūsuf, *Kitāb al-Radd*, p. 43.

either purchased by one of them or taken back by the Muslims as part of the spoil, the tort would be waived but the debt would have to be paid by the purchaser. If the [original] master should purchase the slave at the [real] value or market price, he would be liable to both the tort and the debt. Likewise, if someone obtained the slave as a gift from the inhabitants of the territory of war or if he had purchased him from them, the tort would be waived but he would be liable for the debt. But if the crime were intentional killing, it would not be waived in any case.[28]

202. I asked: If a Muslim merchant were in the territory of war and he and another man who had become a Muslim joined the camp of the Muslims, do you think that those two would each be entitled to a share of a spoil previously taken?

203. He replied: No.

204. I asked: If the Muslims were engaged in battle and these two men fought along with them, would they be entitled to a share in the spoil of that battle as well as in the spoil previously taken?

205. He replied: Yes.[29]

206. I asked: Would the treatment of traders in the army camp be the same as that of the two men in the cases I have mentioned?

207. He replied: Yes.

208. I asked: Would [the ruling] be the same concerning a believer who, having apostatized and gone to the territory of war, repented later and returned to Islam and joined the camp of the Muslim army?

209. He replied: Yes.[30]

[28] Sarakhsī, *Mabsūṭ*, Vol. X, pp. 46-47.
[29] Abū Yūsuf, *Kitāb al-Radd*, p. 44.
[30] Sarakhsī, *Mabsūṭ*, Vol. X, p. 47.

Distribution of "Additional Shares" [31]

210. I asked: If a believer killed an unbeliever and took his salab (prime),[32] do you think that the Imām should give [the killer] that property?

211. He replied: The Imām has no right to give primes to anybody after the property has been captured.

212. I asked: Why?

213. He replied: Because [the property] has become part of the spoil, which belongs to the Muslim [warriors], and the Imām should not give extra primes from the spoil.[33]

214. I asked: Why?

215. He replied: Because the property has become fay' for the Muslims, and the nafal (extra shares) may be promised only before the spoil was taken.[34]

216. I asked: How is the nafal promised?

217. He replied: Extra shares are promised if the Imām says that "whoever kills [an unbeliever in a single combat] will be entitled to his salab (prime), and he who captures anything may take it for himself." [35] Such [promises] were commendable as an encouragement [for warriors] to fight. This narrative has been transmitted by Muḥammad [b. al-

[31] Literally: "Nafal and part of the spoil imported while still collectively owned [by Muslims]." Nafal is the additional or supererogatory portion of the spoil given to a warrior. For meaning of the term, see Sarakhsī, *Sharḥ Kitāb al-Siyar al-Kabīr*, ed. Munajjid, Vol. II, pp. 593-94; Khadduri, *War and Peace in the Law of Islam*, pp. 123-24.

[32] Salab (prime) consists of the clothing and weapons carried by the warrior in battle. See Māwardī, *Kitāb al-Aḥkām*, p. 241; Muṭarrazi, *al-Mughrib*, Vol. I, p. 258.

[33] Abū Yūsuf, *Kitāb al-Radd*, p. 45; Ṭabarī, *Kitāb Ikhtilāf*, pp. 116-17; Sarakhsī, *Mabsūṭ*, Vol. X, p. 47; *Sharḥ Kitāb al-Siyar al-Kabīr*, ed. Munajjid, Vol. II, p. 596.

[34] Additional shares were promised before the spoil was taken for encouraging men to take the field and for raising the morale of the army. See Sarakhsī, *Sharḥ Kitāb al-Siyar al-Kabīr*, ed. Munajjid, Vol. II, p. 594, and *Mabsūṭ*, Vol. X, p. 47.

[35] Bukhārī, *Ṣaḥīḥ*, Vol. II, pp. 286, 287; Ṭabarī, *Kitāb Ikhtilāf*, p. 117, 127-28; Shāfi'ī, *Umm*, Vol. VII, p. 313; Ibn Sallām, *Kitāb al-Amwāl*, p. 309.

Ḥasan] from Abū Ḥanīfa from Ḥammād [b. Abī Sulaymān] from Ibrāhīm [al-Nakhaī].[36]

218. I asked: If a warrior has taken fodder from the spoil and part of it remains [unconsumed] after he has returned to the territory of Islam, what do you think he should do with it?

219. He replied: If the spoil has not yet been divided [the fodder] should be returned; if it has been divided [the fodder] should be sold and [the price] given to the poor.[37]

220. I asked: If he had lent it to another warrior who was in the territory of war?

221. He replied: He should not take any of it back for himself.[38]

Manumission of Women and Children Prisoners of War[39]

222. I asked: If a warrior set free a slave boy or a slave girl from the spoil, do you think that this manumission would be lawful?

223. He replied: No.

224. I asked: Why, since he is entitled to a share of this [spoil]?

225. He replied: Because he does not know what his share is going to be.[40]

226. I asked: If a warrior had sexual intercourse with a

[36] Abū Yūsuf, *Kitāb al-Radd*, pp. 46-47.

[37] Abū Yūsuf, *Kitāb al-Radd*, p. 47; Ṭabarī, *Kitāb Ikhtilāf*, p. 93; Sarakhsī, *Mabsūṭ*, Vol. X, p. 50.

[38] Ṭabarī, *Kitāb Ikhtilāf*, pp. 93-94; Sarakhsī, *Mabsūṭ*, Vol. X, p. 50.

[39] Women and children, taken as prisoners of war, are called sabī and are divided among the warriors who take part in the fighting. See Māwardī, *Kitāb al-Aḥkām*, pp. 232-37.

[40] Contrary to other jurists who permit manumission by the warrior on the ground that the sabī had become Muslim property, Abū Ḥanīfa does not permit the individual warrior to act on behalf of the group. Ṭabarī, *Kitāb Ikhtilāf*, pp. 163-65; and Sarakhsī, *Mabsūṭ*, Vol. X, p. 50.

slave girl [before the spoil was divided] and she became pregnant and he claimed [parentage of] her child?

227. He replied: Punishment [for zina, or fornication] would be waived, but [the warrior] would have to pay the 'uqr [41] and the slave girl and her child remain as part of the spoil until it is divided among the warriors. The parentage of the child would not be established.[42]

228. I asked: If the warrior steals [something] from the spoil, do you think that his hand should be cut off?

229. He replied: No.

230. I asked: Why?

231. He replied: Because he is entitled to a share [of the stolen spoil].[43]

232. I asked: Would you hold the same opinion in a case where the warrior stole from the spoil a slave who had served him when he was in the army?

233. He replied: Yes. In this case also [the warrior's hand] would not be cut off.[44]

234. I asked: Would you hold the same opinion if the warrior's father or mother or son or wife or brother or any of the near of kin—who is lawful to him [to marry]—[stole from the spoil]?

235. He replied: Yes. Nobody will have [his hand] cut off.

236. I asked: If a captive male or female slave, after the spoil was divided, fell in the collective lot of 10 or 100 warriors [45] [and individual distribution has not yet taken place] and one [of the warriors] [46] set him free, do you think that this manumission would be lawful?

[41] The 'uqr (nuptial gift) is the compensation for intercourse with the slave girl.

[42] Abū Yūsuf, *Kitāb al-Radd*, p. 49; Sarakhsī, *Mabsūṭ*, Vol. X, p. 50. The parentage remains unconfirmed because the warrior had intercourse with a woman before clearance of pregnancy was certain. Abū Yūsuf, *Kitāb al-Radd*, pp. 50-51.

[43] Abū Yūsuf, *Kitāb al-Radd*, p. 121; Sarakhsī, *Mabsūṭ*, Vol. X, p. 50.

[44] Abū Yūsuf, *Kitāb al-Radd*, p. 121; Sarakhsī, *Mabsūṭ*, Vol. X, pp. 50-51.

[45] A'rāf (plural of 'arīf, or decurion) a group commanded by a decurion.

[46] Rāya (banner). Each battalion of a hundred men has its banner.

237. He replied: Yes, if [the party of Muslims who set them free] were 100 men or less, and I do not set a time limit on this matter.[47]

238. I asked: Would this [emancipated slave] be like a slave owned by partners, some of whom had set him free?

239. He replied: Yes.[48]

240. I asked: Would the situation be different from the first case, where the slave was set free before the division of the spoil and where [you held] that the emancipation would not be permissible?

241. He replied: The two situations are analogically the same, but in the first I would prefer to abandon the analogy and follow istiḥsān (juristic preference)[49] and hold that the emancipation before the division of the spoil is not permissible.

242. I asked: If the army captured a [married] woman a day or so before her husband, do you think that marital status between the two would remain valid? 137

243. He replied: Yes.[50]

244. I asked: If the span between their respective captures was either equivalent to three menstrual periods or if [the wife] had actually experienced three menstruations and had adopted Islam, but before the army had left the territory of war her husband was [also] captured and became a Muslim, do you think that their marital status would remain valid?

245. He replied: Yes.

246. I asked: Why?

247. He replied: Since they had not yet been taken to the territory of Islam their [marital] status would be regarded as if they had been captured together.[51]

[47] This opinion seems to have been based on the assumption that the group can act separately from the community, having possessed the spoil after division. See Sarakhsī, *Mabsūṭ*, Vol. X, p. 51.

[48] *Ibid.*, p. 51.

[49] A discretionary opinion in breach of analogical deduction. See Khadduri, *Islamic Jurisprudence*, Chap. XIV.

[50] Abū Yūsuf, *Kitāb al-Radd*, p. 53.

[51] Ṭaḥāwī, *Mukhtaṣar*, p. 286.

248. I asked: If the husband were captured before the wife and she after him, do you think that their [marital] status would remain unchanged as you have described it?

249. He replied: Yes.

250. I asked: If one of the two—husband or wife—were captured and taken to the territory of Islam and the other were captured later?

251. He replied: Their marital status would no longer be valid.[52]

252. I asked: Why?

253. He replied: If one of the two [spouses] were taken to the territory of Islam before the other, the wedlock would be broken.[53]

254. I asked: Why is that so?

255. He replied: If the wife had been allotted to the share of one [of the Muslims] and she became a Muslim, do you not think that he would have the right to have intercourse with her or to marry her if he so desired?

256. I said: Yes indeed.

257. He said: Do you not think that her wedlock was dissolved? If her husband, who was in the territory of war, had still preserved the marital bond with her and her wedlock with him were not terminated, the [Muslim] would have no right to have sexual intercourse with her or to marry her, but she would be lawful to the latter if her wedlock with her [former] husband had been broken. It has been related to us that God's saying, "Do not marry . . . married women, except those whom your right hand possesses [i. e., slave women]," [54] was revealed in connection with a woman who

[52] Abū Yūsuf, *Kitāb al-Radd*, p. 55.

[53] The marriage contract between husband and wife is terminated because of the separation of husband and wife, one being in the territory of Islam and the other in the territory of war, not because of capture. Differences in residence between the two constitute cancellation of the marriage contract even if the period of separation is short. See Sarakhsī, *Mabsūṭ*, Vol. V, pp. 50-51.

[54] Q. IV, 28.

had a husband, was taken as a captive, and whose [new] master had intercourse with her, after waiting one menstrual period [to be sure that she was not pregnant]. And it has been related to us from the Prophet that he prohibited [men] from intercourse with pregnant women taken as fay' until they have been delivered and he prohibited [men] from having intercourse even with women who are not pregnant until their clearance from pregnancy is established by one menstrual period.[55]

258. I asked: If a man found in the spoil goods [of daily usage] or clothing or an animal or weapons which the unbelievers had previously captured [from him], do you think [that he would have the right of postliminium]?

259. He replied: If the owner finds them before the spoil is divided, he may take them without paying anything; if the spoil has been divided, he has the right to take them by paying their price.[56]

260. I asked: If he [merely] laid claim to something, would his claim be accepted?

261. He replied: No, unless he produces evidence.

262. I asked: If [the thing] which had been captured from him consisted of [gold] dinārs and [silver] dirhams and [copper] coins, and evidence in his favor had been established?

263. He replied: If he finds them before division [of the spoil], he may take them; if he finds them afterward, he has no right to them.[57]

264. I asked: Why?

265. He replied: Because these are gold [dinārs], silver [dirhams], and [copper] coins and he could take them only by paying their like. Thus, that which he would take would be the same as that which he would give.

266. I asked: If a slave ran away to [enemy] territory

[55] Abū Yūsuf, *Kitāb al-Radd,* pp. 54-55, and *Kitāb al-Āthār,* p. 240.

[56] Abū Yūsuf, *Kitāb al-Āthār,* p. 195; Sarakhsī, *Mabsūṭ,* Vol. X, p. 54.

[57] Sarakhsī, *Mabsūṭ,* Vol. X, p. 54; *Kitāb Sharḥ al-Siyar al-Kabīr* (Hyderabad), Vol. IV, pp. 374-77.

and the Muslims captured him and, having taken him to a place of security, [the original owner] found him in the spoil of war either before or after it had been divided?

267. He replied: Whether found by his master before or after division [of the spoil], a runaway slave could be recovered by his master without payment of the slave's value or anything else.

268. I asked: Why?

269. He replied: Because the unbelievers had not validly placed the slave in a place of security [i. e., they had not legally possessed him], for [the status of] a slave who escapes to them is different from that of one whom they have captured and taken to a place of security.[58]

270. I asked: If [the owner] found his runaway slave in the possession of a man who had taken him as part of his share of the spoil, should [the latter] be compensated if the slave were taken from him?

271. He replied: Yes, he should be compensated by the Imām, who pays the slave's value from the public treasury.[59]

272. I asked: If the owner did not find his runaway slave in the possession of a man who had taken him from the spoil [as his share], but in the possession of a man who had bought him from a purchase from the inhabitants of the territory of war?

273. He replied: If he were a runaway slave, [the original owner] could take him from the purchaser without paying anything wherever he may find him, because [the slave] was not taken to [a valid] place of security by the inhabitants of the territory of war. A runaway slave is not [regarded as] legally capable of being taken to a place of security [by anybody], and he is different [in status] from a slave taken by capture. If the slave were captured by the unbelievers as a

[58] Abū Yūsuf, *Kitāb al-Radd*, p. 56; Sarakhsī, *Mabsūṭ*, Vol. X, p. 55; Ṭaḥāwī, *Mukhtaṣar*, p. 286.

[59] Shaybānī, *al-Jāmi' al-Kabīr*, p. 229; Sarakhsī, *Mabsūṭ*, Vol. X, p. 56.

prisoner [of war] and [the original owner] found him in the possession of a man who had purchased him from the inhabitants of the territory of war, he would have prior right to take him back by paying the price, if he wished. This is the opinion of Abū Ḥanīfa.

However, Abū Yūsuf and Muḥammad [b. al-Ḥasan] held that if a slave were to run away and thereafter were taken as a prisoner [by the enemy] in their territory, [the original owner] could recover him by paying the price in either case [whether recaptured by the Muslims or taken from one who had purchased him in the territory of war].[60]

274. I asked: If the inhabitants of the territory of war had taken the [runaway] slave as a prisoner and had given him as a gift to a man in whose hands the [original] owner found him?

275. He replied: [The original owner] could take him back from the man to whom he was given as a gift by paying the price.[61]

276. I asked: If the man with whom the [original] owner found his slave had purchased the slave from the inhabitants of the territory of war by means of goods or by measurable or weighing commodities, and the owner found [the slave] in his possession, how much would he have to pay for him?

277. He replied: [The owner] may take [the slave] back by paying the price of the goods given in exchange.

278. I asked: If [the slave] was purchased with goods measured or weighed out?

279. He replied: He may take [the slave] back by an equivalent measure or weight [of the goods].

280. I asked: If this possessor has sold the slave to someone else, could [his original owner] take him back?

281. He replied: The [original] owner has the choice of recovering the slave [by paying the price] or of leaving him.

[60] Sarakhsī, *Mabsūṭ*, Vol. X, pp. 56-57; Ṭaḥāwī, *Mukhtaṣar*, p. 286.

[61] Shaybānī, *al-Jāmi' al-Ṣaghīr*, p. 89; Sarakhsī, *Mabsūṭ*, Vol. X, p. 57; Ṭaḥāwī, *Mukhtaṣar*, pp. 286-87.

282. I asked: Should the owner take an oath that he had purchased [the slave] for the specified [price]?

283. He replied: Yes.

284. I asked: If the original owner adduced evidence that [the man] who purchased the slave had paid less [than what he claimed]?

285. He replied: The evidence of the original owner should be accepted.

286. I asked: If a slave was captured by the unbelievers, who sold him to a Muslim for 1,000 dirhams, but the slave was again captured by them and they sold him to another [Muslim] for 500 dirhams, and then the two owners found him jointly [in postliminium], which owner do you think would be more entitled to take back the slave?

287. He replied: The [first] purchaser who had paid 1,000 dirhams for the slave has the greater claim [than the original owner] to recover the slave [in postliminium] by paying 500 dirhams [to the second purchaser]. If he takes him, the original owner should be told that if he wishes he can take him back by paying 1,500 dirhams or leave him.[62]

288. I asked: Why is this so, while the second has greater claim than the first?

289. He replied: Since the latter had paid 1,000 dirhams, he has the greater claim; for if we had rendered the decision in favor of the original owner for only 500 dirhams, the other who had paid 1,000 dirhams would have lost his money.

290. I asked: If the original owner found the slave in the possession of the one who had paid 1,000 dirhams, do you think that he could claim [the slave]?

291. He replied: No. 138

292. I asked: Why?

293. He replied: Do you not think that if the two purchasers came together, the one who paid 1,000 dirhams has greater claim if he paid 500 [to the second purchaser] to recover the

[62] Shaybānī, *al-Jāmiʿ al-Ṣaghīr*, p. 89, and *al-Jāmiʿ al-Kabīr*, p. 361.

slave; the original owner can recover [the slave] if he paid 1,500 dirhams, if he so wishes.

Abū Yūsuf and Muḥammad [b. al-Ḥasan] added that if the slave unintentionally committed a tort or destroyed property or was indebted and was captured by the enemy who accepted Islam, the tort would be waived but the debt would have to be paid [by the owner of the slave].[63]

294. I asked: If the enemy [did not] [64] accept Islam, but the slave was either purchased by a Muslim or was found by the Muslims among the spoil?

295. He replied: The tort would be waived but the debt would have to be paid [by the owner].

296. [I asked:] [65] If the original owner had recovered [the slave] by paying his value or his [market] price?

297. He replied: He would be liable for both the tort and the damages.

298. I asked: If the delict were intentional killing?

299. He replied: The delict would not be waived in any of these situations.

300. I asked: If the enemy captured a believer's slave or some [other] property belonging to him but these were [later] taken as spoil by the Muslims and allotted to one of them as his share; and if the Muslim who received the slave emancipated him [if male] immediately or on terms [to take effect on the owner's death] [66] or, if the slave were female, caused her to become pregnant; or suppose that the postliminium consisted of property destroyed [by someone who received it as a share of the spoil], do you think that the [original] owner would have the right to claim anything?

301. He replied: No, but if he saw it in person he [the original owner] would have the right to claim the property before it is consumed by paying its price, if he wishes.

[63] Sarakhsī, *Mabsūṭ*, Vol. X, p. 58.

[64] Not in Murād Mulla MS, but in 'Ātif and Fayḍ-Allāh MSS.

[65] Not in Arabic MSS.

[66] Tadbīr is an arrangement by which the slave becomes free at the owner's death.

302. I asked: If he found that the [new] owner of the slave woman had given her in marriage to another man, do you think that the original owner could take her back by paying the price of her?

303. He replied: Yes.[67]

304. I asked: Would she be separated from her husband?

305. He replied: No; she [and her husband] remain married, and [the original owner] would have no right to claim even the 'uqr (nuptial gift).

306. I asked: If the slave woman had given birth to a child to her husband, do you think that he [the original owner] has the right to take her back together with her child?

307. He replied: Yes.

308. I asked: Why?

309. He replied: Because [the child came] from her provenance and it [the child] is existing in person.

310. I asked: If the [new] master had emancipated the child or had sold it and spent its price, or had kept it as a slave but expended his earnings?

311. He replied: The [original] owner has the right to take back the slave girl by paying the price [that had been paid by the new owner], if he so desires, or to renounce her, if he so wishes.

312. I asked. If the slave woman's master had married her off and taken her 'uqr or her hand had been cut off and her owner took possession of the arsh [68] paid for her hand, would [the original owner] have the right to recover anything from the 'uqr or the arsh [collected by the new master]?

313. He replied: No.

314. I asked: Why?

315. He replied: Because if [the original owner] had the right to recover the 'uqr or the arsh, he would have [the right] to take her back with a defect—the equivalent of which would

[67] Sarankhsī, *Mabsūṭ*, Vol. X, pp. 58-59.

[68] The arsh is a penalty for certain wounds.

be deducted from the price—but this is unlawful, and nothing should be deducted.

316. I asked: If the [second] owner had purchased [the slave woman] from the enemy for 1,000 dirhams, and she subsequently became blind or acquired some other defect which decreased her value by half, would the original owner have either to pay the full price [in order to be able] to take her back or leave her?

317. He replied: Yes. He has no other alternative.[69]

318. I asked: If the [second] owner emancipated her, do you think that she would be [lawfully] emancipated?

319. He replied: Yes.

320. I asked: Why would you allow her emancipation while she belongs to another [owner]?

321. He replied: The slave woman belongs to the [second] owner and to no one else, but the original owner has only the prior right to take her, if he pays her price.

322. I asked: Would it be lawful for the [second] owner to have sexual intercourse with the slave woman, if he knows her situation?

323. He replied: Yes.

324. I asked: If a slave girl, whose owner was a minor orphan, was captured by the enemy and purchased by another man, do you think that the executor of the [minor] orphan has the right to take her back by paying the price?

325. He replied: Yes.

326. I asked: Has the executor the right to take her for himself?

327. He replied: No, not for himself, but for the [minor] orphan.

328. I asked: Would you hold the same [opinion] if a father purchased a slave girl for his minor son?

329. He replied: Yes.

330. I asked: If a slave girl who had been pledged as

[69] Sarakhsī, *Mabsūṭ*, Vol. X, pp. 59-60.

security for 1,000 dirhams—equivalent to her price—were captured by the enemy and purchased by another man for 1,000 dirhams, do you think that the original owner would have the prior right to [recover] her by refunding the price?

331. He replied: Yes.

332. I asked: If the [first] owner takes possession of her, would she remain in her former status as a pledge [for the debt of the 1,000 dirhams]?

333. He replied: No. Do you not think that the [first] owner has redeemed her by paying 1,000 dirhams? Her situation is the same as if she had committed an offense and the person who held her as security refused to pay the indemnity due for the offense, and the indemnity was paid by the original owner who had given her as security [for his debt]. However, the person who held her as security could if he paid to the original owner the price by which the latter has redeemed her—if this [price] were less than the debt—and recover the slave woman; in such a case she remains as a pledge to the holder, but he has the choice to take or leave her as he wishes.

334. I asked: If a man holds a male or female slave as a deposit or on hire or on loan, but [he or she] is captured by the enemy and taken to a place of security, and then purchased by another man, do you think that the person who held [the slave] on loan or as a deposit or on hire has the right to redeem [the slave]?

335. He replied: He has no such right.

Slave Girl Captured by a Single Warrior Starting from the Muslim Camp and Making an Incursion in the Territory of War[70] 141

336. I asked: If the Imām promised a prime to his companions [in arms] by saying: "He who captures anything from the enemy would be for him," and made [the entire

[70] This section, dealing with the distribution of booty, has been transposed from Chap. IV.

capture] a prime for them; and if one of the Muslims captured a slave girl, do you think that [the warrior] would be entitled to have sexual intercourse with her in the territory of war, provided he waited for her clearance by one menstrual period?

337. He replied: [No] he would not have the right to do so.[71]

338. I asked: If the slave girl were a scripturary?

339. He replied: Even if she were a scripturary.

340. I asked: Would this be true until he had taken her to a place of security and carried her to the dār al-Islām?

341. He replied: Yes.

342. I asked: Would he [even] have no [right] to sell her until he takes her to the territory of Islam?

343. He replied: Yes.

344. I asked: If a group [of warriors] went out from a fortified post or camp and captured spoil and captives from 142
the enemy, do you think that the one-fifth share should be taken out of the spoil and the rest divided among the group and the army [of which it formed a part]?

345. He replied: Yes.

346. I asked: Would the ruling be the same if the party consisted of only one warrior?

347. He replied: Yes.[72]

348. I asked: If [the party] had gone out of the camp without the permission of the Imām?

349. He replied: Even so, the [spoil] acquired would be subject to the [extraction of the] one-fifth [share].[73]

350. I asked: Why is that so?

351. He replied: Since the fortified post and [the army in] the camp provide a support for them, the people of the fortified post would participate in whatever they captured.

352. I asked: If [the warriors] went out from a big city

[71] Sarakhsī, *Mabsūṭ*, Vol. X, p. 72.
[72] Abū Yūsuf, *Kitāb al-Radd*, p. 76; Sarakhsī, *Mabsūṭ*, Vol. X, p. 73.
[73] Ṭaḥāwī, *Mukhtaṣar*, p. 292.

like al-Maṣṣiṣa[74] or Malāṭiya[75] and the Imām sent [them] forth as a detachment and if they captured spoil [from the enemy], do you think that the inhabitants of the city [from which they went out] should participate in the spoil?

353. He said: No.

354. I asked: Why?

355. He replied: These cities are like any other large cities of al-Shām [Syria].[76]

356. I asked: If one or two men went out to the territory of war from a town or a city and captured spoil, do you think that the one-fifth [state] share should be taken out of their spoil?

357. He replied: The one-fifth share would not be taken out of their spoil because the status of these two men would be equivalent to that of adventurers who had taken possession of what [they had plundered]. The spoil belongs to them.[77]

358. I asked: If the Imām dispatched a man in advance of the army as scout and he captured spoil, do you think that the one-fifth [share] should be taken out of the spoil and the residue divided among the rest of the army?

359. He replied: Yes.[78]

360. I asked: How is the latter [situation] different from the status of the two adventurers?

361. He replied: The latter was sent forth from the army by the Imām and the army provided him with the support, whereas the two men [in the former case] did not go forth from the army, but went voluntarily out on their own initiative from a city without the Imām's permission.

362. I asked: If the two adventurers captured a slave girl and one of them purchased the share of the other, do you think that he would have the right to have intercourse with her if he still were in the territory of war?

[74] Modern Missis, near Adana, in Turkey.
[75] In Turkey now.
[76] Sarakhsī, *Mabsūṭ*, Vol. X, p. 73; cf. Ṭabarī, *Kitāb Ikhtilāf*, pp. 71-73.
[77] Sarakhsī, *Mabsūṭ*, Vol. X, p. 74; Ṭaḥāwī, *Mukhtaṣar*, p. 292.
[78] Ṭaḥāwī, *Mukhtaṣar*, p. 292.

363. He replied: No.[79]

364. I asked: Why? As long as she is not subject to the one-fifth [share] and he became owner of her?

365. He replied: Because he had not yet taken her to a place of security and he had not carried her to the territory of Islam.

366. I asked: If a Muslim entered the territory of war under an amām and purchased a Christian slave woman and waited one menstrual period to be sure she was clear of pregnancy, do you think that he would have the right to have intercourse with her?

367. He replied: Yes, if he so desired.[80]

368. I asked: In what respect is the latter [situation] different from the former?

369. He replied: The two are not alike. The latter enjoys an amān [in the dār al-ḥarb] and can buy and sell, whereas the other did not enjoy the amān. Do you not think that if a Muslim army entered the territory of war and encountered those two men who were in possession of the slave girl which they have captured, the army would be entitled to participate in the distribution as booty both of this slave girl and the other spoil which they too may have captured; whereas, if the army encountered the Muslim [merchant] who purchased the slave girl, they would not be entitled to participate in what he had purchased and would have nothing to do against what was in his possession. However, I disapprove for a Muslim to have sexual intercourse with [either] his wife or his slave woman in the territory of war for fear that he might have offsprings [born there].

370. I asked: If a man, who is entitled to a regular share of the spoil, has a very old father in need of support or a son, do you think that his parents or his son would be entitled to receive a portion of the one-fifth [share]?

371. He replied: Yes.

[79] Abū Yūsuf, *Kitāb al-Radd*, p. 79; Sarakhsī, *Mabsūṭ*, Vol. X, p. 74.
[80] Sarakhsī, *Mabsūṭ*, Vol. X, p. 74.

372. I asked: Would the one-fifth [share] be distributed on the same basis as the rest of the spoil?

373. He replied: No, the one-fifth [share] should be distributed among the beneficiaries of the ṣadaqa, not among those who receive the spoil.[81]

[81] Beneficiaries of Ṣadaqa (i. e., taxes collected from Muslims only) are those prescribed in the Qur'ān IX, 60-61; the beneficiaries of the ghanīma (captured from the enemy in war) are those stated in the Qur'ān VIII, 41. See also *ibid.*, pp. 74-75.

Chapter IV

Folio 138

[ON THE INTERCOURSE BETWEEN THE TERRITORY OF ISLAM (DĀR AL-ISLĀM) AND THE TERRITORY OF WAR (DĀR AL-ḤARB)] [1]

Trade between the Territory of Islam and the Territory of War [2]

374. I asked: If a slave girl were captured by the enemy after her master had given her in marriage and thereafter she were purchased by a Muslim who took her back to the territory of Islam without her changing her religion, do you think that she and her husband would be regarded as [still] married?

375. He replied: Yes.[3]

376. I asked: And the capture [by the enemy] would not have a stronger effect in invalidating [her marriage contract] than her sale by her master would?

377. [He replied]: [No], for if her master sold her to another man, her marriage [contract] would remain valid.

[1] The two terms "dār al-Islām" and "dār al-ḥarb," which Muslim jurists apply to the territories under Islamic rule and to territories outside Islamic rule, are not used by Shaybānī consistently; he either uses the terms "ahl al-ḥarb" (people of [the territory of] war) and "dār al-ḥarb" (territory of war) interchangeably, or uses "ahl al-Islām" or merely "al-dār" in place of dār al-Islām (territory of Islam) or even enemy territory. See Translator's Introduction, pp. 11-14, above, and Khadduri, *War and Peace in the Law of Islam*, pp. 52-53, 155-57, 170-71.

[2] Literally: "purchase and sale in the territories of Islam and of war."

[3] Sarakhsī, *Mabsūṭ*, Vol. X, pp. 60-61.

378. I asked: If a Muslim merchant were in the territory of war and the unbelievers captured from the Muslim spoil that included slaves and other objects, do you think that it would be lawful for the [Muslim] merchant to buy from among those slaves a slave girl with whom to have sexual intercourse, an animal to ride, or food to eat, knowing [that these had been captured from the Muslims]?

379. He replied: Yes, but I disapprove of his having intercourse with her before taking her [to the territory of Islam].[4]

380. I asked: Why, since what the believers had done was unlawful?

381. He replied: Because [the unbelievers] took [the slaves] 139
to a place of security and thus became their [lawful] owners. Do you not think that if they [the unbelievers] had become Muslims while in possession [of the slaves] or had made a treaty of peace and had become Dhimmīs, they would be acknowledged as the lawful owners of them?

382. I asked: If [the unbelievers] captured a freedman, an umm walad,[5] mudabbar,[6] or mukātab,[7] and they took him to a place of security and thereafter they either became Muslims while possessing him or made a treaty of peace [by virtue of which] they became Dhimmīs, [what would be his legal status]?

383. He replied: Each would maintain the *status quo ante*: the freedman would be a freedman, the mudabbar would retain his mudabbarship, the umm walad would remain as umm walad, and the mukātab as a mukātab.[8]

[4] Abū Yūsuf, *Kitāb al-Radd*, p. 126; Ṭabarī, *Kitāb Ikhtilāf*, p. 194. Awzā'ī and Shāfi'ī held that the owner may have sexual intercourse with the slave girl if it is clear that she is not pregnant. See Shāfi'ī, *Umm*, Vol. VII, p. 333; Ṭabarī, *Kitāb Ikhtilāf*, pp. 192, 193-94.

[5] An "umm walad" is a slave woman who has given birth to a child to her owner. Right of legal possession of the female slave entitles the owner to have sexual intercourse with her.

[6] A mudabbar is a male slave who has been declared to become free at the time of the death of the owner.

[7] A mukātab is a male slave who has concluded a contract of manumission on the assumption that he pays the price of his freedom by installments.

[8] Ṭabarī, *Kitāb Ikhtilāf*, pp. 190-91; Sarakhsī, *Mabsūṭ*, Vol. X, p. 61.

384. I asked: Would the same be true if [the owners] became Muslims or if [the slave] were sold?

385. He replied: Yes.[9]

386. I asked: Would each be returned to his own people without any compensation?

387. He replied: Yes.[10]

388. I asked: If a man [i. e., a Muslim merchant] purchased from the inhabitants of the territory of war either a mukātab who had been captured by them or a freedman who had asked the merchant to buy him, and thereafter that merchant entered the territory of Islam with that person, do you think that the man who had asked that merchant to buy him would become a freedman as before, and that the mukātab would remain a mukātab, so that the merchant thereby would lose the money [he had paid]?

389. He replied: No. The money paid by the merchant would have to be made good to him both by the mukātab and the freedman since they asked him to buy them; otherwise each would maintain his former status.[11]

390. I asked: If [the merchant] had purchased them without their consent?

391. He replied: He would have no claim against them.

392. I asked: If a slave belonging to the Muslims was captured by the inhabitants of the territory of war and their ruler sold him to a man of that territory, [do you think that] his manumission would be lawful if [the purchaser] emancipated him?

393. He replied: Yes.

394. I asked: Why?

395. He replied: Do you not think that if [the ruler] had sold the slave to a Muslim—who in turn set the slave free—

Mālik agrees with the Ḥanafī doctrine, but Shāfi'ī disagrees. See Ṭabarī, *Kitāb Ikhtilāf*, pp. 189-90.

[9] Ṭabarī, *Kitāb Ikhtilāf*, p. 190; Sarakhsī, *Mabsūṭ*, Vol. X, p. 61.

[10] *Ibid.*

[11] Ṭabarī, *Kitāb Ikhtilāf*, p. 191; Sarakhsī, *Mabsūṭ*, Vol. X. pp. 61-62.

his manumission would be lawful, and that if they [the inhabitants of the territory of war] became Muslims while in possession [of the slave], the slave would be legally theirs? [12]

396. I asked: If the slave was purchased by [another] man from the territory of war who became a Muslim and went over to us with this [slave] and with his family and possessions, would the slave remain his property?

397. He replied: Yes.

398. I asked: Would his [former] owner be entitled to recover him by paying the [slave's] price?

399. He replied: No.

400. I asked: Why?

401. He replied: [Because] the [slave's] status would be the same as if he had been in the possession of [unbelievers] who became Muslims and who would be entitled to retain whatever they had in their possession at the time of their conversion [and the annexation of their territory by Islam].[13]

402. I asked: If the slave's owner entered the territory of Islam under an amām (safe-conduct) and did not become a Muslim but wanted to sell the slave, would the former owner have prior claim to purchase the slave by paying his price?

403. He replied: No.

404. I asked: Why?

405. He replied: Do you not think that if the inhabitants of the territory of war entered into a peace agreement [with the Muslims] and became Dhimmīs, they would be entitled to keep what they possessed at the time they did so?

406. [I asked: Would the ruling be the same concerning Dhimmīs and musta'mins?] [14]

407. He replied: Yes, they and those who were given an amān (safe-conduct) would be treated alike, but [I hold that] they [the Dhimmīs] should be compelled to sell whatever Muslim male or female slaves they might have in their possession.[15]

[12] Sarakhsī, *Mabsūṭ*, Vol. X, pp. 61-62.

[13] Abū Yūsuf, *Kitāb al-Radd*, p. 126; Shāfi'ī, *Umm*, Vol. VII, p. 334.

[14] Not in Arabic MSS, but supplemented.

[15] Sarakhsī, *Kitāb Sharḥ al-Siyar al-Kabīr* (Hyderabad), Vol. IV, pp. 236-37, 239, and *Mabsūṭ*, Vol. X, p. 62.

Prisoners of War Entitled to Funeral Prayer

408. I asked: If the [Muslim] warriors divided the spoil of war among themselves after they had brought it to the territory of Islam and one of them came into the possession (as part of his share) of a male or female child who did not attain the age of understanding Islam [16] up to the time of its death, would the child be entitled to the funeral prayer [as a Muslim] if it died?

409. He replied: If the child enters [the territory of Islam] with one or both of its unbelieving parents, it would retain its religion, and it would not be entitled to [the Islamic funeral] prayer. If one or both of its parents became a Muslim [after entering the territory of Islam], the child would be entitled to [the funeral] prayer. If the [non-Muslim] father and the son enter the territory of Islam together, but from two different directions, the child would not be entitled to [the Islamic funeral] prayer if it dies. If the father enters the territory of Islam before his child, the child would not be entitled to [the funeral] prayer [if it died], because it [would be regarded as having] entered with an unbelieving father. But if the child is brought before the father, it would be entitled to [the funeral] prayer. Thus, I should consider the manner in which [the child] enters [the territory of Islam] and nothing else. If the parents remained in the territory of war and the child died in the territory of Islam before attaining the age of understanding Islam, it would be entitled to [the funeral] prayer.[17]

410. I asked: If the parents were taken captives and came into the possession of a Muslim as part of his share and the child died while the father was [still] an unbeliever, would the child be entitled to the [Islamic funeral] prayer?

411. He replied: [No], it would not be entitled to the prayer.

[16] I. e., professing Islam.

[17] Abū Yūsuf, *Kitāb al-Radd*, pp. 121-22; Shāfi'ī, *Umm*, Vol. VII, p. 332; Sarakhsī, *Mabsūṭ*, Vol. X, p. 62; Kāsānī, *Badā'i' al-Ṣanā'i'*, Vol. VII, p. 104.

412. I asked: If the father died as an unbeliever before his son, would the boy be entitled to [the funeral] prayer?

413. He replied: No.

414. I asked: Why?

415. He replied: Because [the boy] follows his father's religion, unless he has declared himself a Muslim or professed it.[18]

416. I asked: If the parents were in the territory of war and the child died [after he entered the territory of Islam] before he became a Muslim, would he be entitled to [the Islamic funeral] prayer?

417. He replied: Yes.

418. I asked: Why?

419. He replied: Because [the child] came into the possession of the Muslims and was carried to the dār al-Islām; he, therefore, attained the status of a Muslim. For this reason he would be entitled to [the funeral] prayer.

420. I asked: If the captive were a slave girl, mature enough to be lawful for cohabitation, would her master be entitled to have intercourse with her?

421. He replied: Yes.

422. I asked: Why is this so? If she did not accept Islam or profess it, [why do you think that] she would be lawful [to men] and entitled to [the Islamic funeral] prayer?

423. He replied: Because she had come into the possession of the Muslims. Do you not think that I disapprove of Muslims who would sell her to the Dhimmīs?

424. I asked: If the slave girl or the boy were an adult and neither had become a Muslim or professed Islam, would either one be entitled to [the funeral] prayer?

425. He replied: No.

426. I asked: And the slave girl would not be lawful [to her master]?

[18] Abū Yūsuf, *Kitāb al-Radd*, pp. 121-22; Ṭaḥāwī, *Mukhtaṣar*, p. 289.

427. He replied: She would not be lawful unless she were a scripturary.

428. I asked: Do you think that it is objectionable to sell the unbelieving prisoners of war—men and women—to the Dhimmīs, if these prisoners of war have been invited to become Muslims and have refused?

429. He replied: I do not disapprove of that, even if they have not been invited [to become Muslims], but it would be preferable to me if such [a sale] were not made.

430. I asked: Would it be objectionable if they were sold to the inhabitants of the territory of war?

431. He replied: Yes.

432. I asked: Why?

433. He replied: Because they entered the territory of Islam and became Dhimmīs, and I disapprove of their being carried off to the territory of war, whereby they would strengthen the inhabitants of the territory of war against the Muslims.[19]

Muslim Merchants in the Territory of War Seeking to Recover Their Women or Property[20] 140

434. I asked: If the slave woman of a Muslim was captured by the enemy and her master entered the territory of war as merchant or under an amān (safe-conduct), do you think that it would be lawful for him to usurp her?

435. He replied: I disapprove of his doing so.[21]

436. I asked: Would you disapprove of his having intercourse with her?

437. He replied: Yes, I disapprove of his doing so.[22]

[19] Sarakhsī, *Sharḥ al-Siyar*, Vol. IV, pp. 1-5, 107, 369-74; *Mabsūṭ*, Vol. X, pp. 62-63.

[20] Literally: "A man enters dār al-ḥarb as a merchant who steals his slave woman or usurps her and others or recovers his property by force."

[21] Ṭabarī, *Kitāb Ikhtilāf*, p. 194.

[22] It would be objectionable to Abū Ḥanīfa even if the merchant pur-

438. I asked: Why?

439. He replied: Because [the enemy] had taken her to a place of security.

440. I asked: If the woman was a freedwoman, umm walad, mudabbara, or his own wife, whether free or mukātaba [what would be your ruling]?

441. He replied: Anyone of these means would be permissible for him: he may steal or usurp [the slave] from them. He [also] has the right to have intercourse with his umm walad, mudabbara, or wife, if she is a freedwoman. Do you not think that if [the enemy] accepted Islam while in possession of the slave woman, she would be lawfully theirs and the [original] owner would not be entitled to recover her, whereas if [the captive] were the mudabbara, the freedwoman, the umm walad, or the mukātaba, she should be returned to her people? [The merchant] would have no right to have intercourse with the mukātaba, if she were not his wife. Do you not think that if the Muslims recaptured her and the [original] owner found her in the share of another, he would have the right either to recover her by paying her value or leave her, but, if the owner found his mudabbara, umm walad, or mukātaba, [in the shares of others] he would be entitled to recover them without any payment? [Nor] would he have right to have intercourse with the mudabbara, the mukātaba, the freedwoman, and the umm walad. Only the slave woman is capable of [ownership by] sale or capture.[23]

442. I asked: If a man and his slave woman were taken as prisoners of war, would it be lawful [for the man] to recover his slave woman by stealth?

443. He replied: Yes.[24]

444. I asked: Why is it so, since if the same man enters

---

chased her. See Abū Yūsuf, *Kitāb al-Radd*, p. 126. Cf. Shāfi'ī, *Umm*, Vol. VII, p. 333.

[23] Abū Yūsuf, *Kitāb al-Radd*, pp. 124-26; cf. opinions of Awzā'ī and Shāfi'ī in Shāfi'ī's *Umm*, Vol. VII, pp. 332-33. See also Ṭabarī, *Kitāb Ikhtilāf*, pp. 192-94.

[24] Ṭabarī, *Kitāb Ikhtilāf*, p. 194.

the territory of war under an amān it is not lawful for him to have intercourse with her.

445. He replied: Because if the man enters under an amān, he should not violate the pledge he has given [to the inhabitants of the territory of war] or the agreement he has made with them, nor should he break faith with them. He should rather fulfill [all his obligations] to them as they would fulfill them to him. But, if he were a prisoner in their hands and not the possessor of an amān, it would be lawful for him to kill those of them whom he could or steal what he could of their property.[25]

[Status of] the Man in the Territory of War Who Becomes a Muslim While in the Possession of His Property, His Land, His Family, and His Children, after Which the Territory of War Falls under Muslim Rule

446. I asked: If a man from the inhabitants of the territory of war became a Muslim and then the territory fell under Muslim rule, what property or children of his would the Muslims [lawfully] let him keep?

447. He replied: He would be entitled to keep his [movable] property, goods of daily usage, slaves, and all his minor children who follow his religion. [The latter] would not be reduced to slavery, but his adult children would be reduced to slavery and become fay'.[26]

448. I asked: What about [the status of] his land and houses?

449. He replied: They would become fay' for the Muslims.

[25] Abū Yūsuf, *Kitāb al-Radd*, p. 126; Shaybānī, *al-Jāmi' al-Ṣaghīr*, p. 91; Sarakhsī, *Kitāb Sharḥ al-Siyar al-Kabīr* (Hyderabad), Vol. IV, pp. 236-37, and *Mabsūṭ*, Vol. X, p. 66. Cf. opinions of Awzā'ī and Shāfi'ī in Shāfi'ī's *Umm*, Vol. VII, p. 334.

[26] Abū Yūsuf, *Kitāb al-Radd*, pp. 126-27; Sarakhsī, *Mabsūṭ*, Vol. X, p. 66; Kāsānī, *Badā'i' al-Ṣanā'i'*, Vol. VII, pp. 105-6.

450. I asked: Why is the land treated differently from [the movable] property?

451. He replied: Because movable property can be moved 141
from the territory of war [to the territory of Islam], while land cannot.

452. I asked: What would be the status of the [man's] unbelieving wife who is pregnant.

453. He replied: She and the unborn child would be fay' for the Muslims.[27]

454. I asked: Would the unborn child have the same status as she?

455. He replied: Yes.

456. I asked: Why is it so, since his father is a believer?

457. He replied: Because his mother is an unbeliever and has become fay', so her [unborn] child who is [still] in her womb would have the same status.[28]

458. I asked: If a man from the territory of war entered the territory of Islam under an amān and became a Muslim, after which the territory of war [from which he had come] fell under Muslim rule, what would be the status of his family and movable property and dependents?

459. He replied: All would become fay'.[29]

460. I asked: Why?

461. He replied: Because [the man] became a Muslim in the territory of Islam.

462. I asked: If he became a Muslim before he entered the territory of Islam under an amān, what would be the status of his family and dependents and movable property if the territory of war [from which he had come] then fell under Muslim rule?

463. He replied: All would become fay' except the minor

[27] Sarakhsī, *Mabsūṭ*, Vol. X, p. 67.
[28] Shaybānī, *al-Jāmi' al-Ṣaghīr*, p. 91; Sarakhsī, *Mabsūṭ*, Vol. X, p. 67.
[29] Sarakhsī, *Mabsūṭ*, Vol. X, p. 68.

children, who would be [regarded as] Muslims and not liable to capture.[80]

464. I asked: If [the man] had deposited some of his movable property with another man belonging to the territory of war, what would be the status of that property?

465. He replied: It would be regarded as fay' for the Muslims.

466. I asked: If he had deposited [his property] with a Dhimmī who had gone to the territory of war as a merchant or with a Muslim, what would be the status of that property?

467. He replied: It would be given back to its owner.

468. I asked: Why is the case of these two [the Muslim and the Dhimmī just referred to] different from that of the ḥarbī[81] previously mentioned?

469. He replied: If the property were deposited with [another] Muslim or with a Dhimmī, it would have the same status as it would if it were in the possession of its owner in the territory of war; but if it were deposited with one of the inhabitants of the territory of war, it would have the same status as it would have if the owner had departed from the territory of war and left it there, and he had not brought it to the place of security [i. e., dār al-Islām].

470. I asked: If a Muslim or Dhimmī entered the territory of war under an amān and was engaged in trade that resulted in his acquiring movable property, slaves, land, and houses, and thereafter all fell into the hands of the Muslims, his movable as well as immovable property, what would be the status of the goods in his possession as well as slaves and movable property?

471. He replied: He would retain his goods, slaves, and movable property, but all the houses and land would become fay'. [Also] whatever he might have deposited with a ḥarbī

[80] *Ibid.*, p. 68 f.

[81] A ḥarbī is an unbeliever of the inhabitants of the territory of war. See my *War and Peace in the Law of Islam*, p. 163.

or anyone else would be regarded as fay' and would not belong to him.[32]

472. I asked: If adult slaves took part in the fighting against the Muslims, do you think that they would become fay' [if captured]?

473. He replied: Yes.

474. I asked: If a Muslim entered the territory of war under an amān and purchased a minor male or female slave whom he emancipated and, after his return to the territory of Islam, left them behind as unbelievers, do you think that they would become fay' if the territory of war [in which they resided] fell under Muslim rule?

475. He replied: Yes.

476. I asked: Would not the fact that the Muslim emancipated them have the effect of taking them to a place of security [in the dār al-Islām]?

477. He replied: No.

478. I asked: Why?

479. He replied: Because manumission of a slave by a Muslim in the territory of war has no effect.[33]

[32] Sarakhsī, *Kitāb Sharḥ al-Siyar al-Kabīr* (Hyderabad), Vol. IV, p. 238.
[33] *Ibid.*, Vol. II, p. 300, and Vol. IV, p. 203.

Chapter V

Folio 142

[ON PEACE TREATIES] [1]

[*Agreements with the Scripturaries*] [2]

480. I asked: If a group [of scripturaries] made peace [with the Muslims] and became Dhimmīs,[3] do you think that a kharāj [4] should be levied on the men or on the land according to their capacity to pay?

481. He replied: Yes.[5] 143

482. I asked: Has any narrative been transmitted to you concerning the kharāj [imposed] on the Dhimmīs?

[1] Since a state of war was the normal relationship between the dār al-Islām and dār al-ḥarb, conditions of peace were created only by peace treaties which were to last, according to the most liberal opinions (Ḥanafi and Shāfi'ī), no more than ten years. Thus, peace treaties were necessarily of temporary duration, even though the period might not be stated, during which hostile relations were suspended between Islam and enemy territory; they were signed to achieve certain specific purposes. See Abū Yūsuf, *Kitāb al-Kharāj*, pp. 207 ff.; Sarakhsī, *Kitāb Sharḥ al-Siyar al-Kabīr* (Hyderabad), Vol. IV, pp. 60 ff.; Shāfi'ī, *Umm*, Vol. IV, pp. 109 ff.; Ṭabarī, *Kitāb Ikhtilāf*, pp. 14 ff.

[2] Agreements with the People of the Book or scripturaries (people who have scriptures, such as Jews, Christians, Sabians, etc.) were of a somewhat different nature from other peace treaties because they were in the form of permanent covenants or pacts by virtue of which the scripturaries were to become naturalized subjects of the Imām and treated as tolerated religious communities. These agreements may therefore be regarded as constitutional charters. See my *War and Peace in the Law of Islam*, pp. 177-82, 193-95, 213-15.

[3] Scripturaries who entered into a peace treaty with Muslims and became subjects of the Islamic state were called Dhimmīs. This term implies that the scripturaries were in a compact with Islam. See my *War and Peace in the Law of Islam*, pp. 176-77.

[4] The term "kharāj" had the double meaning of land tax or poll tax in early Islam before it was used specifically for land tax. See Chap. X.

[5] Abū Yūsuf, *Kitāb al-Kharāj*, p. 122; Ṭabarī, *Kitāb Ikhtilāf*, p. 199; Sarakhsī, *Mabsūṭ*, Vol. X, p. 77.

483. He replied: Yes, it has been related to us that [the Caliph] 'Umar b. al-Khaṭṭāb imposed on every jarīb [6] of cultivable land [a tax of] 1 dirham [7] [of silver] and a qafīz [8] [of grain]. He imposed on every jarīb [of land] planted with grapevines 10 dirhams and on that planted with perishable fruits, 5. It has [likewise] been related to us that he imposed on every man [either] 12, 24, or 48 dirhams.[9]

484. I asked: Therefore, the poor man who owns no property but earns his living by manual labor should pay 12 dirhams, the one who owns [some] property should pay 24, and the rich man should pay 48?

485. He replied: Yes.[10]

486. I asked: Should we collect anything from the women and children?

487. He replied: No.[11]

488. I asked: Should we collect anything from the blind, the old and very aged, the insane, the crippled, the helpless, and the poor who possess nothing and are incapable of work?

489. He replied: None of them is under obligation to pay [12] the poll tax.[13]

490. I asked: Would the same hold true to slaves, the mukātab, the mudabbar, and the umm walad?

[6] The jarīb is a measure of surface containing 100 square qaṣaba, or 1,952 square meters. See Chap. X.

[7] The dirham is the silver unit of coinage (Māwardī, *Kitāb al-Aḥkām*, p. 267) derived from the Greek *drachma* via Sasanian Iran. See G. C. Miles, "Dirham," *Encyclopaedia of Islam* (2nd ed.), Vol. II, pp. 319-20.

[8] A qafīz is a measure of grain. See Chap. X, n. 5.

[9] Abū Yūsuf, *Kitāb al-Kharāj*, p. 36; Ṭabarī, *Kitāb Ikhtilāf*, pp. 210-11; Sarakhsī, *Mabsūṭ*, Vol. X, p. 78.

[10] Abū Yūsuf, *Kitāb al-Kharāj*, p. 122. For views of other schools of law, see Ṭabarī, *Kitāb Ikhtilāf*, pp. 208-11.

[11] Abū Yūsuf, *Kitāb al-Kharāj*, p. 123; Ṭabarī, *Kitāb Ikhtilāf*, p. 206; Sarakhsī, *Mabsūṭ*, Vol. X, p. 79; Kāsānī, *Badā'i' al-Ṣanā'i'*, Vol. VII, p. 112.

[12] In the 'Ātif MS there is the additional statement: "Nor are their owners under obligation to pay anything," on the assumption that some of the Dhimmīs may be in a state of slavery.

[13] Abū Yūsuf, *Kitāb al-Kharāj*, p. 122; Ṭabarī, *Kitāb Ikhtilāf*, p. 207; Sarakhsī, *Mabsūṭ*, Vol. X, pp. 79-80.

491. He replied: Yes, none of them is under obligation to pay a poll tax nor are their masters to pay anything.[14]

492. I asked: Would the property of Dhimmīs, such as flock of sheep, cattle, camels, and horses, as well as inanimate property, be subject to the kharāj?

493. He replied: No.[15]

494. I asked: Would the land belonging to Dhimmīs who are minors, women, or mukātabs be subject to the kharāj?

495. He replied: Yes, they would have to pay the kharāj just as any adult, healthy, male Dhimmī would.

496. I asked: If a male Dhimmī becomes a Muslim at the end of the year or after the expiration of the year before the poll tax was collected from him, do you think that [the tax] would be collected from him after he had become Muslim?

497. He replied: No.[16]

498. I asked: Why?

499. He replied: Because this [tax] is not a debt which he is liable to pay but a poll tax which should be canceled when he becomes a Muslim, and nothing would be collected from him.

500. I asked: If [the Dhimmī] died as an unbeliever and left an estate, do you think that the poll tax would be taken out of his estate?

501. He replied: No.

502. I asked: Why?

503. He replied: Because [the poll tax] is not a debt which he is liable to pay.[17]

504. I asked: If the Dhimmī was in debt, do you think

[14] Ṭabarī, *Kitāb Ikhtilāf*, p. 207; Sarakhsī, *Mabsūṭ*, Vol. X, p. 80.

[15] Abū Yūsuf, *Kitāb al-Kharāj*, p. 123; Ṭabarī, *Kitāb Ikhtilāf*, p. 218.

[16] Abū Yūsuf, *Kitāb al-Kharāj*, p. 122; Ṭabarī, *Kitāb Ikhtilāf*, p. 207; Sarakhsī, *Mabsūṭ*, Vol. X, p. 80.

[17] Ṭabarī, *Kitāb Ikhtilāf*, p. 212; Sarakhsī, *Mabsūṭ*, Vol. X, pp. 81-82.

that the [unpaid] kharāj would be shared proportionately by his creditors?

505. He replied: No.[18]

506. I asked: And [the poll tax] would be waived and no longer due?

507. [He replied: Yes.] [19]

508. I asked: If a [number of] years passed and [the Dhimmī] failed to pay the poll tax, do you think that he would be liable for the poll taxes of all those years?

509. He replied: No, only the tax for the current year would be collected, because [the poll tax] is by no means a debt the payment of which is obligatory for him.

This is Abū Ḥanīfa's opinion; but Abū Yūsuf and Muḥammad [b. al-Ḥasan] held that he would be liable to pay for all past years, unless his failure to pay was due to sickness or some other [justifying] excuse.[20]

510. I asked: If a piece of land is cultivated with wheat or some other crop twice or three times a year, do you think that the owner would be under obligation to pay the kharāj on all [crops]?

511. He replied: [No], the owner is under obligation to pay only one kharāj consisting of 1 dirham and 1 qafīz [on each jarīb].[21]

512. I asked: [If] a piece of land is planted with many trees, do you think that its kharāj should be levied on the basis of its productive capacity?

513. He replied: Yes.[22]

514. I asked: If a man at the beginning of the year cultivates wheat or some other crops, do you think that he would be under obligation to pay the kharāj on the whole crop?

[18] "They should not be beaten," says Abū Yūsuf, "if they fail to pay the jizya, nor should they be required to stay under the sun . . . but they should be imprisoned until they pay it" (Abū Yūsuf, *Kitāb al-Kharāj*, p. 123).

[19] Not in Arabic MSS. See Sarakhsī, *Mabsūṭ*, Vol. X, p. 82.

[20] Ṭabarī, *Kitāb Ikhtilāf*, p. 232; Sarakhsī, *Mabsūṭ*, Vol. X, p. 82.

[21] Ṭabarī, *Kitāb Ikhtilāf*, p. 223; Sarakhsī, *Mabsūṭ*, Vol. X, p. 82.

[22] Abū Yūsuf, *Kitāb al-Kharāj*, pp. 84-85.

515. He replied: No, he pays only one kharāj consisting of 1 dirham and 1 qafīz on every jarīb of land.

516. I asked: If the crop on a piece of land is completely destroyed by flood or is hit by a blight, do you think that the owner would be under obligation to pay the kharāj on the land?

517. He replied: No, because of the damage that has befallen it.[23]

518. I asked: If [the owner] neglected his land and did not cultivate it?

519. He replied: He still would have to pay the kharāj on it.[24]

520. I asked: Why is there a difference between the two cases?

521. He replied: If he cultivated the land and the crop was struck with a blight he would have an excuse [for not paying], but if the land lay idle and he failed to cultivate it, he would have to pay the kharāj on it, because this would be his own doing. Thus the two [situations] are different.

522. I asked: If a Dhimmī who possesses kharāj land becomes a Muslim, do you think that he would have to pay the kharāj as before?

523. He replied: Yes.[25]

524. I asked: If a Muslim purchased land from an unbeliever, would he be under obligation to continue to pay the kharāj on it?

525. He replied: Yes.[26]

526. I asked: Is it not objectionable that a Muslim should pay the kharāj on the land?

527. He replied: No, because it has been related to us that 'Abd-Allāh b. Mas'ūd and Shurayḥ [b. al-Ḥārith] and others have owned in the Sawād [of southern 'Irāq] lands, the kharāj

[23] Ṭabarī, *Kitāb Ikhtilāf*, pp. 225-26; Sarakhsī, *Mabsūṭ*, Vol. X, p. 83.
[24] *Ibid.*
[25] Ṭabarī, *Kitāb Ikhtilāf*, p. 226; Sarakhsī, *Mabsūṭ*, Vol. X, p. 83.
[26] Abū Yūsuf, *Kitāb al-Kharāj*, pp. 59-60; Ṭabarī, *Kitāb Ikhtilāf*, p. 224; Sarakhsī, *Mabsūṭ*, Vol. X, p. 83.

of which was recorded in the state registry. The same has been reported to us concerning al-Ḥasan b. 'Alī b. Abī Ṭālib.[27]

528. I asked: Would this not be regarded as a humiliation [to the believer]?

529. He replied: No, the humiliation is [the payment of] the poll tax.[28]

530. I asked: Would it not be objectionable to you if a Muslim purchases [kharāj] land from a Dhimmī?

531. He replied: No, that is permissible.

532. I asked: If a group [of scripturaries] made a peace agreement [with the Muslims] on the basis of their becoming Dhimmīs, but later one or all of them accepted Islam, would you not cancel the kharāj from the land and make it 'ushr land (tithe land)? [29]

533. He replied: No, because [the Dhimmī] who owned the land became a Muslim after the land had become a kharāj land.

534. I asked: If a Dhimmī purchased a piece of land which was 'ushr land,[30] do you think that it would become subject to the kharāj?

535. He replied: Yes.[31]

[27] Abū Yūsuf, *Kitāb al-Kharāj*, p. 62; Sarakhsī, *Mabsūṭ*, Vol. X, p. 83.

[28] The idea that payment of the jizya (poll tax) by the unbeliever implies humiliation is based on the Quranic injunction: "Fight against those to whom the Scriptures have been given . . . until they pay the jizya out of hand, and they may be humbled" (Q. IV, 29). See Sarakhsī, *Mabsūṭ*, Vol. X, pp. 77-78, 82, 83. Humiliation, however, was not implied in early Muslim compacts with the Dhimmīs. See my *War and Peace in the Law of Islam*, Chapter XVII; C. D. Dennett, *Conversion and the Poll Tax in Early Islam* (Cambridge, Mass., 1950).

[29] 'Ushr land is land the original owners of which became Muslims, such as that in the Arabian Peninsula, or it may be land occupied by Muslims and distributed among the warriors. The tax imposed on such land was 'ushr, i.e., tithe. See A. W. Poliak, "Classification of Lands in Islamic Law and its Technical Terms," *American Journal of Semitic Languages and Literatures*, Vol. LVII (1940), pp. 50-62; Løkkegaard, *Islamic Taxation in the Classic Period* (Copenhagen, 1950), Chap. III.

[30] 'Ātif MS.

[31] Ṭabarī, *Kitāb Ikhtilāf*, p. 227; Sarakhsī, *Mabsūṭ*, Vol. X, p. 84.

536. I asked: Why, since it was not originally subject to the kharāj?

537. He replied: It would have the same status as residential land transformed into an orchard, thereby becoming subject to the kharāj, whereas no kharāj was paid for it before.

This is the opinion of Abū Ḥanīfa. However, Abū Yūsuf held that the ʿushr tax should be doubled and regarded as a [category of] kharāj. Muḥammad [b. al-Ḥasan] held that the ʿushr should be retained as before and [the land] would be regarded as [in the category of] the zakāt land,[32] because the ʿushr is imposed on land, not on persons. Do you not think that the land of the minor and the mukātab is subject to the ʿushr and [also] the land of the Christians of [the tribe of] Banū Taghlib and that the [principle of] shufʿa (*jus retractum*) is applicable to it?[33]

538. I asked: If a Christian from the [tribe of] Banū Taghlib purchased some kharāj land, do you think that it would be subject to the kharāj?

539. He replied: Yes.[34]

540. I asked: If he purchased some ʿushr land, would it become subject to the kharāj?

541. He replied: No, but the ʿushr would be doubled just as the tax would be doubled on their [i. e., the Taghlibīs] property.[35]

542. I asked: If a Christian woman from [the tribe of] the Banū Taghlib purchased some ʿushr or kharāj land? 144

543. He replied: She would have to pay the kharāj for the kharāj land, but if she purchases ʿushr land, she would have to double the ʿushr. She would have the same status as a man [in this respect].

[32] Zakāt and ṣadaqa are often used interchangeably to mean the tax to be paid by Muslims. See Māwardī, *Kitāb al-Aḥkām*, pp. 208-9.

[33] Abū Yūsuf, *Kitāb al-Kharāj*, p. 69; Ṭabarī, *Kitāb Ikhtilāf*, pp. 226, 227.

[34] Ṭabarī, *Kitāb Ikhtilāf*, p. 227.

[35] Abū Yūsuf, *Kitāb al-Kharāj*, p. 121; Ṭabarī, *Kitāb Ikhtilāf*, p. 228.

544. I asked: Would the same [ruling] apply to a boy if his father or guardian purchased land for him?

545. He replied: Yes.[36]

Muḥammad [b. al-Ḥasan] held that if a land is 'ushr land, it remains so permanently and is unaffected by the ownership of whomever may purchase it. If the land is kharāj land, it also remains permanently as kharāj land. If [the status of] 'ushr land were to be changed on the basis of the ownership of the purchaser, it would change if the land of a mukātab, a Muslim minor, or an insane person were purchased by a Dhimmī or a Taghlibī. Do you think that if land in the sanctuary of Makka were purchased by a Dhimmī or a Christian Taghlibī, [its status] would be changed from that of zakāt and 'ushr land? This cannot happen; it retains its former status as 'ushr land.[37]

546. I asked: If a freed slave of the Banū Taghlib, freed by that [tribe], purchased some kharāj or 'ushr land, what [kind of tax] would he have to pay?

547. He replied: Their freed slave would pay the kharāj, regardless of whether it were 'ushr or kharāj land. The Christian freed slave of the Banū Taghlib should not be in a better position than a Christian freed by a Muslim. If the latter purchases 'ushr or kharāj land he must pay the kharāj; he would have to pay the kharāj on either one of them. On 'ushr land he would not have to pay the zakāt, but the kharāj, according to Abū Ḥanīfa. But Abū Yūsuf held that he would have to pay double the 'ushr.[38]

548. I asked: If a Dhimmī of the Banū Taghlib purchased some 'ushr land and a Muslim pre-empted it [from him], would the Muslim have to pay the kharāj or the 'ushr?

549. He replied: The Muslim would have to pay the 'ushr because he had taken the land by pre-emption (shuf'a or *jus retractum*).

550. I asked: Similarly, if the Dhimmī had bought the land

[36] Ṭabarī, *Kitāb Ikhtilāf*, p. 228.
[37] *Ibid.*, p. 227.
[38] Abū Yūsuf, *Kitāb al-Kharāj*, p. 121.

[from the Muslim] by means of a vicious transaction and then returned the land to him, would the Muslim have to pay the 'ushr as before and not the kharāj?

551. He replied: Yes.

552. I asked: If some of the inhabitants of the territory of war became Muslims in their home and their territory [became part of the dār al-Islām], would the kharāj be imposed upon them?

553. He replied: No. Rather, I should impose the 'ushr on their land.[39]

554. I asked: If a Muslim purchased some of their land?

555. He replied: It would be subject to the 'ushr as before.

556. I asked: If a Taghlibī purchased it?

557. He replied: He would have to pay double the 'ushr.

558. I asked: If the Taghlibī sold it to a Muslim or became a Muslim while he owned the land?

559. He replied: It would be subject to double the 'ushr, because when the Christian of the Banū Taghlib bought it, its status changed from the original one of 'ushr land to that of double-'ushr land. Thus it became like kharāj land. Do you not agree that I should take [the same tax] from land belonging to a minor? This is the opinion of Abū Ḥanīfa based on analogical deduction.[40]

560. I asked: If a man acquires on rent some kharāj land and cultivates it, or cultivates it on the basis of a joint-cultivation arrangement, who would have to pay the kharāj?

561. He replied: The owner of the land who rented the land to the cultivator.[41]

562. I asked: Would the same be true if the owner let the cultivator cultivate the land without paying rent?

563. He replied: Yes.

564. I asked: If the kharāj land belonged to a slave or a mukātab, should we impose the kharāj on it?

[39] Ṭabarī, *Kitāb Ikhtilāf*, pp. 228-29.
[40] *Ibid.*, p. 226.
[41] *Ibid.*

565. He replied: Yes.[42]

566. I asked: If [an unbeliever] enters the dār al-Islām to trade under an amān (safe-conduct), would he be subject to the poll tax?

567. He replied: No.[43]

568. I asked: Why?

569. He replied: Because he was given an amān to trade, not to become a Dhimmī.

570. I asked: If he came to us with an amān to trade, but married a [Dhimmī] woman whom he divorced and then desired to return [to the territory of war], should we refuse to let him go?

571. He replied: No.[44]

572. I asked: If he prolonged his stay and settled down?

573. He replied: If he did so, I should impose the poll tax (al-kharāj) on him.[45]

574. I asked: If he did not stay long, but purchased some land which he cultivated, should we collect the land kharāj from him?

575. He replied: Yes, I should collect from him the land tax and the poll tax, because if he stays in the territory of Islam and cultivates the land, he has settled down there [as a permanent] resident.[46]

576. I asked: If a woman came to us from the territory of war under an amān for trade and married, and later she desired to return [to the territory of war] but her husband refused and wanted to detain her?

577. He replied: She could not leave if she were married, since she had settled down and had become a Dhimmī, for a woman in this situation is not like a man. Do you not think that the woman may not leave [her home] except with

[42] *Ibid.*, p. 228.

[43] Sarakhsī, *Mabsūṭ*, Vol. X, p. 84.

[44] *Ibid.*

[45] The term "kharāj" is used as equivalent to jizya. Abū Yūsuf, *Kitāb al-Kharāj*, p. 189; Sarakhsī, *Mabsūṭ*, Vol. X, p. 84.

[46] Sarakhsī, *Mabsūṭ*, Vol. X, p. 84.

her husband's permission, and that unlike her, he does not have to consult and take permission of his spouse if he wants to leave?

Abū Yūsuf held that if a Dhimmī purchases 'ushr land, the 'ushr on it is doubled.[47]

Peace Treaties with Rulers [of the Unbelievers]

578. I asked: If one of the rulers of the inhabitants of the territory of war owns extensive lands upon which are living some of the people of his realm who are his slaves and whom he sells and deals with as he sees fit, would they [indeed] be the slaves of his?

579. He replied: Yes.[48]

580. I asked: If these [slaves] were captured by some enemy, and later recaptured by the Muslims, from whom [the original owner] obtained them on payment of ransom, would [the slaves] be returned to the previous ownership?

581. He replied: Yes.[49]

582. I asked: If the ruler found that [the slaves] had been divided up [among the Muslims], would he be entitled to take them back by paying their value?

583. He replied: Yes.[50]

584. I asked: If that ruler became a Muslim or he and his people became Dhimmīs, would his people remain his slaves in that case also?

585. He replied: Yes.[51]

586. I asked: If he did not become a Muslim nor was given the benefit of a peace treaty, nor did he become a Dhimmī, but he proposed to the Muslims [a peace treaty] on condition that he be a protected person and pay the Muslims

[47] Ṭabarī, *Kitāb Ikhtilāf*, p. 227.

[48] Sarakhsī, *Kitāb Sharḥ al-Siyar al-Kabīr* (Hyderabad), Vol. IV, p. 115, and *Mabsūṭ*, Vol. X, p. 84.

[49] Sarakhsī, *Mabsūṭ*, Vol. X, p. 85.

[50] *Ibid.*

[51] *Ibid.*

a tribute (kharāj), on condition that he be allowed to exercise over the people of his realm such powers as he wished, such as those of beheading or crucifying, or the like, which are not proper that he should exercise in the territory of Islam, [would such an agreement be made]?

587. He replied: It would not be right for the Muslims to make any peace agreement with him on such conditions.[52]

588. I asked: If [the Muslims] did so and entered into such an agreement with him on such terms and he became a protected person of theirs, [what would be the ruling]?

589. He replied: [The Muslims] would look into those terms of the agreements that were illegal and improper; they would abrogate them and would observe those of the terms that were proper. If the ruler accepted, [well and good]; if not, he and his followers would be allowed to return to their place of safety.[53]

590. I asked: If after having entered into an agreement 145
and having become a protected person of theirs, [the ruler] began to inform the unbelievers of the weak spots in the Muslim defenses, or provide them with guides and give refuge to their spies, would these acts constitute a violation of his pact?

591. He replied: No, but the Muslims should punish him for so doing and throw him into prison.[54]

592. I asked: If he or [one of] the people of his land continued to kill Muslims by surprise attack, would this act constitute a violation of his pact?

593. He replied: No, but [the Muslims] would investigate which one of them committed it; if evidence is established against him, they would behead him in retaliation. But if no evidence were adduced, there could be no case against him.

594. I asked: If they did not know precisely who the murderer [of the Muslim] was, but found him murdered in one of the [ruler's] villages?

[52] Sarakhsī, *Kitāb Sharḥ al-Siyar al-Kabīr* (Hyderabad), Vol. IV, p. 239.
[53] *Ibid.*, pp. 85-86.
[54] *Ibid.*, p. 86; Ṭabarī, *Kitāb Ikhtilāf*, pp. 24-25.

595. He replied: He [the ruler] would be held responsible for the diya (blood-money) after having sworn by God fifty times that neither he, himself, killed him, nor did he know the killer. Thereafter, he would have to pay the diya.

596. I asked: Why would the people of his village not have to swear with him?

597. He replied: Because they are his slaves and slaves neither have to take oaths of innocence nor pay the diya.

598. I asked: If the inhabitants of the village were freedmen?

599. He replied: Then they would have to take the oaths of innocence and pay the diya.

600. I asked: Then they would have the same status as the ruler?

601. He replied: Yes. But God knows best.[55]

Peace Treaties with the Inhabitants of the Territory of War

602. I asked: If some of the inhabitants of the territory of war asked the Muslims to make peace with them for a specified number of years without paying tribute (jizya), do you think that the Muslims should grant the request?

603. He replied: Yes, provided the Imām has considered the situation and has found that the inhabitants of the territory of war are too strong for the Muslims to prevail against them and it would be better for the Muslims to make peace with them.[56]

604. I asked: If [the Imām] made peace with them and found upon reconsideration it was disadvantageous for the Muslims since it was made without any tribute being paid to him, can he give them notice, abrogate the peace agreement, and attack them?

[55] Sarakhsī, *Kitāb Sharḥ al-Siyar al-Kabīr* (Hyderabad), Vol. IV, p. 226, and *Mabsūṭ*, Vol. X, p. 86.

[56] Sarakhsī, *Mabsūṭ*, Vol. X, p. 86.

605. He replied: Yes.[57]

606. I asked: If the Muslims were in a city besieged by the enemy and the enemy asked them to enter into a peace agreement for a period of years whereby they would pay the enemy a fixed annual tribute, do you think that it would be lawful for the Muslims to enter into such an agreement and pay the tribute to the unbelievers, if they were afraid of destruction and realized that an agreement would be better for them?

607. He replied: Yes, that would be permissible in such circumstances.[58]

608. I asked: If some of the inhabitants of the territory of war wished the Muslims to enter into a peace agreement with them for a specified number of years on condition that they would pay a fixed annual tribute to the Muslims, provided that the Muslims abstain from entering their territory or enforce their jurisdiction on them, do you think that the Muslims should make a peace agreement with them on such terms?

609. He replied: No, unless it were better for the Muslims to do so.[59]

610. I asked: And if it were better for the Muslims to do so?

611. [He replied: It would be permissible.] [60]

612. I asked: If it were better for the Muslims to do so and there was signed an agreement that provided that 100 heads [of slaves] were to be delivered annually, do you think that it would be proper for the Muslims to make peace on such terms?

613. He replied: If the 100 heads were taken from among the inhabitants [of the territory of war] or their children, a peace on such terms would not be advantageous and it would

[57] *Ibid.*

[58] Ṭabarī, *Kitāb Ikhtilāf*, p. 17; Sarakhsī, *Mabsūṭ*, Vol. X, p. 86.

[59] Ṭabarī, *Kitāb Ikhtilāf*, p. 17; Sarakhsī, *Kitāb Sharḥ al-Siyar al-Kabīr* (Hyderabad), Vol. IV, p. 2, and *Mabsūṭ*, Vol. X, p. 86.

[60] Not in Arabic MSS.

be incumbent on Muslims not to slay any of them or their offspring since they had given them a pledge of security. Do you not think that if one of the inhabitants of the territory of war sold his son or his father to a Muslim, the sale would not be valid? For the peace treaty applies to these [persons], and their children enjoy the same status as themselves.[61]

614. I asked: If an agreement were made with them whereby 100 predetermined persons would be delivered to the Muslims in the first year [of the coming of the agreement into force], and if they asked in return for a peace agreement for a year, and offered to deliver those predetermined persons and [added]: "We continue the peace agreement for another term of three years on condition that we shall deliver every year 100 heads from among our slaves."

615. He replied: It would be permissible.[62]

616. I asked: If after the agreement were made a Muslim stole a slave girl or some goods from them, do you think that it would be proper [for a Muslim] to purchase [from him] the slave girl or the goods?

617. He replied: No.[63]

618. I asked: If [some other] inhabitants of the territory of war attacked them and captured some of them and enslaved them, do you think that it would be proper [for the Muslims] to purchase from them those slaves?

619. He replied: Yes, because they were not captured by the Muslims, but by [other] inhabitants of the territory of war.

620. I asked: Should [Muslim] merchants be prevented from exporting anything to them?

621. He replied: No, nothing should be prohibited except the kurāʿ (ungulate animals), weapons, iron, and the like.

622. I asked: Why should the kurāʿ be prohibited [from exportation]?

623. He replied: Because the inhabitants of the territory

[61] Ṭabarī, *Kitāb Ikhtilāf*, pp. 17, 19; Sarakhsī, *Mabsūṭ*, Vol. X, p. 87.
[62] Ṭabarī, *Kitāb Ikhtilāf*, p. 20.
[63] *Ibid.*

of war in question are not Dhimmīs, but people having [only] a peace agreement [with the Muslims].

624. I asked: If one of them entered the territory of Islam as a merchant without an amān, except the peace agreement they had made [with the Muslims, what would be the ruling]?

625. He replied: He would enjoy an amān by virtue of that agreement.

626. I asked: Should a one-fifth [share] be taken from the tribute paid by them under the peace agreement?

627. He replied: No. This is tribute (kharāj) and tribute is not subject to the one-fifth [share].[64]

[64] Sarakhsī, *Kitāb Sharḥ al-Siyar al-Kabīr* (Hyderabad), Vol. IV, pp. 12, 24, and *Mabsūṭ*, Vol. X, pp. 87-88.

Chapter VI

Folio 141

[ON AMĀN (SAFE-CONDUCT)][1]

The Granting of the Amān by a Muslim to the Inhabitants of the Territory of War

628. I asked: If a [Muslim] merchant or a [Muslim] captive in the territory of war grants an amān [to an enemy], do you think that [the granting of] such an amān would be valid?

629. He replied: No.

630. I asked: Why?

631. He replied: Because they are living undefended in the territory of war.[2]

632. I asked: Similarly, if a man from the territory of war becomes a Muslim and grants an amān to an enemy, would his amān be null and void?

633. He replied: Yes.

634. I asked: If a Muslim army besieged a city whose inhabitants were well defended and one of the Muslim [warriors] granted an amān to the inhabitants of that city, do you think that his amān would be valid?

[1] Persons who belong to the dār al-ḥarb are individually and collectively in a state of war with Muslims. If anyone of them encounters a Muslim, he is liable to be killed; but he might enter the dār al-Islām without molestation if he obtains a special permission called the amān (safe-conduct), which permits him, along with his family and property, to travel or reside in the dār al-Islām for a limited period. See Khadduri, *War and Peace in the Law of Islam*, Chapter 15; Julius Hatschek, *Der Musta'min* (Berlin, 1920); and Schacht, "Amān," *Encyclopaedia of Islam* (2nd ed.), Vol. I, pp. 429-30.

[2] Abū Yūsuf, *Kitāb al-Kharāj*, p. 204; Ṭabarī, *Kitāb Ikhtilāf*, p. 28; Ṭaḥāwī, *Mukhtaṣar*, p. 292; Sarakhsī, *Sharḥ Kitāb al-Siyar al-Kabīr*, ed. Munajjid, Vol. I, p. 286, and *Mabsūṭ*, Vol. X, p. 69; Kāsānī, *Badā'i' al-Ṣana'i'*, Vol. VII, p. 107.

635. He replied: Yes.[3]

636. I asked: What would be said to the inhabitants of the city?

637. He replied: Islam should [first] be offered to them; if they accept it they are entitled to the same rights and obligations as Muslims. If they refuse they should be asked to pay the jizya; if they agree it should be accepted and they should be left to themselves. If they refuse [to pay the jizya] they should be allowed to return to a place of security and fighting would be resumed.[4]

638. I asked: Would the same hold true if a Muslim woman had granted them the amān?

639. He replied: Yes.[5]

640. I asked: Has any narrative come to your knowledge concerning the granting of the amān by a man or a woman?

641. He replied: Yes. It has been related to us that Zaynab, daughter of the Apostle of God, granted an amān to Abū al-ʿĀṣ b. al-Rabīʿ—her husband—and her amān was carried out by the Apostle. It has also been related to us that [the Prophet] said: " Muslims should support one another against the outsider . . . and the one lowest in status [i. e., the slave] may bind the others, etc. . . ." [6]

642. I asked: If a slave grants an amān, do you think that his amān would be as valid as that granted by a [free] man or woman?

643. He replied: If the slave were fighting along with his master, his amān would be valid; if he were not fighting along with his master, he would [not be regarded as a warrior] but

[3] Ṭabarī, *Kitāb Ikhtilāf*, p. 28; Sarakhsī, *Sharḥ Kitāb al-Siyar al-Kabīr*, ed. Munajjid, Vol. I, pp. 283, 288, 289, 294, 295, and *Mabsūṭ*, Vol. X, p. 69; Kāsānī, *Badāʾiʿ al-Ṣanāʾiʿ*, Vol. VII, p. 107.

[4] Abū Yūsuf, *Kitāb al-Kharāj*, p. 202; Ṭabarī, *Kitāb Ikhtilāf*, p. 28.

[5] Ṭabarī, *Kitāb Ikhtilāf*, pp. 29-30; Sarakhsī, *Sharḥ Kitāb al-Siyar al-Kabīr*, ed. Munajjid, Vol. I, p. 253, and *Mabsūṭ*, Vol. X, p. 69; Kāsānī, *Badāʾiʿ al-Ṣanāʾiʿ*, Vol. VII, p. 106.

[6] Sarakhsī, *Sharḥ Kitāb al-Siyar al-Kabīr*, ed. Munajjid, Vol. I, pp. 252, 253-54, and *Mabsūṭ*, Vol. X, pp. 69-70. See paragraph 50, above.

merely as a servant serving his master and his amān would be void.[7]

However, Muḥammad b. al-Ḥasan held that the slave's amān would be valid in both cases.[8]

644. I asked: If the Dhimmīs who take part in the fighting in support of Muslims [grant an amān], do you think that their amān would be valid?

645. He replied: No, their amān should be null and void.[9]

646. I asked: Has there come to your knowledge any narrative concerning the granting of the amān by a slave?

647. He replied: Yes, it has been related to us that a slave once shot an arrow carrying an amān to some people who were besieged and the [Caliph] 'Umar [b. al-Khaṭṭāb] carried out his amān.[10]

The Musta'min from the Territory of War [Enters the Territory of Islam] [11] 145

648. I asked: If a musta'min from among the inhabitants of the territory of war enters the territory of Islam under an amān to trade and purchases a Muslim slave and thereafter returns with the slave to the territory of war, what would the status of the slave be?

[7] Abū Yūsuf, *Kitāb al-Radd*, p. 68; Sarakhsī, *Sharḥ Kitāb al-Siyar al-Kabīr*, ed. Munajjid, Vol. I, p. 255. Awzā'ī and Shāfi'ī held that the amān granted by a slave is valid regardless whether he was fighting or not. Shāfi'ī, *Umm*, Vol. VII, p. 319.

[8] Abū Yūsuf, *Kitāb al-Kharāj*, p. 205, and *Kitāb al-Radd*, p. 68; Kāsānī, *Badā'i' al-Ṣanā'i'*, Vol. VII, p. 106.

[9] Abū Yūsuf, *Kitāb al-Kharāj*, p. 204; Ṭabarī, *Kitāb Ikhtilāf*, p. 30; Sarakhsī, *Sharḥ Kitāb al-Siyar al-Kabīr*, ed. Munajjid, Vol. I, p. 257, and *Mabsūṭ*, Vol. X, p. 70. Other schools agree with the Ḥanafīs on this point. See Shāfi'ī, *Umm*, Vol. IV, p. 196.

[10] Abū Yūsuf, *Kitāb al-Radd*, pp. 68-69; Sarakhsī, *Sharḥ Kitāb al-Siyar al-Kabīr*, ed. Munajjid, Vol. I, p. 256, and *Mabsūṭ*, Vol. X, pp. 70-71.

[11] The musta'min is the person who enjoys the privilege of amān, whether he is a Muslim in the dār al-ḥarb or a non-Muslim in the dār al-Islām. See note 1, above.

649. He replied: He would be free from the moment [his master] entered with him into the territory of war.[12]

650. I asked: Why?

651. He replied: Because [the slave] is a Muslim purchased in the territory of Islam. Do you not think that if the slave killed his master, took his property, and returned to the territory of Islam, everything that he had taken from his master, whether property or slaves, would be regarded as belonging to him and he would be a freedman and nothing would be held against him.[13]

652. I asked: Would it be lawful for this slave to kill his master?

653. He replied: Yes.

654. I asked: Would you not think that the sale contract [by virtue of which the unbeliever owned the Muslim slave] created a [state of] security (amān) between them?

655. He replied: No. This is Abū Ḥanīfa's opinion. However, Abū Yūsuf and Muḥammad [b. al-Ḥasan] held that the slave would not become free [immediately after his entry into the territory of war] until the Muslims had taken him back by capture or he had returned to the territory of Islam against his master's will. Only in one of these two ways would the slave become free.[14]

656. I asked: If a slave who had accompanied his master to the territory of war became a Muslim and thereafter the slave was either purchased from his master by a Muslim or was captured by some Muslims in a raid [on the territory of war], do you think that he would remain in a state of slavery and become fay', subject to division [as spoil]?

[12] Shaybānī, *al-Jāmi' al-Ṣaghīr*, p. 89; Sarakhsī, *Mabsūṭ*, Vol. X, pp. 89-90.

[13] This is based on Abū Ḥanīfa's doctrine that Muslim rulings are not binding on Muslims in the dār al-ḥarb, nor are decisions made in the dār al-ḥarb binding on persons when they enter the dār al-Islām. See Ṭabarī, *Kitāb Ikhtilāf*, pp. 62-63. Awzā'ī and Shāfi'ī held that Muslim rulings are binding wherever the believer happens to be. See Shāfi'ī, *Umm*, Vol. IV, pp. 162-63; Ṭabarī, *Kitāb Ikhtilāf*, p. 61.

[14] Shaybānī, *al-Jāmi' al-Ṣaghīr*, p. 89; Ṭaḥāwī, *Mukhtaṣar*, p. 291; Sarakhsī, *Mabsūṭ*, Vol. X, p. 90.

657. He replied: No. I hold that, if his case were as you 146
stated, he would be free and nothing would be held against him.[15]

658. I asked: Would the same hold true if a slave from the territory of war became a Muslim while in the possession of his master but then was captured by the Muslims?

659. He replied: He would be free and not regarded as fay'.[16]

660. I asked: If the master became a Muslim before the Muslims captured the slave, what would [the status of] the slave be?

661. He replied: He would remain a slave belonging to his master, and would not become free.[17]

662. I asked: Why?

663. He replied: Because the slave neither came to the dār al-Islām nor did he fall into Muslim hands before his master became a Muslim.

However, Abū Yūsuf and Muḥammad [b. al-Ḥasan] held that if the inhabitants of the territory of war became Muslims and then [the master] sold [his slave] to a Muslim, the slave would remain a slave and would not become free; if the slave were not sold but were captured by Muslims, he would become free.

If a man from the dār al-ḥarb entered the dār al-Islām without an amān and were captured by a man [from the dār al-Islām], he would become a slave of that man, subject to the one-fifth [rule]; but if he had become a Muslim before being captured, he would be free and nothing would be held against him. This is the opinion of Abū Yūsuf and Muḥammad [b. al-Ḥasan]. Abū Ḥanīfa, however, held that if [the man from the dār al-ḥarb] were captured by a Muslim, he would be a fay' for the community [of Muslims], and that

[15] Ṭabarī, *Kitāb Ikhtilāf*, p. 47; Shāfi'ī, *Umm*, Vol. IV, p. 188; Sarakhsī, *Mabsūṭ*, Vol. X, p. 90.

[16] Shaybānī, *al-Jāmi' al-Ṣaghīr*, p. 89; Sarakhsī, *Mabsūṭ*, Vol. X, p. 90.

[17] Ṭabarī, *Kitāb Ikhtilāf*, p. 49; Sarakhsī, *Mabsūṭ*, Vol. X, p. 90.

even if he became a Muslim and were captured thereafter he would belong to the community and not to any single man.

According to Abū Yūsuf and Muḥammad [b. al-Ḥasan], if [the slave] entered the sanctuary [of Makka] before he was captured, he would not be molested or liable to capture, but he should not be given food or water nor be subject to sale. If he left [the sanctuary] and were captured by a man, he would become the slave of that man. Likewise, if a man captured him in the sanctuary and took him out of its precincts, he would become the slave of that man, but this would be an evil act [on the part of the Muslim]. According to Abū Ḥanīfa's analogical deduction, the slave's status does not change; he should not be given food, water, or asylum; but if he leaves [the sanctuary] and is seized he becomes fay' for the community of Muslims.[18]

664. I asked: If a man from among the inhabitants of the territory of war entered the dār al-Islām under an amān and he either purchased a Muslim slave or the slave that may have accompanied him [to the dār al-Islām] became a Muslim, do you think that the man would be permitted to return to the dār al-ḥarb with his slave [in either case]?

665. He replied: No.[19]

666. I asked: What should the ruling be concerning the man and the two [Muslim slaves]?

667. He replied: He should be compelled to sell the slaves [in either case] and not be permitted to take them out.[20]

668. I asked: If the ḥarbī (enemy person) becomes a Muslim in the dār al-Islām while in possession of the two slaves?

669. He replied: They retain their status [as slaves].[21]

[18] Shaybānī, *al-Jāmi' al-Ṣaghīr*, p. 91; Ṭabarī, *Kitāb Ikhtilāf*, pp. 49-50; Sarakhsī, *Mabsūṭ*, Vol. X, pp. 93-94.

[19] Cf. paragraph 648, above. See Ṭabarī, *Kitāb Ikhtilāf*, p. 47; Sarakhsī, *Mabsūṭ*, Vol. X, p. 94.

[20] Ṭabarī, *Kitāb Ikhtilāf*, p. 47.

[21] Other schools of law agree with the Ḥanafī school on this point. See Ṭabarī, *Kitāb Ikhtilāf*, p. 48.

670. I asked: What would you think if [the ḥarbī] becomes a Dhimmī rather than a Muslim?

671. He replied: He should be compelled to sell those [Muslim slaves] and should not be permitted to return with them to the dār al-ḥarb.[22]

672. I asked: If a slave left the dār al-ḥarb with his master [for the dār al-Islām] without becoming a Muslim, but the master set him free after he had brought him [to the dār al-Islām, but later revoked the manumission] and the slave brought action against his master, do you think that the slave would be set free?

673. He replied: Yes.[23]

674. I asked: If the slave's master set him free in the dār al-ḥarb [and then revoked the manumission], would the slave thereby be [lawfully] free?

675. He replied: No.

676. I asked: Why?

677. He replied: Because [his master's] manumission in the dār al-ḥarb is of no consequence.[24]

678. I asked: [Do you hold, then, that] if the master sets [the slave] free after entering the dār al-Islām [and later revokes the manumission], his manumission is valid and [the slave] is free, but that if he sets him free in the dār al-ḥarb [and later revokes the manumission], his manumission is not valid and not worthy of consideration?

679. He replied: Yes.

680. I asked: Why is his manumission in the dār al-ḥarb not valid?

681. He replied: Because his manumission in the dār al-ḥarb is of no consequence. Do you not think that if a man [from the dār al-ḥarb] captured another and held him by force, he could sell that man and the Muslims could purchase him if he had brought that [enslaved person] to them by force

[22] Ṭabarī, *Kitāb Ikhtilāf*, pp. 47-48; Sarakhsī, *Mabsūṭ*, Vol. X, pp. 94-95.
[23] Sarakhsī, *Mabsūṭ*, Vol. X, p. 95.
[24] *Ibid.*

while he was in his captor's possession, even though he was originally a free man like his captor? [25]

682. I asked: What would you think if a ḥarbī entered [the dār al-Islām] with slave girls from among the people of the dār al-ḥarb, some of which were in the status of mudabbaras in the dār al-ḥarb and others umm walads [and later revoked their status as mudabbaras and umm walads]?

683. He replied: He would be entitled to sell his mudabbaras, but not the umm walads.

684. I asked: Why would the status of mudabbaras be different from that of the umm walads?

685. He replied: Because the umm walad has the same status as that of her child, and [the ḥarbī] has no right to sell his child, nor should the Muslim ever purchase [the child] of a man to whom they have given a safe-conduct. The child enjoys the same status as his father. As to the mudabbara, she would be regarded as a slave woman and [her master's] mudabbara arrangement with her in the dār al-ḥarb would be invalid. Therefore, he has the right to sell her if he so wishes. But God knows best! [26]

Property Left behind by the Musta'min Who Returns to the Dār al-Ḥarb or Dies in the Dār al-Islām

686. I asked: What would you think if a musta'min returned to the dār al-ḥarb, having left in the dār al-Islām money lent out to [Muslims], or slaves, property, and the like which he had deposited [with somebody]? And suppose that he had granted to some of the slaves the status of mudabbar in the dār al-ḥarb while to others had granted it in the dār al-Islām. Now suppose that the ḥarbī [i. e., the musta'min who returned to the dār al-ḥarb] was killed and the Muslims took possession of the territory [of war] to which he had

[25] See note 13, above, and Sarakhsī, *Kitāb Sharḥ al-Siyar al-Kabīr* (Hyderabad), Vol. IV, pp. 33, 39-40.
[26] Ṭabarī, *Kitāb Ikhtilāf*, p. 58.

returned. What would be the ruling concerning the disposal of his property, i. e., his slaves, his goods, his loan, and whatever else he had on deposit in the dār al-Islām?

687. He replied: As to the money given on loan by him, it would be waived; the debtors would not be obliged to repay any of it. However, [all] the property on deposit would become fay' for the Muslim [community], save the slaves with whom he had entered into a mudabbar relationship in the dār al-Islām; they would become free—nothing would be held against them—because he set them free in a place where Muslim jurisdiction was operative on him and on them.[27]

688. I asked: Why have you canceled [the debt owing him] and did not declare it fay'?

689. He replied: The said loan cannot be regarded as fay' because it was no longer in the possession [of the debtor], but consumed.

690. I asked: If the owner of the deposited property were taken as a prisoner of war rather than killed, what would be the status of his slaves, deposits, the loan, the property, and mudabbaras?

691. He replied: If the Muslims took possession of the territory [of war] the ruling would be the same, whether the owner was killed or taken as a prisoner of war.

692. I asked: What would you think if a ḥarbī entered the dār al-Islām under an amān and purchased some Muslim and some Dhimmī slaves whom he left behind in the dār al-Islām and returned to the dār al-ḥarb, but thereafter he was taken a prisoner of war [by the Muslims]. Would the slaves become fay'?

693. He replied: Yes.[28]

694. I asked: If he left umm walads in the dār al-Islām, what would be their status?

695. He replied: All of them would be free and nothing would be held against them.[29]

[27] Shaybānī, *al-Jāmi' al-Ṣaghīr*, p. 91; Ṭabarī, *Kitāb Ikhtilāf*, pp. 49-50.
[28] Ṭabarī, *Kitāb Ikhtilāf*, p. 52. [29] *Ibid.*

696. I asked: If the musta'min died in the dār al-Islām, leaving property there, while his heirs were in the dār al-ḥarb, what should be done with his property?

697. He replied: It should be held in custody until his 147
heirs arrive.[30]

698. I asked: If the heirs arrive [i. e. entered the dār al-Islām] under an amān, should the Imām accept their word or should they be asked to produce evidence to [prove] their claim to the inheritance?

699. He replied: They should be asked to produce evidence.

700. I asked: If the evidence were provided by the Dhimmīs, should their testimony be accepted?

701. He replied: I should say no on the basis of analogy, but on the basis of juristic preference [31] their testimony should be accepted and property that has been left should be handed over to the heirs, if they attest that they do not know of any other heirs of his.

702. I asked: Should a guarantor be required for the property delivered?

703. He replied: Yes.

704. I asked: What would you think if [the heirs] produced a letter from the ruler of the territory from which they came, saying that they were the heirs; should it be accepted from them?

705. He replied: I should not accept it.[32]

706. I asked: If it was written in the letter that witnesses had testified to the ruler that [the bearers of the letter] were the heirs?

707. He replied: I should not accept that either.

708. I asked: If some Muslims had testified both to the truth of the claim [before the enemy ruler] and to the genuineness of the seal [before the Muslim court]?

[30] *Ibid.*, pp. 52-53.
[31] Istiḥsān. See p. 46, above.
[32] Ṭabarī, *Kitāb Ikhtilāf*, pp. 53-54.

709. He replied: Even so, I should not accept it.

710. I asked: If evidence that they were the heirs were produced in the dār al-Islām and the property [of the deceased] were delivered to them, do you think that they would be entitled to collect the debt due to them?

711. He replied: Yes.[33]

What the Musta'min May [Lawfully] Take with Him into the Dār al-Ḥarb

712. I asked: If a musta'min wanted to return from the dār al-Islām to the dār al-ḥarb, do you think that he should be allowed to take with him any kurā',[34] weapons, or slaves that he might have purchased from the Muslims or the unbelievers in the dār al-Islām?

713. He replied: [No.] He should not be allowed to take back anything of this kind, save whatever kurā' and weapons he might have brought with him [from the dār al-ḥarb].[35]

714. I asked: Apart from that, would he be allowed to take back garments?

715. He replied: Yes.[36]

716. I asked: Would he be allowed to take back iron?

717. He replied: No.

718. I asked: Why?

719. He replied: Because weapons are made of iron.

720. I asked: If [the musta'min] brought with him a sword which he sold [in the dār al-Islām] and purchased instead

[33] *Ibid.*, p. 54.

[34] Kurā' is a collective term applied to beasts of burden of the category of ungulate animals such as horses, mules, and donkeys. See Muṭarrazī, *al-Mughrib*, Vol. II, p. 148.

[35] Other schools of law agree with the Ḥanafī school on this point. See Abū Yūsuf, *Kitāb al-Kharāj*, p. 188; Ṭabarī, *Kitāb Ikhtilāf*, p. 51; Sarakhsī, *Kitāb Sharḥ al-Siyar al-Kabīr* (Hyderabad), Vol. III, pp. 177-78, 273-74.

[36] Abū Yūsuf, *Kitāb al-Kharāj*, p. 188; Ṭabarī, *Kitāb Ikhtilāf*, p. 50.

a bow or a lance, do you think that he would be allowed to take these back in lieu of the sword?

721. He replied: No, I would not allow him to take back any weapons in lieu of anything. Do you not think that I should allow him to take back only [the weapons] that he had brought with him?[37]

722. I asked: If [the musta'min] exchanged his sword with another sharper than his, do you think that it would be left to him or should he be allowed to take it back with him?

723. He replied: Yes, if he gave another in exchange for it.

724. I asked: If he wanted to take back with him something other than kurā' and weapons, do you think that he would be allowed to do so?

725. He replied: [Yes], if they were not kurā', weapons, iron, and the like; but any slaves which he might have purchased in the dār al-Islām, he would not be allowed to take back anything of this sort.[38]

726. I asked: If the ḥarbī died in the dār al-Islām, do you think that his heirs would have the same status as his in the matters that I have mentioned to you?

727. He replied: Yes.[39]

728. I asked: Is the same true of the Muslim who wants to go to the dār al-ḥarb for trade, namely, that he should not be allowed to take with him kurā' and weapons?

729. He replied: Yes.[40]

730. I asked: If a man from among the inhabitants of the territory of war sent a slave of his to the dār al-Islām under an amān for trade and the slave obtained an amān for his master but thereafter the slave became a Muslim, what would you think should be done [with him]?

[37] Ṭabarī, *Kitāb Ikhtilāf*, p. 51.

[38] *Ibid.*

[39] Shaybānī, *al-Jāmi' al-Ṣaghīr*, p. 91; Ṭabarī, *Kitāb Ikhtilāf*, p. 52.

[40] Abū Yūsuf goes so far as to advise the Imām to set up guard posts on the frontiers to inspect Muslims crossing to the dār al-ḥarb and prevent them from carrying weapons, slaves, and other contraband into it. See Abū Yūsuf, *Kitāb al-Kharāj*, p. 190.

731. He replied: He should be sold and the price received should go to his master.[41] But God knows best! [42]

Persons from [the Territory of] War Who Are Apprehended in the Dār al-Islām

732. I asked: What would you think if a man from the inhabitants of the territory of war were apprehended in the dār al-Islām and claimed that he was an emissary and produced a letter from his ruler [to prove it]?

733. He replied: If it were established that the letter was from the ruler, the emissary would be entitled to an amān until he delivered his message and returned; if the letter turned out to be not from the ruler, [the emissary] and everything with him would become fay'.[43]

734. I asked: If a man from the inhabitants of the territory of war were seized in the dār al-Islām and claimed that he entered under an amān, do you think that he should be believed?

735. He replied: No. He and whatever was with him would become fay'.[44]

736. I asked: If some of the inhabitants of the territory of war entered [the dār al-Islām] to visit some of their relatives from among the Dhimmīs and the Muslims, having been informed of their arrival, went to the village and were told that they were all Dhimmīs, do you think that any one [of the inhabitants of the village] would be held liable to prosecution?

737. He replied: No, not unless one of the inhabitants of the territory of war were personally to be identified, in which case he would be apprehended.

[41] Ṭabarī, *Kitāb Ikhtilāf*, pp. 44-45.

[42] 'Ātif MS.

[43] Abū Yūsuf, *Kitāb al-Kharāj*, pp. 187-88; Ṭabarī, *Kitāb Ikhtilāf*, p. 33.

[44] Awzā'ī and Shāfi'ī held that they would be regarded as musta'mins. See Abū Yūsuf, *Kitāb al-Radd*, pp. 63-64; Shāfi'ī, *Umm*, Vol. VII, p. 317; Ṭabarī, *Kitāb Ikhtilāf*, p. 43.

Application of Ḥudūd Penalties

738. I asked: If some of the inhabitants of the territory of war entered [the dār al-Islām] under an amān for trade and some of them were indebted to others, do you think that any one of them would be held liable for a debt contracted in the dār al-ḥarb?

739. He replied: No.[45]

740. I asked: Why?

741. He replied: Because they entered [the dār al-Islām] under an amān, and any arrangement that they may have entered into in the dār al-ḥarb is none of our concern.

742. I asked: What would you think if some of them became indebted to others in the dār al-Islām, or became indebted to a Muslim, or a Muslim became indebted to them?

743. He replied: I should hold them liable for everything and I should hold others liable [who were indebted to them].[46]

744. I asked: Would they also be held liable if they became indebted to Muslims or Dhimmīs?

745. He replied: Yes.[47]

746. I asked: If either a Muslim had become indebted to them or they had become indebted to him in the territory of war or he had usurped their property or they had usurped his property, do you think that we should concern ourselves with any such matters?

747. He replied: I hold that we should not concern ourselves with such matters and that we should not pass judgment on them.[48]

748. I asked: Would the same be true of any acts of murder or wounds committed in the dār al-ḥarb?

749. He replied: Yes. All such things would be regarded as null and void. 148

[45] Shaybānī, *al-Jāmi' al-Ṣaghīr*, p. 90; Ṭabarī, *Kitāb Ikhtilāf*, p. 61.
[46] Shaybānī, *al-Jāmi' al-Ṣaghīr*, p. 90.
[47] *Ibid.*
[48] Ṭabarī, *Kitāb Ikhtilāf*, p. 62.

750. I asked: Why?

751. He replied: Because they were committed [in a territory] where Muslim rulings are not applicable to them.[49]

752. I asked: If one [of the musta'mins] commits fornication or theft in the dār al-Islām, do you think that we should apply the ḥudūd penalties to him?

753. He replied: No.

754. I asked: Why?

755. He replied: Because they [the persons from the dār al-ḥarb] had made neither a peace treaty [with us] nor had they become Dhimmīs. Thus, Muslim rulings would not apply to them. However, I should make them responsible for any property they might steal, but I should not impose on them the penalty of amputation [of the hand for theft].[50]

756. I asked: If one of them killed a Muslim or a Dhimmī—intentionally or unintentionally—would his case be judged [by the Muslim qādī]?

757. He replied: Yes.[51]

758. I asked: How do the ḥudūd penalties differ from the latter penalties?

759. He replied: The ḥudūd penalties are prescribed for [the right of] God, whereas the case in question involves the rights of Muslims and Dhimmīs; therefore they should be procured in their favor.

760. I asked: If a Muslim cut off the hand of a musta'min or killed him intentionally, do you think that he would be liable to retaliation (*lex talionis*) for such an intentional offense?

761. He replied: I hold that he would not be liable for punishment under *lex talionis*.[52]

762. I asked: Why [do you hold that] the musta'min

[49] *Ibid.* Awzā'ī and Shāfi'ī held an opposing view on this point. See *ibid.*, pp. 60-61.

[50] Abū Yūsuf, *Kitāb al-Kharāj*, p. 189; Ṭabarī, *Kitāb Ikhtilāf*, p. 56; cf. Awzā'ī and Shāfi'ī in Ṭabarī, *Kitāb Ikhtilāf*, pp. 54-55.

[51] Abū Yūsuf, *Kitāb al-Kharāj*, p. 189; Ṭabarī, *Kitāb Ikhtilāf*, p. 56.

[52] *Ibid.*

should not have the same status as the Dhimmī, since you hold that a Muslim would be liable to retaliation for offenses against a Dhimmī, whether for murder or other matters?

763. He replied: [The musta'min] does not enjoy the status of the Dhimmī because he is an enemy person. Do you think that I apply to him [Muslim] rulings and ḥudūd penalties? So any offense committed against him by a Dhimmī or a Muslim, such as cutting off the hand or killing, whether intentional or accidental, would not be punished under *lex talionis* but would be liable to the diya for [the killing] whether intentional or accidental to the extent of the diya paid for the murder of a free Muslim.[53]

764. I asked: If a Muslim entered into a transaction with a ḥarbī involving usury (riba), wine, or corpses (dead animals), do you think that such a transaction would be rejected as null and void?

765. He replied: Yes, if it took place in the dār al-Islām. If it were in the dār al-ḥarb, it should not be regarded as null and void, according to the opinions of Abū Ḥanīfa and Muḥammad [b. al-Ḥasan].[54]

766. I asked: Why? You have said that if a Muslim enters the dār al-ḥarb, it would be permissible for him to sell corpses and take 2 dirhams in exchange for 1.

767. He replied: Yes, it would be quite all right to do so in their land, but not—as in the former situation—in the dār al-Islām, where Muslim rulings are binding on them and where it would not be lawful to do save what is lawful among Muslims. If [on the other hand] the Muslim were in the dār al-ḥarb under an amān, it would be lawful for him to acquire property from them in accordance [with their law] by their own consent, since Muslim rulings would not be binding on them there. This is the opinion of Abū Ḥanīfa and Mu-

[53] Abū Yūsuf, expressing the Ḥanafī doctrine, says that the musta'min who enters the dār al-Islām is not to be treated as a Dhimmī (Abū Yūsuf, *Kitāb al-Kharāj*, p. 189).

[54] *Ibid.*; Ṭabarī, *Kitāb Ikhtilāf*, p. 56; Cf. Awzā'ī and Shāfi'ī, in Ṭabarī, *Kitāb Ikhtilāf*, p. 54-55.

ḥammad [b. al-Ḥasan]. However, Abū Yūsuf held that he would not approve of [a Muslim being involved in] a transaction in the dār al-ḥarb involving riba, wine, or dead animals, and that he rejects it. But God knows best! [55]

The Tithe Duties Imposed on the Inhabitants of the Territory of War

768. I asked: If a musta'min from the inhabitants of the territory of war entered the dār al-Islām under an amān and paid the tithe to the tithe collector, but then returned to the dār al-ḥarb and stayed [only] a few days there and entered [the dār al-Islām] again under an amān, do you think that the tithe collector should collect the tithe for a second time?

769. He replied: Yes.[56]

770. I asked: Why?

771. He replied: Because when he returned to the dār al-ḥarb Muslim jurisdiction ceased to apply to him, so if he came again [to the dār al-Islām] he would have to pay the tithe again since his prior payment would not be counted because Muslim jurisdiction had been interrupted.

772. I asked: Should the tithe be collected each time [the musta'min] comes to us?

773. He replied: Yes.

774. I asked: If the authorities of his land collect from Muslim merchants a duty of one-fifth?

775. He replied: In that case, I should collect a duty of one-fifth from them also.

776. I asked: Should the customs collector examine how much the authorities of the [musta'min's] land collect from Muslim merchants and then collect from their [merchants] similar duties?

777. He replied: Yes. I should collect from each one [who

[55] Abū Yūsuf, *Kitāb al-Kharāj*, pp. 188-89.
[56] *Ibid.*, p. 133.

enters the dār al-Islām] what his authorities collect from Muslim merchants: if they collect more than the tithe, I should collect more; if they collect less, I should collect less. It should be collected from them as much as they collect from Muslim merchants.[57]

778. I asked: If one of the [unbelievers'] children or mukātabs, or slaves or women came before the Muslim tithe collector and [it is known that] they collect duties from Muslim merchants even if they were women, mukātabs, and others, do you think that we should also collect from them?

779. He replied: Yes.

780. I asked: If they do not collect [duties] from those that I have mentioned?

781. He replied: I should not collect from them either, but if they do, I should do so also.[58]

782. I asked: If a ḥarbī enters [the dār al-Islām] carrying with him [merchandise worth] less than 200 dirhams, do you think that we should collect anything from him?

783. He replied: No.[59]

784. I asked: If [the authorities of the dār al-ḥarb] collect duties from Muslim merchants carrying [merchandise worth] less than 200 dirhams, should we also collect from them?

785. He replied: Yes. If they collect [duty for merchandise worth] less than 200 dirhams, I should collect from them on the same basis.

786. I asked: What would you think if one of their men enters [the dār al-Islām] with camels, cattle, sheep, or cloth material and claims that he owes [them as] a debt, or that they are not for trade?

787. He replied: No attention should be paid to what he says; the tithe should be collected on whatever he has with him.

[57] *Ibid.*, pp. 133-35.
[58] Sarakhsī, *Kitāb Sharḥ al-Siyar al-Kabīr* (Hyderabad), Vol. IV, p. 67.
[59] Abū Yūsuf, *Kitāb al-Kharāj*, p. 133.

788. I asked: What would you think about any slaves that he might have with him?

789. He replied: I should collect the tithe on them also.

790. I asked: If he says that one of them was his father or his mother, or the slave-mother of one of his children, should the tithe be collected on them?

791. He replied: No.

792. I asked: If you do not know how much duty the authorities of the land of the man [who enters the dār al-Islām] levy on the property of Muslim merchants, what would you think you should collect?

793. He replied: If I do not know how much they collect from our merchants, I should collect the tithe.

794. I asked: Has any narrative come to your knowledge [on the subject]?

795. He replied: Yes. It has been related to us that [the Caliph] ʻUmar b. al-Khaṭṭāb once asked how much the authorities of the territory of war collected from Muslim merchants, and he was told that they collected the tithe. Thereupon ʻUmar decreed that merchants [from the dār al-ḥarb] should pay the tithe.[60]

796. I asked: Have you heard any narrative concerning your opinion that no kurāʻ or weapons should be exported [to the dār al-ḥarb]?

797. He replied: Yes. Muḥammad b. al-Ḥasan said that Abū Ḥanīfa related to us from Ḥammād [b. Sulaymān] from Ibrāhīm [al-Nakhʻī], who said, "It is [lawful] to export to them [the inhabitants of the dār al-ḥarb] everything except the kurāʻ, weapons, and slaves." But Ibrāhīm said that he preferred that nothing should be exported [to the dār al-ḥarb].[61]

[60] *Ibid.*, p. 135.
[61] Abū Yūsuf, *Kitāb al-Āthār*, p. 195.

The Musta'min's Umm Walad, Mudabbar, Wife, and Freedmen [Who Enter the Dār al-Islām] 149

798. I asked: If a ḥarbī enters the dār al-Islām under an amān with an umm walad of his who [the umm walad] later becomes a Muslim, what do you think would be her status?

799. He replied: She should endeavor to [earn and] repay her value to her master and gain her freedom.[62]

800. I asked: What would you think if [the master] made one of his slaves a mudabbar in the dār al-Islām and the slave accepted Islam?

801. He replied: He and the umm walad should be treated alike; the mudabbar should endeavor to repay his value and become free.

802. I asked: What would you think if the master made the slave a mudabbar in the dār al-ḥarb and thereafter entered the dār al-Islām along with this slave and the slave accepted Islam?

803. He replied: In this case the master would be obliged to sell him. However, this situation is different from the previous one, because the master's making the slave a mudabbar was null and void. It will not be taken into consideration if it was done in the dār al-ḥarb.[63]

804. I asked: If the musta'min—the master—himself became a Muslim in all the [different] situations previously mentioned either before or after [his slaves] accepted Islam, do you think that he would be obliged to sell any of them or that any of them would be required to earn enough to purchase his freedom?

805. He replied: No. Their status vis-à-vis their [master] would remain as it was before [the owner had become a Muslim].

806. I asked: If [the owner] became a Muslim after the judge decided that his umm walad and his mudabbar should

[62] Ṭabarī, *Kitāb Ikhtilāf*, pp. 57-58; Shāfi'ī, *Umm*, Vol. IV, p. 191.
[63] Ṭabarī, *Kitāb Ikhtilāf*, p. 58.

be required to earn and purchase their freedom and they either had paid in part or had not paid anything?

807. He replied: They [the slaves] should continue to pay the installments until they obtain their freedom; he [the master] can no longer turn them into ordinary slaves once the judge passes his judgment; but if they are unable to earn and repay, they revert to their status of slavery as before.

808. I asked: If the mukātab became a Muslim and the master did not, what do you think would be the status [of the mukātab]?

809. He replied: The mukātab will continue to be a mukātab; if he pays his value, he becomes free; if he fails to pay, he reverts to slavery and his master is obliged to sell him.

810. I asked: If the umm walad, the mudabbar, or the mukātab or a Dhimmī accepted Islam, would the situation be the same as in the case of the ḥarbī?

811. He replied: Yes.[64]

812. I asked: If a slave became a Muslim in the dār al-ḥarb and entered the dār al-Islām, leaving his master in the dār al-ḥarb, do you think that the slave would become free?

813. He replied: Yes.

814. I asked: If the master entered the dār al-Islām before his slave and became a Muslim, and thereafter the slave followed him?

815. He replied: He would remain in slavery and would not become free.

816. I asked: If the owner, accompanied by other slaves, entered [the dār al-Islām] after the said slave for trade and thereafter became a Muslim, what would be the status of the slave?

817. He replied: The slave would remain [the property of] the owner.

[64] *Ibid.*

818. I asked: If [the owner] entered the dār al-Islām, but did not become a Muslim, what do you think would be the status of the slave?

819. He replied: I should compel the owner to sell the slave.

820. I asked: If his umm walad became a Muslim and entered dār al-Islām, would she likewise enjoy the status of a freedwoman?

821. He replied: Yes.

822. I asked: Would she have the right to get married at once, if she wished to?

823. He replied: [If she were pregnant, she would] not until she were delivered.[65]

824. I asked: Would she have to observe the ʿidda (waiting period)?

825. He replied: No.[66]

826. I asked: If she were pregnant by her owner and she got married?

827. He replied: The marriage would be void. Abū Yūsuf and Muḥammad [b. al-Ḥasan] held that the umm walad would have to observe the ʿidda, that she would have to wait three menstrual periods, if she were not pregnant.

828. I asked: If she married before the expiration of the ʿidda?

829. He replied: We should invalidate the marriage.[67]

[65] Abū Yūsuf, *Kitāb al-Radd*, pp. 98-99.

[66] Awzāʿī and Shāfiʿī held that she would not be lawful until the expiration of the waiting period (ʿidda). See Shāfiʿī, *Umm*, Vol. VII, p. 326.

[67] According to Ḥanafī doctrine she should first be delivered before marriage. Shāfiʿī held that clearance would be established after one menstrual period. Shāfiʿī, *Umm*, Vol. VII, p. 326.

The Woman of the Inhabitants of [the Territory of] War Who Becomes a Muslim and Enters the Territory of Islam

830. I asked: If a woman from the inhabitants of the territory of war became a Muslim and thereafter entered the dār al-Islām, leaving her husband behind, do you think that she would have the right to get married immediately?

831. He replied: Yes.[68]

832. I asked: Should she not observe the 'idda?

833. He replied: No. Do you not think that if her husband divorced her, the divorce would not be effective? [69]

However, Abū Yūsuf and Muḥammad [b. al-Ḥasan] held that she as well as the umm walad should observe the 'idda; each should wait for three menstrual periods. If she married before the expiration of the 'idda, the marriage would be void. The same ruling should apply if she were pregnant: the marriage would be invalid so long as she were not delivered.[70]

834. I asked: If she were pregnant and got married?

835. He replied: The marriage would be invalid; she has no right to get married until she is delivered.[71]

836. I asked: If her husband became a Muslim and entered [the dār al-Islām] after her either before or after she got married?

837. He replied: In either case he would have no claim against her, because the wedlock between them was dissolved when she entered the dār al-Islām.

838. I asked: If the husband became a Muslim before her

[68] Abū Yūsuf, *Kitāb al-Radd*, pp. 99-100. Awzā'ī and Shāfi'ī held that she would not be lawful for remarriage before the expiration of the 'idda. See Shāfi'ī, *Umm*, Vol. VII, pp. 326-27.

[69] Abū Yūsuf, *Kitāb al-Radd*, pp. 99-100. Cf. Shāfi'ī, *Umm*, Vol. VII, p. 327.

[70] Abū Yūsuf, *Kitāb al-Radd*, pp. 100-2; Ṭaḥāwī, *Mukhtaṣar*, p. 289.

[71] Abū Yūsuf, *Kitāb al-Radd*, p. 103; Shāfi'ī, *Umm*, Vol. VII, p. 327.

and entered the dār al-Islām, would the wedlock between them continue?

839. He replied: No. Nor would she have to observe the ʿidda.[72]

840. I asked: Would her husband have the right to marry four [women] other than her?

841. He replied: Yes.

842. I asked: Would he have the right to marry her sister, if he so wished?

843. He replied: Yes.

844. I asked: Why is this so?

845. He replied: When the husband became a Muslim and entered the dār al-Islām, the wedlock between them was dissolved, because Muslim rulings are not binding in the dār al-ḥarb. Do you not think that if the husband divorced her, the divorce would not be effective, and if he pronounced the ilā'[73] or zihār,[74] these would not be binding on her?

846. I asked: Why do you hold that his ilā' and zihār would not be binding on her, though she became a Muslim and entered the dār al-Islām?

847. He replied: Because the wedlock between them had been dissolved when he left her behind in the dār al-ḥarb, where Muslim jurisdiction is not operative. So his pronouncements of divorce and zihār would not be binding on her, unless he remarried her for the future.

848. I asked: What would you think if a ḥarbī accompanied by his wife entered the dār al-Islām under an amān and they stayed in the dār al-Islām as two musta'mins, and if one of them became [first] a Muslim and the other did so a day later?

[72] Abū Yūsuf, *Kitāb al-Radd*, p. 103; Shāfiʿī, *Umm*, Vol. VII, p. 328.

[73] The husband's oath of abstinence from intercourse with his wife. See Ṭaḥāwī, *Mukhtaṣar*, p. 207; Kāsānī, *Badā'iʿ al-Ṣanā'iʿ*, Vol. III, p. 170.

[74] Repudiation of the wife by the husband by saying to her: "You are for me as untouchable as the back (i. e., the body) of my mother." See Q. LVIII, 3-4; Ṭaḥāwī, *Mukhtaṣar*, p. 212; Kāsānī, *Badā'iʿ al-Ṣanā'iʿ*, Vol. III, p. 229.

849. He replied: Their marriage would remain valid.

850. I asked: If they were in the dār al-ḥarb and one of them became a Muslim a day or a month before the other?

851. He replied: Their marriage would remain valid.

852. I asked: If the woman became a Muslim, how much time would have to pass before the marriage was broken?

853. He replied: If the woman became a Muslim and three menstrual periods passed before her husband became a Muslim, the wedlock would no longer exist between them.[75]

854. I asked: Would the same hold true if the husband became a Muslim and three menstrual periods passed before she became a Muslim? 150

855. He replied: Yes, unless his wife were a scripturary, for then the marriage remains valid as long as the husband does not depart from the dār al-ḥarb and leave her behind.

856. I asked: Would the case be the same regardless whether or not he had consummated his marriage with her?

857. He replied: Yes.

858. I asked: If a man from the inhabitants of the territory of war either pronounced the threefold divorce against his wife or died, after which she became a Muslim and entered the dār al-Islām, do you think that she would be under the obligation to observe the 'idda?

859. He replied: No.

860. I asked: Why?

861. He replied: Because the woman who has a husband and enters [the dār al-Islām] would be in a more difficult situation than [the woman who has no husband] and she [the former] is under no obligation to observe the 'idda. Neither one would be under the obligation of the 'idda because Muslim jurisdiction is not operative in the dār al-ḥarb.[76]

[75] Shāfi'ī holds that the marriage remains valid if the husband becomes a Muslim, regardless of the expiration of the 'idda. See Shāfi'ī, *Umm*, Vol. IV, p. 185.

[76] Cf. *ibid.*

Marital Status of Persons from the Territory of War

862. I asked: If a man and his wife from among the inhabitants of the territory of war became Muslims, but were married without witnesses, do you think that they should be separated?

863. He replied: No, their marriage would subsist.

864. I asked: Why, since such a marriage is invalid?

865. He replied: Because such a marriage was lawful among them. If I were to declare this and similar marriages invalid, I should also have to declare the marriage invalid even if it had taken place in the presence of witnesses, because it is unlawful for a Muslim to marry an unbelieving woman unless she is a scripturary. For if I were to declare valid or invalid for them all that is respectively valid or invalid for Muslims, none of their marriages would be valid, even if they were made in the presence of witnesses. Such marriages are not lawful [to Muslims], but we accept whatever is regarded as marriage according to their religion.[77]

866. I asked: If [the ḥarbī] married a woman who was still observing the ʿidda after the death of her husband or her divorce and both became Muslims, would she be regarded as his wife and would their marriage be lawful?

867. He replied: Yes.

868. I asked: If he divorced his wife with three pronouncements and thereafter remarried her and both became Muslims, do you think that they should be separated?

869. He replied: Yes.

870. I asked: Why?

871. He replied: Because she would not be lawful for him unless [in the meantime] she had married another man [and been divorced].[78]

872. I asked: Why is this case different from the former?

[77] Abū Yūsuf, *Kitāb al-Radd*, pp. 103-7; Shāfiʿī, *Umm*, Vol. VII, p. 328.
[78] See Q. II, 230.

873. He replied: In the former case she would not be unlawful to him unless she were a Muslim married to a Muslim and observing the ʿidda, whereas in the present case she would be permanently unlawful to him until she had married another man [and had thereafter been divorced], just as if a man's wife had died after their marriage had been consummated and he married her mother or her daughter [from an earlier marriage]; they would have to be separated, because either one [the mother or daughter of the former wife] would be unlawful to him in any case.

874. I asked: What would you think if a man from the inhabitants of the territory of war were married to five wives in one or more marriage contracts and thereafter he and they became Muslims?

875. He replied: If [the five wives] were married [to him] by one contract, all should be separated from him; if they were married in more than one marriage contract, the marriage of the first four wives would be lawful and valid, but the marriage to the fifth would be unlawful and she should be separated from him.[79]

876. I asked: Would the same hold true if he married two sisters in one marriage contract or in two different ones?

877. He replied: Yes.

878. I asked: Is it, therefore, your opinion that if he married a woman and her daughter in one marriage contract they should be separated from him; but that if he married them in two separate marriages, the one he married first would be his wife and the other one should be separated from him?

879. [He replied: Yes.] [80]

880. I asked: If he had consummated the marriage in both marriage contracts?

881. He replied: He should be separated from both of them.

[79] Abū Yūsuf, *Kitāb al-Radd*, p. 103. Awzāʿī and Shāfiʿī held that only the fifth (or more) would be divorced in any case. See Shāfiʿī, *Umm*, Vol. VII, p. 328.

[80] Abū Yūsuf, *Kitāb al-Radd*, p. 105; Shāfiʿī, *Umm*, Vol. IV, p. 187.

882. I asked: If he had married a woman and her sister's daughter either in one or in two separate marriage contracts and the marriage was either consummated or not consummated?

883. He replied: Their situation would be the same as that of the two sisters in the case mentioned before.[81]

884. I asked: If he had unlawful intercourse with a woman or kissed her or touched her lustfully or saw her naked [82] and then married her mother and her daughter and thereafter all became Muslims?

885. He replied: He should be separated from both, because neither one would be lawful to him in any case.

886. I asked: If a man [from the inhabitants of the dār al-ḥarb] married a woman of them for whom he had paid a bride-price consisting of a corpse, blood, swine, or wine, and after their marriage was consummated they became Muslims and entered the dār al-Islām, what do you think would be the marital status and the bride-price?

887. He replied: The marriage would be regarded as valid and he would have to pay no [further] bride-price; whatever he had given her would be valid and binding.

888. I asked: Why?

889. He replied: Because they had come to an agreement on something in the dār al-ḥarb and he had given it to her, so she has no further right.

890. I asked: What would you think if he married her without specifying a bride-price at all—a marriage which is lawful in accordance with their religion—and the marriage was consummated, but thereafter they became Muslims and entered the dār al-Islām?

891. He replied: The marriage would be regarded as valid and he would have to pay no bride-price.

[81] Sarakhsī, *Mabsūṭ*, Vol. V, p. 53; Ṭaḥāwī, *Mukhtaṣar*, p. 180.

[82] In Arabic MSS; Farj (vulva). The general sense being that if the man sees a private area of the woman's body when she is naked. See Shāfi'ī's *Risāla*, pp. 349, 351-52 (Khadduri's translation, pp. 176-77).

892. I asked: If he married her on the basis of a specified bride-price and thereafter both became Muslims and entered the dār al-Islām, would she be entitled to demand the bride-price from him?

893. He replied: Yes.

894. I asked: If a woman from the inhabitants of the territory of war married a man while she had another husband, and she and her second husband entered the dār al-Islām and became Muslims, do you think that their marriage would be valid?

895. He replied: No.

896. I asked: Why?

897. He replied: Because [the second husband] married her while she had another husband. It is not lawful in any circumstance for a man to marry a woman who has another husband.

898. I asked: If he made a future marriage contract with her [to be effective] in the dār al-Islām, would such a marriage be lawful for the future?

899. He replied: Yes.

900. I asked: If a man from the inhabitants of the territory of war entered the dār al-Islām under an amān and settled there and became a Dhimmī, while his wife remained in the dār al-ḥarb, what do you think would be the status of his wife?

901. He replied: The wedlock would have been dissolved when the man became a Dhimmī.

902. I asked: Would the situation be the same if a woman entered the dār al-Islām under an amān and settled there, leaving her husband behind, and became a Dhimmī?

903. He replied: Yes, indeed.

Abū Yūsuf and Muḥammad [b. al-Ḥasan] held that if a 151
woman from the inhabitants of the territory of war becomes a Muslim and enters the dār al-Islām, leaving her husband behind, and she is not pregnant, she cannot marry until she waits for three menstrual periods and the expiration of the 'idda. If she marries before that, her marriage would be

vicious. Such a woman should not be considered the same as a prisoner of war. If a ḥarbī married to four wives were taken as a prisoner of war, the marital state between him and them would cease to exist; if two of the wives died before his capture, his marriage to the other two would be regarded as valid, according to Abū Ḥanīfa.[83]

Muslims Entering the Dār al-Ḥarb under an Amān for Trade

904. I asked: What would you think if a Muslim entered the territory of war under an amān and becomes married to a scripturary woman from among the inhabitants of that territory?

905. He replied: I should disapprove his doing so.

906. I asked: But if he married, would such a marriage be valid?

907. He replied: Yes.[84]

908. I asked: Then, why did you disapprove of that?

909. He replied: Because I disapprove of his living in it.[85]

910. I asked: Do you disapprove of [eating] animals slaughtered by the People of the Book (scripturaries)?

911. He replied: It is all right to do so if they are People of the Book. For God, the Most High, made lawful the animals slaughtered by the People of the Book.[86] It has been related to us that [the Caliph] 'Alī b. Abī Ṭālib was once asked about marriage with scripturaries of the territory of war, and he disapproved of it; but when asked about animals slaughtered by them, he saw nothing wrong [in eating them].[87]

912. I asked: Do you hold, then, that if [the inhabitants of the territory of war] are not scripturaries, it is not lawful

[83] Ṭaḥāwī, *Mukhtaṣar*, pp. 178-82.
[84] Shaybānī, *al-Jāmi' al-Ṣaghīr*, p. 92.
[85] Abū Yūsuf, *Kitāb al-Radd*, p. 116; Shāfi'ī, *Umm*, Vol. IV, p. 181.
[86] See Q. V, 8.
[87] Sarakhsī, *Kitāb Sharḥ al-Siwar al-Kabīr* (Hyderabad), Vol. I, p. 101.

[for a Muslim] to eat animals slaughtered by them and to marry their women?

913. He replied: Yes, it is not lawful for him to do so.[88]

914. I asked: If he purchased a slave woman of their religion, would it be lawful for him to have intercourse with her?

915. He replied: No.

916. I asked: If he took her back with him to the dār al-Islām and she was nubile but young and had not yet known anything [of her religion] and had not declared her admission to it, could he have intercourse with her?

917. He replied: Yes, if he so wishes.

918. I asked: Should he perform the [funeral] prayer, if she were to die?

919. He replied: Yes.

920. I asked: Would an animal slaughtered by her be lawful to eat?

921. He replied: Yes.

922. I asked: If a Muslim married a scripturary woman from among the inhabitants of the territory of war and she bore him a child, but the Muslims captured her and her child when she was pregnant, what do you think would be the status of her, her child, and her unborn child?

923. He replied: Her children would be regarded as free Muslims and nothing would be done against them, but the woman and her unborn child would become fay' because the unborn child possesses the same status as its mother.

924. I asked: What would you think if a man entered the dār al-Islām as a Muslim, leaving his Christian wife behind in the dār al-ḥarb?

925. He replied: Her wedlock would be dissolved [from the moment] he entered the dār al-Islām.

926. I asked: Would his divorce of her, or his ilā', or his zihār not be effective on her?

[88] Abū Yūsuf, *Kitāb al-Radd*, p. 116; Shāfi'ī, *Umm*, Vol. IV, pp. 186-87.

927. He replied: No.

928. I asked: If she came to the dār al-Islām for trade, would her husband [lawfully] have intercourse with her on the strength of [the previous] marriage?

929. He replied: No.

930. I asked: If, when he married her in the dār al-ḥarb, she was a scripturary and he was a Muslim and she kept her religion [and her husband came later to the dār al-Islām], would their marriage remain valid?

931. He replied: Yes.

932. I asked: Would the same hold true if they were residing in the dār al-ḥarb and its inhabitants made peace [with the Muslims] and became Dhimmīs?

933. He replied: Yes.[89]

Slaves Purchased by Muslims in the Territory of War

934. I asked: If a Muslim purchased slaves, houses, or land in the territory of war, what would the status of these things be if the Muslims took possession of them?

935. He replied: The land and the houses would become fay' for the Muslims, but the movable property and the slaves would remain his.[90]

936. I asked: Would the same hold true of anything that may have been given him as a gift or purchased by him?

937. He replied: Yes.

938. I asked: Why are the houses and lands treated differently from the slaves and the movable property?

939. He replied: Because he is able to move the slaves and the property to the dār al-Islām, whereas he cannot move the houses and the land.

940. I asked: If a Muslim entered the dār al-ḥarb and deposited his property with a man of that territory or with a

[89] Shāfi'ī, *Umm*, Vol. IV, p. 183.
[90] Shaybānī, *al-Jāmi' al-Ṣaghīr*, p. 91.

Dhimmī, but then it was captured by the Muslims, do you think the Muslims would have to return the property to its owner?

941. He replied: Yes.

942. I asked: If the property were divided among them, do you think that [the owner] would have the right to take it back without paying the value for it?

943. He replied: Yes.

944. I asked: Why?

945. He replied: Because it was the property of a Muslim which the unbelievers [had captured but] had not yet taken to a place of security.

946. I asked: If the unbelievers killed that Muslim while he was in their territory and seized his property, after which the Muslims captured them and the property and the [deceased's] heirs found the property before it was divided?

947. He replied: They [the heirs] would have first claim on it.

948. I asked: If the property had already been divided up?

949. He replied: If it were gold and silver, the heirs would have no claim to it; otherwise, they would have first claim on it [and could take it back] by paying the value for it, if they so wished.

950. I asked: Why would they have to get back in the latter situation by paying the value for it, while in the former case they would not have to pay the value?

951. He replied: Because in the latter situation the unbelievers had placed the property in security when they killed its owner; in the former, they had not placed it in security [by taking possession of it].

952. I said: If the unbelievers, when they killed the Muslim, themselves became Muslims or entered into a peace agreement [with the Muslims] and became Dhimmīs, do you think that they would be liable for the [Muslim's] blood or property?

953. He replied: No.[91]

954. I asked: Why?

955. He replied: Because they captured it in the dār al-ḥarb.

956. I asked: If [a Muslim] who entered the territory of war under an amān killed one of their men or seized some property or slaves and took it to the dār al-Islām, and thereafter the inhabitants of the territory of war became Muslims or Dhimmīs, would you return to them any of the property which [the Muslim] had taken, or would he be held liable for the property or the blood-money [of the unbelievers whom he killed]?

957. He replied: No.[92]

958. I asked: Why? 152

959. He replied: Because [the Muslims] did it in the dār al-ḥarb, where Muslim jurisdiction was not operative.

960. I asked: Would you disapprove of [the Muslim's] committing such acts?

961. He replied: Yes, on the ground of his religion, I disapprove of his dealing treacherously with them.

962. I asked: If he dealt treacherously with them and acquired property and slaves which he carried to the dār al-Islām and a Muslim purchased some of the slaves from him, do you think that this would be permissible?

963. He replied: Yes, all of that would be permissible.[93]

964. I asked: Would you disapprove of a man's purchasing some of those things, if he knew that the other [man] had committed treachery [against the enemy] and had acquired the property treacherously?

965. He replied: Yes, I should disapprove of that for him. But if [someone] purchased them, I should regard it as per-

[91] Abū Yūsuf, *Kitāb al-Radd*, p. 107. Awzā'ī and Shāfi'ī held that all the property and slaves remain in the possession of the Muslim. See Shāfi'ī, *Umm*, Vol. VII, p. 329.

[92] Shāfi'ī, *Umm*, Vol. VII, p. 329.

[93] Ṭabarī, *Kitāb Ikhtilāf*, p. 62.

missible; but if he purchased [a slave woman], I should disapprove of the purchaser's intercourse with her.

966. I asked: If [the Muslim] who entered [the dār al-ḥarb] under an amān was therein when its inhabitants captured prisoners from another [enemy] of the territory of war, do you think that it would be lawful for him to purchase some of those captives?

967. He replied: Yes.

968. I asked: Similarly, if [some of] the inhabitants of the territory in which he was residing had been taken as captives [by some enemy of theirs], would it be permissible for him to purchase some of them?

969. He replied: Yes.

970. I asked: [94] If the Muslims entered into a peace treaty with some of the inhabitants of the territory of war and these were attacked by some persons of [another territory of] war who took captives with them, would it be lawful for that Muslim to purchase any of these captives?

971. He replied: Yes.

972. I asked: If the captors were a group of Muslims who had treacherously attacked the people with whom [the Muslims] had entered into a peace treaty, would it be lawful for the Muslims to purchase any of the captives?

973. He replied: They should not purchase any of them, and if they did I would order them to send them back. This situation would be different from that in which [a single Muslim] entered [the dār al-ḥarb] under an amān [and acted treacherously].

974. I asked: Why?

975. He replied: Because those [in treaty relations with the Muslims] were enjoying an amān and [Muslims] should never attack them treacherously. For a narrative has been related to us from the Apostle of God, in which he said: "The one lowest in status can bind others if he gives a pledge [of security]." [95] If [the inhabitants of the dār al-ḥarb] were

[94] "Similarly" omitted.

[95] See note 6, above.

attacked by others of the territory of war, their captives would be in the hands of people with whom there was no peace treaty [with Muslims]. If those [in peace agreement with the Muslims] were attacked [by their enemy] and captives were taken from them, there would be no harm [if the Muslims purchased their slaves.][96]

Muslims as Musta'mins in the Dār al-Ḥarb

976. I asked: If some Muslims were in the dār al-ḥarb under an amān and that territory were attacked by [some] people of another territory of war, do you think that it would be lawful for those Muslims to fight on their side?

977. He replied: No.

978. I asked: Why?

979. He replied: Because the jurisdiction of the unbelievers prevail there and the Muslims cannot enforce Muslim rulings.

980. I asked: If the Muslims were fearful of their own persons from the enemy, should they fight in defense of themselves?

981. He replied: If the situation were thus, there would be no harm to fight in defense of themselves.

982. I asked: If the inhabitants of the territory of war, among whom there were Muslims under an amān, attacked the dār al-Islām and captured much property and some captives from among free Muslims whom they took over to the dār al-ḥarb, and if they passed by the Muslims who were in that territory under an amān, do you think that those Muslims should denounce their pledge of security [amān] and fight to free the children and women of the Muslims?

982a. He replied: Yes. They would have no choice to do otherwise, if they were able to fight.

983. I asked: If a group of Khārijīs conquered one of

[96] Ṭabarī, *Kitāb Ikhtilāf*, pp. 62-63.

the Muslim cities and ruled it in accordance with [their doctrine of] the untruth, but thereafter they were attacked by some unbelievers who captured some women and children of those Khārijīs and carried them over to the dār al-ḥarb, do you think that the Muslims in the dār al-ḥarb under an amān should denounce their pledge of security and fight to liberate those women and children?

983a. He replied: Yes.

984. I asked: If there was a group of non-Khārijī Muslims in the city [which was in the hands of the Khārijīs] when it was attacked by the inhabitants of the territory of war, would it be incumbent upon the Muslims to fight alongside the Khārijīs in defense of the Muslim community and its inviolable territory?

984a. He replied: Yes. They would have no choice to do otherwise.[97]

[97] Shaybānī, *al-Jāmi' al-Ṣaghir*, p. 90.

Chapter VII

Folio 152

[ON APOSTASY]

General Rules [1]

985. I asked: If a Muslim apostatizes (irtadda) [2] from Islam, what do you think would be the ruling concerning him?

986. He replied: Islam would be offered to him; he has either to accept it or be killed at once, unless he asked for deferment. This would be given him and its [maximum] duration would be three days.[3]

987. I asked: Has any narrative come to your knowledge about this matter?

988. He replied: Yes. It has been related to us from the Prophet [a Tradition] to this effect as well as [narratives] from [the Caliph] ʿAlī b. Abī Ṭālib, ʿAbd-Allāh b. Masʿūd, and Muʿādh b. Jabal. Thus, this ruling is based on the sunna.[4]

[1] Literally: "Rulings concerning apostasy from Islam."

[2] Literally: "Irtadda" means reverted, but legally it applies to Muslims who revert to polytheism or adopt any other religion. See Baghdādī, *Kitāb Uṣūl al-Dīn* (Istanbul, 1928), Vol. I, pp. 328-29; Shāfiʿī, *Umm*, Vol. VI, p. 145; Kāsānī, *Badāʾiʿ al-Ṣanāʾiʿ*, Vol. VII, p. 134; Samuel Zwemer, *Law of Apostasy in Islam* (London, 1924), Chap. 2; Khadduri, *War and Peace in the Law of Islam*, pp. 149-52.

[3] Abū Yūsuf, *Kitāb al-Kharāj*, pp. 179, 180; Sarakhsī, *Kitāb Sharḥ al-Siyar al-Kabīr* (Hyderabad), Vol. IV, p. 162; Kāsānī, *Badāʾiʿ al-Ṣanāʾiʿ*, Vol. VII, pp. 134, 135. Mālik and Shāfiʿī, however, held that the apostate should not be executed before being given three days of grace to afford him time to repent. See Mālik, *Muwaṭṭa'*, Vol. II, p. 737; Shāfiʿī, *Umm*, Vol. VI, pp. 145, 156-57.

[4] While Quranic injunctions do not specifically state the punishment for apostasy should be death (See Q. II, 214; V, 59; XVI, 108), only one, which states: "why are ye two parties on the subject of the hypocrites. . . . If they turn back, then seize them, and slay them wherever

989. I asked: If [the apostate] refused to become a Muslim and the Imām ordered his execution, would his estate be divided among his heirs in accordance with God's commands [concerning the distribution of inheritance]? [5]

990. He replied: Yes.[6]

991. I asked: Has any narrative come to your knowledge concerning this matter?

992. He replied: Yes. It has been related to us from [the Caliph] 'Alī b. Abī Ṭālib that he ordered the execution of an apostate and he divided his estate among his heirs in accordance with God's commands. It has also been related to us similar [narratives] from [the Caliph] 'Alī and 'Abd-Allāh b. Mas'ūd.[7]

993. I asked: If a man who apostatizes from Islam while he is still in the territory [of Islam] and has not [yet] been executed, would his estate be divided among his heirs?

994. He replied: No.[8]

995. I asked: If he had gone over to the territory of war

---

ye find them . . ." (Q. IV, 90-91) refers generally to those who revert and oppose Islam, not necessarily as reversion from the Islamic religion. The practice of the Prophet Muḥammad, as shown in the Ḥudaybiya treaty, seems to indicate that those from among his followers who wanted to return to Makka and join the polytheists were allowed to do so (see Ibn Hishām, *Kitāb Sīrat Rasūl Allāh*, Vol. II, pp. 747-48 [Guillaume translation, p. 504]). However, Traditions have been later ascribed to the Prophet ordering the execution of apostates. For the narratives on the authorities of 'Alī b. Abī Ṭālib, 'Abd-Allāh b. Mas'ūd, and Mu'ādh b. Jabal, see Abū Yūsuf, *Kitāb al-Kharāj*, p. 179; for other authorities, see Abū Dāwūd, *Sunan*, Vol. II, p. 848.

[5] Q. IV, 12-15.

[6] Abū Yūsuf ascribes such a practice to Caliph 'Umar, but Sarakhsī follows Shaybānī. See Abū Yūsuf, *Kitāb al-Kharāj*, pp. 111-12; Sarakhsī, *Mabsūṭ*, Vol. X, p. 100; Kāsānī, *Badā'i' al-Ṣanā'i'*, Vol. VII, p. 138. Shāfi'ī held that the apostate's estate should become fay' and taken over by the state on the strength of the Tradition that a believer cannot inherit from an unbeliever and vice versa. See Shāfi'ī, *Umm*, Vol. VI, pp. 151-52.

[7] Abū Yūsuf, *Kitāb al-Kharāj*, p. 111; Sarakhsī, *Kitāb Sharḥ al-Siyar al-Kabīr* (Hyderabad), Vol. X, p. 100; Kāsānī, *Badā'i' al-Ṣanā'i'*, Vol. VII, p. 138.

[8] Sarakhsī, *Mabsūṭ*, Vol. X, p. 101.

and the matter was referred to the Imām, would his estate be divided among his heirs?

996. He replied: Yes.[9]

997. I asked: Would you regard [his escape] as equivalent to his death?

998. He replied: Yes.[10]

999. I asked: If [the apostate] who went over to the dār
al-ḥarb was indebted and left behind mudabbars and umm 153
walads, and the matter was referred to the Imām?

1000. He replied: The umm walads and mudabbars would be set free [and their prices] deducted from one-third of the estate and the debt would be paid from the residue.[11] If the estate is not enough to pay for the debt, the mudabbars would have to earn and pay the balance of the debt up to two-thirds [of their value].[12]

1001. I asked: If [the apostate] was indebted and [the debt] should be paid at a fixed term, would it have to be paid at once?

1002. He replied: Yes.[13]

1003. I asked: If [the apostate] had made a testament (a will) while he was still a Muslim before he apostatized, would it be executed?

[9] Abū Yūsuf, *Kitāb al-Kharāj*, p. 181; Ṭaḥāwī, *Mukhtaṣar*, p. 258; cf. Kāsānī, *Badā'i' al-Ṣanā'i'*, Vol. VII, p. 138. Shāfi'ī held that the estate should be held in custody until the apostate's ultimate end is known, whether he died in the territory of war or returned to the territory of Islam and repented. If he dies in the territory of war the estate becomes fay'; if he returns to the territory of Islam and repents, his estate should be returned to him. See Shāfi'ī, *Umm*, Vol. VI, p. 151.

[10] Ab Yūsuf, *Kitāb al-Kharāj*, p. 181; Sarakhsī, *Mabsūṭ*, Vol. X, p. 103.

[11] This is on the ground that a will is valid for up to one third of the deceased's estate and has priority over debts. The umm walad and the mudabbars would become immediately free after their master's death. Their manumission takes place in consequence of the will.

[12] Abū Yūsuf, *Kitāb al-Kharāj*, pp. 181, 182; Kāsānī, *Badā'il al-Ṣanā'i'*, Vol. VII, pp. 138-39; cf. Shāfi'ī, *Umm*, Vol. VI, p. 151.

[13] Ṭaḥāwī, *Mukhtaṣar*, p. 258. Shāfi'ī agreed in principle that the debt should be paid, but held that it should be paid at its specified term. See Shāfi'ī, *Umm*, Vol. VI, p. 154.

1004. He replied: No, I would not execute it.[14]

1005. I asked: Why is the ruling concerning the will different from that of tadbīr [for the manumission of slaves]?

1006. He replied: Just as one is entitled to rescind one's own will, so apostasy to me is equivalent to rescission. Do you not think that [the apostate] no longer possesses his estate if he apostatizes and can no longer withdraw the tadbīr [of his slaves]?[15]

1007. I asked: Would you allow his wife to inherit from [the apostate's estate]?

1008. He replied: If he were executed or went over to the dār al-ḥarb while the wife was during the 'idda [the three-month waiting period], I would allow her to inherit from him; but if he were executed after the expiration of the 'idda, I would not allow her to inherit anything from him.[16]

1009. I asked: If [the apostate's] marriage was not consummated, would she have no right of inheritance and be under no 'idda [obligation]?

1010. He replied: That is right.[17]

1011. I asked: Why is [the status of] the woman during the 'idda different from the one whose waiting period has expired?

1012. He replied: It is lawful for [the woman] whose waiting period has expired to remarry. Do you not think that [such a woman] could remarry, if she so wishes? How could she, therefore, inherit from her first husband while she is the wife of another? But if she were during the waiting period she would inherit and she would not have the right to remarry until the expiration of that period.[18]

1013. I asked: If an apostate who had gone over to the territory of war returned repenting, while the governor [dur-

[14] Abū Yūsuf, *Kitāb al-Kharāj*, p. 181; cf. Ṭaḥāwī, *Mukhtaṣar*, p. 258.

[15] Sarakhsī, *Mabsūṭ*, Vol. X, p. 103.

[16] Abū Yūsuf, *Kitāb al-Kharāj*, p. 181; Sarakhsī, *Mabsūṭ*, Vol. X, p. 103.

[17] In MS: "Yes" because in Arabic it is used to confirm the negative answer stated in the question. See Abū Yūsuf, *Kitāb al-Kharāj*, p. 181.

[18] Sarakhsī, *Mabsūṭ*, Vol. X, p. 103.

ing the apostate's absence] set free his umm walads and mudabbars, and paid his debt and divided his estate among the heirs, do you think that he would be entitled to take back anything?

1014. He replied: Nothing would be given back to him save the inheritance; if anything were to be found intact in the hands of the heirs, he would recuperate it.[19]

1015. I asked: What would you think if the Imām did not set free the umm walads nor the mudabbars nor paid the debt [of the apostate] upon his return to the dār al-Islām from the dār al-ḥarb and his repenting?

1016. He replied: The umm walads and the mudabbars remain in their status, the estate and the slaves would be returned to him, and the debt would have to be paid at its specified term.[20]

1017. I asked: If a man apostatized and thereafter entered into sale-purchase transactions, gave a gift, set free a slave, made a tadbīr contract with a slave, made a contract with a slave woman [to be a mukātaba], and later had sexual intercourse with her (who became pregnant and whose child he claimed as his), made a contract with a slave to be a mukātab or set him free against some monetary advantage, and thereafter he returned to Islam, do you think that all of these acts would be regarded as valid?

1018. He replied: Yes.[21]

1019. I asked: If [the apostate] were either executed or went over to the territory of war and his estate were divided, would his sale-purchase transactions, his manumission, his

[19] Abū Yūsuf, *Kitāb al-Kharāj*, p. 182; Sarakhsī, *Mabsūṭ*, Vol. X, pp. 103-4.

[20] Abū Yūsuf, *Kitāb al-Kharāj*, p. 182; Sarakhsī, *Mabsūṭ*, Vol. X, p. 104.

[21] Not all that the apostate may do would be lawful. As indicated in paragraph 1003, the transactions, manumission of slaves, and gifts would be unlawful, but intercourse with a slave woman resulting in her giving birth to a child entitles the child to belong to the father and the slave woman to become an umm walad. See Sarakhsī, *Mabsūṭ*, Vol. VI, p. 104; Kāsānī, *Badā'ī' al-Ṣanā'i'*, Vol. VII, pp. 138-39. Cf. Shāfi'ī, *Umm*, Vol. VI, p. 155.

gifts, and his tadbīr and mukātaba arrangements [which were made during apostasy] be valid?

1020. He replied: None of these would be regarded as valid, except his claim to the child, which I would confirm.[22]

1021. I asked: Would you give the child the right of inheritance along with [other] heirs?

1022. He replied: Yes.[23]

1023. I asked: If the apostate has set free a slave and the [apostate's] only son also set free the same slave and the apostate was later executed, do you think that the manumission of the slave [by the apostate] or his son's manumission would be regarded as valid?

1024. He replied: Neither [one would be regarded as valid].

1025. I asked: Why?

1026. He replied: Because the son did not own [the slave] nor was the apostate's manumission lawful. Do you not think that if the son dies before his father's [execution] or before his father had gone over to the dār al-ḥarb, the slave belongs to someone else? If [the apostate] became a Muslim, he [the slave] no longer belongs to [the son]. Do you not think that [the son] has never been the owner [of the slave]? [24]

1027. I asked: What would you think if the son died when he was in apostasy and thereafter the father was executed for his apostasy. To whom would the father's estate belong, if both the father and the son had freed slaves, provided that the son's freed slave was other than the freed slave of the father? [25]

1028. He replied: The inheritance belongs to the father's freed slave; the son's freed slave would not be entitled to anything.

1029. I asked: If a man apostatized from Islam and earned

[22] Sarakhsī, *Mabsūṭ*, Vol. X, p. 104.

[23] *Ibid.*, p. 164; Shāfi'ī, *Umm*, Vol. VI, p. 153.

[24] Sarakhsī, *Mabsūṭ*, Vol. X, p. 106.

[25] As a rule the father inherits from the son; but the father, having apostatized, would be precluded from inheritance.

some property during his apostasy, do you think that the heirs would be entitled to inherit that property?

1030. He replied: No, it would be regarded as fay', belonging to the state treasury.

1031. I asked: Why?

1032. He replied: Because he would earn it while in the state of apostasy, and the effusion of his blood would be lawful, just as [any person] from among the territory of war. However, Abū Yūsuf and Muḥammad [b. al-Ḥasan] held that whatever [the apostate] earns during apostasy would [also] be inherited by his heirs. They also held that the manumission of slaves during apostasy would be valid and that whatever [the apostate] may earn in the dār al-Islām would not be regarded as fay'. However, Muḥammad [b. al-Ḥasan] held that any manumission of slaves or any sale-purchase transaction [made by the apostate] would be regarded as [acts] equivalent to one who is in a state of sickness.[26]

1033. I asked: Would you think that the apostate's slaughtered animal would be lawful to eat?

1034. He replied: No.[27]

1035. I asked: Even if he had become a Christian [by apostasy]?

1036. He replied: Even if he had [apostatized to Christianity], because he would not enjoy the status of a Jew or a Christian. Do you think that he would be permitted to remain in the religion [he had adopted]? He would have to become a Muslim or else be executed.[28]

1037. I asked: If he marries [during apostasy] a Muslim, a Dhimmī, or an apostate woman, would his marriage [contract] be vicious?

[26] In such a state of sickness, which leads to death, acts of legal consequences are invalidated. Ṭaḥāwī, *Mukhtaṣar,* p. 261; Sarakhsī, *Mabsūṭ,* Vol. X, pp. 106-7.

[27] Abū Yūsuf, *Kitāb al-Radd,* p. 115; Kāsānī, *Badā'i' al-Ṣanā'i',* Vol. VII, p. 135.

[28] Abū Yūsuf, *Kitāb al-Radd,* p. 116; Shāfi'ī, *Umm,* Vol. VI, p. 155.

1038. He replied: Yes.[29]

1039. I asked: If he has an issue from her, would you confirm his parentage?

1040. He replied: Yes. But God knows best! [30]

The Apostate's Offenses

1041. I asked: If an apostate commits a tort intentionally or unintentionally, do you think that the 'āqila [31] would have to bear the responsibility of the damages?

1042. He replied: No.[32]

1043. I asked: Why?

1044. He replied: Because his blood would be as lawful to shed as that of the inhabitants of the territory of war.[33]

1045. I asked: What would be the status of such a tort?

1046. He replied: He [the culprit] must pay the arsh (damages) out of his property.

1047. I asked: Would the ruling be the same for whatever he has usurped or damaged?

1048. He replied: Yes.

1049. I asked: Would you so decide [i. e., payment of these damages], before [the distribution of] inheritance?

1050. He replied: Yes.[34]

1051. I asked: If he did not have any property save what he earned after his apostasy, would [the damages] be paid from that property?

1052. He replied: Yes.

1053. I asked: If a man has apostatized from Islam and

[29] Shāfi'ī, *Umm*, Vol. VI, p. 155.

[30] Sarakhsī, *Mabsūṭ*, Vol. X, p. 106; Kāsānī, *Badā'i' al-Ṣanā'i'*, Vol. VII, p. 136.

[31] The 'āqila consists of the members of the tribe to whom the offender belongs and is responsible for paying the blood money.

[32] Ṭaḥāwī, *Makhtaṣar*, p. 261.

[33] Sarakhsī, *Mabsūṭ*, Vol. X, p. 107. Cf. Shāfi'ī, *Umm*, Vol. VI, p. 153.

[34] Sarakhsī, *Mabsūṭ*, Vol. X, p. 107.

[another] man cut off his hand or destroyed—intentionally or unintentionally—his eye or committed against him any other tort, intentionally or unintentionally, would this [other] man be held liable for anything?

1054. He replied: No.

1055. I asked: Why?

1056. He replied: Since his blood is lawful to shed nobody would be liable for any tort against him, whether cutting off 154 his hand or foot or committing a tort or an injury (wound) against him.[35]

1057. I asked: Would [the ruling] be the same if he accepts Islam and then dies of the wound?

1058. He replied: A person who has committed [the said tort] would not be liable for anything.

1059. I asked: What would you think if a Muslim cut off the hand of another, intentionally or unintentionally, but the victim apostatized from Islam and either went over to the dār al-ḥarb and died there from the injury inflicted upon him or died before he went over or if he returned to Islam and died subsequently?

1060. He replied: The offender would have to pay the diya of the hand in all these cases. If the offense were intentional, the damages would be paid out of his personal property; if it were unintentional, they would be paid by the 'āqila. Only in one particular case, namely if the man's hand were cut off while a Muslim, then he apostatized and returned to Islam and died subsequently of the same wound, the offender would be liable for the full diya (blood-money), whether the offense was intentional or unintentional, provided the diya would be paid by him if the offense were intentional and by the 'āqila if unintentional. This is the opinion of Abū Ḥanīfa and Abū Yūsuf. Zufar and Muḥammad [b. al-Ḥasan] held that even in such a case the offender would not be held liable, except for the payment of the arsh as compensation for [the cutting off of] the hand, because when the victim's

[35] *Ibid.*; Shāfi'ī, *Umm*, Vol. VI, p. 154.

blood became lawful to shed [for apostasy], whatever offense was committed against him would be lawful, regardless whether [the apostate] returned to Islam or not.[36]

1061. I asked: If [the man] who cut off the hand is the one who apostatized from Islam and the one whose hand is cut off were a Muslim, and the offense were intentional, but he who had cut off the hand were punished with death and the injured person either died of the wound or recovered, what do you think would be the ruling?

1062. He replied: If the cutting off [of the hand] were intentional, nothing would be paid to the injured person; if it were unintentional, the diya of the hand would be paid by the 'āqila. If the injured person dies, the 'āqila of the [person] who cut off [the hand] would have to pay the full diya for the loss of life.

1063. I asked: Why should the diya be paid by the 'āqila, if the offender were an apostate?

1064. He replied: Since he committed the offense when he was a Muslim, the 'āqila would have to pay [the diya].

1065. I asked: What would you think if he committed the offense when he was an apostate in the same circumstances as before, and if he were executed for his apostasy?

1066. He replied: If the offense were intentional, nothing would be paid [as damages] to the man whose hand was cut off; if the offense were unintentional, the offender would have to pay the diya of the hand out of his property; but if the man whose hand was cut off died, the offender would pay [the full] diya for homicide out of his personal property.

1067. I asked: If the offender did not own property save what he earned during apostasy, would he be liable to pay from it?

1068. He replied: Yes, indeed.[37]

[36] Sarakhsī, *Mabsūṭ*, Vol. X, pp. 107-8; Kāsānī, *Badā'i' al-Ṣanā'i'*, Vol. VII, p. 137.

[37] Ṭaḥāwī, *Mukhtaṣar*, p. 261; Sarakhsī, *Mabsūṭ*, Vol. X, p. 108; Shāfi'ī, *Umm*, Vol. VI, p. 154.

Female Apostasy [38]

1069. I asked: If a woman apostatized from Islam, what would be the ruling about her?

1070. He replied: Abū Ḥanīfa held that she would not be executed, but imprisoned indefinitely until she returns to Islam.[39]

1071. I asked: Would you not execute women at all?

1072. He replied: No.[40]

1073. I asked: Why?

1074. He replied: It has been related to us from 'Abd-Allāh b. 'Abbās, who said: "If a woman apostatizes from Islam, she should be imprisoned, not killed." [41] It has also been related to us from the Apostle of God that he prohibited the killing of unbelieving women in war. We have therefore waived such [a penalty].[42]

1075. I asked: What would you do with her property?

1076. He replied: It belongs to her.

1077. I asked: If she died in prison or went over to the territory of war, what would be the ruling about her estate?

1078. He replied: Her property would be divided among her heirs in accordance with God's commands [concerning inheritance].[43]

1079. I asked: Would the same be true concerning whatever she may have earned during her apostasy?

1080. He replied: Yes.

1081. I asked: Would her husband be entitled to inherit from her?

[38] Literally: "The woman apostatizes from Islam."

[39] Abū Yūsuf, *Kitāb al-Kharāj*, pp. 179-80; Sarakhsī, *Kitāb Sharḥ al-Siyar al-Kabīr* (Hyderabad), Vol. IV, p. 162; Kāsānī, *Badā'i' al-Ṣanā'i'*, Vol. VII, p. 134.

[40] Shāfi'ī held that if an apostate woman refuses to return to Islam she should be killed. Shāfi'ī, *Umm*, Vol. VI, pp. 159-61.

[41] Abū Yūsuf, *Kitāb al-Kharāj*, pp. 180-81; cf. *Kitāb al-Āthār*, p. 161.

[42] Sarakhsī, *Mabsūṭ*, Vol. X, pp. 108-10; Kāsānī, *Badā'i' al-Ṣanā'i'*, Vol. VII, p. 134.

[43] Q. IV, 12-15.

1082. He replied: No.

1083. I asked: Why?

1084. He replied: Because she would be [immediately] divorced from him if she apostatized.

1085. I asked: Why have you given the wife the right to inherit from the husband if he apostatizes while you did not give him the right to inherit from her?

1086. He replied: Do you not think that if the man divorces his wife thrice in his sickness, she would still inherit from him if he died while she were in her waiting period ('idda); but if she died, he would not inherit from her? So the apostate's status is equivalent to the man who divorces [his wife] in [the last] sickness.[44]

1087. I asked: If a woman apostatized when she was sick and died during her waiting period, do you think that her husband would be entitled to inherit from her?

1088. He replied: Yes, if she died during her waiting period.

1089. I asked: Why is her apostasy in sickness different from her apostasy when she is not?

1090. He replied: If she apostatized in sickness she would be in my opinion in the same status as a woman who renounces [the right of] inheritance. So if the waiting period expired before her death, he would not be entitled to inherit from her.

1091. I asked: If she goes over to the territory of war, would her husband have the right to marry four women before the expiration of her waiting period?

1092. He replied: Yes.

1093. I asked: Why?

1094. He replied: Because her apostasy and her flight to the territory of war would be equivalent to her death.

1095. I asked: Would he have the right to marry her sister, if he so wishes?

[44] Sarakhsī, *Mabsūṭ*, Vol. X, p. 112; Shāfi'ī, *Umm*, Vol. VI, pp. 161-62.

1096. He replied: Yes.

1097. I asked: If she were taken [by Muslims] as a captive from the territory of war, would she be executed?

1098. He replied: No, she would be [enslaved and] divided as part of the spoil and obliged to accept Islam.

1099. I asked: Would this [capture] have any effect on her [former] husband's [marriage to the] women he married after her?

1100. He replied: No.

1101. I asked: If she were not taken as a captive, but she became a Muslim and returned to the territory of Islam, do you think that this would vitiate any of her [former] husband's [subsequent] marriages?

1102. He replied: No.

1103. I asked: Would she have the right to remarry immediately, if she so wishes?

1104. He replied: Yes.

1105. I asked: Would she be under no [obligation of the] 'idda?

1106. He replied: No.

1107. I asked: If she did not adopt Islam, but she gave birth to a child in the territory of war and both [she and her child] were later captured [by Muslims], do you think that they would become fay'?

1108. He replied: Yes.

1109. I asked: If [the apostate woman] went over to the territory of war, leaving behind a mudabbar and the matter was brought up to the Imām, do you think that he would set him free?

1110. He replied: Yes.

1111. I asked: If she were indebted and [the debt] had to be paid at a specified term, would [the debt] have to be paid immediately [from her estate]?

1112. He replied: Yes.

1113. I asked: If she had entered into sale-purchase transactions during her apostasy, would those transactions be regarded as valid by the Imām?

1114. He replied: Yes.

1115. I asked: Would her manumission [of slaves], her gifts, and her sale-purchase transactions be regarded as valid? 155

1116. He replied: Yes.

1117. I asked: Would she not be regarded in [all] such matters in the same status as the man?

1118. He replied: She would not be in the same status as the man [because] the man would be liable to be executed [for apostasy], while she would be imprisoned.

1119. I asked: What would you think if [a woman] apostatized from Islam, but when she was brought before the Imām she said: "I did not apostatize at all and I profess that there is no god but God and that Muḥammad is the Apostle of God." Would this [declaration] constitute repentance?

1120. He replied: Yes.

1121. I asked: Would the same be true if the man [said so]?

1122. He replied: Yes.

1123. I asked: If a woman apostatized from Islam and was married during her apostasy either to a Muslim, to an unbeliever apostate, to a Dhimmī, or to any other, do you think that such a marriage would be valid?

1124. He replied: No.

1125. I asked: Would the same hold true if the man [so acted]?

1126. He replied: Yes.

1127. I asked: Would it be lawful to eat an animal slaughtered by a male or female apostate?

1128. He replied: No.

1129. I asked: Not even if [the apostate] became a Jew or a Christian?

1130. He replied: Even if they became [Jews or Christians]. Do you not think that I should not allow the man to remain in apostasy, for he must return to Islam or otherwise be executed?

I would not accept him to pay the poll tax as Dhimmīs do, but I should imprison the woman until she returns to Islam.

However, Abū Yūsuf and Muḥammad [b. al-Ḥasan] held that the apostate woman would be liable to execution unless she returns to Islam. But Abū Ḥanīfa held that she would be in the same category as a very old man.[45]

Apostasy of [Male] Slaves, Mukātabs, and Female Slaves[46]

1131. I asked: If a slave apostatizes from Islam, what would be the ruling concerning his [action]?

1132. He replied: Islam would be offered to him; he must accept it or else be executed. The same would hold true for the mudabbar, the mukātab, and the slave who is partially freed and is required to earn and pay the rest of his value.

1133. I asked: Would these be able to enjoy the status of a free Muslim?

1134. He replied: Yes.

1135. I asked: What would be the ruling concerning the slave woman, umm walad, the mudabbara, the mukātaba, and the slave woman who is partially freed and is required to earn and pay the balance of her value, if any one of them apostatizes?

1136. He replied: Islam would be offered to her; if she accepts it, that would be satisfactory; if she refuses, she should be imprisoned until she returns to Islam, but no one of them should be executed.

1137. I asked: If [she] were a servant [whose earning] was essential for the family, would she be imprisoned?

1138. He replied: No. If she were in such a situation, Islam would be offered to her; if she refuses, she should be given to her family so as to compel her to return to Islam.

[45] Sarakhsī, *Mabsūṭ*, Vol. X, pp. 112-13.

[46] Questions relating to male and female slaves are discussed in Sarakhsī, *Mabsūṭ*, Vol. X, pp. 114-16; Kāsānī, *Badā'i' al-Ṣanā'i'*, Vol. VII, p. 135.

1139. I asked: If a male or a female slave, an umm walad, or a mudabbar earned property during apostasy, to whom would you think the property belongs?

1140. He replied: It belongs to the master.

1141. I asked: Would the same be true if the slave and the mudabbar were executed for their apostasy; would their property belong to the master?

1142. He replied: Yes.

1143. I asked: Similarly, if the mukātab earned property during his apostasy and was executed for his apostasy, what would be the ruling concerning what the mukātab has earned?

1144. He replied: Whatever he has earned up to the amount equivalent to the contract price [of manumission] would belong to the owner, but the residue, if any, would become an inheritance to the heirs.

1145. I asked: If what he earned was not sufficient to pay for the contracted price?

1146. He replied: It all belongs to the master.

1147. I asked: If the slave commits a tort during apostasy or a tort is committed against him, what would be the ruling?

1148. He replied: In the case of his committing a tort, the ruling would be the same as before he apostatized; but if the tort were committed against him during his apostasy, the offender would not be liable for anything.

1149. I asked: If [the slave] were punished with death while in apostasy and committed a tort before his master could compel him [to return to Islam], would the master be liable for anything?

1150. He replied: No.

1151. I asked: Why have you annulled [the liability] if the tort is committed against [a slave] during his apostasy?

1152. He replied: Do you not think that if a free Muslim apostatizes and a tort was committed against him, the offender would not be liable for anything?

1153. I asked: Similarly, if an offense were committed

against the [apostate] mukātab and the mudabbar, the offender would not be liable for anything?

1154. He replied: Yes.

1155. I asked: If a mukātab committed a tort while in apostasy and was thereafter executed, would [the compensation] be paid out of [the mukātab's] property?

1156. He replied: The [compensation for] offense and the value [of the mukātab] would be compared and [the mukātab] would be held liable for the lesser of the two.

1157. I asked: If a slave woman apostatized and committed a tort?

1158. He replied: Her master will either have to hand her over [to the victim] or pay ransom for her.

1159. I asked: If a tort were committed against [the slave woman] in apostasy, would the offender be held liable for anything?

1160. He replied: No.

1161. I asked: Why, if you do not approve of the execution of women?

1162. He replied: Since some of the jurists hold that apostate women should be executed, I hold that a tort committed against them would not render [the offender] liable.

1163. I asked: Would the same hold true if a free woman apostatized and a man killed her or committed a tort against her—he would not be held liable?

1164. He replied: Yes, he would not be held liable for anything.

Sale of the Male and Female Slave Apostates[47]

1165. I asked: If a slave woman apostatized from Islam and her master sold her to another man and concealed [the

[47] Abū Yūsuf, *Kitāb al-Kharāj*, pp. 182-83; Ṭaḥāwī, *Mukhtaṣar*, p. 261; Sarakhsī, *Kitāb Sharḥ al-Siyar al-Kabīr* (Hyderabad), Vol. IV, pp. 190-92; Kāsānī, *Badā'i' al-Ṣanā'i'*, Vol. VII, p. 137.

fact of] her apostasy from him, do you think that this would be [regarded as] a defect for which she could be returned [to the vendor]?

1166. He replied: Yes.

1167. I asked: If the vendor told [the purchaser] about her [apostasy] for which he would no longer be responsible, would [the sale] be valid?

1168. He replied: Yes.

1169. I asked: If he were a male slave, would you [first] offer Islam to him in [the presence of] the purchaser so that he had either to accept Islam or be executed?

1170. He replied: Yes.

1171. I asked: If he refused to accept Islam and went over to the dār al-ḥarb, but thereafter he was captured [by Muslims] and either died or returned to Islam, would the slave belong to the master as he was [before apostasy]?

1172. He replied: Yes.

1173. I asked: If he had earned some property while in the territory of the enemy and he were captured [by Muslims] along with his property and thereafter he returned to Islam, would all his property be given to the master?

1174. He replied: Yes.

1175. I asked: If he refused to return to Islam and was executed, would his property be given to the master?

1176. He replied: Yes. 156

1177. I asked: Would the same be true if a mukātab apostatized and went over to the dār al-ḥarb, was captured [by Muslims], refused to return to Islam, and was executed—his property would be given to his master?

1178. He replied: Yes.

1179. I asked: If he adopts Islam, would the property in his possession belong to him?

1180. He replied: Yes.

1181. I asked: Would the same be true if a slave is set

free up to half [of his price] and is required to earn and pay the balance of the value [in installments]?

1182. He replied: Yes.

1183. I asked: What would you think if a slave woman, a mukātaba, an umm walad, or a mudabbara apostatized and went over to the territory of war but later was taken as a captive by the Muslims?

1184. He replied: She would be imprisoned until she returns to Islam, but she should not be executed, and she belongs to her master as was before.

1185. I asked: If her master (whether she were a slave woman, a mudabbara, or an umm walad) died in the territory of Islam when she was in the territory of war and was later captured [by the Muslims] but refused to return to Islam, what would be the ruling concerning her?

1186. He replied: She would become fay'.

The Apostasy of a [Free] Man and His Slave [48]

1187. I asked: If both a man and his slave apostatized and went over to the territory of war, but the master died there and the slave was captured [by the Muslims], do you think that [the slave] would become fay'?

1188. He replied: Yes.

1189. I asked: If the slave refuses to return to Islam, would he be executed?

1190. He replied: Yes.

1191. I asked: Why would he become fay' in such a situation?

1192. He replied: Since his master went over to the territory of war along with him, anything taken by him to the territory of war and [later] captured [by Muslims] would become fay'.

[48] See Abū Yūsuf, *Kitāb al-Kharāj*, p. 182; Shāfi'ī, *Umm*, Vol. IV, p. 203; Ṭaḥāwī, *Mukhtaṣar*, p. 261; Sarakhsī, *Sharḥ al-Siyar al-Kabīr* (Hyderabad), Vol. IV, pp. 194-205.

1193. I asked: If the master came to us from the dār al-ḥarb in a raid and took back with him [from the dār al-Islām] some of the property which had been divided among the heirs and returned to the territory of war where he was executed for his disbelief, but the property which had been taken by him was captured [by the Muslims], would it become fay'?

1194. He replied: No, because the property which he had taken belonged to the heirs and they would have the right to take it back if they found it before the division of the spoil. If they found it after it was divided up, they would have the right to take it by paying its value.

1195. I asked: If a slave apostatized from Islam and went over to the territory of war taking with him some of his master's property, but thereafter he was killed and his property was captured [by Muslims], do you think that the property would become fay'?

1196. He replied: No, it would be returned to his master.

1197. I asked: If a slave apostatized from Islam and his master sold him to another man but concealed [the fact of his] apostasy from the purchaser, do you think that this would constitute a defect for which the slave could be returned [to the vendor]? [49]

1198. He replied: Yes.

1199. I asked: If he were executed while in the possession of the purchaser, after Islam had been offered to him and he had refused to accept it, would the vendor have to return the price to the purchaser?

1200. He replied: Yes, according to Abū Ḥanīfa.

However, Abū Yūsuf and Muḥammad [b. al-Ḥasan] held that the [two] values of the slave—when he was in immunity and when it was lawful to shed his blood—would be estimated, and [the purchaser] would be entitled to recuperate the difference [from the vendor].

[49] See paragraph 1165.

Capture of Apostates [50]

1201. I asked: If a group [of Muslims], including their wives and children, apostatized and attacked the Muslims and captured one of their cities in the territory of war and no Muslim remained in that city [but] the apostates went on fighting until the Muslims conquered it, captured [apostate] women and children, and killed some [of their] men, do you think that all [the captives] would become fay'?

1202. He replied: Yes, and they would be [also] subject to the one-fifth [share of the state].

1203. I asked: Would women be compelled to return to Islam?

1204. He replied: Yes.

1205. I asked: If women refused to return to Islam, would they be executed?

1206. He replied: No.

1207. I asked: If a woman refused to return to Islam and she either fell in the share of one of the Muslims or was purchased by him, do you think that it would be lawful for him to have intercourse with her?

1208. He replied: No.

1209. I asked: Even if she had become a Jewess or a Christian?

1210. He replied: Even so. Do you not think that she should be obliged to return to Islam?

1211. I asked: If she returned to Islam, would her master have the right to have intercourse with her by right of ownership?

1212. He replied: Yes.

1213. I asked: If she were indebted in the dār al-Islām?

1214. He replied: The debt becomes void; it is canceled by capture.

[50] See Ṭaḥāwī, *Mukhtaṣar*, p. 261; Sarakhsī, *Mabsūṭ*, Vol. X, pp. 119-20; Kāsānī, *Badā'i' al-Ṣanā'i'*, Vol. VII, p. 137.

1215. I asked: If some Muslims captured [an apostate] who refused to return to Islam, do you think that he would become a slave?

1216. He replied: No, he should be executed.

1217. I asked: Why?

1218. He replied: Because he had apostatized from Islam, and no Muslim who apostatizes should be permitted to reside in the dār al-Islām, for he should either return to Islam or be executed.

1219. I asked: If he returned to Islam, would he become fay'?

1220. He replied: No, he becomes a free man.

1221. I asked: Why?

1222. He replied: No [Muslim] Arab should become fay', and whoever refuses to return to Islam should be executed. But whoever becomes a Muslim would be free and not liable to anything.

1223. I asked: Would their [apostate] women and children become subject to capture if they were in the territory of war?

1224. He replied: Yes.

1225. I asked: If the men and women of a Muslim city apostatized and took control of the city—except some Muslims who remained in it in security—and the city was later captured by the Muslims, what do you think would be the ruling concerning the women and children?

1226. He replied: All of them would be regarded as free men, but they should be compelled to return to Islam.

1227. I asked: Why?

1228. He replied: Because there were with them a group of Muslims.

1229. I asked: If there were no Muslims with them, and the women did not apostatize, would the children become slaves?

1230. He replied: No.

1231. I asked: Why?

1232. He replied: Because they would be regarded as Muslims, following the religion of their mothers.

1233. I asked: If they and their women apostatized and captured the city, but immediately afterwards [the Muslims] recaptured it, do you think that the women and children would become slaves?

1234. He replied: No, they would not become slaves.

1235. I asked: Would the women be compelled to return to Islam?

1236. He replied: Yes.

1237. I asked: Would the men be invited to return to 157
Islam so that if they returned that would be acceptable; if they refused, they would be executed?

1238. He replied: Yes:

1239. I asked: If a man and his wife apostatized from Islam and went over to the territory of war with a small child, but thereafter the man was killed and the woman and the child were captured [by the Muslims], do you think that they would become fay'?

1240. He replied: Yes, she and the child would become fay'.

1241. I asked: If a man apostatized and went over to the dār al-ḥarb taking with him a small child, leaving behind in the dār al-Islām his wife who remained a Muslim, but thereafter the man was killed and the child was captured by [Muslims], would the child become fay'?

1242. He replied: No, he would be returned to his mother.

1243. I asked: Why, if the father had taken him to the territory of war?

1244. He replied: Because his mother is a Muslim and the child follows its mother's religion.

1245. I asked: If the mother died before the father apostatized, would the child become fay'?

1246. He replied: No, he would not become fay' because the mother died as a Muslim before the father had apostatized [and the child would follow her religion].

1247. I asked: Would the same hold true if the mother were a Christian or one of the People of the Book or a Dhimmī?

1248. He replied: Yes, since this and the foregoing situation would be the same.

1249. I asked: If a man and his wife apostatized and went over to the territory of war where children were born to them, but thereafter the father and mother died and the children grew up as unbelievers and gave birth to other children who were captured by the Muslims, would [the grandchildren] become fay' [if captured]?

1250. He replied: Yes.

1251. I asked: Would they not be compelled to become Muslims?

1252. He replied: No.

1253. I asked: Why, since they have been the descendants of apostates?

1254. He replied: The apostate himself or his immediate child would be compelled to return to Islam, but not their grandchildren.

1255. I asked: Why?

1256. He replied: If some of the captives had a Muslim grandfather or a grandmother, do you think that I should oblige them to accept Islam? If I did, then anyone ever taken as a captive should be obliged to accept Islam, since all men are the descendants of Adam and Eve,[51] peace be upon them.

Breach of Dhimmīs' Agreement [with the Muslims][52]

1257. I asked: If a group of Dhimmīs violated their covenant [with Islam] and fought the Muslims and took control of their [Dhimmī] city and their rule was established there, but some Muslims remained there in security and thereafter [Muslim rule] was re-established, do you think that [the Dhimmīs] would become captives?

[51] Murad Mulla MS: Noah; but in 'Ātif and Fayd-Allāh MSS: Eve.

[52] See Ṭaḥāwī, *Mukhtaṣar*, p. 261; Sarakhsī, *Mabsūṭ*, Vol. X, pp. 116-17.

1258. He replied: No.

1259. I asked: Why?

1260. He replied: Because the territory did not become [a part of the] dār al-ḥarb. Do you not think that the Muslims lived there in security and the territory continued to be a dār al-Islām as it was [before the violation of the agreement]?

1261. I asked: If [the Dhimmīs] killed the Muslims who were in the city and took their children as captives and ruled the city for a very long time maintaining their domination and enforcing the rulings of unbelievers so that no Muslim could live there in security and there was no Muslim population between them and the inhabitants of the territory of war, but later Muslim rule prevailed and killed [all] their combatants, would their women and children be taken as captives?

1262. He replied: Yes.

1263. I asked: If the Dhimmīs violated their covenant and fought the Muslims, do you think that their status would be equivalent to that of the apostates who go over to the dār al-ḥarb?

1264. He replied: Yes.

1265. I asked: Would their women and children be taken as captives?

1266. He replied: Yes.

1267. I asked: Would the men also be taken as captives?

1268. He replied: Yes, because these should be treated differently from male apostates.

1269. I asked: If they asked for peace and became Dhimmīs again after they had violated their covenant, and if some of them had committed bodily injuries and seized property before they violated their covenant, would they be held responsible [for all previous acts]?

1270. He replied: Yes.

1271. I asked: Would they receive retaliation for any tort where *lex talionis* is possible?

1272. He replied: Yes.

1273. I asked: Do you think that they would be held

responsible for any property that they may have destroyed during their fighting [with the Muslims] or any blood that they may have shed?

1274. He replied: No.

1275. I asked: Why is the latter situation different from the former?

1276. He replied: As to a tort that they may have committed in the dār al-Islām when they observed the covenant and were in peace with Muslims, they would be held liable for such acts, and the existence of the covenant would not render them null and void; but as to the offenses committed during the fighting they would be unavenged because [the state of] war is different from that of peace.

1277. I asked: If [the rebels] made no peace agreement, but [the Muslims] attained victory over them and took them as fay' [i. e., slaves], would they be held liable for offenses committed in the dār al-Islām?

1278. He replied: No, because those would be waived by their becoming captives.

1279. I asked: Would the apostates and these be treated alike?

1280. He replied: Yes.

1281. I asked: If a Dhimmī violated his covenant [with Islam] and went over to the dār al-ḥarb with his young children, but thereafter he was killed and his children taken as captives, do you think that they would become fay' if their Dhimmī mother were residing in the dār al-Islām?

1282. He replied: No, they would not become fay' if their mother were in the dār al-Islām, but they would be given back to their mother and their status would be the same as their mother's.

1283. I asked: Would the same hold true if the mother had died in the dār al-Islām before the father violated the covenant [with the Muslims]?

1284. He replied: Yes.

1285. I asked: If both the father and mother violated the covenant and went over to the territory of Islam, leaving behind them a little boy in the dār al-Islām, would he become fay'?

1286. He replied: No, he continues to enjoy the same status as before.

1287. I asked: If the parents had taken with them another young son to the dār al-ḥarb and thereafter the son was taken as captive, would he become fay'?

1288. He replied: Yes.

1289. I asked: Why?

1290. He replied: Because they took him with them to the dār al-ḥarb and he would have the same status as that of the people [of that territory].

1291. I asked: If the Dhimmī in question entered again into a peace agreement [with the Muslims] and he had destroyed [Muslim] property and shed [Muslim] blood while he was fighting them, do you think that he would be held liable for anything?

1292. He replied: No.

1293. I asked: If he had left behind in the dār al-Islām a Dhimmī wife and then made a peace agreement with the Muslims, would his marriage with her remain valid?

1294. He replied: His marriage with the wife he had left in the dār al-Islām remains no longer valid, but his marriage with the wife who violated the agreement along with him
would be valid if she made peace and returned along with 158
him [to the dār al-Islām].

1295. I asked: Why is her situation different from the other?

1296. He replied: Because when he went over to the territory of war, where Muslim rulings are not binding on him, the wedlock bond between him and his wife [who remained in the dār al-Islām] was dissolved.

1297. I asked: Would the same be true in the case of the apostate?

1298. He replied: Yes.

1299. I asked: If the wife of the apostate apostatized and went along with him to the territory of war, and later both returned to Islam, would their marriage remain valid?

1300. He replied: Yes.

1301. I asked: If he left his apostatizing wife in the dār al-Islām and after his return [to dār al-Islām] both adopted Islam, [would their marriage remain valid]?

1302. He replied: Marital relations between them would be discontinued because when he went over to the territory of war, leaving her behind in the territory of Islam, the wedlock was dissolved.

Apostate Ascendancy in Their Territory[53]

1303. I asked: If a group [of Muslims] apostatized from Islam and—possessing resisting power—established their ascendancy in the territory in which they were living and no Muslim or Dhimmī remained there with them and the territory became a territory of unbelievers and an adjunct part of the territory of war,[54] and they acquired there property belonging to Muslims and Dhimmīs, and acquired also captives from the territory of war, but thereafter they returned to Islam while in possession of what they had acquired, do you think that they would have the right to keep all what they acquired [during apostasy]?

1304. He replied: Yes.

1305. I asked: If they had in their possession persons whom they had captured from Muslims or Dhimmīs, or if they had captured an umm walad or a mudabbar or a mukātab?

[53] See Sarakhsī, *Kitāb Sharḥ al-Siyar al-Kabīr* (Hyderabad), Vol. IV, pp. 164-69.

[54] It becomes a separate territory having the same status as the territory of war.

1306. He replied: They all would have to be returned to their people.

1307. I asked: If the Muslims had captured from the belligerents [of the territory of war] some of their children, property, slaves, and booty which they divided up as spoil, and these [belligerents] later returned to Islam, would anything [of the slaves or property] acquired be returned to them?

1308. He replied: No.

1309. I asked: Why?

1310. He replied: Because at the time Muslims captured these objects it was lawful for them to divide whatever they had taken as spoil.

1311. I asked: What would you think if the apostates asked the Muslims to treat them as Dhimmīs and said they would pay the poll tax?

1312. He replied: They should not be allowed to do so.

1313. I asked: Would the Muslims be allowed to make a peaceful agreement with them for a year so that [the apostates] might consider their position?

1314. He replied: If this were advantageous to the Muslims or if the Muslims were unable to defend themselves [against their attack], there would be no harm in making a peace agreement with them; but if Muslims were capable of prevailing over them and war [seemed] to be more advantageous than peace, no agreement should be made with them but they should be captured.

1315. I asked: Would [the Muslims] collect the tribute (kharāj) if they made an agreement with them?

1316. He replied: I disapprove of that, but if they ever did I would regard it as lawful. But God knows best!

Arab Polytheists[55]

1317. Muḥammad b. al-Ḥasan from al-Ḥasan b. 'Umāra from al-Ḥakam [b. 'Utayba] from Miqsam [b. Bujra] from ['Abd-Allah] b. 'Abbās, who said:

The Apostle of God gave Arab polytheists no alternative than conversion to Islam or execution. Abū Ḥanīfa, Abū Yūsuf, and Muḥammad [b. al-Ḥasan] accepted this ruling.

1318. I asked: If the Arab polytheists refused to adopt Islam, do you think that they would be allowed to make peace with the Muslims and become Dhimmīs?

1319. He replied: They should never be allowed to do so, but they would be invited to accept Islam. If they became Muslims, that would be acceptable on their part; otherwise, they should be forced to surrender because it has been related to us that such was the ruling and they should not [be treated] like other unbelievers.[56]

1320. [I asked:] If the Muslims attacked them and took their women and children as captives and their men as prisoners of war, what would be the ruling concerning them?

1321. He replied: The women and children would become fay' and divided up as spoil, out of which the one-fifth [share] would be taken; but of the men, those who adopt Islam would be free (and nothing would be done against them), but those who refuse to adopt Islam would have to be executed.

1322. I asked: What is the ruling concerning the scripturaries of Arabia?

1323. He replied: The ruling concerning them is the same as that of other unbelievers.[57]

[55] See Sarakhsī, *Kitāb Sharḥ al-Siyar al-Kabīr* (Hyderabad), Vol. IV, pp. 192-94, and *Mabsūṭ*, Vol. X, pp. 117-19.

[56] In Arabic MSS: Like other Muslims is an error.

[57] I. e., like the scripturaries of any other country.

The Group of Muslims in the Territory of War Who Apostatize[58]

1324. I asked: If [the Muslims] attacked the territory of war and some of them apostatized and left the army and fought separately the unbelievers, and both they and the Muslims captured spoil, but thereafter the apostates repented and returned to Islam before they left the dār al-ḥarb, do you think that they would be entitled to participate along with the Muslims in the spoil of war?

1325. He replied: No.

1326. I asked: Would they be allowed to keep what they had acquired?

1327. He replied: Yes.

1328. I asked: But if they encountered the enemy later [after their return to Islam] and fought along [with the Muslims], would they participate in the division of the spoil?

1329. He replied: Yes.

Apostate Liable To Be Executed[59]

1330. I asked: If a group [of Muslims] apostatized from Islam and were attacked by [other] Muslims without [first] having been invited to adopt Islam, do you think that those [who attacked] would be liable for anything?

1331. He replied: No.

1332. I asked: Why? According to the sunna they should be invited [to adopt Islam] before being fought.

1333. He replied: Even so, they would not be liable for anything.

1334. I asked: Would the same be true if a single man apostatized from Islam and was killed by another before he was invited [to return] to Islam?

[58] See Sarakhsī, *Mabsūṭ*, Vol. X, pp. 119-20.
[59] See *ibid.*, pp. 121-22.

1335. He replied. Yes.

1336. I asked: Would the same [ruling] apply to a woman?

1337. He replied: Yes.

1338. I asked: Would the same [ruling] apply to a male or a female slave? 159

1339. He replied: Yes.

1340. I asked: Why?

1341. He replied: Men [who apostatize] would be liable to be executed, regardless whether they were slaves or free.

1342. I asked: But what about women, although you do not [approve] killing them?

1343. He replied: Because some jurists hold that they should be executed if they left Islam.

1344. I asked: If a lad apostatized from Islam before he reached puberty, do you think that he would be executed?

1345. He replied: No.

1346. I asked: Would the same hold true if he had come of age while still an unbeliever?

1347. He replied: I would order his imprisonment rather than execution, because he had never professed Islam after he had come of age.

1348. I asked: If the lad who apostatized from Islam was capable of understanding but had not yet reached puberty, do you think that he would have the right to inherit from his father and be entitled to [the Islamic funeral] prayer if he died?

1349. He replied: I would say yes on the strength of analogical reasoning, but I would rather abandon analogy in this case because it is too ugly [to apply analogy], so I would neither eat from his slaughtered animal, nor say the [funeral] prayer for him, nor allow him to inherit.

1350. I asked: If a Magian lad has grown up and become capable of understanding but he has not yet reached puberty and adopted Islam, would you eat from his slaughtered animal and would you say the [funeral] prayer for him?

1351. He replied: Yes.

1352. I asked: Would he have the right to inherit from his Magian father or could his father or mother inherit from him?

1353. He replied: No [neither one would have the right to inherit from the other]. This is the opinion of Abū Ḥanīfa, Muḥammad [b. al-Ḥasan], and the former opinion of Abū Yūsuf. However, Abū Yūsuf later held that if the lad were capable of understanding, he would regard his Islam as [a veritable] Islam, but would not regard the disbelief of such [an adolescent] as a [veritable] disbelief.

1354. I asked: If a man who apostatized from Islam repented and returned to Islam, and then apostatized again to repent later and repeated this act several times, do you think that [his repentance] would be acceptable?

1355. He replied: Yes.

1356. I asked: Even if this has been repeated on his part?

1357. He replied: [Yes], even if it were repeated. But God knows best!

Apostasy of the Intoxicated Person[60]

1358. I asked: If a man drank [heavily] until he was intoxicated and lost his reasoning power and while in such a state he apostatized from Islam but thereafter he recovered and observed [the rules of] Islam, do you think that his wife would be separated from him?

1359. He replied: I would say yes on the strength of analogical reasoning, but I should rather abandon analogy and follow juristic preference [on the strength of which] I hold that the intoxicated person who loses his reasoning ability would be treated in this case like the insane; therefore his wife would not be separated from him.

[60] Ṭaḥāwī, *Mukhtaṣar*, p. 259; Sarakhsī, *Mabsūṭ*, Vol. X, p. 123; Kāsānī, *Badā'i' al-Ṣanā'i'*, Vol. VII, p. 134.

1360. I asked: If the ruler of the unbelievers forces a Muslim to abandon Islam and the man reverted, but when he was released he returned to his wife, do you think that the wife would be separated from him if he had [apostatized] under duress?

1361. He replied: I would say yes on the strength of analogical reasoning because we do not know what the inward feeling [of the man] had been, but I should abandon analogy [in such a situation] and would not separate the wife from him.

1362. I asked: If a man apostatized from Islam, but when asked to repent he said that he had never apostatized?

1363. He replied: His declaration would be regarded as repentance and I should accept it on his part.

1364. I asked: If a man apostatized from Islam and acquired property during his apostasy, and his heirs claimed that before his death he had returned to Islam and that his property belonged to them as an inheritance, what would be the ruling in this case?

1365. He replied: The property would be regarded as fay', unless the heirs produce evidence that he had returned to Islam before his death.

1366. I asked: If the Dhimmī breaks the covenant [with the Muslims], fights the Muslims, and goes over to the territory of war, leaving behind [in the dār al-Islām] property and children, what would be done with his property? Should it be confiscated or left to his children?

1367. He replied: It would be treated like the property of a Muslim who apostatized from Islam and went over to the territory of war, i. e., it would be divided among the heirs in accordance with God's commands [concerning the distribution of inheritance].[61]

1368. I asked: If he had a debt to be paid at a specified term, would it have to be declared payable immediately and charged as such [having priority over heirs]?

[61] Q. IV, 12-15.

1369. He replied: Yes.

1370. I asked: If he had mudabbaras and umm walads, would they be set free?

1371. He replied: Yes.

However, Abū Yūsuf and Muḥammad [b. al-Ḥasan] held that whatever the apostate earns during apostasy would have the same status as his former property and should not be regarded as fay'. Likewise, all his sale-purchase transactions, his manumisson of slaves, and his gifts would be regarded as valid.[62]

[62] Shāfi'ī, *Umm*, Vol. VI, p. 148; Sarakhsī, *Mabsūṭ*, Vol. X, p. 123.

Chapter VIII

Folio 159

[ON DISSENSION AND HIGHWAY ROBBERY]

Khārijīs (Dissenters) and Baghīs (Rebels) [1]

1372. [Abū Sulaymān al-Juzjānī] said: Muḥammad b. al-Ḥasan told us from al-Ajlaḥ b. 'Abd-Allāh from Salama b. Kuḥayl from Kathīr b. Tamr al-Ḥaḍramī,[2] who said:

I entered the Mosque of Kūfa through the Kinda gates where I met five men cursing [the Caliph] 'Alī [b. Abī Ṭālib]. One of them, covered with a burnus,[3] said: " I have made a covenant with God that I shall kill him." Whereupon, I kept close [to this man] while his companions dispersed, and I took him to 'Alī and said: " I heard this man saying that he has made a covenant with God that he will kill you." " Bring him nearer [to me]," said

[1] Whoever departs from the " truth " (al-'adl), or the generally accepted sunna, and follows a heterodox creed would be regarded as belonging to the party of Baghī or dissenters. If the dissenters do not renounce the authority of the Imām, they would not be denied residence in the territory of Islam; but if they denounce the authority of the Imām and resort to arms they would be subject to the jihād and liable to be killed. Those who took arms and fought the Caliph 'Alī b. Abī Ṭālib (called the Khārijīs) were crushed in the battle of al-Nahrawān (36/658). For a discussion of their creed see Abū al-Ḥasan al-Ash'arī, *Maqālāt al-Islāmiyyīn*, ed. M. Muḥī al-Dīn 'Abd al-Ḥamīd (Cairo, 1950), Vol. I, pp. 156-96; Abū al-Fatḥ al-Shahrastānī, *al-Milal wa al-Niḥal*, ed. Aḥmad Fahmī Muḥammad (Cairo, 1948), Vol. I, pp. 170-96; Ibn Ḥazm, *al-Faṣl Fī al-Milal wa al-Ahwā' wa al-Niḥal*, ed. 'Abd al-Raḥmān Khalīfa (Cario, 1347/1928), Vol. III, p. 119-26; J. Wellhausen, *Die Religiös-politischen Opposition parteiem im alten Islam* (Göttingen, 1901), and *The Arab Kingdom and its Fall* (Calcutta, 1927).

[2] Ṭabarī cites the name as Kathīr b. Bahzal-Ḥaḍramī. See Ṭabarī, *Ta'rīkh al-Rusul wa al-Mulūk*, ed. M. Abū al-Faḍl Ibrāhīm (Cairo, 1963), Vol. V, p. 73.

[3] Anglicized as burnous or burnouse, a cloak with a hood.

['Alī] and added: "woe to you, who are you?" "I am Sawwār al-Manqurī," replied the man. "Let him go," said 'Alī. Thereupon, I said: "Shall I let him go, though [he said that] he made a covenant with God to kill you?" "Shall I kill him even though he has not [yet] killed me?" replied 'Alī. "He has cursed you," [said I]. "You should then curse him or leave him," said 'Alī.

It has been related to us that while [the Caliph] 'Alī b. Abī Ṭālib was once making a sermon on Friday, [some] Khārijīs, from one side of the Mosque, pronounced the formula: "Judgment belongs to none save God." "A word of Truth to which is given a false meaning,"[4] said 'Alī [and he added]: "we shall not prohibit you from entering our mosques to mention His [God's] name; we shall not deny you [your share of] the fay', so long as you join hands with us; nor shall we fight you until you attack us."[5] Then he resumed his [Friday] sermon.

It has also been related to us that [the Caliph] 'Alī b. Abī Ṭālib said in the Battle of the Camel: "Whoever flees [from us] shall not be chased, no [Muslim] prisoner of war shall be killed, no wounded in battle shall be dispatched, no enslavement [of women and children] shall be allowed, and no property [of a Muslim] shall be confiscated.[6]

1373. I asked: If there were two parties of believers, one of

[4] This statement was made in condemnation of 'Alī's acceptance of arbitration as a means to settle his dispute with Mu'awiya, Governor of Syria, when 'Alī refused to resume fighting after the battle of Ṣiffīn (37/658).

[5] Ṭabarī, *Ta'rīkh al-Rusul*, Vol. V, pp. 73-74; Shāfi'ī, *Umm*, Vol. IV, p. 136; Māwardī, *Kitāb al-Aḥkām*, p. 96; Sarakhsī, *Mabsūṭ*, Vol. X, pp. 124-25.

[6] Abū Yūsuf, *Kitāb al-Kharāj*, pp. 214, 215; Sarakhsī, *Mabsūṭ*, Vol. X, p. 126. The rule that rebels are liable to be fought if they refuse to submit is based on a Quranic injunction which runs as follows: "If two parties of the believers fight, put things right between them, and if one of the two parties oppresses the other, fight the one which is oppressive until it returns to God's command. If it returns, set things right between them justly and act fairly. Verily God loves those who act fairly" (Q. XLIX, 9). The jurists advised calling the rebels to submission before attacking them on the strength of this Quranic communication. See Shāfi'ī, *Umm*, Vol. IV, pp. 133-34.

them is rebellious (party of baghī) and the other loyal (party of justice),[7] and the former was defeated by the latter, would not the loyal party have the right to chase the fugitives [of the other party], kill their prisoners, and dispatch the wounded?

1374. He replied: No, it should never be allowed to do so 160
if none of the rebels has survived and no group remained with whom refuge might be taken; but if a group of them has survived with whom refuge might be taken, then their prisoners could be killed, their fugitives pursued, and their wounded dispatched.[8]

1375. I asked: If the loyal [army] acquired weapons, kurā', and other materials from the rebels, what would be done with them?

1376. He replied: If anyone of the rebels has survived, there would be no harm for the loyal army to use the weapons and kurā' against him; but when the war comes to an end, everything should be returned to its [original] owners. However, anything acquired, other than weapons and kurā', should be returned to them [even] before the war comes to an end. If none of the rebels has survived, the weapons, kurā', and other material should be returned to their [rightful] owners. [For] it has been related to us from [the Caliph] 'Alī b. Abī Ṭālib that he deposited everything he had acquired [at the battle] of Nahrawān on the plain so that anyone who recognized something that belonged to him could take it back. Thus the last person who had recognized an iron pan belonging to him took it.[9]

[7] "Ahl al-'adl" is the Party of Justice or Party of the Truth, i.e., the loyalists (see Māwardī, *Kitāb al-Aḥkām*, p. 96).

[8] Sarakhsī, *Mabsūṭ*, Vol. X, p. 126. Shāfi'ī, however, held that the fighting of rebels was based on a Quranic injunction and Caliph 'Alī's precedent; accordingly, he disagreed with the Ḥanafī doctrine that only those who were supported with others should be fought and killed. See Shāfi'ī, *Umm*, Vol. IV, pp. 137, 142-43.

[9] Sarakhsī *Mabsūt*, Vol. X, pp. 126-27. Shāfi'ī held that it was more appropriate to take possession of the property and weapons of the rebels if they were liable to be fought and killed. See Shāfi'ī, *Umm*, Vol. IV, pp. 143-44.

1377. I asked: If a group of the rebels prevailed over a country where it was residing and dominated its people and collected from them the taxes (ṣadaqāt), such as camels, cows, and sheep as well as the poll tax from the Dhimmīs, but thereafter the loyal army reconquered the land, do you think that the latter should collect [again] the poll tax from the Dhimmīs and the taxes due on the camels, cows, and sheep, not taking into account what the rebels have collected from them?

1378. He replied: They should not collect anything from them [for the period in which the rebels had ruled] because these [tax payers] were neither protected from the rebels nor did the rulings [of the lawful authorities] apply to them, but they would be held liable for payment of all dues in the future.[10]

1379. I asked: If a woman took part in the fighting along with the rebels and was taken as a prisoner, do you think that she would be liable to be executed if the rebel army (preserving its forces) were still fighting?

1380. He replied: She should not be executed, but imprisoned.[11]

1381. I asked: What would you think if a freeman and a slave who was fighting along with the rebels were taken prisoners while the rebel army, preserving its forces, was still fighting the loyal army?

1382. He replied: Whoever of those [two] categories is captured could be executed.

1383. I asked: If a noncombatant slave in the service of his [combatant] master and a combatant woman were taken prisoners, would they be liable to be executed?

1384. He replied: No, but they would be imprisoned.

1385. I asked: How long should such a woman or such a slave remain in prison?

[10] Shāfi'ī, *Umm*, Vol. IV, p. 139.

[11] Abū Yūsuf, *Kitāb al-Kharāj*, p. 214; Shāfi'ī, *Umm*, Vol. IV, pp. 137-38; Sarakhsī, *Mabsūṭ*, Vol. X, p. 127; Kāsānī, *Badā'i' al-Ṣanā'i'*, Vol. VII, p. 141.

1386. He replied: Until no one of the rebels remains fighting.[12]

1387. I asked: [13] What would be the status of the kurāʿ and weapons which [loyal] Muslims may capture and for which they have no need?

1388. He replied: The kurāʿ may be sold and its prices retained, but the weapons should be returned to its owners after the war is over.[14]

1389. I asked: If the rebels want to enter into a peace agreement with the lawful authorities (the loyalists) for a specified number of days or for a month until they reconsider their position, would it be lawful to do so?

1390. He replied: Yes, if this were advantageous to the loyalists.[15]

1391. I asked: If [the loyalists] asked [the rebels] to pay a specified amount of property [as a *quid pro quo* for peace], do you think that this would be lawful to accept from them?

1392. He replied: No.

1393. I asked: Why?

1394. He replied: Because [the rebels] are Muslims; therefore, nothing should be taken from their property, for this would amount to kharāj.[16]

1395. I asked: If the rebels repented and joined the loyalists, do you think that they should be held liable for whatever property or life they destroyed during the war?

1396. He replied: No, unless something tangible remained which should be returned to its owners.[17]

1397. I asked: Would the same hold true for whatever property the loyalists had captured and consumed and would

[12] Sarakhsī, *Mabsūṭ*, Vol. X, p. 127; Kāsānī, *Badā'i' al-Ṣanā'i'*, Vol. VII, p. 141.

[13] "Similarly" is omitted.

[14] Cf. Shāfi'ī, *Umm*, Vol. IV, pp. 143-44.

[15] Sarakhsī, *Mabsūṭ*, Vol. X, p. 127.

[16] *Ibid.*

[17] Abū Yūsuf, *Kitāb al-Kharāj*, p. 215; Sarakhsī, *Mabsūṭ*, Vol. X, pp. 127-28.

any blood they had shed be left unavenged—they would not be liable for that?

1398. He replied: Yes [they would not].

1399. I asked: What do you think concerning the wounds inflicted [on the loyalists] by the rebels and the property usurped from them?

1400. He replied: These also would be waived, unless some [of the property] remained unconsumed, which should be returned to its owners.

1401. I asked: If the rebels sought the assistance of a group of Dhimmīs, who took part in the fighting along with them, do you think that [the Dhimmīs' participation in the fighting] would be regarded as a violation of their agreement [with the Muslims]?

1402. He replied: No.

1403. I asked: Why?

1404. He replied: Because they were in the company of a group of Muslims.[18]

1405. I asked: Would the killing or wounds or destruction of property inflicted [on the loyalists] by the Dhimmīs be treated in the same way as those by the rebels?

1406. He replied: Yes.

1407. I asked: Why should not the rebels be held liable for whatever of those things that they have committed?

1408. He replied: Because [loyal Muslim] rulings do not apply to them [in their territory] and they would be regarded as having been separated [from the Muslims] like the inhabitants of the territory of war.[19]

1409. I asked: Why should not the loyalists be held liable for whatever [injuries] they inflicted on the rebels, if these [the rebels] repented?

1410. He replied: Because it had become lawful for the loyalists to fight [the rebels] and therefore they would not be held liable.

[18] Sarakhsī, *Mabsūṭ*, Vol. X, p. 128. Cf. Shāfi'ī, *Umm*, Vol. IV, p. 138.
[19] Sarakhsī, *Mabsūṭ*, Vol. X, p. 128.

1411. I asked: Would the loyalists have to invite the rebels to accept the Just [20] if they meet them?

1412. He replied: Yes.[21]

1413. I asked: If [the loyalists] fought them without such an invitation, would they be held liable?

1414. He replied: No.

1415. I asked: Why?

1416. He replied: Because they [the rebels] had known what the invitation would be, although an invitation would be commendable, for they might yet return [to the truth].[22]

1417. I asked: Would it be objectionable to you if the loyalists shot [the rebels] with arrows, inundated [their positions] with water, attacked them with manjanīqs (mangonels), and burned them with fire?

1418. He replied: No harm in doing anything of this sort.

1419. I asked: Would a sudden attack at night be objectionable to you?

1420. He replied: No harm in it.[23]

1421. I asked: If the loyalists made a peace [agreement] with the rebels for a month, allowing them to reconsider their position, and each party [agreed] to send hostages to the other so that if either one attacked the other [the execution of] his
hostages would be lawful to the other, and if the rebels 161
attacked [first] and killed the hostages in their hands, do you think that the loyalists should execute the hostages in their hands?

1422. He replied: No.

[20] "al-'adl," i. e., the "right path" or the truth.

[21] Abū Yūsuf, *Kitāb al-Kharāj*, p. 214; Shāfi'ī, *Umm*, Vol. IV, p. 133; Kāsānī, *Badā'i' al-Ṣanā'i'*, Vol. VII, p. 140.

[22] Sarakhsī, *Mabsūṭ*, Vol. X, p. 128; Kāsānī, *Badā'i' al-Ṣanā'i'*, Vol. VII, p. 140.

[23] Sarakhsī, *Mabsūṭ*, Vol. X, pp. 128-129; Kāsānī, *Badā'i' al-Ṣanā'i'*, Vol. VII, p. 141; Māwardī, *Kitāb al-Aḥkām*, pp. 97-99.

1423. I asked: What should they do with them?

1424. He replied: They should be imprisoned until all the rebels perished and returned [to the truth] or repented.[24]

1425. I asked: Would the same hold true if such an agreement were made between the Muslims and the unbelievers and it was the latter who committed treachery and killed the Muslim hostages in their hands? Should the Muslims kill the hostages [of the unbelievers] in their hands?

1426. He replied: No. They should be imprisoned permanently unless they become Muslims or Dhimmīs, whereupon they would be released.

1427. I asked: If one of the loyalists gave an amān to a rebel, do you think that such an amān would be valid until [the recipient of amān] returned to his place of security?

1428. He replied: Yes.[25]

1429. I asked: [26] Would the amān be valid if [the man who granted it] said: "No harm"?

1430. He replied: Yes.

1431. I asked: Would the same hold true if he said, "No harm to you," in Persian or in the Nabatean language?

1432. He replied: Yes.

1433. I asked: Would the same hold true if a woman of the loyalists said the same to one of the rebels?

1434. He replied: Yes.

1435. I asked: Would the same hold true if a slave [granted an amān]?

1436. He replied: No, [it would not be so] if he were not fighting along with his master, but if he were fighting his amān would be valid. This is the opinion of Abū Ḥanīfa.[27]

1437. I asked: If a Dhimmī were fighting along with the loyalists and gave an amān to one of the rebels?

[24] Shāfi'ī, *Umm*, Vol. IV, p. 140; Māwardī, *Kitāb al-Aḥkām*, p. 99; Sarakhsī, *Mabsūṭ*, Vol. X, p. 129.

[25] Sarakhsī, *Mabsūṭ*, Vol. X, pp. 129-30.

[26] "Similarly" is omitted.

[27] Sarakhsī, *Mabsūṭ*, Vol. X, p. 130.

1438. He replied: Both the slave who does not fight and the Dhimmī who fights are alike and are not entitled to give amān; but if the slave takes part in the fighting and he is a Muslim, his amān to the unbelievers and to the rebels would be valid.

1439. I asked: In accordance with what you said, would it be valid if a male or female Muslim gave an amān to an unbeliever from the inhabitants of the territory of war?

1440. He replied: Yes.

1441. I asked: If the loyalists captured kurā' and weapons from the rebels and were in need of them, do you think that it would be lawful for the Imām to divide it up among them, giving the horse-rider two shares and the foot-warrior one, after deducting the one-fifth [share]?

1442. He replied: No. This [property] should not be regarded as spoil taken from the unbelievers, but the Imām may give out of it to each according to his need; when the war would be over, the whole [property] should be returned to its original owners.[28]

1443. I asked: If women were fighting along with the rebels against the loyalists, do you think that it would be lawful for the loyalists to kill them?

1444. He replied: Yes, it is [29] lawful to kill them.[30]

1445. I asked: If a prisoner of the loyalists fell in the hands of the rebels, or loyal merchants went to the rebel camp and one of the merchants killed another merchant or cut off his hand and thereafter the loyalists reconquered [the land], do you think that one [of the two merchants] would be liable for retaliation for the offense committed against the other?

1446. He replied: No.

1447. I asked: Would the same be true if one of the prisoners committed that against the other?

1448. He replied: Yes.

[28] See paragraph 1337, above; Māwardī, *Kitāb al-Aḥkam*, pp. 99-100.

[29] In Arabic MSS: "it is not"—an error. See Sarakhsī, *Mabsūṭ*, Vol. X, p. 127.

[30] Kāsānī, *Badā'i' al-Ṣanā'i'*, Vol. VII, p. 141.

1449. I asked: Why?

1450. He replied: Because they committed the offenses in a place where Muslim rulings were not binding on them; we have thus waived [the penalties].[31]

1451. I asked: If the judge of the rebels wrote a letter to the judge of the loyalists confirming the [property] right of a man of the rebels, based on the witnesses of the rebels and confided a man from the loyalists [to transmit it], do you think that the judge of the loyalists should regard the letter and the testimony of his witnesses as valid?

1452. He replied: No, for if [the judge of the loyalists] accepts the validity of the letter of the judge of the rebels, the rebels would then be able to take away all the property of the loyalists.[32]

1453. I asked: If the rebels took control of one of the cities and appointed as judge one of the men of that city who was not a rebel and who wrote a letter confirming the [property] right of a man in that city, or even a rebel, certified by witnesses from the people of that province, do you think that the judge of the loyalists should accept the validity [of that letter] if the agent of that man appeared before the judge and the witnesses certified him [to be the agent]?

1454. He replied: If the judge who received the letter knew the witnesses who gave evidence before the other judge and that judge was not a rebel, I hold that the letter should be accepted, but if the judge [of the loyalists] did not know [the witnesses], I hold that the letter should not be accepted.[33]

1455. I asked: If a man in the said city under the rule of rebels cut off the hand of another or killed him intentionally and the matter was brought to the judge, would he be entitled to pass judgment as the judge of the loyalists?

1456. He replied: Yes.

[31] Sarakhsī, *Mabsūṭ*, Vol. X, p. 130; Kāsānī, *Badā'i' al-Ṣanā'i'*, Vol. VII, p. 141.

[32] Shāfi'ī, *Umm*, Vol. IV, p. 139; Sarakhsī, *Mabsūṭ*, Vol. X, p. 130; Kāsānī, *Badā'i' al-Ṣanā'i'*, Vol. VII, p. 142.

[33] Shāfi'ī, *Umm*, Vol. IV, p. 140; Sarakhsī, *Mabsūṭ*, Vol. X, p. 130.

1457. I asked: Would he be competent to impose the ḥudūd penalties even as the judge of the loyalists?

1458. He replied: Yes, because it would not be possible for him to do otherwise.

1459. I asked: If it were a qiṣāṣ (retaliation) or an arsh (damage), would he have to carry them out?

1460. He replied: Yes.

1461. I asked: Would the judge impose the ḥudūd in that city just as the judge of the loyalists does?

1462. He replied: Yes.[34]

1463. I asked: If the rebels captured property or committed offenses before starting rebellion or before they engaged in fighting, and the Imām thereafter made peace with them after they had rebelled on condition that he waive [all the said unlawful acts], do you think that this would be lawful?

1464. He replied: No, it would not be lawful for the Imām to make peace with them on such [conditions]; on the contrary, they should be held liable for them.

1465. I asked: [Do you hold, therefore, that] for whatever involves the qiṣāṣ (retaliation), they should be held liable for it; for whatever involves unintentional killing, [the blood-money] should be paid by the 'āqila; for whatever involves quasi-intentional tort to body falling short of life, qiṣāṣ should be imposed; for whatever involves loss of life, the highest diya should be paid by the 'āqila of the offender, and for whatever property is destroyed, damages should be paid?

1466. He replied: Yes.

1467. I asked: Why is that so?

1468. He replied: Because they committed all of the said [acts] before they went to war [with the loyalists] and Muslim rulings were binding on them at that moment just as upon all other Muslims.[35]

[34] Sarakhsī, *Mabsūṭ*, Vol. X, pp. 130-31; Kāsānī, *Badā'i' al-Ṣanā'i'*, Vol. VII, p. 141.

[35] Shāfi'ī, *Umm*, Vol. IV, p. 140; Sarakhsī, *Mabsūṭ*, Vol. X, pp. 130-31; Māwardī, *Kitāb al-Aḥkām*, pp. 99-101.

1469. I asked: If one of the loyalists were killed in the camp of the rebels, do you think he would be entitled to be treated as a martyr?

1470. He replied: Yes.

1471. I asked: If the loyalists prevail over the rebels,[36] 162
would those [from among the rebels] who were killed be entitled to [funeral] prayer?

1472. He replied: No.

1473. I asked: Why? Are they not Muslims?

1474. He replied: Yes. Even though they are Muslims, I would give that up for them.

1475. I asked: Would you order that [their dead] be buried?

1476. He replied: Yes.[37]

1477. I asked: Would you disapprove of carrying the heads [of their killed persons] to the Imām?

1478. He replied: Yes, I disapprove of that because it amounts to mutilation. Nothing has been related to us from [the Caliph] 'Alī b. Abī Ṭālib that he ever did so in any of his wars, nor did he order any head to be carried [at the point of the lance].[38]

1479. I asked: What do you think if one of the loyalists killed his father or a brother participating in the war;[39] would he be entitled to inherit from him?

1480. He replied: Yes.

1481. I asked: Why?

1482. He replied: Because such killing was right.

1483. I asked: What do you think if a warrior of the party of the Baghī kills his father or his grandfather; would he be entitled to inherit from him?

[36] In Arabic MSS: "And their dead."

[37] Abū Yūsuf, *Kitāb al-Kharāj*, p. 214; Sarakhsī, *Mabsūṭ*, Vol. X, p. 131. Shāfi'ī, however, held that they would be entitled to prayer and to be buried. See Shāfi'ī, *Umm*, Vol. IV, pp. 140-41.

[38] Shāfi'ī, *Umm*, Vol. IV, p. 141; Sarakhsī, *Mabsūṭ*, Vol. X, pp. 131-32.

[39] Literally: "Among the people of war."

1484. He replied: Yes, because he killed him in accordance with his own interpretation [of the law]. This is the opinion of Abū Ḥanīfa and Muḥammad [b. al-Ḥasan], but Abū Yūsuf held that he would not be entitled to inherit.[40]

1485. I asked: Would you disapprove of a man of the loyalists killing his father or brother from among the rebels?

1486. He replied: Yes, but it would be commendable if someone else did so in his place.

1487. I asked: Would the same hold true if the father were an unbeliever while fighting [against Muslims]?

1488. He replied: Yes.

1489. I asked: Would you disapprove if he were to kill a brother, paternal or maternal uncle, if they were unbelievers?

1490. He replied: No harm in that.[41]

1491. I asked: If the father, as an unbelieving warrior, wanted to kill his son, do you think it would be lawful for the son to fight his father in self-defense?

1492. He replied: Yes.

1493. I asked: If the father did not directly intend [to kill] his son, would you disapprove of the son's taking the initiative against the father?

1494. He replied: Yes.

1495. I asked: If one of the loyalists happened to be in the ranks of the rebels and was killed by a [loyal] Muslim, do you think that the latter would be liable for the diya?

1496. He replied: No.

1497. I asked: Why?

1498. He replied: Because it is lawful for him to kill anyone who happened to be in the ranks of the rebels.

1499. I asked: If one of the rebels entered the camp of the loyalists under an amān and was killed by one of the loyalists, do you think that [the latter] would be liable for the diya?

[40] Abū Yūsuf, *Kitāb al-Kharāj*, p. 214; Sarakhsī, *Mabsūṭ*, Vol. X, p. 132.
[41] Shāfiʿī, *Umm*, Vol. IV, p. 141; Sarakhsī, *Mabsūṭ*, Vol. X, p. 132.

1500. He replied: Yes.[42]

1501. I asked: Why?

1502. He replied: Because [the victim] had entered under an amān.

1503. I asked: Would the same hold true if a warrior of the unbelievers entered [the dār al-Islām] under an amān and was killed by a Muslim?

1504. He replied: Yes.

1505. I asked: If the loyalists encountered the rebels and fighting takes place and one of the loyalists attacks a rebel, but the latter says that he repents and lays down his arms, do you think that the former should refrain [from attacking him]?

1506. He replied: Yes.

1507. I asked: Would the same hold true if the man said: "Refrain from me until I reconsider my position; maybe I would follow you," and he laid down his arms?

1508. He replied: Yes.[43]

1509. I asked: If he said: "I follow your religion," but he did not lay down his arms?

1510. He replied: He is right in what he said and he is of the same religion, yet one need not refrain [just for his saying so].

1511. I asked: If one of the rebels takes to flight, do you think that the loyalists should kill him?

1512. He replied: Yes, if there were a group [of rebels] with whom he might take refuge.[44]

1513. I asked: If a group of rebels captured a city and took control of it, but [later] they were attacked and defeated by another group of rebels who sought to take [Muslim] women and children as captives, would it be lawful for the [Muslim] inhabitants of the city to fight in defense of the women and children?

[42] Sarakhsī, *Mabsūṭ*, Vol. X, pp. 132-33; Kāsānī, *Badā'i' al-Ṣanā'i'*, Vol. VII, p. 141.

[43] Abū Yūsuf, *Kitāb al-Kharāj*, p. 215.

[44] Shāfi'ī, *Umm*, Vol. IV, p. 141; Sarakhsī, *Mabsūṭ*, Vol. X, p. 133.

1514. He replied: Yes. They have no choice but to do so.[45]

1515. I asked: If the rebel combatants made a peace agreement with a group of the unbelievers of the territory of war for a specified number of days, but later the rebels committed a treachery and took them as captives and killed their men, would it be [lawful] for the loyalists to purchase any one of those captives?

1516. He replied: No.

1517. I asked: Why? For the peace concluded by the rebels and the amān given by them were not correct [i. e., not binding on the loyalists].

1518. He replied: Indeed, those who made the peace agreement with them were Muslims, and a narrative from the Apostle of God has reached us in which he said: "The person least in status can give a binding oath on behalf of other [Muslims]."[46]

1519. I asked: If the rebels defeat some of the loyalists and force them to escape into the territory of the unbelievers, would it be lawful for them to join in an attack launched by unbelievers against other unbelievers?

1520. He replied: No.

1521. I asked: Why?

1522. He replied: Because the jurisdiction of unbelievers prevails there [over the Muslims].

1523. I asked: Would it be lawful for the said group of the loyalists [who had entered the territory of unbelievers] to seek the support of unbelievers against Muslim rebels where the jurisdiction of unbelievers prevails?

1524. He replied: No, they should never do so.

1525. I asked: Why?

1526. He replied: Because the jurisdiction of unbelievers prevails there. Do you not think that the loyalists had entered the territory [of the unbelievers] under an amān? I disapprove

[45] Sarakhsī, *Mabsūṭ*, Vol. X, p. 133.

[46] *Ibid.*, pp. 133-34, and paragraph 50, above.

of Muslims fighting along with unbelievers against unbelievers; it is even worse if they fight along with unbelievers against Muslims [i. e., the rebels].[47]

1527. I asked: If a group of unbelievers attacked the territory where [the group of Muslim refugees] is residing and took captives from them, but the Muslims who obtained an amān became afraid for their lives, would it be lawful for them to fight in self-defense?

1528. He replied: Yes. There is no harm in fighting in such circumstances.

1529. I asked: Similarly, if those who attacked were [Muslim] rebels who defeated the unbelievers and took some of them as captives, and later turned on the loyal Muslims who were [residing there] as musta'mins and tried to attack them, do you think that it would be lawful [for the loyalists] to defend themselves?

1530. He replied: Yes. There is no harm to fight in such a state of affairs.

1531. I asked: If the unbelievers defeated the [Muslim] rebels and took their women and children and those of the Dhimmīs as captives, and then passed along with those [captives] by the [Muslim] musta'mins, do you think that these [Muslims] should refrain from attacking them, even if they were strong enough to fight?

1532. He replied: No, they could not afford [to refrain]; on the contrary, they should fight to rescue the women and children from their hands.

1533. I asked: Would they have to denounce the peace agreement that was between them and the inhabitants of the territory of war?

1534. He replied: Yes. It would not be lawful to make a pact [to the contrary].

1535. I asked: If the rebels were in [control of] a city in which a group of the loyalists were under subjugation, but [the city] attacked by unbelievers from the territory of war

[47] Shāfi'ī, *Umm*, Vol. IV, p. 138; Sarakhsī, *Mabsūṭ*, Vol. X, pp. 133-34.

who defeated the rebels and tried to take the women and children as captives, would you think that the Muslims are under obligation to fight in defense of the women and children of the rebels?

1536. He replied: Yes, they could afford to do nothing but fight against the unbelievers to defend Muslim women and children. 163

1537. I asked: If the loyalists were afraid that the rebels might attack them, do you think that it would be lawful for them to seek the support of Dhimmīs, provided that the loyalists would be in command?

1538. He replied: Yes. There is no harm in so doing.

1539. I asked: Would it be all right for them to seek the support of one group of Muslim rebels against another?

1540. He replied: Yes, provided the loyal Muslims would be in command over the rebels and their rule prevails over them. No harm in such a case, if they seek their support.

1541. I asked: If two groups of the rebels were fighting one another and a [third] loyalist group was not involved in that fighting, do you think that the latter could take sides and fight with the one against the other if the command were in rebel hands? Moreover, provided it was possible for [the loyal Muslim] to separate from them if they received some reinforcement.

1542. He replied: It would not be lawful for them to fight in such conditions.

1543. I asked: Would it be lawful for them to remain idle, if they were not strong enough to fight against the rebels?

1544. He replied: Yes.[48]

[48] Shāfi'ī, *Umm*, Vol. IV, pp. 138-39; Sarakhsī, *Mabsūṭ*, Vol. X, pp. 133-34.

[*Status of*] *Highway Robbers, Adventurers, and Muta'awwils* [49]

1545. I asked: If one or two men rebel against a city as muta'awwils and fight and kill, but thereafter asked for an amān, do you think that they would be liable for anything they have done?

1546. He replied: Yes.[50]

1547. I asked: Why?

1548. He replied: Because they did not constitute a fighting force [as warriors] but would be regarded as highway robbers.

1549. I asked: In a case of killing, or wounds, where retaliation is possible, would you order *lex talionis* against them; and where wounds cannot be retaliated would you order damages to be paid? [51]

1550. He replied: Yes.

1551. I asked: If the two men attacked a group and menaced them by brandishing arms and the latter resisted and fought in self-defense, do you think that [the latter group] would be liable for anything?

1552. He replied: No.

1553. I asked: Why?

1554. He replied: Because it is lawful for them to defend themselves against such persons.

1555. I asked: If they went so far as to kill [the two men]?

1556. He replied: Yes [it would be lawful for them to do so].

1557. I asked: If a man in a city brandished against another a stick or a stone, do you think that it would be lawful for the menaced [person] to kill him?

1558. He replied: This case does not resemble the other.

1559. I asked: Why?

[49] "The Muta'awwil" is he who follows his opinion or interpretation of a doctrine. See Shārīf 'Alī al-Jurjānī, *Kitāb al-Ta'rīfāt*, ed. G. Flügel (Leipzig, 1845), pp. 206-7; Māwardī, *Kitāb al-Aḥkām*, pp. 101-2.

[50] Abū Yūsuf, *Kitāb al-Radd*, pp. 76-78; Sarakhsī, *Mabsūṭ*, Vol. X, p. 134.

[51] Structure of sentence is slightly changed for clarity.

1560. He replied: Because [the two men] brandished arms, while this man did not brandish any arms.

1561. I asked: Do you think that if the menaced [person] killed by a stick the man who menaced by brandishing something [other than arms], it is the 'āqila who would have to pay the compensation, but if he did that by an iron instrument, he should be punished with death?

1562. He replied: Yes.

1563. I asked: Would the ruling be the same if the menacing [person] menaced someone by pretending that he was brandishing something, but in fact had nothing in hand?

1564. He replied: Yes [the homicide would be liable]. This is the opinion of Abū Ḥanīfa.

However, Abū Yūsuf and Muḥammad [b. al-Ḥasan] held that if the menacing person menaced someone by brandishing something [such as a stick] or by an iron instrument, and the menaced person killed him, the shedding of the latter's blood would be left unavenged; indeed the menaced person would have the right to kill [the menacing one].[52]

1565. I asked: If a man attacked another in his house at night in order to steal his property and menaced him by means of arms or a stick but the owner of the house killed him and produced evidence to establish his case, do you think that [the owner of the house] would be liable for anything?

1566. He replied: No.

1567. I asked: Why?

1568. He replied: Because the one menaced the other at night.

1569. I asked: If [the thief] menaced him during the day with a weapon or something else and was killed by the owner of the house?

1570. He replied: If [the thief] had menaced him during the day with a weapon, the owner of the house would not be liable for anything, but if he had menaced him by brand-

[52] Sarakhsī, *Mabsūṭ*, Vol. X, pp. 134-35; Kāsānī, *Badā'i' al-Ṣanā'i'*, Vol. VII, p. 141.

ishing something other than a weapon and the owner killed him with a stick, the 'āqila [of the owner of the house] would have to pay the diya.

1571. [I asked:] If the [menaced person] killed the other by means of a weapon, would he have to be punished with death?

1572. He replied: Yes.

1573. I asked: Would the same hold true if [the attacking person] were a slave in all [the foregoing situations]?

1574. He replied: Yes [the ruling would be the same].

1575. I asked: If a group of men intercepted travelers on the highways and menaced them with other than arms, do you think that it would be lawful for the Muslims to fight them in order to defend themselves?

1576. He replied: Yes.

1577. He asked: If one of the thieves were killed, would they be liable for anything?

1578. He replied: No.

1579. I asked: If a man were attacked [by another] in the city with other than arms and the attacking man was killed, would the killer be liable for the diya if he killed him with other than arms; and if he killed him intentionally, would the killer be liable to be executed?

1580. He replied: Yes.

1581. I asked: Why is this case different from the other?

1582. He replied: Because those who intercept [travelers] on the highway and menace [them] are unlike those who do so in the city during the day; the victims of the latter are in a position to call people and to seek support against these [culprits], while those in the highway would be unable to call people and to seek the support of others against them.

1583. I asked: If the man were menaced in his house at night and [the attacking person] was killed, do you think that the blood [of the attacking person] would be unavenged and that his case would be like the one [engaged] in a highway robbery?

1584. He replied: Yes [that is right].

1585. I asked: If a group of men were not muta'awwils but adventurers or the like who occupy a region and kill some of its [Muslim] inhabitants and capture their property and consume it, and thereafter [the forces of] the lawful authorities captured them, do you think that you would make a decision in favor of the owners of the property and those whose blood was shed against them?

1586. He replied: Yes.

1587. I asked: Why?

1588. He replied: Because these are not regarded as muta'awwils but as marauding adventurers.

1589. I asked: If a group of rebels takes control of a city and appoints a judge who makes decisions relating to [such matters as] marriage, manumission of slaves, divorce, extortion, and [the enforcement of] penalties in *lex talionis,* but thereafter the loyal forces re-establish their rule over that city and the men against whom the judge of the rebels made the decision take up the case to the judge of the lawful authorities, but the defendants, in whose favor the judge [of the rebels] made the decision, produce evidence in support [of the judgment], would the judge [of the lawful authorities] confirm and carry out such a judgment if it were just; or declare it null and void, if it were unjust; or would he carry it out if it were in accordance with the opinion [even] of some of the jurists?

1590. [He replied: Yes, he would do so.] [53]

If the Rebels Fight along with the Muslims against the Unbelievers [54] 164

1591. I asked: [55] If the rebels take control of a city and then attack the territory of war when the loyalists are engaged

[53] Sarakhsī, *Mabsūṭ*, Vol. X, p. 135; Kāsānī, *Badā'i' al-Ṣanā'i'*, Vol. VII, p. 142; Māwardī, *Kitāb al-Aḥkām*, pp. 102-7.

[54] The problems discussed in this section are summed up in Sarakhsī, *Mabsūṭ*, pp. 135-36; and Kāsānī, *Badā'i' al-Ṣanā'i'*, Vol. VII, p. 142.

[55] See 'Ātif and Fayḍ-Allāh MSS.

in attacking the [same] territory of war and the two armies meet and fight together the unbelievers and capture spoil of war, what would be the ruling concerning the spoil and would both be entitled to participate in it?

1592. He replied: Yes.

1593. I asked: Would it be divided among them?

1594. He replied: Yes.

1595. I asked: Who would be entitled to the one-fifth [share]?

1596. He replied: The lawful authorities who would distribute it among those entitled to it.

1597. I asked: If the rebels refuse and ask to be given their portion of the one-fifth [share] to divide it among whomever they wanted?

1598. He replied: They should never be given [such a portion of the one-fifth share].

1599. I asked: [56] If an Imām entered the territory of war at the head of a Muslim army and died there, but opinion in the army was divided as to who would be the successor and they came into armed conflict with each other but later encountered unbelievers whom they fought and from whom they captured spoil, would such spoil be subject to the one-fifth share and would they participate in the division [of the four-fifths shares]?

1600. He replied: Yes.

1601. I asked: Similarly, if one of the two groups captured spoil and the other did not, but thereafter they [settled their differences] and followed the truth while in the territory of war, would the spoil be subject to the one-fifth [share] and would it be divided up among them [all]?

1602. He replied: Yes.

1603. I asked: If a group of warriors went out of a [Muslim] city to fight without the permission of the Imām and captured spoil, would the spoil be subject to the one-fifth [share] and would the residue be divided up among them?

[56] "Similarly" is omitted.

1604. He replied: Yes, because such [an attack] would be different from a raid by one or two men who go out from a city to plunder.

1605. I asked: In the above-mentioned case of the rebels and loyalists, if the loyal forces captured spoil and the two groups were later reconciled [to one another], would the rebels be entitled to participate in the spoil?

1606. He replied: Yes.

1607. I asked: If the rebels made a peace agreement with some people of the territory of war, do you think that the loyalists should [ever] attack them?

1608. He replied: No, they should not do so, since it is some Muslims who have made peace with them, for the Apostle of God in accordance with a narrative from him said that "the person least in status can give a binding oath on behalf of other [Muslims]." [57]

1609. I asked: If a group of the loyalists made a peace treaty with the inhabitants of the territory of war, but these people were attacked by a party of [Muslim] rebels who captured from them women and children as captives, do you think that it would be lawful for the loyalists to purchase any of those captives?

1610. He replied: No.

1611. I asked: Why?

1612. He replied: Because they had made a peace treaty with them and it was not lawful for the rebels to attack them when the loyalists had made peace with them.

1613. I asked: Similarly, if the rebels made peace with some people of the territory of war and thereafter they violated [the agreement] and attacked them and captured prisoners from them, could not the loyalists purchase any [of the captives]?

1614. He replied: No, because it is a group of Muslims who has made peace with them.

1615. I asked: If the rebels attacked some people of the

[57] See note 46, above.

territory of war and penetrated into their territory and took captives from them, although the loyalists had made a peace agreement for a specified number of years, but thereafter the rebels repented and reconciled [their differences with the loyalists] while the captives remained in their possession, should the loyal authorities return the captives to the inhabitants of the territory of war?

1616. He replied: Yes.

1617. I asked: If a group of the rebels sought the support of some of the inhabitants of the territory of war in their fighting with the loyalists, but the latter attained victory over them, would the people of the territory of war who supported the rebels be liable to be taken as captives?

1618. He replied: Yes.

1619. I asked: Do you not think that the support sought by the rebels constitutes an amān to them?

1620. He replied: No.

1621. I asked: Similarly, if the rebels made a peace agreement with some people of the territory of war, and the latter attacked the loyalists, who fought and attained victory over them [the unbelievers], would it be lawful [for the loyalists] to take captives from them?

1622. He replied: Yes.

1623. I asked: If one of the loyal warriors went over to the rebels and fought against the loyalists, would his property be divided among his heirs?

1624. He replied: No.

1625. I asked: Why would he not be regarded as an apostate if he goes over to the territory of war?

1626. He replied: Do you not think that the wife [of such a person] is still in valid marriage [with him] and she inherits from him if he dies just as he inherits from her if she dies. So how could he be an apostate, so long as he is a Muslim, save he is a rebel?

Chapter IX

Folio 164

SUPPLEMENT TO THE KITĀB AL-SIYAR [1]

1627. Muḥammad b. al-Ḥasan said that Abū Yūsuf said: I asked Abū Ḥanīfa [his opinion] concerning the spoil taken by the Muslims from the unbelievers in the territory of war, and how they should divide it, whether [2] its division should take place in the territory of war or in the territory of Islam after they have taken it there. Also what would he assign to the horse-rider and the foot-warrior, and whether he would give preference to certain kinds of horses over others? How would he divide up the one-fifth [share]? Would the slaves be entitled to any share of the spoil? Would the women be entitled to any share of the spoil? What would be the status of the territory conquered by Muslims; would it be regarded as household property [to be divided as spoil among the warriors] or not?

1628. Abū Ḥanīfa replied: If the Muslims captured any spoil, it should never be divided in the territory of war because they would not have yet taken it to a place of security. Its security would be achieved after they take it to the dār al-Islām. But if they ever divided it in the territory of war, it would be permissible, although it would be more commendable if they divided it after they have taken it to the dār al-Islām. So also held Abū Yūsuf and Muḥammad [b. al-

[1] Literally: "what Muḥammad [b. al-Ḥasan] has added by way of a supplement at the end of the *Kitāb al-Siyar*." This chapter is in the main a summary of Ḥanafī doctrines discussed in Chap. II-IV, above, to which Shaybānī added a few more hypothetical situations. It is deemed unnecessary to reproduce the annotations provided in earlier chapters.

[2] "He said" is omitted.

Ḥasan]. However, Abū Yūsuf held that if the Imām could not find transport to carry it [to the dār al-Islām], he may divide it in the dār al-ḥarb.

Abū Ḥanīfa held that the slave is not entitled to a share of the spoil, but if he participated in the fighting he would be entitled to compensation, not to a share. He held the same opinion concerning women and mukātabs. Abū Yūsuf and Muḥammad [b. al-Ḥasan] held similar opinions. 165

Abū Ḥanīfa held that the volunteer who joins an army and the warrior whose name [is registered] in the dīwān [of the permanent army] receive equal [shares]. But[3] [Muslim] merchants who enter [the enemy territory] in pursuit of their trade and find themselves in the Muslim army would not be entitled to anything of the spoil.

Abū Ḥanīfa held that the horse is entitled to one share and the foot-warrior one share because, he said, he would disapprove of rating the animal higher than an individual Muslim. But Abū Yūsuf and Muḥammad [b. al-Ḥasan] held that the horse should be given two shares and the foot-warrior one on the strength of the ḥadīth and the sunna.

Abū Ḥanīfa held that two or more horses [i. e., owned by one warrior] would not be entitled to more [than the share of one horse] because, he said, if two horses were to be given [two separate] shares, then three horses or more should be given, too. So also held Muḥammad [b. al-Ḥasan] but Abū Yūsuf held that he was in favor of giving [separate] shares to two horses, but not to more.

Abū Ḥanīfa held that a thoroughbred horse, a hybrid, and a jade would be entitled to equal shares, making no distinction between one and the other on the strength of God's command in His Book [the Qur'ān], in which no preference is given [to the horse] over other [riding animals].[4] So also held Abū Yūsuf and Muḥammad [b. al-Ḥasan].

Abū Ḥanīfa held that if the Imām conquered a territory of the unbelievers he would have the choice to do whatever

[3] "He said" is omitted.

[4] See Q. XVI, 8: "And horses, and mules, and asses [He created] for you to ride . . ."; see also Q. LIX, 6.

appeared to be more advantageous and acceptable to the Muslims. If he decides to take out of the land and property the one-fifth [state share] and divide the four-fifths among the warriors who captured it, he may do so. The one-fifth would be [then] divided into three parts: one for the poor, one for the orphans, and one for the wayfarer. But, Abū Ḥanīfa said, if the Imām decides to immobilize the land and leave it to its people as Dhimmīs who would be obliged to pay for themselves and their land [the poll tax and] the kharāj, as [the Caliph] ʿUmar b. al-Khaṭṭāb had decreed for the Sawād [territory], he may do so.

1629. Abū Yūsuf said: I asked Abū Ḥanīfa [his opinion] concerning men who would be called to take part in an expedition and those who do not take part in it but instead would contribute (i. e., pay scutage) to those who take the field.

1630. [Abū Ḥanīfa] replied: If the Muslims were short in spoil or fay', no harm is there if they help each other. But if the Muslims had sufficient fay', I would disapprove of giving it.

1631. I said: I asked Abū Ḥanīfa [his opinion] about [the Muslim] who takes an animal from the fay' for a ride or wears a garment, whether he disapproves of that and prohibits it.

1632. He replied: If [the Muslim] were wounded and was afraid of its [effect] on his life, it would be all right to take the animal for a ride or use the clothing, if he were in need of them.

1633. I said: I asked [Abū Ḥanīfa his opinion] about the man who takes weapons from the fay' to fight with them.

1634. [He replied]: It would be objectionable for him [to do so].

1635. I asked: If he were in need of them?

1636. [He replied]: No harm then if he were in need and could not find any other [weapons].

1637. I asked: If an enemy shoots [the Muslim] with an arrow and the latter shot it back to him or snatched a sword from the hand of the enemy and struck them with it, do you think that there would be any harm in that?

1638. He replied: There is no harm in it.

1639. I asked: If a man hamstrung his own animal and, fearful of any enemy [attacking] him, found an animal belonging to the enemy on which he rode and returned to his people, do you think that there would be any harm in that?

1640. He replied: No harm in it, if he were frightened, or hungry, or in need [of the animal], or [was afraid] of treachery.

1641. I said: I asked [Abū Ḥanīfa his opinion] about the killing of women and children and very old men chronically ill and incapable of fighting?

1642. [He replied: He said] he would prohibit [such killing] and he disapproved of it.

1643. I asked: If [a Muslim] captures a prisoner of war, would it be lawful to kill him or should he be brought to the Imām?

1644. He replied: Whatever he did would be all right. Abū Yūsuf and Muḥammad [b. al-Ḥasan] held that he should do whatever he deems good or advantageous to the Muslims.

1645. I said: I asked [Abū Ḥanīfa his opinion] about the corpse of an enemy killed by the Muslims, whether [it would be all right] to sell it to the unbelievers.

1646. He replied: No harm in doing so in the dār al-ḥarb, i. e., outside the army camp of the Muslims. Do you not think that it is lawful for the Muslims to take away the property [of the enemy]? So, if such [property] were taken in lieu of their corpses, it would be all right. However, Abū Yūsuf disapproved of such [an act] and prohibited it. He held that it is unlawful for the Muslims to sell corpses, to transact with interest, to sell wine or swine, whether to the inhabitants of the territory of war or others.

1647. I said: I asked [Abū Ḥanīfa his opinion] about an army if it attacks the territory of war and takes spoil and thereafter another Muslim army which had not taken part in the fighting would join it before the spoil is taken to the dār al-Islām and before it is divided up.

1648. He replied: [The second army] would be entitled to participate in the spoil, because the first had not yet taken it to a place of security and was still in the dār al-ḥarb.

1649. [I said:] I asked [Abū Ḥanīfa his opinion] about the commander of an army who attacks the territory of war, whether he has the right to promise primes before the taking of spoil by saying, "He who captures anything may have for himself such-and-such [a portion of it]."

1650. [He replied: As to that, I would say "yes"] but as to offering primes after the spoil has already been captured, he [the commander] should not do it.

1651. [I said:] I asked [Abū Ḥanīfa his opinion] whether there is any harm for the Muslims in seeking the assistance of unbelievers [in a war] against the inhabitants of the territory of war and whether they would be entitled to any [regular] share of the [captured] spoil.

1652. He replied: There is no harm in seeking their assistance, provided the command is in the hands of the Muslims, but if the command were in the hands of the unbelievers, the Muslims should not participate in the fighting along with unbelievers, unless they were fearful of their safety—[in such a case it would be all right to fight with them] in self-defense. But [5] [if the unbelievers participate with the Muslims] they would not be entitled to any share, save to compensation.

1653. I said: I asked [Abū Ḥanīfa his opinion] about the prisoner of war, whether he would be killed, released on ransom, or divided [as spoil]?

1654. He replied: He should not be released on ransom; he should be killed or taken as fay'. The Imām can make a choice and do whatever he deems advantageous to the Muslims.

1655. [I said:] I asked [Abū Ḥanīfa]: Would it be lawful to exchange Muslim prisoners for prisoners of the unbelievers?

[5] "He said" omitted.

1656. He replied: There is no harm in it, but I disapprove of ransoming prisoners of the unbelievers with property.

1657. I said: I asked [Abū Ḥanīfa his opinion] about men who take spoil consisting of camels, horses, and sheep and are unable to drive them or about any of the animals belonging to the Muslims that resist being driven.

1658. He replied: I disapprove of hamstringing or mutilating them, but there is no harm in slaughtering them and burning them so that the enemy would not get any benefit of
them. 166

1659. Abū Ḥanīfa said: If the unbelievers captured a slave or a riding animal or clothing [from the Muslims] and the Muslims recaptured [any of] them as spoil and the owner found it before the spoil was divided, he may take it without paying anything [as a right of postliminium], but if he found it after the spoil was divided he may take it by paying its value, unless it were gold or silver or anything to be weighed or measured; then, Abū Ḥanīfa added, the owner would not have to take it if he found it after the spoil was divided, for he would have to take something by paying as much in weight or measure.

1660. Abū Ḥanīfa said: If a slave ran away to the enemy and was taken [by one of them] and thereafter was recaptured by the Muslims, his master may take him back without paying anything, whether before or after the spoil was divided, because the runaway slave is unlike the prisoner of war or the property captured and taken to a place of security.

1661. Abū Ḥanīfa said: If a riding animal escaped [to the territory of war] and was captured [by the unbelievers], and thereafter recaptured by the Muslims, the owner may take it back without paying anything if he found it before the spoil was divided, but he must pay its value if he found it after the spoil was divided. Thus the runaway slave is treated differently from the riding animal which ran away.

However, Abū Yūsuf and Muḥammad [b. al-Ḥasan] held that these cases should be treated alike if [the unbelievers] captured them in their territory, regardless whether [the captive] were a runaway slave, an expelled person, or a prisoner of war. If the owner found him before the spoil is divided, he may take him without paying anything; if he found him after the division, he must pay its value. Abū Ḥanīfa held that if an unbeliever entered the dār al-Islām under an amān along with the said slave and sold him there, nobody would have the right to claim ownership [of the slave], according to the opinion of all [the jurists], except in the case of the runaway slave, whose master, according to Abū Ḥanīfa, has the right to take him wherever he may find him without paying anything.

1662. Abū Ḥanīfa said: If a Muslim slave is captured by the unbelievers and a Muslim purchases this slave from them, his master has the right to take him back by paying his value, if he so wishes. But if he did not take him back and the unbelievers recaptured him and [the slave] was purchased by another man, Abū Ḥanīfa held that [the first] owner would have no right to take him back until purchased by the second owner who takes him back by paying the price of the second sale; thereafter the first owner takes him back on payment of both prices. Abū Yūsuf and Muḥammad [b. al-Ḥasan] held the same opinion.

1663. Abū Yūsuf and Muḥammad [b. al-Ḥasan] said: If a slave girl became blind in the hand of the purchaser or suffered a defect and her [first] master wanted to take her back, deducting from her price a portion equivalent to the [value of the] defect, it would not be lawful for him to do so. He should either take her by paying the full price or leave her. This is also the opinion of Abū Ḥanīfa, as far as Abū Yūsuf knows. Do you not think that if a man sold a slave to another and the slave became blind while in the possession of the vendor, the purchaser would be told that he can take the slave by paying the full price or leave him?

1664. If a man cuts off the hand of the slave girl and her master collects the arsh (damages) and the [first] owner from whom the unbelievers had captured the slave girl wanted to take her back and demanded to deduct from her price a portion equal [to the value of the defect], it would not be lawful for him to do so; if he wants to take her back, he has either to pay the full price or leave her. [For] do you think that if [the owner], in whose hand was the slave girl, caused the loss of her eye, he can deduct anything from her price? If this [case] were like any other sale transaction, deduction from the price [equivalent to the value of the defect] would be lawful. If it were also like the shuf'a (*jus retractum*) sale, deduction from the price would be lawful. And [also] like the purchase [of a house], if part of it is destroyed, a portion of the price equal [to the value of that part] would be deducted from the price to be paid by the pre-empting purchaser.

1665. Do you not think that if [the person] who has purchased [the slave girl] from the enemy had intercourse with her, nothing would be deducted from her price and the [first] owner could take her back [only] by paying the full [price], and the intercourse with her would be lawful? If she gave birth to a child and the owner in whose hand was [the child] set him free and the [first] owner took the slave girl back by paying the full price, nothing would be deducted from her price. If the child were killed and an arsh were paid [to the owner], the [first] owner could [still] take the mother by paying the full price or could leave her.

1666. If [the mother] gave birth to a child and the mother were set free [by the owner] and the first owner wanted the child, he should either pay the full price [of the mother] or leave him. Such a purchase is neither like [an ordinary] sale nor the shuf'a sale, for [in this situation] the man [the first owner] has a priority right of purchasing the thing by paying the [full] price in the condition in which it is found, regardless of changes over which he had no control, and he must pay the full price [if he wishes to take it back].

1667. If the price could proportionately be divided between the mother and the arsh [paid] for the injury of the child, or if it could be divided between the mother and the defect caused to her, then the price could be proportionately divided between her and the defect caused to her when [for instance] she is blinded by her possessor. Similarly, one could divide the price between her and the nuptial gift due to her, if her possessor had intercourse with her, provided he has to pay damages to her, not being the owner of her entire person, [and] if any accident takes place, the price would be diminished proportionately. If such were the case it would not be lawful [for the owner] to set her free. Do you not think that the pre-empting purchaser (shāfiʿ) would be entitled to purchase a house by the shufʿa right from the vendor and annul the payment of price on the part of the [frustrated] purchaser? But if the owner of the slave girl set her free, his manumission would be lawful, and if he sold her, his sale would be lawful; if the [first] owner wishes to take her back, he would have to pay the price offered by the second purchaser. But if she were given as a gift [to another man], the first owner would be entitled to take her back by paying her value to the person to whom she was given as a gift. Such [a transfer] is at any rate neither like [an ordinary] sale nor the shufʿa sale. Do you not think that if a man sold a slave woman, it would not be lawful for him to resell her or set her free or give her as a gift after his first sale [to another man] is achieved, while the latter [owner] would have the right to sell her or give her as a gift, and if he had intercourse with her, the intercourse would be lawful, and if she gave birth to a child, she would become an umm walad for him? But if the vendor had intercourse with her [after selling her], the intercourse would be unlawful, and if she gave birth to a child for him, she would not become an umm walad for him, in case the purchaser wanted to take her as well as her child. Thus, such [a transaction] would be neither like a shufʿa, nor a sale, nor a gift.

1668. If a man gave a [female] servant as a gift to another man and her value increased by him, he who gave her as a gift has no right to take her back. If a man gave a gift to a member of his near of kin who is unlawful to him [in marriage] and [the beneficiary] obtained possession, he who gave 167
the gift has no right to take it back. If the female slave were captured by the unbelievers [and sold to the near of kin], the

[first] owner would have the right to take her back from the near of kin or any other, whether her worth has increased or not—together with her children—but the person who gave her as a gift would not have the right to take the child if the child were born when she was in the possession of the receiver of the gift.

1669. If a mukātaba were mortgaged with a man and was [thereafter] captured by the unbelievers as a prisoner from Muslim hands and purchased by another man from them [the unbelievers], the [original] owner would not have the right to take her back until the man in whose hand she was mortgaged would pay her price and from whom the owner would take her by paying the debt and the price. Such [a transaction] is neither like a sale, nor gift, nor shuf'a.

1670. If a man sold a slave woman but, before the purchaser obtained possession and paid the price, the inhabitants of the territory of war captured her and another man purchased her [from them], the [first] purchaser would not have the right to claim her until the original vendor had recovered her from the one who had purchased her from the enemy by paying her price. If he obtains her on paying the price, then the [first] purchaser would have the right to take her by paying the original price with which he had purchased her and the other price which the [original] owner had paid to redeem her.

1671. If a slave, liable both to a debt and a tort, were captured by the unbelievers and purchased [later by a Muslim] from them, the latter would be liable for the debt [of the slave] but not for the tort. If the [original] owner took him back by paying the price, he would be liable for [both] the debt and the tort. If [the slave] returned to the first owner, he would be liable to the tort and the debt; if he did not return to the first owner, the tort would be waived, but he would remain liable for the debt. [For] do you not think that if a slave in debt were sold by his master, the debt remains binding on him but the tort would be waived if he goes out of the ownership of the master, but not if he were set free?

[And] do you not think that the debt for which a slave was mortgaged would be disregarded until [the original mortgagee] takes [the mortgaged slave] back on paying [the purchaser] the price and thus receives his mortgage, and thereafter the original owner could redeem him by paying the debt?

1672. If the inhabitants of the territory of war captured a male or female slave or any property from the Muslims and thereafter became Muslims while still in possession of these objects, then the slave would become their property, [so much so] that the [original] owner would not have the right to take him back; if the slave were in debt, [the new owner] would remain liable for debt; if he were liable to a tort, [the new owner] would not be liable for it. If the [captured] property were a mortgage, it would not revert to the charge of mortgage, and the debt for which [the property] was given in mortgage would be waived, if the value of the [mortgaged property] were equal to the debt.

1673. If a free man were captured by the inhabitants of the territory of war and those people while in possession [of the free man] became Muslims, the free man would remain free and would never become a slave. The same would hold true in the case of the mudabbar, the umm walad, and the mukātab, who revert to their original status and do not become slaves [of the captor]. This applies to any property which is not lawful to be sold and which the people of the territory of war capture—those people would not have the right to own it if they capture it.

1674. If a free man asked another man to purchase [him from the unbelievers] he would remain a free man and the merchant who purchased him would have the right to recuperate from him [i. e., the prisoner] the price [paid to the enemy]. Likewise, if a mukātaba, an umm walad, and a mudabbara [were made prisoners and purchased at their demand from the enemy], the purchaser will have the right to recuperate from [the mukātaba, etc.] the price paid [to the enemy] after these [mukātaba, etc.] obtain their freedom.

1675. If a free man asked another to purchase for him a

named free man [a prisoner in the hands of the enemy] from the dār al-ḥarb and if the other purchased him, the free man who has been purchased would not have to pay the price at all, but the commanded person has the right [to recuperate the price] from the man who gave the order, provided he had guaranteed the price, or had said, "Purchase [him] for me." On the other hand, if he said: "Purchase him for yourself and consider it a charity," he would not be liable [to reimbursing].

1676. If a man purchased a slave from the unbelievers [in the dār al-ḥarb], who had captured him from the Muslims, and the [new] purchaser mortgaged him, and if the original [Muslims] owner arrived later, he would not have the right to redeem [the slave] until he paid the debt [for which the slave was mortgaged] and separated the different charges. Thereafter, the [original Muslim] owner can recuperate him on payment of the price [paid to the enemy]. If the owner wanted to pay the debt to the mortgagee and also the price, and if [the mortgagee] voluntarily renounced the debt, he might do that; but the [original] owner would not constrain him to redeem until he takes him back with payment of the debt.

If [the slave] were hired [while in the hands of the purchaser], the hiring would be permissible and the [original] owner may take back [the slave] and cancel the hiring for the remaining period [if he wishes to do so]. The hiring is different from the amount of mortgage. For do you not think that the hiring is a divisible thing, if it is made for a number [of days, for instance]? The present case is likewise [divisible]. But God knows best!

The King's Prerogatives in His Realm and Who Are To Be Considered as His Slaves from among His Subjects

1677. Muḥammad b. al-Ḥasan said:

If a group of the inhabitants of the territory of war conquered another group equally at war [with the Muslims] and captured them as slaves on behalf of their ruler and thereafter the ruler and the inhabitants of his country became Muslims while in possession of those slaves, the warriors who fought [with the ruler] would be regarded as free men, with nothing to do against them. Those who were captured and reduced to slavery would be the slaves of the ruler, who would have the right to sell or give as a gift any of them as he wished, before or after he became a Muslim or a Dhimmī. The warriors who fought with the ruler would be free and not subject to slavery.

1678. If the ruler designated his property and gave it in inheritance to some of his children to the exclusion of others and the ruler made such an arrangement before he became a Muslim or a Dhimmī and thereafter the children became Muslims, the inheritance would be valid as arranged by the ruler. But if the arrangement were made after the ruler became a Dhimmī or a Muslim, it would not be regarded as valid and all his male and female slaves whom he had acquired through conquest would be inherited by all the heirs in accordance with God's commands [in the Qur'ān].[6] If the arrangement were made when [the ruler] was at peace with the Muslims, who require the payment of an annual tribute to them, and Muslim rulings were not binding on him, whatever arrangement he had made would be regarded as valid.

1679. If the ruler divides his lands among his children at his deathbed, assigning to each one a particular province of his realm and all the male and female slaves in it, such an arrangement would be regarded as valid if he made it while he was at peace [with the Muslims] before he became a Muslim or a Dhimmī. If he made the arrangement after he became a Muslim or a Dhimmī, but on the deathbed, it would be regarded as null and void and all the male and female slaves would be inherited by his heirs.

1680. If the [ruler] bequeathed [his estate] to one of his children to the exclusion of others while he was at peace [with

[6] Q. IV, 12-15.

the Muslims] and another son inherited from him after his death and he either killed his brother or exiled him to the Islamic territory or any other territory and took possession of all his property, and thereafter all [the children] became
Muslims or Dhimmīs, all that the usurping son had done 168
would be regarded as valid and all the male and female slaves would be his property. If the usurping son had made [his usurpation] after the deprived son became a Muslim or a Dhimmī, anything which was taken from him would be returned to him and [the usurping son] would be ousted. If the usurping brother made [his usurpation] when he was in a state of war with the Muslims, his action would be regarded as valid if [later on] he became a Muslim or a Dhimmī.

1681. If the Muslims captured any of the said male and female slaves [of the ruler], the first son would have the right to take them back without paying anything if he found them before the division of the spoil, but if he found them after the division of the spoil, he would have the right to take them back by paying their value, if he so wishes.

1682. If Muslim merchants went to the second son [i. e., the usurper] and purchased from him some of those male and female slaves, it would be lawful for them to do so. But if they took them to the dār al-Islām, the first son, the victim of usurpation, would have the choice of recovering them by either paying the price or leaving them, if he so wishes. If the usurping son takes [possession of the inheritance] while he is a Muslim or a Dhimmī and his brother, the victim of usurpation, was [also] a Muslim or a Dhimmī, the Muslim [merchants] should not purchase any one of the sold slaves, and if they ever did and took them to the dār al-Islām [he would have the right to recover them] paying neither their price nor their value.

1683. If the deprived son were a Muslim or a Dhimmī when his brother did so to him and the brother were [also] a Muslim or a Dhimmī, and thereafter the usurping son apostatized from Islam or renounced his status as Dhimmī and fought the Muslims in defense of his land and enforced the rulings of the unbelievers there, but thereafter either the land was captured [by Muslims] or some of the female slaves were taken by them as captives, the deprived son would have the right to recover them without paying anything if he found them before the spoil were divided. If he found them after the spoil were divided, he would have the right to recover them by paying their value, if he so wishes. But God knows best!

Chapter X

Folio 169

KITĀB AL-KHARĀJ (THE BOOK OF TAXATION)[1]

Kharāj Land

1684. Muḥammad b. al-Ḥasan said that the entire lands of al-Sawād [of Southern 'Irāq], the mountainous lands, and the lands watered by the Tigris and the Euphrates are [in the category of] kharāj land.[2] Indeed, any land that was conquered by the Muslims is kharāj land.[3]

1685. All the kharāj land, low and high,[4] that has access to water and is cultivable, whether it is cultivated or not, pays a tax of 1 qafīz [of grain][5] and a dirham [of silver][6] on each jarīb[7] per year, regardless of whether its owner raises one

[1] A great portion of this book is reproduced verbatim by Ṭabarī in his *Kitāb Ikhtilāf*, pp. 223-25, 226-27, 228-29, 232, 236, 238, 240-41.

[2] The term "kharāj," which is specifically applied by many a classical writer to the land tax, was used in the early Islamic period in the broader sense of tax or taxation. In the present text, Shaybānī uses the term in the dual sense of land tax and poll tax (jizya). For a discussion on the meanings of kharāj and jizya, see my *War and Peace in the Law of Islam*, pp. 187-93; Dennett, *Conversion and Poll Tax in Early Islam*; Løkkegaard, *Islamic Taxation in the Classic Period.*

[3] Abū Yūsuf, *Kitāb al-Kharāj*, pp. 28 ff.; Yaḥya b. Ādam, *Kitāb al-Kharāj* (Cairo, 1347/1928), pp. 22 ff.; Ibn Sallām, *Kitāb al-Amwāl*, pp. 57-59; cf. Shāfi'ī, *Umm*, Vol. IV, pp. 192-93.

[4] "Ghāmir and 'āmir" means land which is accessible to tidal water and highland which is not.

[5] The qafīz is a measure of grain and was known at the time of the Prophet as al-ṣā'. It is equivalent to 12 manns. See Māwardī, *Kitāb al-Aḥkām*, p. 265; Walther Hinz, *Islamische Masse und Gewichte* (Leiden, 1955), p. 48.

[6] A silver unit of coinage. See Chap. V, n. 7.

[7] The jarīb is a measure of land equivalent to 100 square qaṣabas or 1,592 square meters. See Māwardī, *Kitāb al-Aḥkām*, p. 265; Hinz, *Islamische Masse und Gewichte*, pp. 38, 65.

crop on it per year, or more than that, or whether it is all cultivated simultaneously. Each year, 1 qafīz and a dirham must be paid on every jarīb of land. The qafīz [in question] is that of the Ḥijāz; it is one-fourth of the hāshimī—like the ṣā'—which was current in the time of the Prophet, and is equal to 8 riṭls.[8] This is equivalent to the measure that is used for wheat and barley today, plus 2 handfuls. This [tax] is imposed on every jarīb [of land sown to] wheat or barley.[9]

1686. All land sown to graminiferous crops, like rice, sesame, vegetables, perfumed herbs, and other cultivated crops—except lucerne and vines—and all cultivable kharāj land that is [deliberately] not cultivated by its owner pays [a tax of] 1 qafīz of wheat and 1 dirham per jarīb. But if the owner has planted the land and [the crops] have been totally destroyed by hail, fire, flood, or anything else, he does not pay any tax for that year. If most of the crop has been ruined but the value of what remains is equivalent to 2 dirhams and 2 qafīzs or more per jarīb, then [a tax of] 1 qafīz and a dirham per jarīb should be collected. If the value per jarīb of the remaining crop is less than 2 qafīzs and 2 dirhams, only half [of the remaining crop] is due.[10]

1687. No [tax] is imposed on date palms and [other] trees. But for every jarīb of grapevines 10 dirhams are due, and for every jarīb of lucerne, 5 dirhams. If the crop is blighted and the owner has no benefit from it, no tax is due. If the value of the remaining grapevines is equivalent to 20 [dirhams] or more per jarīb, 10 dirhams are due. If the value is less than 20, the value of half [of the harvest] is due. If the value of the lucerne left in every jarīb is 10 dirhams or more, 5 dirhams per jarīb are due. If the value is less, half of that is due.[11]

[8] See Muṭarrazī, *al-Mughrib*, Vol. II, p. 48; Māwardī, *Kitāb al-Aḥkām*, p. 257.

[9] Abū Yūsuf, *Kitāb al-Kharāj*, pp. 36, 38, and *Kitāb al-Āthār*, p. 194; Yaḥya b. Ādam, *Kitāb al-Kharāj*, pp. 23, 55, 72; Ibn Sallām, *Kitāb al-Amwāl*, pp. 69, 71. For views of Awzā'ī, Mālik, and Shāfi'ī, see Ṭabarī, *Kitāb Ikhtilāf*, pp. 218-22.

[10] Abū Yūsuf, *Kitāb al-Kharāj*, p. 52.

[11] Abū Yūsuf, *Kitab al-Kharāj*, pp. 36, 38, and *Kitāb al-Āthār*, p. 194.

1688. With regard to land containing dense stands of date palms or [other] trees under which no other crops can be cultivated, [the tax] per jarīb should be levied according to the capacity of the land, and this on the same basis as in the case of grapevines, namely, 10 dirhams on every jarīb.[12]

1689. [Shaybānī] said: The jarīb is 60 by 60 royal cubits. The royal cubit is divided into 7 masābiq, which is the same as 7 hand-widths (qaṣabāt). This [cubit] exceeds the common cubit by 1 hand-width. The dirham is the one that 10 pieces are minted from—7 mithqāls [of silver] as is commonly known today. The dirhams which people use today for purchases are the basis of 7 mithqāls.[13]

1690. [Shaybānī] said: If a man possesses a kharāj land, part of which is salinated (sabkha) and uncultivable and not supplied with water, [this part] is not subject to the kharāj. But if water is available and it could be reclaimed and cultivated, a kharāj of 1 qafīz and 1 dirham is due on every jarīb.[14]

1691. [Shaybānī] said: If a man plants 100 jarībs of land with grapevines sufficient for only 60 jarībs, the annual kharāj would be 1 qafīz and 1 dirham [on every jarīb] until they matured; after they have developed and yielded ripe fruit, the kharāj would be 10 dirhams on each jarīb. But if the [value of the] produce of each jarīb were less than 20 dirhams, [the kharāj] on each jarīb would be half [of the harvest]. If the [value of the] produce of each jarīb were 20 dirhams or more, [the kharāj] would be 10 dirhams [per jarīb, not more.] If the [value of the] produce were either more or less than 1 qafīz and 1 dirham, [the kharāj] would be 1 qafīz and 1 dirham.

1692. [Shaybānī] said: Likewise, if a man cultivates lucerne on kharāj land and it matures but the plants are scattered and the produce is so meager that [the value] per jarīb is less than 10 dirhams, [the kharāj] is levied on [only] half of the

[12] Abū Yūsuf, *Kitāb al-Kharāj*, pp. 36, 37.

[13] Muṭarrazī, *al-Mughrib*, Vol. 1, pp. 78-79; Māwardī, *Kitāb al-Aḥkām*, p. 265.

[14] Māwardī, *Kitāb al-Aḥkām*, p. 263.

produce. However, if the value of the remaining half is more[15] than 1 qafīz and 1 dirham, [the kharāj] is 1 qafīz and 1 dirham.

1693. If a man plants his kharāj land thickly with palms or other trees so that no other crops can be cultivated between them and the fruits do not ripen, [the kharāj] per jarīb is [only] 10 dirhams, like that for grapevines. But if the produce 170
is so meager that each palm produces [only] 1 or 2 clusters or so and the value of the dates produced per jarīb is 20 dirhams or more, [the kharāj] on each jarīb is 10 dirhams. If the value of the dates [per jarīb] is less than 20 dirhams, [the kharāj] would be levied on only half of the value, unless this half of the value were less than 1 qafīz and 1 dirham, in which case [the kharāj] would be 1 qafīz and 1 dirham on each jarīb.[16]

1694. As to cultivation other than that of date palms and other trees, such as wheat, barley, rice, and other grains, and such crops as vegetables, sweet basil, saffron [za'farān], safflower ('uṣfur), and the like [the kharāj] of each jarīb is I qafīz and 1 dirham, regardless of whether the value [of the purchase] is greater or lesser.[17]

1695. If a man possesses a thicket on a kharāj land where game is abundant, no kharāj is due on the game. But if the land produces reeds (qaṣab)—whether in abundance or not—tamarisks (ṭarfa), plane-trees (dulb), ḥalfa (alfa or esparto grass), stone pines, or the like that can be cut or sold, [the kharāj] is 1 qafīz and 1 dirham on each jarīb, if the value of the produce of each jarīb is 2 dirhams and 1 qafīz or more. If the value is less, [the kharāj] is levied on half of the value of the produce of each jarīb.[18]

1696. [Shaybānī] said: If the kharāj land produces salt,

[15] "Less," in Arabic MSS, obviously an error.

[16] The Imām may lower the tax if there is sufficient ground to believe that the produce is less than the regular annual produce. See Abū Yūsuf, *Kitāb al-Kharāj*, pp. 85-86; Māwardī, *Kitāb al-Aḥkām*, pp. 260-61.

[17] Abū Yūsuf, *Kitāb al-Kharāj*, pp. 36, 50; Māwardī, *Kitāb al-Aḥkām*, pp. 256-57.

[18] Abū Yūsuf, *Kitāb al-Kharāj*, pp. 56, 71.

regardless of whether it is much or little, or if it produces bitumen (qīr) or naphtha, or if it contains bees and honey and the like, and the land is cultivable but water is not available, then [no kharāj] is due. But if the land is cultivable and water is available, [the kharāj] is 1 qafīz and 1 dirham on each jarīb. This is the opinion that we follow.[19]

The Status of Kharāj Land If Its Owners Become Muslims or Unable to Work on It or Abandon It[20]

1697. [Shaybānī] said: In the Sawād, whoever owns kharāj land, whether he is a Muslim, a Dhimmī, a mukātab, or a slave, or is in debt or not, must pay the kharāj. If he owns kharāj land, he must pay, like others in similar circumstances, on every cultivable jarīb 1 qafīz and 1 dirham. On every jarīb of grapevines [the kharāj] is 10 [dirhams]; on every jarīb of lucerne 5 [dirhams]; no distinction is made between date palms and other trees. If the date palms or other trees are thickly planted, the kharāj is levied according to what we have already explained.[21]

1698. [Shaybānī] said: If a Dhimmī who owns kharāj land becomes a Muslim, the status of his land remains unchanged; he continues to pay the kharāj on the land, but he is relieved of the kharāj on his head [i. e., the poll tax]. If a Muslim rents out his kharāj land [to a Dhimmī] or becomes his partner in cultivating it (muzāraʿa), the owner of the land pays the kharāj. Also, if he puts someone in charge of the land to improve it, the owner pays the kharāj, unless it is cultivated with grapevines, vegetables, or thick trees and thick palm groves. But if the tenant or the borrower plants the land with grapevines and lucerne, he would have to pay the kharāj at the rate of 10 dirhams on every jarīb of grapevines and 5

[19] *Ibid.*, pp. 55, 56, 70.

[20] Literally: "Rulings concerning kharāj land if its tenants become Muslims or [either] neglect it or abandon it."

[21] Abū Yūsuf, *Kitāb al-Kharāj*, pp. 59-60; Yaḥya b. Ādam, *Kitāb al-Kharāj*, p. 54; Ibn Sallām, *Kitāb al-Amwāl*, pp. 87-88; Māwardī, *Kitāb al-Aḥkām*, pp. 261-62.

on every jarīb of lucerne. If a renter or a borrower plants the land thickly with date palms or other trees so that nothing else can be grown between them, the borrower pays the kharāj. If [the owner] sells the land, gives it as a gift, or gives it as charity either to his minor son or to a stranger, the purchaser [respectively, the beneficiary of gifts, etc.], be he minor or major, pays the kharāj on the date palms and other trees. [Shaybānī] said: If he has sold it or given it in charity before the kharāj is collected, the kharāj would be due from the purchaser or the beneficiary of the charity. If the date palms and other trees are thickly planted the kharāj is as we have described.[22]

1699. [Shaybānī] said: If the owner of kharāj land is unable [to cultivate it] or neglects it or abandons it, the Imām 171
has the right to take it from him and give it to whoever is willing to cultivate it. If he does not find anyone who will take it and pay the kharāj, he may give it to anyone who is willing to cultivate it in return for a third or a fourth or less of the produce, depending on the capacity of the land and the capability of him who receives it. The same arrangement applies to date palms and other trees that might be on the land; payment [of the kharāj] would be on the basis of one-half or one-third or less of the produce, depending on the capacity of the land and the capability of whoever is found to work on the land. So [the Imām] would give out that land as he deems fit.[23]

1700. If [a Christian] from the tribe of Taghlib or Najrān purchases kharāj land, he must pay the kharāj just as Muslims must. If kharāj land becomes the property of a minor, an orphan, a woman, or a Dhimmī, they also must pay the kharāj just as Muslims must. This is the opinion that we follow.[24]

[22] Abū Yūsuf, *Kitāb al-Kharāj*, p. 86; Yaḥya b. Ādam, *Kitāb al-Kharāj*, pp. 21-25, 61; Ibn Sallām, *Kitāb al-Amwāl*, pp. 80, 87, 91; Māwardī, *Kitāb al-Aḥkām*, p. 263.

[23] Abū Yūsuf, *Kitāb al-Kharāj*, pp. 85-86; Māwardī, *Kitāb al-Aḥkām*, p. 264.

[24] Abū Yūsuf, *Kitāb al-Kharāj*, p. 121; cf. Yaḥya b. Ādam, *Kitāb al-Kharāj*, p. 29.

The Kharāj and the Jizya on the Heads of Adult Males[25]

1701. [Shaybānī] said: All adult Dhimmī males of the people of the Sawād, including the inhabitants of al-Ḥīra and other cities—whether they are Jews, Christians, Magians, or idolaters—must pay the jizya (poll tax), except the Christians of [the tribes of] Banū Taghlib and those of Najrān. The jizya is to be paid annually only by the male population.[26]

1702. The rich are to pay 48 dirhams, those who have a medium [income] pay 24 dirhams, and the artisans and the needy pay 12 dirhams. This [tax] is to be collected annually, and if they are unable to pay it in any other way [i. e., in cash] and offer to pay it in kind, it should be accepted, provided it equals the amount due. But neither swine nor wine nor dead animals are acceptable for the jizya.[27]

1703. If a portion of the jizya is deferred, the balance should be collected in the following year. But if one of them dies and part of his jizya has not been paid, it should not be deducted from his estate nor should it be collected from his heirs, because the jizya is not considered a debt. If any of them becomes a Muslim and part of his jizya has not been paid, the unpaid part would be waived and he would no longer be responsible for it. Nor shall he be responsible for any future payment, if he becomes a Muslim. Likewise, if anyone becomes blind or poor and is no longer able to pay

[25] Literally: "[Rulings] concerning the kharāj on the heads and the jizya on the heads; how much should be and how it should be imposed on the basis of narratives and opinion."

[26] Abū Yūsuf, *Kitāb al-Kharāj*, pp. 122 ff.; Ṭabarī, *Kitāb Ikhtilāf*, pp. 199-200; Yaḥya b. Ādam *Kitāb al-Kharāj*, pp. 71-77. For a discussion of the use of the term "jizya" and the forms of its application to the people of the occupied territory outside Arabian Peninsula, see my *War and Peace in the Law of Islam*, pp. 176-77, 177-87.

[27] The jizya varied from one province to another, for it was left to the governor to fix its amount. In 'Irāq it was fixed as reported by Abū Yūsuf and Shaybānī, representing the Ḥanafī viewpoint. See Abū Yūsuf, *Kitāb al-Kharāj*, p. 122. For the amount fixed in Arabia and Syria (i. e., one dinār), see Yaḥya b. Ādam, *Kitāb al-Kharāj*, pp. 70, 72, 73. For various other rates, see Ṭabarī, *Kitāb Ikhtilāf*, pp. 208-11.

the remainder of his jizya, it is waived and he is no longer obliged to pay it.[28]

1704. Dhimmī women and children do not have to pay the jizya, nor do those of them who are blind, crippled, helplessly insane, chronically ill, too old to work, or who are too poor to be able to pay. Priests, monks, and abbots are to pay if they own property. But Dhimmī slaves, mudabbars, and mukātabs do not have to pay the jizya. If a Dhimmī minor reaches the age of puberty at the beginning of the year, before the jizya is levied on adult males, provided he is of a well-to-do family, he would have to pay the jizya for that year. But if he reaches puberty toward the end of the year, after the jizya has been levied on adult males, he would not have to pay it for that year, but would pay in the following year.[29]

1705. Likewise, if a Dhimmī slave who is an artisan is set free at the beginning of the year before the jizya is levied on [free] men, the jizya is levied on him also; but if he is set free at the end of the year after the jizya has been levied on other men, the jizya is not to be levied on him for that year but for the following year. If a poor Dhimmī who is not an artisan comes into the possession of property at the beginning or the end of the year, the jizya is levied on him for that year. If some people of the territory of war became Dhimmīs at the beginning of the year before the jizya is levied on those who are to pay it that year, it is to be levied on them the following year and thereafter.[30]

1706. Shaybānī said: As to the blind, the crippled, the chronically ill, and the insane, the jizya is not to be levied on them, even if they are rich. If a person remains ill for several years and does not recover, we should not levy the jizya on him; if he recovers at the beginning of the year before the jizya is levied, it is not to be levied on him. If he completely

[28] Abū Yūsuf, *Kitāb al-Kharāj*, pp. 122-23; Ṭabarī, *Kitāb Ihktilāf*, pp. 206-7; Kāsānī, *Badā'i' al-Ṣanā'i'*, Vol. VII, p. 112.

[29] Abū Yūsuf, *Kitāb al-Kharāj*, pp. 122-23; Ṭabarī, *Kitāb Ikhtilāf*, pp. 206-8; Yaḥya b. Ādam, *Kitāb al-Kharāj*, pp. 72-73; Kāsānī, *Badā'i' al-Ṣanā'i'*, Vol. VII, p. 112.

[30] Ṭabarī, *Kitāb Ikhtilāf*, p. 207; Sarakhsī, *Mabsūṭ*, Vol. X, p. 80.

recovers, the jizya is to be levied on him the following year and thereafter. As to the Christians of [the tribe of] the Banū Taghlib, the jizya is not to be imposed on them, because peace was made with them [by the Muslims] on the basis that [the tax] collected on their land would be double that collected from the Muslims. Nor is the jizya to be collected from the Christians of Najrān. These are under obligation to pay in 172
garments [instead of in cash] on their heads which [the Caliph] 'Umar imposed on their heads and on their land.[31]

Limitations on the Dhimmīs with Respect to Their Dressing and Riding Mounts[32]

1707. [Shaybānī] said: None of the Dhimmīs should be allowed to imitate Muslims in his clothing, in his mode of riding, or in his appearance. Dhimmīs should rather be obligated to wear around their waist a girdle (kustīj) coarse and tied in the middle. They should also wear a multicolor cap and use saddles bearing a pomegranate-like [ornament] on the saddlebow. Moreover, the thongs of their sandals should be rugged and different from those of Muslims. Nor should they be allowed to wear shawls (ṭaylasān) like those of Muslims or robes like their robes.[33]

1708. [Dhimmīs] should be allowed to build neither new synagogues nor churches but only [to repair] those already in existence when they became Dhimmīs and located in cities other than those inhabited by Muslims. Nor should Dhimmīs be permitted to reside in cities inhabited by Muslims, for [as stated in a Tradition] the Apostle expelled them from

[31] On the special status of the Christians of Najrān and Banū Taghlib, see Abū Yūsuf, *Kitāb al-Kharāj*, pp. 71-75, 120-21; Yaḥya b. Ādam, *Kitāb al-Kharāj*, pp. 24-25, 26, 30, 65-68, 119; Ṭabarī, *Kitāb Ikhtilāf*, pp. 227-28. See also Khadduri, *War and Peace in the Law of Islam*, pp. 198-99.

[32] Literally: "[Rules] concerning the people of the Dhimma: that they are not allowed to wear clothes similar to Muslims or ride [on horses], based on narratives and opinions."

[33] Abū Yūsuf, *Kitāb al-Kharāj*, pp. 127-28; Ṭabarī, *Kitāb Ikhtilāf*, pp. 240-41; Kāsānī, *Badā'i' al-Ṣanā'i'*, Vol. VII, p. 113.

Madīna, and it is related concerning [the Caliph] ʿAlī [b. Abī Ṭālib] that he expelled them from Kūfa. If anyone of them possesses a house in a Muslim city, he should be compelled to sell it; if he purchases a house in such a city, the purchase is [legally] valid, but he should be compelled to sell it. However, there is no harm for them to live outside of a [Muslim] city and resort to it to buy and sell by day, returning to their houses [at night].[34]

1709. [Shaybānī] said: [The Dhimmīs] should be permitted to build neither a synagogue nor a church nor a fire temple in a Muslim city or in any other city in the lands of the Muslims. But if they have retained a synagogue or a church or a fire temple in cities other than those resided in by Muslims, and conceded to them under the peace agreement, they may keep it, and if it should be destroyed they should be permitted to rebuild it. But if the Muslims establish a city [for themselves] in that place, they should take and tear down the synagogues and churches there, but the Dhimmīs should be allowed to build similar ones outside that city. This is the opinion that we follow.[35]

Pacts of the Prophet and His Companions Concerning the People of Najrān and the Tribes of Banū Taghlib[36]

1710. [Muḥammad's Pact with the People of Najrān:]

In the name of God, the Compassionate, the Merciful. This is the pact which has been issued by the Prophet Muḥammad, peace be upon him, to the People of Najrān, to whom his rulings shall extend—their fruit, their gold and silver money and their slaves. All these are left to them except the payment of 2,000 garments (ḥulal al-awāqī), of which 1,000 are to be

[34] Abū Yūsuf, *Kitāb al-Kharāj*, p. 127; Kāsānī, *Badā'i' al-Ṣanā'i'*, Vol. VII, pp. 113-14.

[35] Abū Yūsuf, *Kitāb al-Kharāj*, pp. 127, 138; Ṭabarī, *Kitāb Ikhtilāf*, p. 238.

[36] Literally: "What has been provided by the Prophet, peace be upon him, and his Companions concerning the people of Najrān and Banū Taghlib, and the rulings concerning them and [their] produce."

paid [each year] in the month of Rajab and 1,000 in the month of Ṣafar; the value of each is an ounce of silver. If the value exceeds or becomes less than the [prescribed] kharāj (the tribute), it should be taken account of. If the people of Najrān pay the tax in the form of coats of mails, horses, camels, and other objects, that would be acceptable and the value should be in proportion to the prescribed tribute. They must also entertain and provide supplies for my messengers for a maximum period of twenty days, but these must not be kept with them more than a month. If there is war or trouble in al-Yaman, they must lend thirty coats of mails, [thirty horses],[87] thirty arcs, and thirty camels. If some of what was lent to my messengers is destroyed or perished, in the form of coats of mails and horses, it remains in charge of my messengers and [the people of Najrān] shall be compensated. They shall have the protection of God and the guarantee of Muḥammad, the Apostle of God, that they shall be secured their lives, property, lands, creed, those absent and those present, their buildings, and their churches. No bishop or monk shall be displaced from his parish or monastery and no priest shall be forced to abandon his priestly life. All their belongings, little or much, remain theirs. No hardships or humiliation shall be imposed on them nor shall they be pressed for pre-Islamic bloodshed. They shall not be called for military service, nor shall they pay tithe nor their land be traversed by [our] army. Those who seek justice shall have it: there will be no oppressors nor oppressed at Najrān. Those who practice usury in the future shall have no protection from me. No one shall be subject to reprisal for the fault of another. For the continuation of this compact, the guarantee of God and the assurance of Muḥammad, Apostle of God, sanction what has been written until God manifests his authority so long as the people of Najrān remain faithful and act in accordance with their obligations, giving no support to oppression. Witnessed by Abū Sufyān b. Ḥarb, Ghaylān b. 'Amr, Mālik b. 'Awf of [the tribe of] the Banū Naṣr, al-

[87] Abū Yūsuf, *Kitāb al-Kharāj*, p. 72.

Aqra' b. Ḥabīs al-Ḥanzalī, and al-Mughīra b. Shu'ba; Abū Bakr acted as secretary.[38]

1711. [Abū Bakr's Renewal of the Pact:]

[The people of Najrān approached the Caliph 'Abū Bakr after the Prophet's death in 10/632, and he confirmed the principles embodied in the pact as follows:]

In the name of God, the Compassionate, the Merciful. This is the pact which the servant of God Abū Bakr, successor to the Prophet Muḥammad, issued to the people of Najrān. They shall have the protection of God and the guarantee of Muḥammad, Apostle of God, for their persons and their lands, creed, property, dependents, buildings, those absent and those present, and their bishops and monks, churches, and all that they possess, whether it be much or 173
little. No conscription or tithe shall be imposed on them, nor shall any bishop or monk be displaced from his office, in fulfillment of the pact which Muḥammad issued to them and in accordance with the promises given in this document. May the protection of God and the guarantee of Muḥammad forever be upon this document so long as [the people of Najrān] remain faithful and act in accordance with their rightful obligation. Witnessed by al-Mustawrid [b. 'Amr]; by 'Amr, the freed slave of Abū Bakr, by Rashīd B. Ḥadhīfa; and by al-Mughīra [b. Shu'ba].[39]

1712. ['Umar's Renewal of the Pact:]

[The people of Najrān approached the Caliph 'Umar b. al-Khaṭṭāb, after having been obliged to emigrate from Arabia to southern 'Irāq, who wrote to them:]

In the name of God, the Compassionate, the Merciful. This is what was written by the servant of God 'Umar,[40] Commander of the Believers, for the people of Najrān. Who-

[38] See Abū Yūsuf, *Kitāb al-Kharāj*, pp. 72-73; Abū al-'Abbās Aḥmad b. Yaḥya b. Jābir al-Balāḍurī, *Kitāb Futūḥ al-Buldān*, ed. M. J. de Goeje (Leiden, 1866), p. 65; Ibn Sallām, *Kitāb al-Amwāl*, p. 188; Hamidullah, *Majmū'at al-Wathā'iq al-Siyasīya* (Cairo, 1958), pp. 111-13; and my *War and Peace in the Law of Islam*, pp. 179-80.

[39] See Abū Yūsuf, *Kitāb al-Kharāj*, p. 73.

[40] In Arabic MSS: 'Uthmān, obviously an error.

ever emigrates shall have God's security and no harm shall befall him from any Muslim; the pact issued to them by the Prophet Muḥammad and [the Caliph] Abū Bakr shall be fulfilled.

Wherever [the people of Najrān] may settle, whether under the jurisdiction of the Amīr of 'Irāq or under that of the Amīr of al-Shām (Syria), let them be permitted to till the soil. And whatever they may build there shall be theirs and their children's as charity for God's sake, in lieu of their lands [from which they departed] and no one shall bother or hinder them.

Whoever of the Muslim [officials] may be present among them shall support them against whoever may do them injustice, for they are a people who have been granted the status of Dhimmīs. Their jizya is waived for twenty-four months after they have arrived [at their new home] and they shall not be obligated to pay it until after they have settled down, nor shall any injustice be done to them, nor shall they be oppressed. Witnessed and written by 'Uthman [b. 'Affān] and Mu'ayqib.[41]

1713. [Shaybānī] said: [The people of] Najrān, for their persons and the tilled lands of Najrān [in 'Irāq], are under obligation to pay [only] the garments (al-ḥulal al-Najrānīya), each year 2,000 garments, the minimum value of each being 50 dirhams. No garment shall be accepted if its value is less than 50 [dirhams]. One thousand are to be paid in [the month of] Ṣafar and another 1,000 in [the month of] Rajab. The payment of this number is to be divided among those men who have not yet become Muslims as a poll tax and as a tax on their lands in Najrān. If some of them sell their land to a Muslim or a Dhimmī or a Taghlibī, the payment of the 2,000 garments would be estimated on the basis of the quantity of their land and number of those men among them who did not become Muslims. The tax in garments levied on the lands shall be divided among all the lands of Najrān,

[41] See Abū Yūsuf, *Kitāb al-Kharāj*, pp. 73-74; cf. Ibn Sallām, *Kitāb al-Amwāl*, p. 99.

and the tax on the men shall be levied according to the number of men. But whoever becomes a Muslim will no longer be subject to the poll tax, and the tax paid in garments will be redivided among the remaining men and land.

1714. [Shaybānī] said: If a man of Najrān buys a piece of land in Najrān, he must pay kharāj of 1 qafīz and 1 dirham [per jarīb], but he does not have to pay proportionately any of the tax of 2,000 garments due on the land of Najrān, regardless of whether the purchaser is a slave, a free man, a mukātab, a Dhimmī, a minor, or a woman.

1715. [Shaybānī] said: The people of Najrān are no longer under obligation to entertain or provide supplies for anyone, including any messenger that may come to them or any governor appointed over them. It was in the time of the Apostle of God, when he sent his messengers to Najrān in the neighborhood of al-Yaman, that such obligations were imposed. But today [when they reside elsewhere], they are no longer under any such obligation; rather, they should be treated kindly and well and the covenant which the Prophet Muḥammad issued regarding them should be observed. Whoever violates the covenant commits evil and sin and acts wrongfully.

1716. [Shaybānī] said: The decree that God issued to them through the Prophet Muḥammad should be fulfilled. Neither their old men nor their boys are subject to the poll tax (jizya), whether in the form of garments or otherwise, nor should they be prevented from building chapels, monasteries, or churches in their lands. They should be subject to neither conscription nor the tithe, and someone should be sent to collect the tax from them [rather than their being required to come and pay it]. If anyone is unable to cultivate his land and abandons it, the Imām may give the land to someone else who, he believes, will work on it on the basis of receiving one-half or one-third or more or less. The Imām also may hand over date palms and other trees to whoever will look after them and lend them on the basis of receiving one-third or one-quarter [of the produce] or more or less, according to his capability. If the Imām should decide to give it to someone instead on the basis of his paying the [normal] land tax or on the basis of a share of the produce, he may do so.[42]

1717. [Shaybānī] said: The [tribes of] Banū Taghlib are under obligation to pay on their land double the tax that is paid by the Muslims. If they possess a kharāj land, they must pay the kharāj on it. If one of them sells his land to a Muslim or to a Dhimmī, the Muslim or the Dhimmī would have to pay double the tithe on the land, just as the Taghlibī did.

1718. [Shaybānī] said: If the clients [of freed slaves] of Banū Taghlib are Christians, the jizya is levied on them just as it is levied on the Dhimmīs. [The kharāj] is also levied on their lands just as in the case of the Dhimmīs. This is the opinion that we follow.[43]

The Regime of the Kharāj[44]

1719. [Shaybānī] said: The governor [of a province] should appoint as collector of the kharāj a man who must treat the inhabitants kindly and justly. He should collect the kharāj 174
from them when the crop has been harvested and according to the size of the crop so that their kharāj may be paid by the end of the year. The rate of the kharāj is 5 dirhams on each jarīb of cultivable land whether high or low land. On every jarīb of grapevines [the kharāj] it is 10 dirhams, and on every jarīb of lucerne, 5 dirhams. If they fail to pay any part of the kharāj, no harm should be done to them nor should their property be seized or should they be persecuted, but [the collector] may withhold the crops from them until the

[42] Ibn Sallām, *Kitāb al-Amwāl*, pp. 531-40.

[43] For rights and duties of the tribe of Banū Taghlib, see Abū Yūsuf, *Kitāb al-Kharāj*, pp. 120-21; Balādhurī, *Kitāb Futūḥ al-Buldān*, pp. 181-83; Ibn Sallām, *Kitāb al-Amwāl*, pp. 540-42. The Christians of Banū Tanūkh were accorded similar status by the Caliph 'Umar b. al-Khaṭṭāb. See my *War and Peace in the Law of Islam*, pp. 198-99.

[44] Literally: "[Rules] concerning the collector of the kharāj, how he should act, who are subject to the kharāj, and other [rulings] based on narratives and opinion."

kharāj is fully paid. If a blight befalls the crop of anyone after the end of the year, he should be excused [from the tax] owing to the blight. This is the opinion that we follow.[45]

The Enfeoffment of Uncultivated and Waste Lands[46]

1720. [Shaybānī] said: Uncultivated or waste lands for which water is not available, whether such lands be in the Sawād or Kūfa or mountain country or elsewhere, may be allotted by the Imām to whoever is willing to cultivate it and improve it or pay the tithe on it. And whatever is developed or created on such lands without the permission of the Imām shall belong to the person who cultivates the land, and he pays the tithe on it. Similarly, whoever finds a spring or digs a well in a waterless desert in the kharāj land category is entitled to develop and to improve that land, and he pays the tithe on it. Also, whoever brings in a flowing well in a desert or wasteland is the owner of the well and an appertinent area of 500 [square] cubits around it. No one else is allowed to dig a flowing well within that area and the owner may exploit it for himself. And whoever rents a main irrigation canal or takes over a branch canal and brings water from the Euphrates or the Tigris or another source to wasteland is entitled to an area of 500 [square] cubits on each side [of the main or branch canal] and no one else is allowed to use it.

1721. [Shaybānī] said: Whoever digs a well and pulls up water from it [by means of] camels, and the land [in which the well is located is] in open country, a desert, a steppe, or any unowned land, is entitled to an appertinent area of 60 [square] cubits around it which he may exploit and develop and do with it as he pleases. If he digs a well for his animals in order to water camels, cattle, and sheep, the appertinent area around it to which he is entitled is 40 [square] cubits. He

[45] Abū Yūsuf, *Kitāb al-Kharāj*, pp. 124-25; Ṭabarī, *Kitāb Ikhtilāf*, p. 232; Māwardī, *Kitāb al-Aḥkām*, p. 264.

[46] Literally: "[Rules] concerning the enfeoffment of land: the lawful enfeoffment of 'ushr (tithe) and mawāt (waste) lands."

is entitled to do whatever he wants with it to the exclusion of anyone else. This is the opinion that we follow.[47]

Tithe Land and the Rights and Duties of Those Who Cultivate It[48]

1722. [Shaybānī] said: Any 'ushr land watered by waterwheels, buckets, or camels is subject to half the tithe, but the land watered by flowing water, rivers, wādīs (temporary rivers), or rain is subject to the [whole] tithe. On the produce of tithe land, such as wheat, barley, rice, dates, unripe dates, raisins, all kinds of vegetables, sweet basil, and all kinds of trees which yield fruit by God's will, whether in abundance or scarcity, the tithe is due, regardless of whether they are watered by streams or by rain. If [the land] is watered by waterwheels or buckets, it is subject to half the tithe. Likewise, on any [crops] given by God's will such as fruits, safflower seeds, beans, broadbeans, flax, cotton, saffron, safflower, or anything else, whether produced in abundance or in scarcity, the tithe is due whether watered by a stream or by rain. But if it is watered by buckets or waterwheels, it is subject to half the tithe. If the produce is a handful of vegetables or sweet basil, it is subject either to the [whole] tithe or to half the tithe. No tithe is due on straw, date palms, firewood, or grass, nor on palm leaves, reeds, tamarisk, leeks, stone pines, ḥalfa (alfa), or any kind of fuel wood.[49]

1723. [Shaybānī] said: If the tithe land is used for trade or partnership or if it is in the hands of hired agent, an orphan, a mukātab, a slave, or a mudabbar, it is subject to the [whole] tithe or to half the tithe. But if the land has been rented out by the owner, the tenant has to pay the tithe.[50]

[47] Abū Yūsuf, *Kitāb al-Kharāj*, pp. 51-53; Yaḥya b. Ādam, *Kitāb al-Kharāj*, pp. 115-23.

[48] Literally: "[Rulings] concerning the 'ushr land and [the rights and duties] of whoever repairs it or to whom it is enfeoffed."

[49] Abū Yūsuf, *Kitāb al-Kharāj*, pp. 51-52.

[50] *Ibid.*, p. 134.

1724. [Shaybānī] said: The tax on whatever is produced by the land of Banū Taghlib is double that paid by the Muslims. Thus the produce [of a land] watered by streams or rain 175
is 20 [dirhams], that is one-fifth (khums), and [the tax] on the produce [of a land] watered by buckets or waterwheels would be the regular [tax]. All minors, women, men, mukātabs, insane persons, and slaves belonging to the Banū Taghlib must pay [the tax] on any 'ushr land they own, as is paid by their adult men, regardless of whether they are in debt or not in all the cases that we have described.

1725. [Shaybānī] said: If a piece of 'ushr land owned by a Taghlibī were purchased by a Muslim, he would have to pay single tithe. But if the Taghlibī purchased a piece of 'ushr land from a Muslim, the former would have to pay double the tithe. If a Taghlibī purchased a piece of kharāj land from a Christian, or a Christian purchased a piece of 'ushr land from a Taghlibī, the purchaser would have to pay double the tithe. Likewise, if a piece of 'ushr land were purchased by a Christian from a Muslim, the tithe would be double. If a Muslim purchased a piece of 'ushr land from a Christian or a Taghlibī, [only] one tithe would be paid by him, whether it were watered by a stream or by rain. But it would pay half the tithe if it were watered by buckets or waterwheels.

1726. [Shaybānī] said: Christian clients of the Banū Taghlib who [own land] are to be treated like other Christians of the Dhimmī [community] in the matter of the payment of the tax. Likewise, if these Christians were clients of a Muslim, they would be treated like other Dhimmīs with regard to the land tax. If a Taghlibī becomes a Muslim, he pays on his land only the tithe [like other Muslims]. This is the opinion that we follow.[51]

1727. [Shaybānī] said: If a Muslim owns a piece of 'ushr land, he must neither conceal nor hide any [of the produce]

[51] Abū Yūsuf, *Kitāb al-Kharāj*, pp. 66, 120-21, 134-35, 137; Yaḥya b. Ādam, *Kitāb al-Kharāj*, pp. 68-70; Ṭabarī, *Kitāb Ikhtilāf*, pp. 224, 227, 228-29; Ibn Sallām, *Kitāb al-Amwāl*, pp. 540-46.

before the 'ushr is levied on it. He should not pay [the tithe] by means of bad produce, but by good produce. If some of the produce subject to the 'ushr is overlooked [by the assessor] or if the owner has concealed some of it and it has not been discovered, the owner should—since the matter is between him and God—give it away as a charity because it is not permissible for him to consume it; he must give it in charity. The same is true of the land of kharāj: if the tax is neglected or if he conceals it, or if he flees from the governor who is unable to find him out, it is necessary that the land owner make a charity [of the unpaid tax], and it is not permissible for him to consume it, but he must pay it as kharāj tax.[52]

1728. [Shaybānī] said: If a man owns a village containing a market place, houses, and villas situated on his kharāj land, no kharāj is due on the land, whether the buildings are rented out or not. Likewise, if a man owns 'ushr land and a village is situated on it, no tithe is due on the land or the village whether they are rented out or not.

1729. [Shaybānī] said: If a man owns a villa in a town situated on land planned for urban use, and the owner establishes an orchard on the land belonging to that villa or plants date palms producing dates, no tithe or kharāj would be due either on the date palms or the other trees. But if he turns the entire land originally designed for urban use into a garden, the tithe is due. This is the opinion that we follow.[53]

1730. [Shaybānī] said: If a man owns 'ushr land used as a place for fishing, hunting gazelles, or for any similar purpose, neither the tithe nor the kharāj is due on it, even if it is a kharāj land. If the land contains a source of salt, asphalt, pitch, or naphtha, or if it contains beehives, neither the tithe nor the kharāj is due on any of it. This is the opinion that we follow.[54]

[52] Ṭabarī, *Kitāb Ikhtilāf*, pp. 231-32.

[53] Abū Yūsuf, *Kitāb al-Kharāj*, pp. 102 ff.; Māwardī, *Kitāb al-Aḥkām*, p. 263.

[54] Abū Yūsuf, *Kitāb al-Kharāj*, pp. 87-88; Yaḥya b. Ādam, *Kitāb al-Kharāj*, p. 32.

Chapter XI

Folio 177

BOOK ON 'USHR (TITHE) ACCORDING TO DĀWŪD B. RUSHAYD[1]

1731. Dāwūd b. Rushayd said: I heard Muḥammad b. al-Ḥasan say that Abū Ḥanīfa said:

On all green produce that 'ushr land produces, whether in abundance or in scarcity, and whether it bears permanent fruit or not, a tithe is due, regardless of whether it is watered by streams or by rain. On those [crops that] have been watered by buckets or waterwheels [only] half of the tithe is due. But no tithe at all is due on [such product] as firewood, grass, and straw. [Abū Ḥanīfa] held this [opinion] on the strength [of a narrative] transmitted by Ibrāhīm al-Nakha'ī, who maintained that [only] half the tithe is due on what I have just described. This narrative was transmitted by Mujāhid [b. Jubayr] who, however, said that he did not subscribe to it.

1732. It is well known that the Apostle of God said: "No tax shall be taken from a dhawd (herd) of camels numbering less than five, nor from anything weighing less than 5 ounces." The other Tradition, also well known, says that the Prophet sent Mu'ādh b. Jabal to al-Janad [in South Arabia] and ordered him not to collect the tax on green produce. By green

[1] For a brief account of Ibn Rushayd, see pp. 55-56, above. It is deemed unnecessary to reproduce the references used in the previous chapter, since the subject matter is essentially the same. For general source material on the subject, the reader is referred to Abū Yūsuf, *Kitāb al-Kharāj*, pp. 47-57, 63-67, 69-71, 76-79, 88-93, 94-105; Ibn Sallām *Kitāb al-Amwāl*, pp. 468-525; Māwardī, *Kitāb al-Aḥkām*, pp. 194-216, 308-22. See also article " 'ushr," *Shorter Encyclopaedia of Islam*, ed. H. A. R. Gibb and J. H. Kramers (Leiden and London, 1953), pp. 610-11; Løkkegaard, *Islamic Taxation in the Classic Period*, Chap. 3; Aghnides, *Mohammedan Theories of Finance*, Part II, Chap. 2-3.

produce we mean that which does not produce permanent fruit such as vegetables, lucerne, melons, cucumbers, snake cucumbers, onions, garlic, and the like, and all kinds of flowers such as myrtle, roses, dye plants, and the like, for which no tax is due if they are grown on 'ushr lands. The same applies to all seeds that are of no use except as seeds, such as the seeds of lucerne, vegetables, melons, and the like; no taxes are due on them, neither tithe nor anything else, whether they are produced in abundance or in scarcity.

1733. If 'ushr land produces plants bearing permanent fruit such as wheat, barley, figs, raisins, rice, millet, and shilb, as well as walnuts, almonds, pistachios, hazel nuts, ḥabba khaḍra, and the like, a tithe would be due. But nothing is due if the produce amounts to less than 5 wasqs. The wasq is equivalent to 60 ṣā's, according to the ṣā' that existed in the time of the Apostle of God. Our ṣā' of today is equivalent to 8 'Irāqī riṭls, according to Abū Yūsuf; and 5⅓ 'Irāqī riṭls according to the jurists of the Hijāz. Thus, on every 5 wasqs of the above-mentioned produce, the whole tithe is due if it was not watered by streams or rain; half the tithe is due if it was watered by buckets or waterwheels. Likewise, on produce of permanent fruit that is measured by any measure, no tithe is due if the amount is less than 5 wasqs—each wasq as I have stated is equal to 60 ṣā's—and the tithe would be on the quantity of the produce, not on the oil [contained in it, for example]. Thus, if olives amounted to 5 wasqs, a tithe would be due; if they were less, no tithe would be due. If the produce consisted of 2 wasqs of dates, 2 of wheat, and 2 of raisins, they should not be lumped together; if each were less than 5 wasqs, no tithe would be due, since neither the dates nor the raisins nor the wheat amount to 5 wasqs by themselves. Likewise, all pulses such as lentils, beans, broad beans, Indian pease, and the like should not be lumped together, unless each one amounts separately to at least 5 wasqs. If the produce [is of the same species], but some is white and some is black, the two can be lumped together. If the produce consisted of 5 wasqs of dried dates or raisins, a tithe would be due on it. If [the produce] were to be sold as fresh dates, fresh grapes, or unripe dates, [the tithe] would be estimated on the same basis as if they were dry dates or raisins. If the quantity is estimated to be 5 wasqs, a tithe would be due; if not, nothing would be due.

1734. If the produce of the tithe land were saffron and wars (a dye plant) or anything calculated by weight in riṭls and manns, rather than by measure of capacity, in calculating the tithe the largest unit of weight should be adopted, and the largest unit of weight for honey is the farq. Just as we have previously stated that no ṣadaqa is due on any quantity less than 5 wasqs, so no ṣadaqa is due on honey if it amounts to less than 5 farqs. Likewise, the largest unit of weight used for saffron and wars is the mann. If a quantity of saffron or wars amounts to less than 5 manns, no tax is due on it, but if it amounts to 5 manns, the tax is due. Also, if cotton amounts to less than 5 ḥimls, no ṣadaqa is due. The ḥiml is equivalent to 300 farqs.

1735. Safflower and flax produce seeds which are measured according to capacity. If the safflower produces 5 wasqs of seeds, the tithe is due on all the seeds as well as on the safflower that produces them, but only half tithe is due if the seeds have not been separated from the safflower. If the produce is less than 5 wasqs of seeds, nothing is due, and there is no tax due on the safflower itself. Also, if flax produces seeds amounting to 5 wasqs, the tithe would be due on both the seeds and the flax. But if the produce were less than 5 wasqs, nothing would be due on either the seeds or the flax. As to 178
hemp, if the amount of seeds produced were 5 wasqs, the tithe would be due; if the amount produced were less than that nothing would be due. But no tax at all is due on the hemp itself, because it is similar to wood, and no tax is due on wood and [unproductive] date palms. [For] do you not think that we levy the tax on wheat, but not on straw? Similarly, wood, and the tar which is expected from it, and pitch, do not pay anything. Indeed, anything produced from wood is free. If the produce of the stone pine amounts to 5 wasqs, the tax is due on it; but if it were less, the same is due. No tax at all is due on the wood of the stone pine. The tithe and the half-

tithe are due only on plants brought forth by the soil (i. e. that are cultivated).

1736. Nothing is due on salt or on bitumen, naphtha, or any similar liquid. Only in the nonperishable fruit of plants which people and animals eat is subject to the tithe or the half-tithe. Sugar cane that does not yield sugar does not pay anything, but sugar juice is subject to the tithe, if it amounts to 5 farqs. The farq is equivalent to 36 'Irāqī riṭls. But no tax is due on any amount less than 5 farqs.

1737. Ṣadaqa is due on any quantity of caraway, cumin, coriander, and mustard that amounts to [at least] 5 wasqs. But nakhwa, mustard, thyme, savin, shunir (black seeds), and the like do not pay anything, because they are used as medicine, even though the first named is usually used as food and the last named is used in place of coriander. The marshmallow, the cypress, ushnān (saltwort), and the like do not pay anything, because they are poisonous; if they were useful, they would be regarded as in the same category as vegetables, but they are all alike. Pomegranate seeds that are sold dry are subject to the tithe on every 5 wasqs, but if the seeds are not permanent and are not stored up, no [tithe is due] and they are regarded in the same category as dates; if the amount is 5 wasqs the tax is due. The same applies to the jujube. But peaches, pears, apples, nabq (lotus jujube), apricots, and mulberries do not pay anything, either on the leaves or the fruit, because most of them are not storable or capable of being dried. The same applies to bananas, myrobalan, carobs, fenugreeks, capers, and dye plants.

If a man owns two parcels of land, each situated on a different irrigation canal, and together they produce 5 wasqs of produce of the kind that is subject to the tax the tithe is also due on it. If the two parcels of land are widely separated and are located in two different regions or if there are a number of parcels of land, the produce should be lumped together. If it totals 5 wasqs of produce of the kind that is subject to the ṣadaqa, the ṣadaqa is collected on it. If there is only one owner, it makes no difference if his lands are scattered and are located in different regions.

If a piece of land is owned in common by two different men and it produces only 5 wasqs of produce of the type subject to the tax, tax is not due until the share of each one amounts to 5 wasqs.

1738. On whatever is produced from mountains in the way of gold, silver, copper, lead, iron, and mercury, whether in abundance or in scarcity, [a tax of] one-fifth [of its value] is due. But no tithe is due on [such minerals as] arsenic, kuḥl (antimony), bizm (bismuth), zāj (green vitriol), and the like. Also, no [tithe is] due on [such precious stones as] corundum, chrysolite, and turquoise that are extracted from the mountains. They all belong to whoever finds them. [For] it has been related to us from the Prophet that he said, "No taxes are due on stones," and we follow this ruling.

1739. Likewise, whatever is taken from the sea, such as ambergris, pearls, fish, etc., are not subject to the tax. These all belong to whoever obtains them.

Dāwūd b. Rushayd said: Muḥammad b. al-Ḥasan related to me from Sufyān b. 'Uyayna from 'Amr b. Dīnār from his father [Dīnār al-Jumaḥī] from ['Abd-Allāh] Ibn 'Abbās that he was once asked whether a one-fifth [ṣadaqa] is due on ambergris. [Ibn 'Abbās] replied, "It is something thrown up by the sea." We also hold that nothing is due on it, as does Abū Ḥanīfa. Abū Yūsuf for a long time was of the same opinion, but later held that pearls and ambergris taken from the sea were subject to the one-fifth [tax]. Nothing is due on fish, because it is not a plant. He also held that nothing is due on al-dawra or its stalk, for they are in the category of flowers and scents. We also follow the same [rulings] based on analogical deduction from the opinions of Abū Ḥanīfa and Abū Yūsuf, as I have already described.

Muḥammad b. al-Ḥasan was once asked whether ambergris were subject [to tax]. He replied, "Yes." He was asked, "Do you hold that the tithe is due regardless of whether it is owned by anyone or not?" "Yes," he replied. Praises be to God, the Most High, the Guide to Truth. End of the Book of Tithe. Peace be upon His Prophet and [the Prophet's] family and Companions.

END

TRANSMITTERS OF TRADITIONS AND NARRATIVES

'Abd-Allāh b. 'Abbās
Companion; traditionist and jurist; Makka; d. 68/687

'Abd-Allāh b. Abī Ḥumayd
Traditionist (obscure); Baṣra; n. d.

'Abd-Allāh b. Abī Awfī
Companion (last surviving); traditionist; Madīna and Kūfa; d. 86 or 87/705

'Abd-Allāh b. Abī Najīḥ
Traditionist; Makka; d. 132/750

'Abd-Allāh b. Burayda b. al-Ḥuṣayb
Traditionist; judge of Merv; Madīna and Merv; d. 115/733

'Abd-Allāh b. 'Umar
Companion (son of Caliph 'Umar); traditionist; Madīna; d. 74/693

'Abd al-Malik b. Abī Sulaymān b. Maysara
Traditionist; Madīna; d. 145/762

'Abd al-Raḥmān b. 'Abd-Allāh b. Mas'ūd
Son of Companion Ibn Mas'ūd; traditionist; Kūfa; 165/781

Abū 'Abd-Allāh Makḥūl
Traditionist; Damascus (Syria); d. 113/731

Abū 'Abd-Allāh Nāfi'
Freed slave of, and transmitter from, Ibn 'Umar; Madīna; d. 120/737

Abū Bakr 'Abd-Allāh b. Abī Quḥāfa
Companion (first caliph); Makka and Madīna; d. 12/634

Abū Bakr b. 'Abd-Allāh
Traditionist and judge; Madīna and Baghdad; d. 162/778

Abū Ḥanīfa (*see* Nu'mān b. Thābit)

Abū Isḥāq (*see* Sulaymān b. Abī Sulaymān)

Abū Ja'far (*see* Muḥammad b. 'Alī b. al-Ḥusayn)

Abū Ṣāliḥ (*see* Dhakwān al-Sammān)

Abū Sulaymān al-Juzjānī
Jurist (Shaybānī's disciple and transmitter of his writings); Baghdad; d. *ca.* 200/815.

Abū 'Uthmān al-Nahdī
Traditionist; Kūfa and Baṣra; died during the governorship of al-Ḥajjāj
Abū Yūsuf (*see* Ya'qūb b. Ibrāhīm)
Abū al-Zubayr (*see* Muḥammad b. Muslim b. Tadrus)
Al-Ajlaḥ b. 'Abd-Allāh al-Kindī
Traditionist; Kūfa; d. 145/762 (Shi'ī)
'Alī b. Abī Ṭālib
Companion (fourth Caliph); jurist and traditionist; Madīna and Kūfa; d. 40/660
'Alqama b. Marthad
Traditionist; Kūfa; d. 120/737
'Āmir b. 'Abd-Allāh b. 'Ubayd al-Sabī'ī
Traditionist; Kūfa; d. 127/744
'Āmir b. Sharāḥīl al-Sha'bī
Traditionist and jurist; Kūfa; d. 104/722
'Amr b. Dīnār al-Jumaḥī
Traditionist; Makka; d. 126/743
'Amr b. Shu'ayb b. Muḥammad b. 'Amr b. al-'Āṣ
Traditionist; Madīna; d. 118/736
Ash'ath b. Sawwār
Traditionist (judge of al-Ahwāz); Kūfa; d. 130/747
'Āsim b. Sulaymān al-Aḥwal
Traditionist; Baṣra; d. 141/758
'Atā' b. Abī Rabāḥ
Traditionist; Makka; d. 114/732
Burayda b. al-Ḥuṣayb al-Aslamī
Companion; Madīna, Baṣra, and Merv; d. 62 or 63/681 or 682
Daḥḥāk b. Muzāḥim al-Hilālī
Traditionist; Madīna and Khurāsān; d. 102/720
Dhakwān al-Sammān, Abū Ṣāliḥ
Traditionist; Madīna; d. 101/719
Ḥajjāj b. Arṭāt al-Nakha'ī
Traditionist; judge of Baṣra; Kūfa and Baṣra; d. 147/764
Ḥakam b. 'Utayba
Traditionist; Kūfa; d. 115/732
Ḥammād b. Abī Sulaymān
Jurist (teacher of Abū Ḥanīfa); Kūfa; d. 120/737
Ḥasan b. Abī al-Ḥasan al-Baṣrī
Traditionist (son of the theologian al-Ḥasan al-Baṣrī); Baṣra; d. 110/728
Ḥasan b. 'Umāra al-Bajalī
Traditionist; Kūfa; d. 153/770
Ḥasan b. Ziyād al-Lu'lu'ī
Jurist; judge of Kūfa; Kūfa; d. 204/819

Hishām b. Sa'd
    Traditionist; Madīna; d. 161/777
Ibn 'Abbās (*see* Abd-Allāh b. 'Abbās)
Ibn Abī Najīḥ (*see* 'Abd-Allāh b. Abī Najīḥ)
Ibrāhīm b. Yazīd al-Nakha'ī
    Jurist; Kūfa; d. 95 or 96/713 or 714
Ismā'īl b. Umayya b. 'Amr b. Sa'īd
    Traditionist; Makka; 140/757
Jābir b. 'Abd-Allāh al-Anṣārī
    Companion; traditionist; Madina; d. 78/697
Jābir b. Zayd al-Azdī
    Traditionist; Madīna and Baṣra; d. 93 or 103/711 or 721
Jarīr b. 'Abd-Allāh al-Bajalī
    Companion; traditionist; Madīna and Kūfa; d. 54/673
Jubayr b. Muṭ'im
    Companion; Madīna; d. 59/678
Kalbī (*see* Muḥammad b. al-Sā'ib)
Makḥūl (*see* Abū 'Abd-Allāh Makḥūl)
Maymūn b. Mihrān
    Traditionist; judge of Kūfa; Kūfa and Raqqa; d. 117/735
Miqsam b. Bujra
    Traditionist; Madīna; d. 101/719
Mis'ar b. Kidām
    Traditionist; Kūfa; d. 153/770
Mu'āwiya b. Abī Sufyān
    Companion (first Umayyad Caliph); Madīna and Damascus; d. 61/680
Muhājir b. 'Umayra
    Traditionist (obscure); n. d.
Muḥammad b. 'Abd-Allāh b. Shihāb al-Zuhrī
    Traditionist; Madīna; d. 124 or 125/741 or 742
Muḥammad b. 'Abd al-Raḥmān b. Abī Layla
    Traditionist; jurist and judge; Kūfa; d. 148/765
Muḥammad b. Abī al-Mujālid
    Traditionist (obscure); n. d.
Muḥammad b. 'Ali b. al-Ḥusayn b. Abī Ṭālib (known as al-Bāqir)
    Traditionist (Shi'ī Imām); Madīna; d 114/732
Muḥammad b. Isḥāq
    Traditionist and historian; Madīna; d. 151/768
Muḥammud b. Muslim b. Shihāb al-Zuhrī
    Traditionist; Madīna; d. 124/742
Muḥammad b. Muslim b. Tadrus
    Traditionist; Makka; d. 126/743
Muḥammad b. al-Sā'ib al-Kalbī
    Traditionist; Kūfa; 146/763

Muḥammad b. Sīrīn
Traditionist; Madīna and Baṣra; d. 110/728
Muḥammad b. Zayd
Traditionist (obscure); n.d.
Mujāhid b. Jubayr
Traditionist; Makka; 103/721
Mujālid b. Sa'īd b. Umayr
Traditionist; Kūfa; d. 144/761
Nāfi' (*see* Abū 'Abd-Allāh Nāfi')
Najda b. 'Āmir
Khārijī traditionist (transmitted from Ibn 'Abbās); 'Irāq; d. 69/688
Nu'mān b. Thābit (Abū Hanīfa)
Jurist; Kūfa; d. 150/767
Qatāda b. Di'āma al-Sadūsī
Traditionist; Baṣra; d. 107/725
Sabi'ī (*see* 'Amr b. 'Abd-Allāh b. 'Ubayd)
Sa'd b. Abī Waqqāṣ
Companion; Madīna; d. 55 or 58/674 or 677
Sa'īd b. al-Mussayyib
Jurist and traditionist; Madīna; d. 93 or 94/711 or 712
Salama b. Kuhayl
Traditionist (Shī'ī); Kūfa; d. 121/738
Sha'bī (*see* 'Āmr b. Sharāḥīl)
Shurayḥ b. al-Ḥārith
Judge of Kūfa; Madīna and Kūfa; d. 80/699
Sufyān al-Thawrī
Jurist; Baṣra; 161/777
Sulaymān b. Abī Sulaymān (Abū Isḥāq)
Traditionist; Kūfa; d. 138/755
Sulaymān b. Burayda
Traditionist; Madīna and Merv; d. 105/723
Sulaymān b. Mihrān
Traditionist; Kūfa; d. 148/765
Ṭāwūs b. Kaysān
Traditionist; Makka; d. 105 or 106/723 or 724
'Ubayd-Allāh b. 'Umar b. Ḥafs b. 'Āṣim
Jurist (one of the seven jurists of Madīna); Madīna; d. 144 or 145/761 or 762
'Umar b. al-Khaṭṭāb
Companion (second caliph); Madīna; d. 23/643
'Umar b. Shu'ayb b. Muḥammad b. 'Abd-Allāh b. 'Amr b. al-'Āṣ
Traditionist; Madīna and Tā'if; d. 118/736
'Umayr (freed slave of Abī al-Laḥm)
Companion; traditionist (obscure); Madīna; n.d.

Yaḥyā b. Abī Unaysa
Traditionist (obscure) ; n. d.
Ya'qūb b. Ibrāhīm al-Anṣārī (Abū Yūsuf)
Jurist and judge; Kūfa and Baghdad; d. 182/798
Yazīd b. 'Abd-Allāh b. Qasīṭ
Traditionist; Madīna; d. 122/739
Yazīd b. Ḥabīb
Traditionist (obscure) ; n. d.
Yazīd b. Hurmuz
Traditionist; Madīna; died in the reign of the caliph 'Umar b. 'Abd al-'Azīz
Zayd b. Abī Unaysa
Traditionist; Kūfa; d. 124 or 125/741 or 742
Zayd b. Ḥāritha
Companion (freed slave of the Prophet) and father of Usāma; d. 8/629
Ziyād b. 'Ilāqa
Traditionist; Kūfa; d. 125/742
Zuhrī (*see* Muḥammad b. Muslim b. Shihāb)

GLOSSARY

'Abd: slave
Ābiq: runaway slave
'Adūw: enemy
Ahl al-Dhimma: non-Muslim subjects of the Islamic state
Ahl al-Ḥarb: subjects of enemy territory
Ahl al-Kitāb: non-Muslims who possess a scripture; scripturaries
Ama: slave woman
Amān: safe-conduct; pledge of security
Amīr: prince; commander
Arḍ: land; territory
Arḍ al-Ḥarb: territory of war or enemy territory
Arsh: damage or compensation for an injury or wound
Asīr: prisoner of war
Athar (pl. āthār): narrative; tradition; precedent
Baghī (pl. bughāt): dissenter; rebel
Ba'th (pl. bu'ūth): expedition
Bāṭil: void; invalid
Bay': exchange; sale transaction
Ḍamān: responsibility; liability
Dār: house; abode; territory
Dār al-ḥarb: enemy territory or territory of war
Dār al-Islām: territory of the Islamic state
Da'wa: invitation to adopt Islam; claim
Dharārī: children captives
Dhimmī: *see* Ahl al-Dhimma
Dīnār: gold unit of coinage, derived from Latin *denarius*, through Greek into Arabic
Dirham: silver unit of coinage, from Greek *drachma*
Dīwān: army record
Diya: blood money

Faqīh (pl. fuqahā') : jurist
Fāris (pl. fursān) : horse rider
Fāsid: defective; voidable
Fay': property taken from non-Muslims without war or violence
Fidā': ransom
Fiqh: jurisprudence
Ghanīma: spoil of war; booty
Ghaṣb: usurpation
Ghāzī: warrior
Ghazūw: raid
Ghulūl: treachery
Ḥadd (pl. ḥudūd) : fixed penalties for certain crimes (as provided in the Qur'ān)
Ḥadīth: Tradition
Ḥalāl: permitted
Ḥarām: forbidden
Ḥarb: war
Ḥarbī: enemy person; person from the territory of war
Ḥirz: place of security (i. e., territory of Islam)
Ḥukm (pl. aḥkām) : judgment; decision; ruling
Ḥurr: freeman
'Idda: waiting period for a woman after divorce or death of husband
Iḥrāz: *see* ḥirz
Ikrāh: *see* makrūh
Imām: leader; caliph; supreme authority
'Iṣma: wedlock; impeccability
Istiḥsān: juristic preference
Jā'iz: permissible
Ju'l: scutage
Jarīb: a measure of land; 100 square qaṣaba (or 60 square cubits)
Jāriya: girl slave
Jaysh: army
Jihād: just war (popularly holy war)
Jizya: poll tax
Kāfir: infidel; unbeliever
Kharāj: land tax
Khums: one-fifth state share (of the spoil of war)
Kitāb-Allāh (or al-Kitāb) : Book of God; Qur'ān

Kurā': ungulate animals
Makrūh: objectionable
Māl (pl. amwāl): property
Mamlūk: slave
Mawāt: waste land
Mawla: master; owner; client
Mithla: mutilation
Mudabbar: a slave whose manumission is arranged by tadbīr so that it takes effect at the death of the owner
Mudabbara: as above for female slave
Muftī: jurisconsult
Muhādana: peace agreement
Muḥtalim: a youth who has reached puberty
Mukātab: a slave whose manumission is obtained by installments
Murtadd: apostate
Mushrik (pl. Mushrikūn): polytheist; unbeliever
Musta'min: person who enjoys temporary safe-conduct
Muwāda'a: peace agreement
Nafal: compensation from the spoil in addition to an assigned share (supererogatory)
Naskh: abrogation
Nikāḥ: marriage; marital relations
Qāḍī: judge
Qafīz: a certain measure of capacity (consisting of 10 makūks or 12 manns)
Qatl: killing; homicide
Qīma: price
Qitāl: fighting, battle
Qiyās: legal reasoning by analogy
Rahn: security; hostage
Rājil: foot-warrior
Raqīq: slave
Rasūl: emissary; messenger; apostle
Ra'y: opinion
Riṭl: a unit of measure consisting of 12 ounces (1 ounce equals 40 dirhams)
Rumḥ: lance

Sā': a certain measure of capacity consisting of 5 riṭls (the Ḥijāz) and 8 ('Irāq)

Sabī: women and children captives

Ṣadaqa: charitable alms, often used in the sense of Zakāt

Sahm: fixed share (of the spoil)

Salab (pl. aslāb): prime, or the spoil of an enemy killed in a duel or battle, such as his clothes, weapons, etc.

Ṣalāt: ritual prayer

Sarīya: detachment

Sharī'a: Islamic law

Shirk: *see* mushrik

Sīra (pl. siyar): course; conduct of state

Ṣulḥ: peace treaty; agreement

Sunna: custom or precedent based on the Prophet's acts or sayings

Ta'wīl: individual interpretation of a religious or legal doctrine

Thaman: value

Umm Walad: slave woman who has borne a child to her owner

'Uqr: compensation for unintentional adultery; nuptial gift

'Ushr: tithe

'Utq: manumission

Wasq: a certain measure of capacity consisting of 60 sā's (*see* sā').

Zakāt: legal alms

SELECT BIBLIOGRAPHY

It is the purpose of this bibliography neither to compile and set forth a complete list of works on the Islamic law of nations, nor to reproduce all those cited in the footnotes, but rather to provide the fundamental primary and modern works that have bearing on Shaybānī's life and works, especially those relating to the subject of the siyar. Fairly exhaustive bibliographies of classical works can be found in Ḥajjī Khalīfa's *Kashf al-Zunūn*, ed. G. L. Flügel (Leipzig and London, 1835-38); Ibn al-Nadīm's *Kitāb al-Fihrist*, ed. G. L. Flügel (Leipzig, 1871); and C. Brokelmann's *Geschichte der Arabische Literatur*, 2nd ed. (Leiden, 1942-44). The reader may also refer to the relevant articles in the *Encyclopaedia of Islam* (old and new editions) and the *Shorter Encyclopaedia of Islam.*

Primary Sources

Abū Dawūd, Sulaymān b. al-Ash'ath. *Sunan.* 40 vols. Cairo, 1935.

Abū Ḥanīfa, al-Nu'mān b. Thābit. *Kitāb al-Musnad*, ed. Ṣafwat al-Saqqā. Aleppo, 1382/1962.

Abū Yūsuf, Ya'qūb b. Ibrāhīm al-Anṣārī. *Kitāb al-Āthār*, ed. Abū al-Wafā al-Afghānī. Cairo, 1355/1936.

———. *Kitāb al-Kharāj.* Cairo, 1352/1933. French translation, *Le livre de l'impôt foncier*, E. Fagnan. Paris, 1921.

———. *Kitāb al-Radd 'ala Siyar al-Awzā'ī*, ed. Abū al-Wafā al-Afghānī. Cairo, 1357/1938.

Balādhurī, Abū al-'Abbās Aḥmad b. Yaḥya b. Jābir. *Kitāb Futūḥ al-Buldān*, ed. M. J. de Goeje. Leiden, 1886. English translation, *Origin of the Islamic State*, Philip Hitti. New York, 1916.

Bukhārī, Abū 'Abd-Allāh Muḥammad b. Ismā'īl. *Kitāb al-Jāmi' al-Ṣaḥīḥ*, ed. M. Ludolf Krehl. 4 vols. Leiden, 1862-1908.

Dārimī, Abū Muḥammad 'Abd-Allāh b. 'Abd al-Raḥmān b. Faḍl b. Bahram. *Sunan.* 2 vols. Damascus, 1349/1930.

Dhahabī, Abū 'Abd-Allāh Muḥammad b. Aḥmad b. 'Uthmān. *Manāqib al-Imām Abī Ḥanīfa wa Ṣaḥibayhi Abī Yūsuf wa Muḥammad b. al-Ḥasan*, ed. M. Zāhid al-Kawtharī and Abū al-Wafā al-Afghānī. Cairo, 1366/1947.

Ibn 'Abd al-Barr, Abū 'Umar Yūsuf b. 'Abd-Allāh b. Muḥammad. *Kitāb al-Intiqā' fī Faḍā'il al-Thalātha al-A'imma al-Fuqahā'*. Cairo, 1350/1931.

———. *Kitāb al-Istī'āb fī Manāqib al-Aṣḥāb*, ed. Abū Muḥammad al-Bijawī. 4 vols. Cairo, n. d.

Ibn 'Ābidīn, Muḥammad Amīn. *Majmū'at Rasā'il: al-Risāla al-Thāniya: Sharḥ al-Manẓūma al-Musammāt Bi'uqūd Rasm al-Muftī*. Vol. I. Istanbul, 1325/1907.

Ibn Ādam, Yaḥya. *Kitāb al-Kharāj*, ed. Aḥmad Muḥammad Shākir. Cairo, 1347/1928. English translation, *Taxation in Islam*, A. Ben Shemesh. Leiden, 1958.

Ibn Ḥajar al-'Asqalānī, Shihāb al-Dīn b. 'Alī. *Kitāb al-Iṣāba fī Tamyīz al-Ṣaḥāba*. 4 vols. Cairo, 1358/1939.

Ibn Ḥajar al-Haythamī, Shihāb al-Dīn Aḥmad. *Kitāb al-Khayrāt al-Ḥisān fī Manāqib al-Imām al-'Aẓam Abī Ḥanīfa al-Nu'mān*. Cairo, 1304/1886.

Ibn Ḥanbal, Aḥmad. *al-Musnad*, ed. Aḥmad Muḥammad Shākir. 15 vols. (incomplete). Cairo, 1304/1886.

Ibn Hishām, Abū Muḥammad 'Abd al-Malik. *Kitāb Sīrat Sayyidina Muḥammad Rasūl Allāh*, ed. Ferdinand Wüstenfeld. 2 vols. Göttingen, 1858-60. English translation, *The Life of Muhammad*, A. Guillaume. London, 1955.

Ibn al-'Imād al-Ḥanbalī, Abū al-Falāḥ 'Abd al-Ḥayy. *Shadharāt al-Dhahab fī Akhbār Man Dhahab*. 8 vols. Cairo, n. d.

Ibn Kathīr, 'Imād al-Dīn al-Fidā' Ismā'īl b. 'Umar. *Kitāb al-Bidāya wa al-Nihāya fī al-Ta'rīkh*. Vol. X. Cairo, n. d.

———. *Kitāb al-Ijtihād fī Ṭalab al-Jihād*. Cairo, 1347/1928.

Ibn Khallikān, Abū al-'Abbās Shams al-Dīn Aḥmad b. Muḥammad b. Abī Bakr. *Wafayāt al-A'yān*, ed. M. Muḥī al-Dīn 'Abd al-Ḥamīd. 6 vols. Cairo, 1948.

Ibn Māja, Abū 'Abd-Allāh Muḥammad b. Yazīd al-Qazwīnī. *Sunan*, ed. M. Fu'ād 'Abd al-Bāqī. 2 vols. Cairo, 1373/1954.

Ibn Qutayba, Abū Muḥammad 'Abd-Allāh b. Muslim. *Kitāb al-Ma'ārif*, ed. Tharwat 'Ukkāsha. Cairo, 1960.

Ibn Sa'd, Muḥammad. *Kitāb al-Ṭabaqāt al-Kabīr*. 9 vols. Beirut, 1957-58.

Ibn Sallām, Abū 'Ubayd al-Qāsim. *Kitāb al-Amwāl*, ed. M. Ḥamīd al-Fiqqī. Cairo, 1353/1954.

Ibn Taymīya, Taqī al-Dīn Abū al-'Abbās Aḥmad b. 'Abd al-Ḥakīm. "Qā'ida fī Qitāl al-Kuffār," in *Majmū'at Rasā'il*, ed. M. Ḥamīd al-Fiqqī. Cairo, 1368/1949.

Kirdarī, Muḥammad b. Muḥammad b. Shihāb. *Manāqib al-Imām al-A'ẓam* (printed with Makkī's Manāqib). Hyderabad, 1321/1903.

Kāsānī, 'Alā' al-Dīn Abū Bakr b. Mas'ūd. *Kitāb Badā'i' al-Ṣanā'i'*. Vol. VII. Cairo, 1328/1910.

Khaṭīb al-Baghdādī, Abū Bakr Aḥmad b. 'Alī. *Ta'rīkh Baghdād.* 14 vols. Cairo, 1349/1931.

Makkī, Abū al-Mu'ayyad al-Muwaffaq b. Aḥmad. *Manāqib al-Imām al-A'ẓam Abī Ḥanīfa.* 2 vols. Hyderabad, 1321/1903.

Mālik b. Anas. *al-Muwaṭṭa'*, ed. Muḥammad Fu'ād 'Abd al-Bāqī. 2 vols. Cairo, 1951.

Māwardī, Abū al-Ḥasan 'Alī b. Muḥammad b. Ḥabīb. *Kitāb al-Aḥkām al-Sulṭānīya*, ed. M. Enger. Bonn, 1853. French translation, *Les statuts gouvernementaux, ou règles de droit public et administratif*, E. Fagnan. Algiers, 1915.

Muslim, Abū al-Ḥusayn Muslim b. al-Ḥajjāj. *Ṣaḥīḥ*, with Nawawī's Commentary. Vols. 12-13. Cairo, 1929-30.

Nawawī, Abū Zakariya Yaḥya. *Kitāb Tahdhīb al-Asmā'*, ed. F. Wüstenfeld. Göttingen, 1842-45.

Nu'mān, Qāḍī Abū Ḥanīfa. *Da'ā'im al-Islām*, ed. Āṣif 'Alī Aṣghar Fayḍī [A. A. A. Fyzee]. Vol. I. Cairo, 1951.

Qur'ān. Translations used are as follows:

A. J. Arberry, *The Koran Interpreted.* 2 vols. London, 1955.

Richard Bell, *The Qur'ān*, 2 vols. Edinburgh, 1937-39.

E. H. Palmer, *Qur'an.* London, 1928.

J. M. Rodwell, *The Koran.* London, 1909.

Ṣafadī, Ṣalāḥ al-Dīn Khalīl b. Aybak. *Kitāb al-Wāfi bil-Wafayāt*, ed. S. Dedering. Vol. II. Istanbūl, 1949.

Sarakhsī, Shams al-Dīn Muḥammad b. Aḥmad b. Sahl. *Kitāb al-Mabsūṭ.* Vol. X. Cairo. 1324/1906.

———. *Sharḥ al-Siyar al-Kabīr* [li Muḥammad b. al-Ḥasan al-Shaybānī]. 4 vols. Hyderabad, 1335-36/1916-17.

———. *al-Siyar al-Kabīr lil-Imām Muḥammad b. al-Ḥasan al-Shaybānī*, ed. Muḥammad Abū Zahra and Muṣṭafa Zayd. Vol. I (incomplete). Cairo, 1958.

———. *Sharḥ Kitāb al-Siyar al-Kabīr li-Muḥammad b. al-Ḥasan al-Shaybānī*, ed. Ṣalāḥ al-Dīn al-Munajjid. 3 Vols. (incomplete). Cairo, 1957.

Shāfi'ī, Abū 'Abd-Allāh Muḥammad b. Idrīs. *Kitāb al-Risāla*, ed. Aḥmad Muḥammad Shākir. Cairo, 1938. English translation, *Islamic Jurisprudence: Shāfi'ī's Risāla*, tr. M. Khadduri. Baltimore, 1961.

———. *Kitāb al-Umm.* 7 vols. Cairo, 1321-25/1904-8.

Shawkānī, Muḥammad b. 'Alī b. Muḥammad. *Nayl al-Awṭār.* 8 vols. Cairo, 1952.

Shaybānī, Muḥammad b. al-Ḥasan. *Kitāb al-Āthār.* Lucknow, n. d.

———. *Kitāb al-Aṣl.* Part I: Kitāb al-Buyū' wa al-Salam, ed. Shafīq Shiḥāta. Vol. I. Cairo, 1954.

———. *Kitāb al-Jāmi' al-Kabīr*, ed. Abū al-Wafā al-Afghānī. Cairo, 1356/1937.

———. *Kitāb al-Jāmi' al-Ṣaghīr*. Cairo, 1310/1892. German translation of the chapter on sale with an introduction by Iwan Dimitroff, "Asch-Schaibani und sein corpus juris al-gami as-Sagir," *Westasiatische Studien*, pp. 60-206. Berlin, 1908.

Ṭabarī, Abū Ja'far Muḥammad b. Jarīr. *Kitāb Ikhtilāf al-Fuqahā': Kitāb al-Jihād wa Kitāb al-Jizya wa Aḥkām al-Muḥāribīn*, ed. J. Schacht. Leiden, 1933.

———. *Ta'rīkh al-Rusul wa al-Mulūk*, ed. M. J. de Goeje. 15 vols. Leiden, 1879-1901.

Ṭaḥāwī, Abū Ja'far Aḥmad b. Muḥammad b. Salama. *Kitāb al-Mukhtaṣar*, ed. Abū al-Wafā al-Afghānī. Cairo, 1370/1950.

Tirmidhī, Abū 'Īsa Muḥammad b. 'Īsa b. Sawra. *Sunan*, ed. Aḥmad Muḥammad Shākir. 2 vols. (incomplete). Cairo, 1356/1937.

Modern Works

Abū al-Wafā al-Qurashī, Muḥī al-Dīn Abū Muḥammad 'Abd al-Qādir. *al-Jawāhir al-Muḍiya fī Ṭabaqāt al-Ḥanafīya*. 2 vols. Hyderabad 1332/1913.

Abū Zahra, Muḥammad. *Abū Ḥanīfa: Ḥayatuh wa 'Aṣruh, Arā'uh wa Fiqhuh*, 2nd ed. Cairo, 1947.

Armanazi, Nagib. *Les principes islamiques et les rapports internationaux en temps de paix et de guerre*. Paris, 1929.

Dennett, Daniel C. *Conversion and the Poll Tax in Early Islam*. Cambridge, Mass., 1950.

Hamidullah, Muḥammad. *Document sur la diplomatie musulmane à l'époque du prophète et des khalifes orthodoxes*. Paris, 1935.

———. *Muslim Conduct of State*. 3rd ed. Lahore, 1953.

Hatschek, Julius. *Der Musta'min*. Berlin, 1920.

Jenks, C. Wilfred. *The Common Law of Mankind*. London, 1958.

Kawtharī, Muḥammad Zāhid b. al-Ḥasan. *Bulūgh al-Amānī fī Sīrat al-Imām Muḥammad b. al-Ḥasan al-Shaybānī*. Cairo, 1355/1937.

———. *Ḥusn al-Taqāḍī fī Sīrat al-Imām Abī Yūsuf al-Qāḍī*. Cairo, 1368/1948.

———. *Lamḥāt al-Nazar fī Sīrat al-Imām Zufar*. Cairo, 1368/1948.

Khadduri, Majid. "International Law," *Law in the Middle East*, ed. M. Khadduri and H. J. Liebesny, Vol. I, pp. 349-72. Washington, 1955.

———. "Islam and the Modern Law of Nations," *American Journal of International Law*, Vol. 50 (1956), pp. 358-72.

———. "The Islamic System: Its Competition and Co-Existence with Western Systems," *Proceedings of the American Society of International Law*, 1959, pp. 49-52.

———. "The Islamic Theory of International Relations and its Contemporary Relevance," *Islam and International Relations*, ed. J. H. Proctor, pp. 24-39. New York, 1965.

———. *War and Peace in the Law of Islam.* 2nd ed. Baltimore, 1955.

Khallāf, 'Abd al-Wahhāb. *Al-Siyāsa al-Shar'īya wa Niẓām al-Dawla al-Islāmīya.* Cairo, 1350/1931.

Kruse, Hans. *Islamische Völkerrechtslehre.* Göttingen, 1953.

———. "al-Shaybani on International Instruments," *Journal of the Pakistan Historical Society,* Vol. I (1953), pp. 90-100.

———. "The Notion of Siyar," *Journal of the Pakistan Historical Society,* Vol. II (1954), pp. 16-25.

———. "The Foundation of Islamic International Jurisprudence," *Journal of the Pakistan Historical Society,* Vol. III (1955).

Løkkegaard, Frede. *Islamic Taxation in the Classic Period.* Copenhagen, 1950.

Nussbaum, Arthur. *A Concise History of the Law of Nations.* Rev. ed. New York, 1954.

Qurā'a, 'Alī. *al-'Alāqāt al-Dawlīya fī al-Ḥurūb al-Islāmīya.* Cairo, 1374/1955.

Rabbath, Edmund. "Pour une théorie du droit international musulman," *Revue Egyptienne de Droit International,* Vol. VI (1950), pp. 1-23.

Rāziq, 'Alī 'Abd. *al-Islām wa Uṣūl al-Ḥukm.* Cairo, 1925.

Rechid, Ahmad. "L'Islam et le droit des gens," *Académie de Droit International, Recueil des Cours,* 1937, Vol. II, pp. 375-504. Paris, 1938.

Sanhoury, A. *Le Califat: Son évolution vers une Société des Nations Orientales.* Paris, 1926.

Schacht, Joseph. *The Origins of Muhammadan Jurisprudence.* Oxford, 1950.

Wright, Quincy. "Asian Experience and International Law," *International Studies Quarterly Journal of the Indian School of International Studies,* Vol. I (1959), pp. 71-87.

———. "The Influence of the New Nations of Asia and Africa upon International Law," *Foreign Affairs Reports* (Indian Council of World Affairs), Vol. VII (1958), pp. 33-39.

Zwemer, Samuel M. *The Law of Apostasy in Islam.* London, 1924.

INDEX

The Islamic Law of Nations

Shaybānī's Siyar

by
Majid Khadduri

designer : Athena Blackorby
typesetter : J. H. Furst
typefaces : Baskerville (text), Weiss (display)
printer : J. H. Furst
paper : Perkins & Squier GM
binder : Moore and Company
cover material : Holliston Aldine Linen

Printed in the United States
3824

9 780801 869754